RECLAIMING
the
EUROPEAN STREET

Speeches on **EUROPE** *and the*
EUROPEAN UNION, *2016–20*

MICHAEL D. HIGGINS

RECLAIMING *the* EUROPEAN STREET

Speeches on **EUROPE** *and the* **EUROPEAN UNION**, *2016–20*

Edited by
JOACHIM FISCHER
and
FERGAL LENEHAN

THE LILLIPUT PRESS
DUBLIN

First published 2021 by
THE LILLIPUT PRESS
62–63 Sitric Road, Arbour Hill
Dublin 7, Ireland
www.lilliputpress.ie

Copyright © 2021 Michael D. Higgins
Introduction © Joachim Fischer and Fergal Lenehan

ISBN 9781843517948

All rights reserved. No part of this publication
may be reproduced in any form or by any means
without the prior permission of the publisher.

A CIP record for this title is available
from The British Library.

10 9 8 7 6 5 4 3 2 1

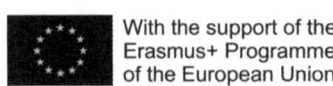
With the support of the Erasmus+ Programme of the European Union

The Lilliput Press gratefully acknowledges the financial support of the Arts Council/An Chomhairle Ealaíon.

Set in 11.5 pt on 15.5 pt Arno by iota (www.iota-books.ie)
Printed in Poland by Drukarnia Skleniarz

Contents

Preface by Michael D. Higgins, Uachtarán na hÉireann   ix
Introduction by Joachim Fischer and Fergal Lenehan   xv

I. EUROPEAN HISTORY AND MEMORY

In Honour of Roger Casement
Speech at the official state commemoration in honour of Roger Casement, Banna Strand, Ardfert, Co. Kerry, 21 April 2016.   3

A Forgotten Polish Hero of the Great Irish Famine: Paul Strzelecki's Struggle to Save Thousands of Lives
Speech at the official opening of a Polish exhibition on the Great Famine, Royal Irish Academy, Dublin, 8 May 2019.   10

The Great Flu of 1918–19: Why Remember? Why Forget?
Speech at a reception commemorating the Great Flu Epidemic of 1918–19, Áras an Uachtaráin, 31 May 2019.   16

Remembering the Holocaust
Speech at the Holocaust Memorial Day Commemoration 2020, Mansion House, Dublin, 26 January 2020.   24

II. TOWARDS A SOCIAL EUROPE

A New European Mind and the Need to Rejuvenate Discourse
Speech at the launch of the Jean Monnet Centre of Excellence in the New Political Economy of Europe, UCD, 28 March 2019.   33

Trade Unions and the European Future
Speech at the European Federation of Public Service Unions' Annual Congress, 'Trade Unions and the Future', RDS, Dublin, 4 June 2019.   47

Contents

Parliamentary Democracy in the European Union
Speech at a reception for the European Association of Former Members of Parliament, Áras an Uachtaráin, 9 June 2017.   61

Solidarity in Europe: Achieving Authenticity on the European Street
Lecture at the European University Institute, Florence, Italy, 10 May 2018.   66

III. THINKING ABOUT EUROPE

On the State of Democracy in Our Changing World
The Aristotle Address 2019, the Stoa of Attalos at the Ancient Agora of Athens, 10 October 2019.   81

Overcoming Disciplinary Boundaries
Speech to the European Research Council, Iveagh House, Dublin, 12 October 2016.   95

Ethical Challenges for the European Union
Address at the Pontifical Irish College, Rome, 22 May 2017.   100

The Idea of Home
Speech at the Galway International Arts Festival, NUI Galway, 21 July 2018.   105

IV. CONNECTING EUROPEAN CULTURES

Of Greece and Ireland: An Ancient and Enduring Relationship Full of New Possibilities
Lecture at the University of Athens, 23 February 2018.   123

Pangur Bán
Reception for Imogen Stuart to mark the installation of the sculpture Pangur Bán, Áras an Uachtaráin, 21 January 2020.   130

Ireland and Germany
Toast on the occasion of the state dinner hosted by Frank-Walter Steinmeier, President of the Federal Republic of Germany, and Ms Elke Büdenbender, Schloss Bellevue, Berlin, 3 July 2019.   134

Ireland and the Netherlands
Speech at a state dinner in honour of Their Majesties King Willem-Alexander and Queen Máxima of the Netherlands, Áras an Uachtaráin, 12 June 2019. ... 138

Ireland and Sweden
Speech at a state dinner in honour of Their Majesties King Carl XVI Gustaf and Queen Silvia of Sweden, Áras an Uachtaráin, 22 May 2019. ... 144

Ireland and Lithuania: Towards a Shared Future Within the European Union
Speech at the Vytautas Magnus University, Kaunas, 20 June 2018. ... 150

Ireland and Croatia
Speech at a state dinner in honour of Kolinda Grabar-Kitarović, President of Croatia, Áras an Uachtaráin, 3 April 2017. ... 160

V. THE FUTURE OF THE EUROPEAN UNION

Giving the European Union a Future That Will Engage Citizens: A Shared Challenge
Speech at the inaugural event of the Brexit Institute, Dublin City University, 25 January 2018. ... 169

The Future of Europe: Re-Balancing Ecology, Economics and Ethics
Speech at the University of Leipzig, 4 July 2019. ... 188

Europe and Africa: Towards a New Relationship
Webinar address to the Institute of International and European Affairs, Áras an Uachtaráin, 10 June 2020. ... 206

VI. A MULTILINGUAL EUROPE – TRANSLATIONS INTO IRISH, FRENCH AND GERMAN

Pangur Bán
Fáilte roimh Imogen Stuart chun suiteáil na deilbhe, Pangur Bán, *in Áras an Uachtaráin, 21 Eanáir 2020 a chomóradh.* ... 225

Une certaine idée de « la maison »
   Discours prononcé au Festival international des Arts de Galway (Galway International Arts Festival), NUI Galway, le 21 juillet 2018.   230

Die Zukunft Europas: Ökologie, Wirtschaft und Ethik – Eine neue Balance finden
   Rede an der Universität Leipzig, 4. Juli 2019.   248

Postscript on the COVID-19 Crisis: Towards a Europe Resolute in Its Vindication of the Most Vulnerable Among Us
   From a letter to the President of the Hellenic Republic, 9 April 2020.   271

Bibliography	273
Notes	283
Index	297

Illustrations between pages 128 and 129.

Preface

This collection of some of my recent speeches covers a five-year period from 2016 to 2020, a tumultuous time that commenced with the Brexit vote in the United Kingdom and the election of Donald Trump in the United States and concludes with the onslaught of the COVID-19 pandemic with all its personal, social, cultural and economic consequences.

These speeches I gave in that period were to European audiences drawn from the institutional matrix of the European Union. That matrix had, and still has, a specific form of discourse. I was conscious, however, of a more raucous, angry and, at times, disappointed discourse echoing from the European Street. It was from a public bearing not just a memory, but a retained set of experiences that were still being felt as a result of the responses made to the banking-sourced financial and economic disaster of 2008. The name given by so many in the European Street to that response was 'austerity'.

In so many of the speeches that follow, I sought to address the assumptions of the economic model that had brought us to both the crisis of 2008 and the response that had been made to it. The reception I received was encouraging in some settings. In a few places, a particular speech might draw a bad-tempered dismissal of my opinion and the sources I quoted as the words of mavericks who did not understand economics; that their decision or mine to critique or even to speak of 'neo-liberalism' was to use a cliché.

Preface

I believe that a new challenge with a global response has changed all that. What was not tolerated in the discourse is now part of the necessary response to COVID-19 – a source of policy for an activist and even entrepreneurial state, social protection and collective responses that now can allow for a discussion of the ecological, social and economic intermix that is unavoidable for policy.

The global loss of life and disruption to our daily lives resulting from COVID-19 is unprecedented in living memory. Indeed, it was only in 2019 that I held a seminar at Áras an Uachtaráin to mark the centenary of the last pandemic of similar magnitude, that of the so-called and misnamed Spanish flu, the address from which is included in this book.

From COVID-19 we have been reminded through tragedy and suffering that we have a shared, globalized vulnerability that is common to all humanity, one that knows no borders. We are learning how we must make urgent changes to improve resilience in a range of essential areas, such as work, healthcare and housing. We have been forced to recognize our dependence on our public-sector frontline workers, and the state's broader role in mitigating this crisis and saving lives.

COVID-19 has magnified the shortcomings of an insufficient, narrow, indeed failed and failing paradigm of economy with all its imbalances, inequities and injustices. Yet, responding to COVID-19 has proved, if ever proof were required, that government is needed, and can act decisively when the will is there. It has reminded us of how so many are only ever one wage payment away from hardship; how the self-employed or workers in the so-called 'gig' economy lack security and basic employment rights; how private tenants in under-regulated housing markets are at the mercy of their landlords; how many designated 'key workers', those providing essential services, are shamefully undervalued and underpaid.

How regrettable it is that it has taken a pandemic of this magnitude to demonstrate these stark facts so vividly. What a tragedy it is that it has required the pandemic's toll, the millions of lives cut short across the world, to establish, or rekindle, widespread appreciation of work in the public sphere and the importance in the economy of the public good – and, in terms of our shared future, the state's benign and transformative capacity. Averting our gaze from these grim truths is no longer an option.

There is now a widespread, recovered recognition across the streets of Europe, and indeed beyond, not only of the state's positive role in managing such crises, but of how it can play a deeper, entrepreneurial, transformative role in our lives for the better. The erosion of the state's role, the weakening of its institutions, and the undermining of its significance for over four decades has left a less just and more precarious society and economy, one ill-prepared for seismic shocks such as COVID-19.

The role of the state, thus, needs to be recovered, understood, accepted and defined anew, as well as the concept of sovereignty, in such a way that sovereignty is shared, can flow for the benefit of citizens beyond borders, can have a comparative and regional character; one that has the capacity to be exemplary for global economic systems.

Better ideas that will generate more inclusive, transformative and transparent policies are now required – ideas based on equality, universal public services, equity of access, sufficiency, sustainability. Better ideas are fortunately available for an alternative paradigm of sustainable social economy within ecological responsibility. We now have a rich contemporary discourse, to which scholars such as Ian Gough,[1] Mariana Mazzucato,[2] Sylvia Walby,[3] Kate Raworth[4] and others are contributing; scholars who advance progressive alternatives to our destructive, failed paradigm. The regular contributions to *Social Europe* from such scholars and so many others offer opportunities for a necessary discourse. Such scholarship indicates that we are neither at the end of history or of ideas, to reference the hubristic construct of Francis Fukuyama.[5]

Out of respect for those who have suffered greatly, those who have lost their lives, and indeed the bereaved families, we must not drift into some notion that we can recover what we had previously as a sufficient resolution, nor can we revert to the insecurity of where we were before, through mere adjustment of fiscal- and monetary-policy parameters. That would be so wholly insufficient to the task now at hand. A brighter horizon of opportunity must emerge, one which offers hope.

It is not only the case that the COVID-19 pandemic provides us with an opportunity to do things better; it also enables us to realize what is destructive of social cohesion and the environment. We must have the courage to examine critically the assumptions that brought us to this point. This crisis will pass eventually, but there will be other viruses and other crises. We cannot allow ourselves to be in the same vulnerable position again. On the most basic level, we should recover and strengthen instincts of moral courage we may have suppressed, which the lure of individualism may have driven out, displacing a sense of the collective, of shared solidarity, allowing the state's value and contribution to be derided and disregarded, so that a narrow agenda of accumulation could be pursued.

We have to ask, too, if that narrow furrow which we ploughed for our teaching of economics has brought us to sources of policy based on abstract ideological assumptions rather than those transparent or open to empirical verification, and, thus, to a culpable incompetence, inability, and a confused silence, rather than a wide understanding of economics and the policies that might flow from it. We must, from now surely, do things in a different, in a more responsible and integrated way.

As well as highlighting the unequivocal case for a new form of political economy based on ecological and social sustainability, the pandemic has also demonstrated, I suggest, the critical importance of having universal basic services that will protect us in the future, as Anna Coote and Andrew Percy[6] have suggested, and of enabling people to have a sufficiency of what they need, as Ian Gough has contended.[7]

In these speeches, I have sought to place global solidarity at the core of our new paradigm if we are to avoid healthcare collapse in many developing countries, including in sub-Saharan Africa. COVID-19 has all but halted migration as countries across the globe close borders, severely restricting mobility. This has implications for those seeking asylum, fleeing persecution and conflict. Such individuals are particularly at risk to COVID-19 because they often have limited access to water, sanitation systems and health facilities. I have written that we must ensure that people forced to flee are included in preparation and response plans for COVID-19.[8]

In these pieces, I have felt it necessary to repeat some, as I see it, essential messages. For example, we require enhanced attempts at the global level to build a new international architecture, to reverse the policy of fragmentation and institutional damage that has, in recent years, affected the United Nations and other multilateral organizations.

In all of Europe, transformative actions are now required. Good work is underway. For example, analysis by Ireland's National Economic and Social Council (NESC) published in 2020 provides a framework within which the transition to a new political economy may be a just transition.[9] This will require social dialogue and a deliberative process, as NESC suggests, which should be framed in the wider context of discussions on how we embed the just economy and society now so urgently needed and desired by the citizenry.

Successful crisis management is no guarantee of durable reform. We must turn the hard-earned wisdom from this crisis into strong scholarly work that can inform policy and institutional frameworks – this is the great challenge from a political-economy perspective.

There are great sources from which we are yet to adequately draw. For example, culture – the resource of ideas that are available in literary imagination, art, music and literature specifically – is rarely articulated in considerations as to the future of Europe. Yet words matter: words such as the declaration which called for a European Union. Now language and culture are underutilized, even neglected. This is a neglect for which the European Union has paid a heavy price. It is so reflected in the language of spokespersons who read minima to an anonymous citizen, but who achieve merely an echo of what on the European Street is perceived as not only insufficient but as inauthentic. As I write, cultural practitioners have been among the most impacted in terms of income and practice as a result of COVID-19, and we must all – governments and concerned citizens – show our solidarity by helping our writers and artists through this difficult time.

The scale of the change that is now required is, to my mind, similar to that which occurred in the late 1980s and early 1990s in Central and Eastern Europe, an invocation of a moral future of peace similar perhaps in scale, scope and significance to that advocated in the *Ventotene Manifesto* in its day by Altiero Spinelli and Ernesto Rossi.[10]

Our challenge now is surely to draw on the best of indomitable instincts of solidarity and ingenuity as COVID-19 confronts 21st-century society and its world economy with a new kind of emergency hazard. We must galvanize those sentiments across the citizenries of the globe, invite a discussion on the inherent flaws of our current model, and create the capacities needed for embracing a new paradigm founded on universalism, sustainability and equality.

Looking ahead, my vision, of which I continue to write and speak as I try to avoid any Adornoesque pessimism, is of a Europe with quality public services at its core and decent jobs in the public sector. We must remember that the services the public sector delivers are not a cost to society, but an investment in our communities. This message must be taken to, and accepted in, the heart of Europe. It can help restore credibility and build a partnership with the European Street and its discourse. The 'unaccountable' – speculative flows of insatiable capital, a global, unregulated, financialized version of economy – represents the greatest threat to democracy, the greatest source of an inevitable conflict, and the greatest obstacle to us achieving an end to global poverty or achieving sustainability.

The lessons of necessity and solidarity learnt during the pandemic must now inform a European-led transition to a just and ecologically sustainable society in its aftermath. I am hopeful that, within an enlightened eco-social framework, we may respond together in a transformative, inclusive way to the COVID-19 pandemic, climate change, the impact of digitalization, rising inequality and the unaccountable, and, in doing so, address the democratic crisis facing so many societies in Europe and beyond.

May I express, as I did in my previous collection, *When Ideas Matter*, my deepest appreciation and thanks to those who helped me prepare speeches, as well as to the editors, Joachim Fischer and Fergal Lenehan, the translators and the publishers who are making this publication possible, and to the readers and students who I hope will elaborate, contest, improve and even apply its messages.

Michael D. Higgins, Uachtarán na hÉireann
December 2020

Introduction

THE BREXIT SHOCK

The United Kingdom's decision to leave the European Union has resulted in the resurgence of the political slogan upon Ireland's neighbouring island. Thus we have had, for example, 'Brexit means Brexit,' while the need to 'get Brexit done' probably won an election in late 2019. As the material and geopolitical consequences of Brexit become clearer, however, the catchy slogans have all but dried up. For many in the European Union the Brexit referendum of June 2016 has acted as a wake-up call; for political and economic leaders, as well as for parliamentarians and civil society. The realization has dawned on many that the multilateral values taken for granted in western Europe since 1945 are not necessarily written in stone, that in the face of the utter ignorance and disconnect all too evident in the UK a lot more needs to be undertaken to engage citizens with the European Union, which is still essentially an unfinished political project. It has led to a new focus upon the social aspect of the Union and renewed vigour to engage citizens in the debate of where the EU, and its integration project, may feasibly go. Under Jean-Claude Juncker, on 1 March 2017, the *White Paper on the Future of Europe* was published starting a process of public debates in all Member States, with a preliminary end before the parliamentary elections in June 2019. In April 2017 the reflection paper on the noticeably more citizen-focused social dimension of Europe appeared followed by the Social Summit for Fair Jobs and Growth in Gothenburg in November 2017.

In Ireland also the debate about the European Union, and Ireland's place within it, is gathering pace, and may be seen as branching out beyond the narrowly political, economic or fiscal aspects traditionally dominating commentary. Never before has the European Union been so present in the Irish media as it has been since 2016. Alongside the public arena major European policy initiatives have been engaged upon by the Irish government, beyond the immediate actions required by Brexit, with strategy papers taking a noticeably broader view than the traditional, often myopic, utilitarian focus, as evidenced by those dealing with Ireland's relations with key EU Member States, such as *Ireland in Germany: A Wider and Deeper Footprint* (2018), a year later supplemented by *Global Ireland: Ireland's Strategy for France 2019–2025: Together in Spirit and Action*. Both contain a strong cultural dimension and the acknowledgment that wider knowledge of European cultures and other EU languages are key to participating more fully in EU-wide discourses. The policy document *Languages Connect: Ireland's Strategy for Foreign Languages, 2017–2026* demonstrates – after a decade-long evasion of the issue of a languages strategy – a new urgency within the Department of Education and Skills, no doubt strongly encouraged by business and industry concerned about language shortages in the new economic environment. There is a clear consciousness that Ireland will have to connect to the EU and continental Member States much more intensely and directly post-Brexit, both in a material, i.e. economic, and an immaterial, i.e. political and intellectual sense.

The new context explains why the speeches of Ireland's Head of State and President Michael D. Higgins since 2016 have become ever more European in outlook. But they not only echo the renewed interest in Europe, they also critically reflect upon the past, present and future of the European Union, and on what may have been missing in this debate, not only in Ireland. Whether it in fact reaches the 'European Street' is one of the key questions asked in these interventions. Undeniably, this is an appropriate time to present the President's collected speeches in the accessible format of a book; a further contribution to the renewed European-wide interest in the future of Europe and the EU.

Introduction

Some speeches in this volume were delivered within the wider context of Future of Europe Citizens' Debates.¹ Similarly to their fellow EU citizens, members of the Irish public also participated in several day-long national Citizens' Consultations on the Future of Europe in Dublin and elsewhere, between November 2017 and May 2018. The final report of the Citizens' Consultations of November 2018 states: 'the abiding message was that the Irish people see Europe at the heart of their future and Ireland at the heart of Europe'.² This bold statement might serve as a starting point for a brief review of Irish public discourses regarding Europe since joining the EU in 1973.

IRISH PUBLIC DISCOURSES ON EUROPE

In the most recent *Eurobarometer* survey (no. 92) conducted in November 2019, Ireland had the most positive image of the European Union of all Member States. For 63 per cent of Irish respondents the EU conjured up positive associations. Only 7 per cent had a negative image, with 29 per cent retaining a neutral stance.³ The highest percentage in all of the EU Member States again (73 per cent) saw themselves as satisfied with the way democracy works in the EU, while only 17 per cent (again the lowest figure) expressed their unhappiness in this regard. No doubt these results are influenced by recent events in the context of Brexit and the EU's substantial support for the Irish position, in which the Union centred Irish concerns in relation to the implementation of the Good Friday Agreement and the maintenance of an open border on the island. There is widespread confidence that whatever Brexit settlement is eventually arrived upon, significant EU support for Ireland, as the country most directly exposed to the fallout from the British decision of 2016, will be forthcoming. It should indeed not be a surprise if the approval ratings were to climb further as the economic consequences of COVID-19 become more obvious and Ireland, like all Member States, will for the foreseeable future become dependent on massive financial support underwritten eventually by the European Central Bank and the EU.

We are obviously in a new phase of Ireland's membership of the European Union, one in which the fortunes of the country have become intertwined with that of the Union as a whole to an unprecedented level. In terms of approval ratings we are approaching the situation at the very

Introduction

commencement of membership when, in May 1972, 83 per cent voted for entry into the then European Economic Community. In the standard work on the subject (sadly somewhat out of date at this stage), Brigid Laffan and Jane O'Mahony identify three distinct phases in Ireland's membership of the EU, and its predecessors, up to 2008.[4] Phase I from 1973 to 1986 they regard as an adjustment phase characterized by what the authors call a 'begging-bowl mentality', while Phase II from 1986 they view as an increasing integration phase hastened by the economic crisis of the late 1980s. The third phase encompasses economic recovery and the accelerating boom of the so-called Celtic Tiger, and with this a more sceptical attitude towards the EU. This found expression in the now infamous Boston vs Berlin speech of then Tánaiste Mary Harney of 2000[5] (on which more below) and the two rejected referenda of Nice and Lisbon (though reversed in the subsequent years, in both cases). We can readily add two more recent phases following the appearance of Laffan and O'Mahony's 2008 book: the bailout/austerity phase of 2009–16, while Brexit marks the beginning of the present phase, which is the one primarily reflected in this volume.

Ireland has been, indeed, a very active and committed member of the European Union. It has played a key role in some of the most momentous developments within the EU. These include – during the EU Council presidency from January to June 1990 – the facilitation of the easy accession of the former East Germany (much appreciated by Helmut Kohl's German Government) and, during another presidency from January to June 2004, the welcoming of ten new members into the EU, mostly from the former Soviet bloc. Ireland has also supplied key EU politicians such as the late former Commissioner Peter Sutherland and the former President of the European Parliament Pat Cox; there are indications that the former European Parliament's First Vice President and now Commissioner Máiréad McGuinness may become an even more influential Irish politician in Brussels. They are complemented by key figures in past EU administrations, such as Catherine Day and David O'Sullivan as well as the impressive and influential European Ombudsman, Emily O'Reilly. Maura Adshead has rightly judged that 'considering its small population, Ireland has enjoyed disproportionate influence in the European Union'.[6]

The figures mentioned at the outset point – relatively speaking – to a generally positive and unambiguous relationship between the EU and Ireland in recent years. But it is also true to say that much of this support may be seen as somewhat shallow and based upon utilitarian motives and, therefore, may actually be quickly lost; as transpired in the early 2000s when Irish citizens rejected the EU's agreed political position on two occasions, or indeed when strictures were imposed upon citizens – rather than bondholders – during the bailout phase. This may also be the outcome of a relatively narrow and superficial public discourse on the European Union, often confined to economics and lacking in any great critical depth. In particular the broader objectives of the European Union as a response to two world wars, the meaning of European citizenship, the future of the Union – including the concept of its *finalité* – and the necessary institutional changes required for its more effective functioning have received little sustained public debate. As in many other Member States, the debate about Europe and its future has remained a largely elite discourse, closed off from general citizens on the 'European Street'; the small number of participants in the Citizens' Consultations, while very welcome, did not fundamentally change the overall picture.

This has not been helped by the low priority the European Union and the concept of European citizenship has within the Irish education system. Quite rightly the results emanating from the Citizens' Consultations unequivocally highlight this issue: 'Education was seen as key.'[7] Even though Ireland joined in 1973 it took more than forty years for an appropriate space to be created for EU Studies in the Politics and Society Leaving Certificate curriculum, first examined in 2018.[8] There is widespread ignorance not only concerning the political structure of the EU and its institutions, but also around the distribution of competencies (the principle of subsidiarity). As a result the EU, often backed by national politicians, is regularly blamed for decisions which are in fact national responsibilities, or which the government itself had first formally agreed to in Brussels. In this regard, Ireland is no different to other Member States.

From a party-political perspective Irish discourses on the European Union, constructive ones at least, have been particularly closely related to the Fine Gael party. It very easily and quickly after Ireland's accession found a political home in the European People's Party, the European Parliament's largest political grouping whose constituent parties have many heads of government in their midst, not least Angela Merkel and her predecessor as German Chancellor, Helmut Kohl. Fine Gael and the European People's Party generally retain conservative and pragmatic positions favouring a smooth running of the capitalist market economy, seeing the EU as a facilitator of the existent order. Parties with a strong nationalist element in their ideological core, such as Sinn Féin, have always struggled with the concept of shared sovereignty. The left has, to a significant degree, marginalized itself within constructive public EU discourse, even if members of the Labour Party have been influential figures at European level, such as the longstanding MEP Proinsias de Rossa, the Irish member of the European Court of Auditors, Barry Desmond, or the co-founder (1989) of the Institute of European Affairs (now the Institute for International and European Affairs), the late Brendan Halligan.[9] At the more extreme end of the political spectrum on the left we can also find Eurosceptic condemnation of the EU as a capitalist, neo-liberal and at times even neocolonial venture. For a while strongly Euro-critical positions were also held within the Labour Party, indeed also by Michael D. Higgins himself: in the 1980s, as the largely ceremonial but influential Chairman of the Labour Party he belonged to the radical left wing of the party and actively campaigned against the Single European Act of 1987 and the Maastricht Treaty on the basis of Irish neutrality.[10] And yet, those who read (or remember) his statements from that period[11] will still find in the present speeches more evidence of the values-based consistency of a socialist rather than an ideological flexibility indebted to age or office held. Higgins' argument against the Maastricht Treaty was also the low priority and dilution the social dimension was accorded in that document; the speeches presented here prove that it has remained a key concern of his.[12] This is also, of course, for readers themselves to judge. It is true to say that outside of President Higgins' articles and speeches there have been few attempts by Irish intellectuals to popularize a constructive left-wing European position, which has for many years crystallized around the concept of a social Europe. We will pay particular attention to this here.

Introduction

CONTINENTAL EUROPEAN DEBATES

Closely related to Brexit, the evident resurgence of nationalism has also been a major issue for public intellectuals engaging with Europe, with some seeing this as endangering the European Union itself.[13] Indeed, dealing internally with the increased nationalism of Union members, such as Poland and Hungary, may well be the most important EU question of future years. More recently the Bulgarian commentator Ivan Krastev has actually taken a benign view on the neo-nationalism of Brexit, which he does not see as an existential threat to the Union. In the 2020 edition of his publication *After Europe* he writes: 'But if there is one single factor that is most responsible for Europe making its peace with the idea of maintaining the Union in some form, it is Brexit. Since 2016, Great Britain has been transformed in almost unimaginable ways. It has become provincial, disoriented, and unimportant.'[14]

In his recent pandemic book, *Is It Tomorrow, Yet? How the Pandemic Changes Europe*, Krastev argues that COVID-19 could actually lead to the consolidation and further integration of the European Union, as the global pandemic shows the necessity for both international cooperation and, at least partial, de-globalization.[15]

Indeed, the surge in nationalism in Europe has also resulted in the creation of a number of grassroots pro-EU movements from the 'European Street', which see themselves as inherently anti-nationalist. Trans-continental pro-European movements – with a defined and large social media presence and which organize pro-European events and demonstrations – include Pulse of Europe, the Young European Collective, the Democracy in Europe Movement 25 (DiEM25), We Are Europe and Stand Up for Europe.[16] These movements are not uniform. For example, Pulse of Europe, which organized large pro-EU demonstrations throughout the continent following Brexit in 2016 and 2017, sees itself as reacting to radicalism and chooses not to identify as left or right; DiEM25, on the other hand, would like to reform the EU and sees post-capitalism and a new Green Deal as necessarily central to this; Stand Up for Europe sees a federal Europe, with a president, government and a shared budget, as their ultimate goal. While it is probably easy to criticize such movements as broadly liberal and middle class, it is also undeniable that there have been distinct stirrings upon the 'European Street', although substantially less

Introduction

so in Ireland, where the rather mainstream European Movement still remains the prime forum for civic engagement.

The political scientist Claus Leggewie has catalogued many of these grassroots movements in his book *Europa Zuerst!* (Europe First!). He sees these organizations as a direct reaction to increased nationalism and authoritarianism and, if Stalin were the midwife of a European Community post-1945, then Trump and Putin may conversely be seen as preparing the ground for a European Renaissance, Leggewie believes.[17] He views these movements as agents of change that are joined together by an emphasis on democratic participation, solidarity and social and ecological sustainability; each group engages with a transnational problem central to the further development of wider European democracy. Leggewie includes in his discussion, for example, the Romanian anti-corruption movement that resulted in large demonstrations against the Romanian government in 2016; an association in Hungary that works with the Roma in direct confrontation with Viktor Orbán's government; the Irish marriage equality movement preceding the referendum of 2015, of European importance within the context of increased homophobia within and outside of Europe; Polish women's rights demonstrators protesting against their government's increased social conservatism; the large number of pro-cycling associations attached to the European Cyclists' Federation; Green economy campaigners in Greece; supporters of a universal basic income in Switzerland whose initiative resulted in a state-wide referendum; and academics in France looking for a more honest engagement with French colonialism.[18]

What is the connection between such movements and the European Union, beyond a general if perhaps vague idea of internationalist solidarity? Some of these groupings were financed by the European Union, others draw on the EU as a source of symbolic liberal-democratic support, or see it as an historical and institutional source of genuine social liberalization, as well as an organization symbolizing a more honest and balanced engagement with a dark past.

There is a particularly vibrant European debate, especially since 2016, in the German-speaking lands. These include more radical – even utopian – visions of a Europe of the future, such as that of the German political scientist Ulrike Guérot who has called for the creation of a new European Republic, in which the people hold sovereignty, with regions and cities as the foremost political agents.[19] Far too little is known in the anglophone world, and in Ireland specifically, of such visions, although English-language translations of key works are readily available.[20] One does not have to agree with such arguments – in fact in Guérot's homeland few probably do – but her ideas are stimulating and worth discussing. Together with her Austrian collaborator, the writer Robert Menasse, Guérot has also co-authored a manifesto for a European Republic. Menasse has argued for the creation of a new, post-national democracy beyond the nation state. He has also published the award-winning novel *Die Hauptstadt*, translated into English as *The Capital* and often hailed as the first EU novel, in which one of the characters makes a startling proposal for the relocation of the EU capital.[21] The novel is evidence of a broadening discourse, of a branching out into the cultural and literary field, and thus precisely in the direction Michael D. Higgins advocates in his speeches. France has contributed the more applicable, though equally radical, anti-capitalist proposal by Stéphanie Hennette, Thomas Piketty and others.[22] Otherwise, beyond President Macron's European initiatives (acknowledged by President Higgins), France appears to be, to outside observers at least, too absorbed in internal political struggles to continue the vibrant debate of previous decades, with Edgar Morin's *Penser l'Europe* (1987) being the outstanding example of this earlier engagement with the concept of Europe.

IRELAND AND INTELLECTUALS

What about Irish contributions to this debate? Is it possible that 'continental countries', albeit to varying degrees in respective societies, still admire and live the tradition of intellectuals more in an age that is increasingly losing respect for intellectual work? Before we examine Irish thoughts on Europe some reflections upon the particular role of intellectuals are appropriate here, not least as President Higgins has always been viewed in his home country as the quintessential Irish public intellectual. What exactly a public intellectual *is*, however, remains open to debate. Mary Corcoran sees a public intellectual as having a bridging function between academia and the general public; the political scientist Tom Garvin sees the purpose of the public intellectual as one of encouraging a wider audience to think; while the sociologist Pat

Introduction

O'Connor sees the role as 'creating new agendas and raising issues those in power currently wish to avoid'.[23] The post-colonial theorist Edward Said perceives the public intellectual as challenging 'both an imposed silence and the normalised quiet of unseen power'.[24] The German literary scholar Heinz Drügh views public intellectuals as formulating concepts and ideas that are inherently abstract and have not taken material or physical form yet, while personal popularity is also unavoidable for the more successful of the type.[25] All of these views retain a degree of validity, making any 'mapping' of the landscape of public intellectualism a somewhat onerous task.

The question might be asked, is Ireland an unwelcoming place for intellectuals? Describing twentieth-century Britain, Stefan Collini has written of the hostility towards the figure of the intellectual, of how the intellectual has often been conceived as essentially other; a figure of other societies and other ages, not the here and now.[26] Many would probably argue that this view is also relevant for Britain's neighbouring island: is intellectualism not seen as an element of the distant Yeatsian past? Something that takes place somewhere else, in Paris perhaps? Ireland no longer now has what can be described as a dedicated journal of ideas. The *Irish Review* valiantly struggled to replace the formidable *Crane Bag* since the mid-1980s when the latter ceased publication, eventually succumbing to market pressures in early 2020. Indeed Irish culture has been notably chided for its perceived anti-intellectualism. Historian Joe Lee has memorably stated that twentieth-century Irish culture is 'more sub-intellectual' than anti-intellectual, as 'anti-intellectualism is too intellectually demanding'; the sociologist Mary Corcoran has also more recently argued that Ireland is becoming increasingly anti-intellectual.[27] Indeed, while the Irish literary imagination has been extremely well researched by Irish and international academics, Irish intellectual history and culture has received, comparatively, scant attention.[28]

Perhaps paradoxically then, Michael D. Higgins has made the public communication of complex and abstract ideas central to his presidency. He has also been a president of unprecedented popularity, not least among younger people.[29] Should we, thus, actually talk about 'subtle-intellectualism' rather than sub-intellectualism within contemporary Irish culture? Certainly the Irish landscape of public intellectuals is now complex and diverse, while communication itself takes place among a variety of media. Public intellectuals are more likely to communicate via social media, podcasts or recently established websites, rather than traditional print media or RTÉ television. Indeed, the webzine the *Dublin Review of Books*, which publishes long-form argumentative essays usually based upon recent publications, lists up to 600 contributors, mostly Irish or Irish-based, suggesting that any lingering idea of Irish anti-intellectualism is an historical rather than contemporary reality.[30] While academic commentators have often suggested that a strong male gendering of public intellectualism in Ireland is evident,[31] this has probably become less defined.

The sociologist Liam O'Dowd suggests that in Ireland 'the contested nature of nation- and state-building and the lack of congruence between state and nation have ensured a political prominence for public intellectuals who narrate the "national story" or the "national-predicament".'[32] The 'national' certainly remains the dominant frame of reference for intellectual debate, whether in relation, for example, to discussion concerning the past or contemporary feelings of belonging.[33] President Higgins' reflections on the concept of 'home' respond, at least partly, to this national narrative. But, in contrast to the dominant discourse, he has always gone beyond it, to Europe and the wider world.

IRISH INTELLECTUALS AND EUROPE

While political scientists and political sociologists who specialize in the transnational European Union, such as Brigid Laffan and Katy Hayward, have had an undoubted wider presence in recent public intellectual life, much of the post-Brexit commentary has dealt with Ireland and Britain rather than an abstract or visionary idea of Europe itself.[34] Indeed, Fintan O'Toole – probably the best-known Irish public intellectual in the wider English-speaking world – has journeyed in recent years from incisively analysing Irish culture and politics to de-robing the pomposities of Brexit Britain and Trump's America; remaining distinctly however within a national frame of reference, even if the nations he deals with have changed in a fundamental fashion.[35] Michael D. Higgins is the sole contemporary public intellectual to regularly engage with an abstract idea of an alternative European space; the sole Irish intellectual looking to consistently reimagine Europe.

Introduction

This is not to say, of course, that Irish intellectuals have ignored the topic. Katy Hayward has argued that Irish visionary engagement with Europe has largely taken place within the dominant conceptual frameworks of Catholicism and nationalism.[36] In the 1940s Seán Ó Faoláin and Hubert Butler argued in favour of a future European federation that would enhance Irish nationhood as Ireland could engage with other small nations, while social democrat and constitutional Irish nationalist John Hume in the 1980s looked to a realigned European federal space within a new Europe of the Regions.[37] Examining Irish state discourse during the first thirty years of EEC/EU membership, Hayward also contends that 'a symbiotic relationship between national and supra-national ideologies' has existed; the language of Europe has simply been incorporated into the language of constitutional Irish nationalism, she convincingly argues.[38] Drawing on anarchist thought and postmodern theory, the philosopher Richard Kearney also looked to reimagine European space in the 1980s and early 1990s, although his thinking often tended towards an ambivalently defined united Ireland within Europe and, thus, also remains within the general framework of constitutional nationalism.[39]

Michael D. Higgins' writings on Europe largely exist outside of these nationalistic paradigms. The wider intellectual context within which to situate his writing and speeches on Europe – based as it is upon a transnational vision beyond capitalism – is actually within a left-oriented Social Europeanism, which has had, otherwise, little purchase in Ireland (as the Labour Party found out during the European election campaign of 2019). The philosophical core of this position can be found in the writings of Jürgen Habermas. Michael D. Higgins could indeed be described as an Irish Habermassian; the work of the German philosopher permeates his thought, as is clearly evident from the present collection. Habermas' Social Europeanism is based upon a number of consistent ideas: the need for post-nationalist government beyond the nation state, secularization, a belief in the management potential of the state in economics and the necessity for a strong solidarity-orientation within society.[40] The most significant argument, for Habermas, in favour of greater European integration is the fact that an unwieldy, globalized form of capitalism, which can very easily go beyond borders, requires an effective transnational institution to act as a controlling mechanism and which also functions beyond the confines of the nation state.[41] The website www.socialeurope.eu[42] brings together a number of contemporary authors, many inspired by Habermas, who write from a Social Europeanist perspective on issues such as inequality, the future of work, just transition, the refugee crisis and rising populism.[43]

RECLAIMING THE EUROPEAN STREET

The present volume should be seen within this wider European context; President Higgins' frequent reference to continental political thinkers and philosophers is no coincidence. His is an Irish contribution to the Europe-wide debate concerning the future of Europe, arguably the first of its kind. It intends to invigorate and broaden the debate, but retains a clear direction and focus.

President Michael D. Higgins' political home is the Labour Party. The vision of the European Union developed here is that of a social Europe founded on values; an ethical union, which places citizens and workers – and specifically the materially disadvantaged – at the centre of the EU's concern. It is a vision that is critical of globalized, financialized capitalism and neo-liberalism, which, these speeches make clear, have also been adopted by EU policymakers and integrated into European treaties, such as that of Lisbon. But rather than arriving at a Eurosceptic conclusion, the speeches return to the founding documents of the European integration project, the *Ventotene Manifesto* and the Treaty of Rome. The speeches are to be read as examples of a left-wing pro-European constructive criticism. The vision of a sustainable economy echoes the objective of the European Green Deal, the centrepiece of the new Commission's work plan. President Higgins' vision is also a gendered vision within which women are not just given equal rights but where the 'female' values of community, communication and cooperation move close to the centre.[44] The title of the volume is deliberately ambivalent: it highlights the need to engage with the 'street' while also critiquing the violence stirred by nationalist populist agitators and the ideologues articulating themselves there; the latter is seen as a result of the failure of the former. The streets of Europe need to be reclaimed from the dangers and vanities of populist nationalism. Advocates of socially and ecologically aware internationalism need to make their arguments more forcefully.

Introduction

Irish discourses concerning the European Union are often characterized by their complete exclusion of the cultural dimension. President Higgins regularly makes a point of including and quoting European writers and philosophers, from Aristotle to Friedrich Schiller and Czesław Miłosz. A poet himself, he aims to integrate the imaginative and utopian dimensions integral to art and literature into the European discourse. This not only broadens the debate and makes it more future-oriented rather than pragmatic and present-focused, it also adds colour, vibrancy and excitement to an EU discussion that has tended towards the stale and dreary, where legal, economic and often distant political aspects predominate.

Linked to this is the linguistic dimension. A fluent speaker of Irish, President Higgins also connects the language question to the European discourse, including lesser-used languages as expressions of minorities and marginalized communities. He emphasizes linguistic and cultural diversity and its preservation as an integral part of the Union's identity, a value which native speakers of the EU's effective *lingua franca* English often only insufficiently acknowledge. Its corollary is that an openness towards Europe cannot be achieved without a positive attitude towards learning its languages. Irish citizens decrying the distance of Brussels from their everyday lives rarely reflect upon the added distance the language of the Brussels administration creates for other citizens in the EU, 98.5 per cent of whom post-Brexit speak another language as their native tongue.

President Higgins' speeches also proudly describe the European intellectual heritage and its influence globally in terms of political and philosophical traditions, specifically in terms of human rights and democratic principles emanating from the Enlightenment period. These are also placed in more specific national contexts in the speeches on Ireland's cultural relations with individual Member States, where both parties remain part of broader European traditions of thought. The regular references to recent and contemporary continental thinkers and intellectuals, be they Paul Ricoeur, Jürgen Habermas, Wolfgang Streeck or Hartmut Rosa, mean that these speeches must be seen as part of a continent-wide European conversation, continuing in a fashion the tradition of Humanists from all of Europe corresponding with Erasmus of Rotterdam. This highlights a tension that the author is very well aware of. One could argue that this volume by an unashamedly public intellectual continues

Introduction

the elitist discourse on Europe; this would however be utterly misreading its thrust. The constant insistence on practical application and implementation in terms of social policy is only one aspect: the conviction that philosophy concerns itself with ethics and values is another. In this sense, thinking philosophically about Europe serves a very practical and social purpose, and ultimately aims to improve the lives of all citizens.

THE PRESENT EDITION

This volume contains twenty-three speeches grouped into five sections plus a Postscript on COVID-19, taking the collection right up to present concerns. It brings together all of President Higgins' major speeches on the topic of Europe since 2016.

As already stated, the Brexit decision in the UK has fundamentally altered Ireland's relationship with the European Union, and has exponentially increased interest in European matters in public debates in this country. But there are also other reasons for choosing the start date of 2016. The Centenary celebrations of the Easter Rising offered an opportunity to reflect upon the European dimension in Irish history. The role and function of historical memory is an issue President Higgins addresses frequently; its European dimension provides the theme for the first group of speeches. The start date of 1 January 2016 is also to avoid any overlap and repetition with an edition of President Higgins' speeches with a far wider remit entitled *When Ideas Matter*, which appeared in 2017.

The volume encompasses interventions on historical aspects, bilateral cultural links, citizens' involvement in the European project, workers' rights, trade unionism, third-level education and ecological concerns. A long-standing campaigner for human rights on behalf of the so-called 'developing world', President Higgins' finishing speech focuses on the EU's southern neighbours, reminding us that the EU has responsibilities for the wider world and especially for the continent of Africa, on which it may very well depend for its long-term future. That Europe is the first destination for refugees lends immediate urgency to the issue. The question of migration is presented as a consequence of global inequality and the speech reiterates the point that politics is, ultimately, a moral and ethical issue.

Introduction

We also include three translations into Irish, French and German of three selected speeches. The translation into Irish responds to the President's particular concern for Ireland's first official language – due to be given full official status in Brussels in 2022 – which he showed during his tenure as Minister for Arts, Culture and the Gaeltacht 1994–97 when Teilifís na Gaeilge, now TG4, Ireland's public Irish-language television channel, was established. The translations into French and German, the most widely spoken native languages in the EU and two of its three 'procedural languages' in which the Commission conducts its internal affairs (alongside English), highlight the multilingual nature of the European Union, but they are also included in order to increase the book's international appeal. Despite the President's active travel schedule (as evidenced by the venues mentioned in this book), little is known about Irish discourses on Europe, the EU and its future outside of Ireland. We hope that this volume will make an important contribution in this regard. As an intervention by Ireland's First Citizen we hope it will meet with interest in Brussels, among European politicians and in leading intellectual circles and think-tanks in other Member States, perhaps even on the European Street.

Non-Irish readers may find it surprising that the volume contains little on arguably the two most frequently talked about Irish issues EU-wide since 2016: Northern Ireland and the country's dogged defence of its taxation policy, specifically its corporation tax strategy. It must be openly acknowledged that what are presented here are the speeches of the Irish Head of State whose limits are narrowly defined by the Irish Constitution. The President of Ireland cannot, of course, openly interfere in (and much less criticize) government policy and the political process, even though President Higgins is well known for continuously testing the limits of his brief; this was perhaps the very reason why he was re-elected with a landslide majority. Rather than disappointment, we hope the volume may generate surprise about the trenchant criticism of neo-liberal capitalism expressed here, emerging from a country whose international stereotype is still infused with rurally-based conservative Catholicism. The speeches are a sign of a profound political change in Ireland which mirrors – but also deviates from – EU-wide trends.

It is well worth remembering that President Higgins was overwhelmingly re-elected in 2018 at a time of relative economic stability, a time usually not favourable to left-wing critics. This volume indicates an Ireland that has become more secular, open, critical and in party-political terms has noticeably shifted to the left. Recent elections, as in other EU countries, have seen a decline of the traditional (conservative) popular parties Fianna Fáil and Fine Gael, from which the President's original political home, the Irish Labour Party, has however not benefited: as in other Member States, decades of collaboration with a system which many voters regard as incapable of solving the problems of growing inequality and the erosion of workers' rights, have taken their toll. That nearly half of Ireland's MEPs elected in the last European election of 2019 are of a left or ecological left persuasion is an expression of the new political climate. The volume is a document of an Ireland in flux, a country on the periphery, yet even without Brexit well on its way to embracing EU political 'normalcy': not a few outsiders may be surprised to hear that the percentage of Ireland's population not born in the state is actually higher than in Germany.

Lastly, the speeches highlight to what extent Irish culture has always been intertwined with that of other European countries and is, thus, very much part of the collective European heritage. Mary Harney's statement that 'geographically we are closer to Berlin than Boston … spiritually we are probably a lot closer to Boston than Berlin' was questionable in 2000, and is arguably even more so now twenty years later.

Many of the speeches were first delivered to non-Irish audiences, and the key point in Michael D. Higgins' speeches applies to all EU citizens. There is a need for all citizens of the EU to take a broader perspective and an ethical view of the European Union, a view that goes beyond our narrow individual and national needs and considers the ultimate purpose for which the European Union and its predecessors were established. Frequently President Higgins refers to the *Ventotene Manifesto*, its peaceful, internationalist and tolerant spirit centring on the improvement of citizens' lives. Only when a united Europe – whatever its eventual political structure – becomes a project not only for but also of its citizens does the EU have a long-term future.

The speeches have been slightly edited but retain their flavour of oral delivery. Certain repetitions have been removed but some remain in order not to interfere with the integrity of the texts. We have also retained occasional

Introduction

passages in Irish as delivered on the occasion. English translations are given in footnotes.

We would like to thank President Higgins for suggesting the idea of this book to us following his state visit to Germany in 2019 and for granting us access to all of his speeches and additional notes. We would like to thank especially Claire Power, Adviser to the President, for her instant responses to all our enquiries and her help with the numerous photographs accompanying this edition. We are grateful to our three translators, Pádraig de Bhaldraithe, Dominique Le Meur and Rolf Höfig for delivering their translations within a very short timeframe. Our thanks are also due to Antony Farrell of The Lilliput Press for readily and enthusiastically engaging in the project and to the editorial team for bringing it through the editing stages in a timely fashion. All of us were keen to bring out this book as soon as possible as it responds to issues of the day. Lastly, we would like to acknowledge the financial support of the European Union's Jean Monnet Programme as part of, arguably, the most successful programme the EU has ever undertaken, ERASMUS, now expanded into ERASMUS+. While many other programmes have generated rivalry and competition, ERASMUS has had, since 1987, no other purpose than bringing young people together, without whose involvement and engagement the EU has no future. It is thus quite appropriate that President Higgins should also highlight it in several instances in his speeches.

Joachim Fischer (Limerick)
Fergal Lenehan (Jena)
December 2020

I
EUROPEAN HISTORY AND MEMORY

In Honour of Roger Casement

Speech at the official state commemoration in honour of Roger Casement, Banna Strand, Ardfert, Co. Kerry, 21 April 2016.

Roger Casement was not just a great Irish patriot, he was also one of the great humanitarians of the early twentieth century – a man who is remembered fondly and respectfully by so many people across the world for his courageous work in exposing the darkness that lay at the heart of European imperialism. In his own time, few figures attracted the sympathy and admiration of their contemporaries as widely as Roger Casement. Striking in appearance, his photograph was widely distributed and displayed in the homes of Ireland, and Roger Casement was described by many as a man of considerable charm and distinction. Those who knew him – his friends in the Irish nationalist movement, those in the Congo Reform Association, his colleagues in the British Foreign Service – have all emphasized Roger Casement's idealism, his passionate empathy for the hopeless and the oppressed. His friend Bulmer Hobson thus said of him: 'I have known no one who was so stirred at the thought of injustice and wrong, whether it was in Africa, America or Ireland. I have not met his equal for courtesy or kindliness or generosity ... I do not expect to meet his like again.'[1]

And yet, none of the leaders of 1916 has excited as much controversy just before their death and ever since. Casement was undoubtedly a complex personality, and he was centrally involved in one of the most contentious episodes of the Irish revolutionary period.

A hundred years on, with the benefit of hindsight, we are able to see in a new light the life and legacy of Roger Casement. We are better able to grasp how the multiple layers of his identity and allegiances, as an Irishman and a sensitive humanitarian at the turn of the last century, were played out in the life of Roger Casement. We can more readily discern, too, the complexities of his personality, the impact of early childhood and separation, but also the coherence of his journey, from his membership of the British colonial administration to his most fundamental critique of Empire, and his ultimate commitment to the cause of Irish independence.

As we come together at the location of Roger Casement's last stand as an Irish revolutionary, it is appropriate that we recall the crucial part that he played in the lead-up to the Easter Rising of 1916. Indeed it was here, on this 'lonely strand', that Roger Casement, Robert Monteith and Daniel Bailey came ashore in the early hours of the morning of Good Friday, 21 April 1916. The three men had arrived to Kerry aboard the German submarine *U19* and they had expected to meet the *Aud*, a German ship disguised as a neutral Norwegian freighter, which was carrying a supply of arms for the men and women who, across Ireland, were getting ready for an armed uprising scheduled to happen on the following Easter Sunday. Due to failures in communication, the two vessels failed to meet in Tralee Bay. Casement, Bailey and Monteith set off for the shore in a small wooden boat, which capsized. Drenched, exhausted, and suffering from a recurrence of the malaria he had contracted in the Congo, Roger Casement remained in hiding at McKenna's Fort while his two companions walked ahead to Tralee to seek help. At around 1.30 pm that same day, Roger Casement was discovered and arrested by Constable Bernard O'Reilly and Sergeant John Hearn of the Ardfert RIC; he spent the night in Tralee's police barracks, where he was treated with kindness by Head Constable John A. Kearney, before he was transferred to London to be interrogated and tried for treason. Meanwhile, out at sea, having evaded British naval patrols and survived several violent storms, the *Aud* and its arms shipment had arrived in Tralee Bay on Thursday 20 April. When they discovered that there was no pilot to guide them into Fenit, Officer of the Imperial German Navy Captain Karl Spindler and his crew of twenty-two men, all of whom had volunteered for the perilous mission, decided to wait in the bay throughout the day. Eventually trapped, the *Aud* was escorted by HMS *Bluebell* to Queenstown [Cobh Harbour], where the crew decided to scuttle the ship rather than surrender their cargo. These men spent the subsequent war years in prison for the part they played in supporting the plans for an Irish armed rebellion, and both they and their families paid a price for these actions. Some of the crew, including Raimund Weisbach, Wilhelm Augustin, Otto Walter, Hans Dunker and Friedrich Schmitz, participated in the official Irish State ceremonies of 1966, and they travelled to Kerry to witness the laying of the foundation stone of this memorial at which we stand today. Again today, fifty years after 1966, and a century on from April 1916, it is appropriate that Ireland acknowledges the debt of gratitude we owe to these men for their actions in support of Irish freedom.

The events that unfolded here in Kerry a hundred years ago are notorious – they are remembered in song and in legend; but the background to these events, and, above all, their many ramifications and consequences abroad are sometimes cloaked in confusion although they are of immense importance in understanding the events that would take place in Dublin during that Easter week. It is well known, for example, how, upon learning that Casement had been captured and that the arms were lost, leader of the Irish Volunteers Eoin MacNeill issued his countermanding order calling off the Rising. However, popular memory has often omitted to register that, upon coming back to Ireland, Roger Casement's intention had been to try and prevent the planned rebellion from taking place. Indeed, Casement believed that any Irish insurrection would be easily suppressed unless it received substantial assistance from Germany. In October 1914 he had travelled to Berlin as the envoy of Irish-American nationalist leaders, to lead discussions with high-ranking German officials and try and form an Irish Brigade from among thousands of Irish prisoners of war held in Germany. The eighteen months Roger Casement spent across the Rhine were, overall, a failure: he managed to recruit only fifty-six volunteers for his Irish Brigade;[2] and, eventually, disillusioned with the minimal character of imperial Germany's support to an Irish uprising, and anxious to avoid an unnecessary bloodshed, he resolved to go back to Ireland to advise the nationalist leaders that any armed uprising was doomed and should, therefore, be aborted.

When reflecting back on those founding events of our state, it is essential to locate the Easter Rising within its global and European contexts, and particularly within the 'game of embattled giants' that was World War I, in the words of Roger Casement. In the eyes of many Irish Republicans, that imperialist war was both an appalling loss of life in which 'small nationalities' were mere 'pawns'[3] and a catalyst for the great Irish revolt they were calling forth. The reference to Germany as 'our gallant allies in Europe', in the Proclamation of 1916, must be read in that context. We might find such intervention of a belligerent nation against which many Irishmen were then fighting from within the British army an uncomfortable fact to acknowledge. Yet it is important that we refrain, at a distance of one hundred years, from any simplistic judgment – whether apologetic or condemning. It is important that we endeavour to do justice to the motivations of the actors of the time, and to the manner in which they judged or were induced to seize the opportunities afforded by that wider context to advance a cause they believed was just; however it was to be attained. Regardless of how ambivalent in their relation to great powers Irish Republicans might have been, the Irish Citizen Army was not – as is reflected in the banner 'We serve neither King nor Kaiser, but Ireland' they put up on Liberty Hall in the lead-up to the Rising.

Roger Casement, having seen through the moral breakdown of the free-trading Empire he had willingly served for several decades, was in no doubt, by Easter 1916, where his loyalty lay. As he put it in his famous speech from the dock, of which we have just heard several moving excerpts:

> Loyalty is a sentiment, not a law. It rests on love, not on restraint. The government of Ireland by England rests on restraint, and not on law; and, since it demands no love, it can evoke no loyalty.
>
> That blessed word Empire, that bears so paradoxical resemblance to charity! For if charity begins at home, Empire begins in other men's homes, and both may cover a multitude of sins. I, for one, was determined that Ireland was much more to me than Empire, and that, if charity begins at home, so must loyalty.[4]

Today we must also recall how, in a true Republican spirit, Roger Casement's generous vision for the Ireland of the future was one that included all of the people of Northern Ireland, in the diversity of their beliefs, origins and history. This was a vision which Casement recalled in that same speech from the dock, when he said: 'We aimed at uniting the Ulster Volunteers to the cause of United Ireland. We aimed at uniting all Irishmen in a natural and national bond of cohesion based on mutual self-respect.'[5]

This reminds us that throughout his life, Roger Casement always thought of himself as an Ulsterman. When he and a small number of his friends, including Bulmer Hobson, Erskine Childers and Alice Stopford Green, took the initiative of the Howth and Kilcoole gun-runnings, in the summer 1914, they had in mind the example of the Ulster Volunteers, who had imported guns from Germany a few short months earlier. Sharing a common Antrim background, both Roger Casement and Eoin MacNeill also shared an admiration for the determination of the Ulster Unionists, and Roger Casement was slow to relinquish his hopes that they might be won over to the struggle for Irish Home Rule.

Notwithstanding what some have described as the naivety of such views, today we must appreciate the rich and multilayered sense of belonging to Ireland that underpinned all of Roger Casement's actions. A boy brought up in the Protestant faith, first in Co. Dublin and then between Ulster and Liverpool, he admired and identified with the Irish rebels of the past, as well as with the legendary Ulster heroes. Those figures featured prominently, for example, in 'The Dream of the Celt', an epic Roger Casement began on his way out to Loanda (and which would go on to be the title of Mario Vargas Llosa's fictional biography of Casement).[6] Roger Casement himself claimed that it was his Irish identity that allowed him to fully grasp the oppressive nature of European colonial rule in the Congo and the Amazon. Indeed, he would become the whistle-blower of imperial colonial greed in two continents. Although Casement's transformation is indeed quite an astonishing one – five years after being knighted in recognition of his investigations in the Putumayo on behalf of the British Foreign Office, he was put on trial for his separatist revolutionary activities and hanged for high treason – there is coherence and integrity to this journey.

I. European History and Memory

Recent scholarship has shown how Casement's 'reading' of Ireland as a victim of conquest informed his outlook on the oppression of the indigenous peoples of Africa and South America. In turn, his experience in these sites of plunder, exploitation and degradation probably crystallized his view of Ireland's subjugation to British imperialism. Tellingly, two of the most significant junctures in Roger Casement's professional life as a British diplomat – the publication of his report on the Congo in 1904, and on the Putumayo in 1911 – also correspond to two thresholds in his involvement with the Irish revolutionary movement. In 1904, after travelling to remote areas of the Upper Congo, Roger Casement presented convincing evidence that the collection of rubber in the territory under the direct control of King Leopold of Belgium, the so-called 'Congo Free State', was widely associated with extortion of taxes, forced labour, murder, mutilation and depopulation. As a formidable indictment of a system based on the crudest violations of human rights, Roger Casement's findings contributed to boosting international pressures that eventually led to a reform of the administration of the Congo. It was in June of that same year, 1904, that Casement attended the Feis of the Glens in Antrim – a festive occasion that bonded him for the next decade with a circle of Irish cultural and civic activists, and sparked his deepening interest in the Irish language and the revival movement. Seven years later, in March 1911, Roger Casement completed a second report for the Foreign Office, in which he documented the atrocities associated with the activities of an Anglo-Peruvian rubber company operating in the frontier region of the north-west Amazon. The publication of this report coincided with the culmination of Casement's estrangement from the British Diplomatic Service, from which he resigned in 1913. From thereafter, Roger Casement moved decisively towards separatist activities, up to that fateful Good Friday 1916, when he was captured in McKenna's Fort near Banna Strand.

Roger Casement was hanged in Pentonville Prison, in London, in the early morning of 3 August 1916, following a trial that attracted the attention of writers, humanitarians and lawyers from around the world. While much of the controversy surrounding the trial has revolved, up to our times, around the question of Roger Casement's sexuality, the more important question always related to the various distortions of justice that characterized these legal proceedings. The trial was outrageous for its imperilling of an adequate defence by the circulation of material that would strike a populist note and blacken the defendant in an extra-judicial attempt at undermining the international campaign for clemency. Beyond and above all these considerations, the ongoing commemorations offer an important opportunity, I believe, to engage with the fundamental questions Roger Casement raised about power and human rights, about the rights of communities and indigenous peoples, and about the rules guiding foreign policy and international trade. His was an epoch that is sometimes referred to as that of the 'first globalization' – an era when capital moved freely between countries and when the flow of goods exchanged within and between Europe's huge colonial empires increased dramatically; an era, too, when tens of millions of Europeans left the old continent to seek their fortunes in what was called the New World.[7] It is only now, despite the pioneering humanitarianism of such as Casement, that the degradation of indigenous peoples has grown into a central issue in human rights discourse. At the same time, it is in those very regions visited by Casement that we continue to see today the greatest damage to ecosystems and communities – and where, outrageously, once again immunity is being sought by irresponsible but powerful commercial interests in sectors such as logging and mining.

Is deis íontach é Comóradh an Chéid seo dúinn díriú ar na ceisteanna moráltachta bunúsacha a d'árdaigh Ruairí Mac Easmainn lena chomhghleacaithe a scrúdú athuair - ceisteanna atá fós le freagairt againn céad bliain níos déanaí. Is cúis mórtais dúinn idéalachas Mhic Easmainn sa lá atá inniu ann, agus is ceart dúinn a bheith bródúil as an méid a rinne sé ar son chosmhuintir an domhain, agus cur chun cinn na saoirse, in Éirinn agus thar lear.[8]

May I, here in Kerry, at the site of his last efforts in the name of that freedom, quote once more Roger Casement's own words, conveying his beliefs and his life's purpose: 'The faculty of preserving through centuries of misery the remembrance of lost liberty, – this surely is the noblest cause ever man strove for, ever lived for, ever died for.'[9]

A Forgotten Polish Hero of the Great Irish Famine: Paul Strzelecki's Struggle to Save Thousands of Lives

Speech at the official opening of a Polish exhibition on the Great Famine, Royal Irish Academy, Dublin, 8 May 2019.

Ireland and Poland have much in common. Our shared history is enriched by deep economic, cultural and personal ties, as well as our shared membership of the European Union. Contemporary Irish–Polish relations are dynamic and growing, bolstered in no small part by the vibrant Polish community in Ireland; men and women who have chosen to make Ireland their home and who, may I acknowledge, are making such a vital contribution to our society.

Together with our experience of being caught in the injustices of empires, their conflicts and our struggle for independence, it is perhaps our mutual, shared and sometimes painful histories of migration that provide such a striking commonality. For those of us who have been students of migration, the seminal work on Polish migration to America by Thomas and Znaniecki, *The Polish Peasant in Europe and America*,[10] remains one of the classical founding studies on migrants at points of origin and destination.

A Forgotten Polish Hero of the Great Irish Famine

Today we are recognizing a special friend of the Irish, Paul (Paweł) Edmund Strzelecki, one of the great Polish humanitarians of the nineteenth century. This exhibition tells the captivating story of Strzelecki, an explorer and geologist by profession, thanks to whose efforts perhaps some 200,000 children were saved from starvation during the Great Irish Famine of the nineteenth century. Strzelecki was the main agent of the British Relief Association, a charity established by a group of prominent philanthropists in 1847 that was the largest private provider of relief during the Great Irish Famine and Scottish Highland Potato Famine of the 1840s.

Strzelecki developed a visionary and effective mode of assistance: feeding starving children directly through the schools. He extended daily food rations to schoolchildren across the most famine-stricken western part of Ireland, while also distributing clothing and promoting basic hygiene. At its peak in 1848, around 200,000 children from all denominations were being fed, many of whom would have otherwise perished from hunger and disease.

On an occasion like today, at which we discover the detail of his heroic work and formally mark Polish links to the Great Famine in Ireland, it is important to recall all those who suffered and perished during this most defining event in the making of contemporary Ireland. That catastrophe in terms of human impact was, as we now recognize is true of all famines, ultimately political and economic in its origins. We are morally challenged to reject any suggestion that its human toll was unavoidable, inevitable, or indeed, as some sources put it, an act of God.

By 1849 the nation was in the midst of the apocalyptic conditions of the fourth year of famine, at a time when the responsibility for public action had, in effect, been abdicated by the British government and passed to the indebted Irish Poor Law Unions. In this year, one of the first professors recruited to the newly established University College Cork was the distinguished mathematician George Boole, who described what he witnessed on his rail journey from Dublin to Cork: 'There is over the whole country an air of utter destitution and abandonment.'[11] This was a theme that was recorded earlier in a number of accounts by European travellers, including the 1837 account of the Hungarian Baron József Eötvös.[12] A decade before the arrival of potato blight, the precarious position of a large swathe of the population was already a matter of public record. The script for the devastation that was to follow ten years later had largely been written.

It is impossible, in my view, to adequately deal with the Great Famine without reference to the plantations, dispossessions and exclusions that created a particular congested dispersal of population on impossible holdings of land and serf-like conditions. George Cornewall Lewis' *Remarks on the Third Report of the Irish Poor Inquiry Commissioners*[13] is a particularly interesting account because it provides an insight into what insiders at the time admitted (it is rarely admitted now) as to the British government's real intentions in relation to Ireland: to clear the land of tenants and secret organizations through harsh workhouse regimes.

As a surviving people in appalling conditions with an enforced migratory diaspora, Ireland and Irish people would become totally changed by the Famine. We are only now, assisted with recent advances in new scholarship such as UCC's *Atlas of the Irish Famine*,[14] and encouraged by new cultural endeavours, such as that which is represented here today, taking into ourselves the depth of the complexity of the Great Famine and, thus, feel able to confront the consequences of the tragic events which took place on our island 170 years ago. Our own past, the dynamics of our own history and its relationship with our neighbours, the changes in social forces in our own country and how it would inform our politics, cannot be understood without an understanding of the Great Famine.

We know from the 1841 census that some 40 per cent of Irish families were recorded as living in nearly half a million of what was called a *bothán*, a one-room mud hut described on the census as 'fourth-class houses' that were considered generally unfit for human habitation. The families who lived in a *bothán* were drawn overwhelmingly from either the over 3 million landless agricultural labourers in Ireland at the time, or the nearly 1.5 million cottiers that were leasing tiny plots of land, often barely enough to keep their families alive. They, like the tenant categories above them, had no security of tenure, but were frequently without the means of survival itself, and, with nothing to sell, were without the means to flee. The English journalist Joseph Kay was appalled to learn that their homes were simply destroyed when they were evicted: 'If they do not pay their rent at the proper time, they are liable to be turned adrift, even in the middle of the night, into the bleak road, without a shelter, and with their helpless wives and children. No notice is necessary; no notice is given.'[15]

These classes of men, women and children in the lower reaches of the class pyramid – the labourers and the cottiers – bore the very worst consequences of the Famine. It is they who are, in statistical terms, more likely to be found amongst the more than 1 million who died. If some were lucky enough to be assisted, such as those 200,000 children helped by Paweł Strzelecki, they are among the 2 million who subsequently emigrated to places like Britain, North America and Australia.

There are of course countless others who, without the resources to emigrate, gathered in the large towns and cities; for between 1844 and the 1850s many, including pregnant women, took to the roads to survive. The 1851 census records only 135,000 habitations described as *bothán*, testament not to any programme of assistance, but to the obliteration and destruction of any record that these families had even lived their lives on the land.

The Great Famine, *an Gorta Mór*, though not the sole foundation event in the formation of the Irish diaspora – after all, over a million Irish people had emigrated to North America between 1815 and 1845 – must yet still be considered the single most important event in the formation of a distinct Irish-American cultural identity. Some 2.1 million people left this island in the decade between 1846 and 1855, more than in the previous two-and-a-half centuries combined, and 1.5 million of them settled in the United States, even if it was Canada that had been their point of arrival.

Their migration made a legacy that had been foretold with apprehension. In 1860 the *Times* of London was quoted as saying the following:

> If this goes on as it is likely to go on … the United States will become very Irish … So, an Ireland there will still be, but on a colossal scale, and in a new world. We shall only have pushed the Celt westwards. Then, no longer cooped between the Liffey and the Shannon, he will spread from New York to San Francisco, and keep up the ancient feud at an unforeseen advantage … We must gird our loins to encounter the nemesis of seven centuries' misgovernment. To the end of time a hundred million spread over the largest habitable area in the world, and, confronting us everywhere by sea and land, will remember that their forefathers paid tithe to the Protestant clergy, rent to the absentee landlords, and a forced obedience to the laws which these had made.[16]

Indeed, this article was prescient, as, by 1901, more people born in Ireland were living outside the island of Ireland than living within it. They, the Irish abroad, would play a crucial role in the cultural revival and the preparations for independence, both parliamentary and military.

I am struck by the parallel Polish experience of emigration, in particular to the United States. In the period from the early 1800s to the beginning of World War II, records indicate that approximately five million Polish emigrated to the United States. These Poles fled their country for various reasons: some left to escape conscription, others left to seek better opportunities in the United States, and some fled from religious persecution.

The Ireland of the late 1840s had not experienced the impact of the public health reforms championed by Edwin Chadwick. Sanitation and water supplies were compromised, leading to a huge incidence of diseases such as typhus, yellow fever and cholera. In his testimony to a House of Lords Committee in 1847, Father Theobald Mathew, whose statue adorns Cork's St Patrick's Street, described his efforts to bury the dead: 'Each day there was a large pit dug, and all that died that day were put down; the pit was covered up; I had four men employed. Some days there were sixty or seventy a day buried, and some days more.'[17]

Accounts such as this, which lay bare the 'averted gaze' as I have written elsewhere[18] and demonstrate an absence of, as Father Mathew suggested, solidarity and empathy for human suffering, should be grounds for our reflection. We have also to place such an account alongside the extraordinary accounts of the visit of Queen Victoria to Cobh and Cork, in the midst of jubilant crowds of prosperous citizens, while unseen to the visiting monarch, those whom contemporaries termed 'shadows and spectres', 'ghastly skeletons' and 'phantoms' wandered the streets of the city.[19] Father Mathew issued a statement that is a credit to his obvious anger, criticizing Cork Council for having beggars routinely rounded up every night: 'Under the Authority of an Act of Parliament they take up sturdy beggars and vagrants, they confine them at night in a Market Place, and the next morning send them out in a cart five miles from the town, and there they are left, and a great part of them perish, for they have no homes to go to.'[20]

There are lessons that can be drawn from the obvious crisis and destitution of the people and the indifference to it. Only a pernicious and dangerous economic orthodoxy could morally sanction poverty amidst plenty, conspicuous consumption amidst mass slaughter – an ideology that elevated the right of property above any version of natural law, even while it relegated the duty of humanity and of solidarity to the arena of charity. Were it not for those like Paweł Strzelecki, the numbers who died of starvation would, of course, have been even higher. In February 1847 Strzelecki reached Westport and wrote, 'No pen can describe the distress by which I am surrounded.'[21] His testimony broke the silence as it was published by several British newspapers and helped to illuminate the plight of the suffering in Ireland.

Despite this, the British government, which had sanctioned the withdrawal of government support in the midst of Black '47, also, as scholars Amartya Sen and Mike Davis have reminded us, attempted to rationalize the monumental catastrophes suffered in the same manner as those experienced by the Indian people and the inaction of the British Raj during the Indian famines of 1876–78, 1896–97 and 1899–1900.[22] Despite the British government cutting state-backed famine relief in 1847, Strzelecki remained in Ireland, assisting poor families until 1849, even though he himself was suffering from the effects of typhoid fever contracted in Ireland.

Strzelecki also helped impoverished Irish families to seek new lives in Australia where he had been an explorer in the years before arriving in Ireland. During his three years in Ireland he never sought any remuneration for his work. His commitment was widely recognized and praised by his contemporaries, and it is appropriate that, in May 2015, a plaque honouring Strzelecki's efforts was unveiled by Lord Mayor Christy Burke and the Mayor of Poznán, Mr Jacek Jaśkowiak, and can be found on Sackville Place in the heart of Dublin's city centre. This exhibition this evening ... rightly endeavours to bring his achievements and legacy more widely into the public eye.

How should we now reckon with the Famine? Let us do so with new histories, new intellectual work to inform policy that does not eschew moral purpose, that does not accept bogus inevitabilities, that tests assumptions, and is dedicated to telling the story of the people; let us do so through a renewed commitment to solidarity, in a spirit of hope and a generous welcome to all models of possibility, with all those who still now suffer as our ancestors, at home and overseas, once did.

The Great Flu of 1918–19: Why Remember? Why Forget?

Speech at a reception commemorating the Great Flu Epidemic of 1918–19, Áras an Uachtaráin, 31 May 2019.

Just over one hundred years ago, as World War I was drawing to a fitful close, an influenza virus, unlike any before or since, swept across the world, felling soldiers and civilians alike. The global death toll was inconceivable: according to the most recent estimates, between 50 million and 100 million people worldwide perished in the three pandemic waves between the spring of 1918 and the winter of 1919, making it one of the deadliest natural disasters in human history. Indeed, the pandemic caused mortality that was similar in scale to that which resulted from the Black Death in the fourteenth century. If one adjusts for population growth, the death toll would be equivalent in terms of impact to between 200 million and 425 million deaths today. As with other twentieth-century epidemics and pandemics, such as HIV/AIDS, Africans and Asians suffered proportionately more than Europeans and North Americans. Thus, while the average case mortality in what we term the developed world was about 2 per cent, in India, where 18.5 million perished, it was

6 per cent, and in Egypt, where 138,000 died, it was 10 per cent. In isolated regions in which populations had no immunity to flu, the impact was truly astonishing: in Western Samoa, for example, a quarter of the population died, while in Alaska some entire Inuit communities died as a result.

Infectious disease had already limited life expectancy in the early twentieth century. However, in the first year of the pandemic, life expectancy in the United States was shortened by about twelve years as a direct result. Mark Honigsbaum, the author of *Living with Enza: The Forgotten Story of Britain and the Great Flu Pandemic of 1918*, has written extensively about the pandemic's probable origin.

Few epidemiologists believe the pandemic began in Spain, pointing instead to pre-pandemic waves in Copenhagen and other northern European cities in the summer of 1918. Where the virus first leapt from birds to humans or some other mammal is even more perplexing, with some scientists favouring a Kansas point of origin and others northern France or China.[23]

Spanish flu was so called because neutral Spain was one of the few countries in 1918 where correspondents were free to report on the outbreak. To maintain morale in countries at war, wartime censors minimized early reports of illness and mortality in Germany, the United Kingdom, France and the United States. Papers were free to report the epidemic's effects in neutral Spain (such as the grave illness of King Alfonso XIII). This created a false impression of Spain as especially hard hit, thereby giving rise to the pandemic's moniker, 'Spanish flu'.

In a 2007 analysis of medical journals from the period of the pandemic, it was found that the viral infection itself was no more aggressive than any previous influenza, but that the special circumstances of the context, both structural and contingent of the epidemic (malnourishment, overcrowded medical camps and hospitals, poor hygiene) promoted bacterial super-infection that would kill most of the victims, typically after a prolonged deathbed.

However, there remain many mysteries associated with the pandemic, perhaps chief of which relates to why the Spanish flu proved so deadly to young adults. Here, present-day science has some interesting hypotheses to offer but, it appears, no conclusive answers. One suggestion is that the elderly enjoyed greater immunity because, as children, they had been exposed to a pandemic virus with a similar genetic makeup to what was called the Spanish flu. Conversely, those aged twenty-eight and under had an immunological blind spot because their first exposure had been to the 1890 'Russian flu', a virus with a completely different configuration of genes. Another explanation, posited by Honigsbaum, is that the unusual mortality pattern seen in 1918 was the result of an as yet unidentified environmental exposure, or stressor, peculiar to young adults at the time. Answering these questions is important because genes from the Spanish flu continue to circulate in human and pig populations to this day. Some of these genes are direct descendants of the 1918 virus; others have reasserted themselves with other pandemic viruses, such as the 1968 Hong Kong flu and the virus responsible for the 2009 swine flu pandemic.

The pandemic reached Ireland, most likely in spring 1918, as troops sailing home took the flu into Dublin and Cork. The first recorded outbreak was on USS *Dixie*, off Cobh, in May. From the ports the disease swept across Ireland in three waves: mild in spring 1918; lethal in autumn 1918; and moderate in early 1919. It disrupted Irish society and politics, as has been skilfully recounted by Dr Ida Milne [...] Her doctoral research in Trinity College Dublin, which has been published as a book entitled *Stacking the Coffins: Influenza, War and Revolution in Ireland, 1918–19*,[24] is the first Irish history of the disease that includes statistics where an attempt is made to analyse which groups were most affected. It is all the more valuable for also drawing from personal accounts of individuals affected.

Léiríonn an leabhar gur chuir spré an ghalair na bailte ina dtost; dhún sé na scoileanna, na cúirteanna, agus na leabharlanna, laghdaigh sé méid na trádála, líon sé na hospidéil, agus chuir sé brú as cuimse ar na dochtúirí agus iad ag cuir cóir leighis ar na céadta othar gach lá.[25]

Dr Milne also reveals how the pandemic became part of a major row between nationalists and the government over interned anti-conscription campaigners. Indeed, Dr Milne and Dr Patricia Marsh from Queen's University Belfast [...] have analysed how, across the whole island of Ireland, there were more than 23,000 recorded deaths as a result of the virus. However, due to a lack of diagnosis and documentation, it is thought that up to 800,000 people in Ireland – about one-fifth of the population at the time – could have been infected.

I am [...] pleased to be able to welcome to the Áras today some family members of those who died tragically and of central figures who helped those affected by the pandemic in Ireland, as well as others involved in preventing and combating pandemics today.

I wish to focus today on the legacy of the Spanish flu pandemic in terms beyond the scientific mysteries and devastating statistics that it gave rise to. By this I mean I would like to consider the link between the pandemic, and indeed other tragic historical events, and human memory. I believe this is a worthwhile endeavour because the Spanish flu began to fade from public awareness quickly, especially over the decades of the twentieth century until the arrival of news about bird flu and other pandemics in the 1990s and 2000s. Indeed, although it claimed many more lives than the Easter Rising, the War of Independence and the Civil War combined, the Great Flu is rarely incorporated into the narrative of twentieth-century Ireland. This has led some historians, such as A.W. Crosby and Caitriona Foley, to label the Spanish flu a 'forgotten pandemic'.[26]

The challenge of remembering ethically was a significant part of the Ethics Initiative, which I launched as the second President of Ireland Initiative of my presidency. In addressing the need to 'remember ethically', I turned to the philosophical writings of Hannah Arendt, Paul Ricoeur, Avishai Margalit and Richard Kearney. The emphasis was on the need to respect a pluralism of narratives of shared events, including sources of conflict, its delivery, consequences, as material for revived hate, fear, xenophobia, or indeed by some necessary but rare forgiveness. The concept of collective memory, initially developed by Halbwachs, has been explored and expanded from various angles across different disciplines of research. Our collective memory of events can be constructed, shared and passed on by large and small social groups. Memories survive and take shape through a relationship with others, evolving over time, and are open to reinterpretation and reconsideration as we strive to transact a relationship that will ideally release us from the weight of past events, and that will allow a moving forward, however tentatively, to new beginnings by loosening the lid on, what I call in one of my poems, the 'mouldering jar of memory'.

The historian Professor Guy Beiner [...], an authority on memory and history on Ireland, has criticized the unreflective use of the adjective 'collective' in many studies of memory. In his essay, 'Troubles with Remembering, or, the Seven Sins of Memory Studies', he asserts:

> The problem is with crude concepts of collectivity, which assume a homogeneity that is rarely, if ever, present, and maintain that, since memory is constructed, it is entirely subject to the manipulations of those invested in its maintenance, denying that there can be limits to the malleability of memory, or to the extent to which artificial constructions of memory can be inculcated. In practice, the construction of a completely collective memory is, at best, an aspiration of politicians, which is never entirely fulfilled and is always subject to contestations.[27]

In its place, Professor Beiner has promoted the term 'social memory' and has also demonstrated its limitations by developing a related concept of 'social forgetting'.

Why do some major historical events occupy the forefront of the collective consciousness, while profound moments, such as the pandemic we are discussing today, sometimes stand distantly behind? Ricoeur reflects in his book, *Memory, History, Forgetting*, on whether it is possible that history 'overly remembers some events at the expense of others,'[28] revealing how this attempted symbiosis of what are contested and conflicting versions, and the mould into which they are poured, influences both the perception of historical experience and the production of historical narrative. The philosophical paradoxes of memory, the aporias of forgetting, and the mediating role of history are all issues we need to consider in understanding such a profound, complex and interconnected question. Our ambivalence about remembering perhaps expresses ambivalence about our own identities. The basic dialectic of memory and amnesia is, thus, not only about remembering and forgetting certain events or people. Viet Thanh Nguyen argues that, in the context of war, it is instead more fundamentally about remembering our humanity and forgetting our inhumanity, while conversely remembering the inhumanity of others and forgetting their humanity:

> A just memory demands instead a final step in the dialectics of ethical memory – not just the movement between an ethics of remembering one's own and remembering others, but also a shift toward an ethics of recognition, of seeing and remembering how the inhuman inhabits the human.[29]

No wonder, then, that for Jorge Luis Borges, remembering is a 'ghostly verb'. Memory is haunted, not just by ghostly others, but by the horrors we have done, seen and condoned, or by the unspeakable things from which we have profited. The troubling weight of the past is especially evident when we speak of war and our limited ability to recall it. Haunted and haunting, human and inhuman, war remains with us and within us, impossible to forget but difficult to remember.

According to Avishai Margalit, shared memory in a modern society travels from person to person through institutions, such as archives, through historiographic texts, and through communal mnemonic devices, such as speeches enunciated by public representatives, monuments and the names of streets; all of these reflect a distribution of power.[30]

Memory, indeed, constitutes one of the greatest sources of interrogation bequeathed to us by the twentieth century, with its cortege of pandemics like the one we are remembering today, mass crimes and fateful experimentations with totalitarianism. How and what are we to remember? How are individual and collective memories articulated? What must never become the subject of amoral amnesia? In what ways does the 'duty of memory' summon us to do justice to the dead? To what extent are we to allow ourselves to be changed as we listen to the narrative of the Other? What is the relationship between memory and history? These are first-order moral questions. They are central to the work of important thinkers such as Maurice Halbwachs, Hannah Arendt and Paul Ricoeur – work that I find myself returning to again and again as I attempt an answer to such questions.

There really can never be a new moment; rather, it is that from the fragments of the old, as in nature itself, something new seeks to be born, often against the impediments of the old, and thus arrives with a scream that in time may become a smile. Edith Wyschogrod, in *An Ethics of Remembering: History, Heterology and the Nameless Others*, attempts to answer the question, 'can the historian ever bring back that which has gone by, ever tell the truth about the past?'[31] Wyschogrod is concerned with the cataclysm: mass annihilations of the twentieth century such as the flu pandemic. Realizing the philosophical impossibility of ever recovering 'what really happened', Wyschogrod nevertheless acknowledges a moral imperative to speak for those who have been rendered voiceless, to give countenance to those who have become faceless, and hope to the desolate.

Various theories of why there is something of a collective amnesia regarding the Spanish flu include: first, the rapid pace of the pandemic, which killed most of its victims in the United States, for example, within a period of less than nine months, resulting in limited media coverage; second, the fact that, as the historical epidemiologist Carla Morrissey has pointed out,[32] the general population was familiar with patterns of pandemic disease in the late-nineteenth and early-twentieth centuries, with typhoid, yellow fever, diphtheria and cholera all occurring near the same time, possibly lessening the significance of the influenza pandemic for the public; third, in many areas the flu was not reported on, the only mention being that of advertisements for medicines claiming to cure it, as discussed by Benedict and Braithwaite;[33] fourth, the outbreak coincided with the deaths and media focus on World War I, which took precedence, according to A.W. Crosby;[34] and fifth, related to this, the majority of fatalities, from both the war and the epidemic, were among young adults, with the deaths caused by the flu potentially overlooked, according to Simonsen and others,[35] owing to the large number of deaths of young men in the war or as a result of injuries.

It seems highly plausible that, particularly in Europe, where the war's toll was extremely high, the flu may not have had a great, separate psychological impact, or may have seemed just another terrible extension of the war's tragedies. The flu-related deaths appear to have been absorbed into the public consciousness side by side with those deaths directly attributable to the war. The duration of the pandemic and the war could have also played a role. The disease would usually only affect a certain area for a month before leaving, while the war, which most had initially expected to end quickly, had lasted for four years by the time the pandemic struck.

Historian Nancy K. Bristow has argued that the pandemic, when combined with the increasing number of women attending college at the time, contributed to the success of women in nursing. This was due in part to the inability of medical doctors, who were predominantly men, to contain and prevent the illness. Nursing staff, who were predominantly women, felt more inclined to celebrate the success of their patient care and less inclined to identify the spread of the disease with their own work, according to Robin Lindley's interview with Nancy Bristow, author of *The Forgotten American Pandemic*.[36]

Our consideration today reminds me again of how the interpretation of silence, gaps and exclusions are – in assessing the historiography of this time, of the importance of new approaches – reworkings. We have had some good work on the silence that followed An Gorta Mór.[37] We now have to deal with the War of Independence and the Civil War. However, is there a continuing thread we ignore, the thread from which respectability is knitted, a garment commenced, when land was secured, surplus population gone in involuntary migration? An atmosphere where being born from a chesty family damaged marital prospects, but above all the holding on of the land. 'Keep yourself nice,' Samuel Beckett has Winnie say in *Happy Days*.[38]

I wish to conclude, if I may, with a short quotation from French philosopher Paul Ricoeur, who remarked: 'to be forgotten is to die twice'. Initiatives, such as the one I am taking today, may I hope play a modest but meaningful role in remembering the tragic loss of the millions of lives that occurred during a catastrophic event in recent history, ensuring these mostly young men and women are not forgotten, and are allocated their rightful space in our shared historical memory.

Remembering the Holocaust

*Speech at the Holocaust Memorial Day Commemoration 2020,
Mansion House, Dublin, 26 January 2020.*

As anti-Semitism, xenophobia, racism and intolerance are once again on the rise across Europe and many parts of the world, we must remember the Holocaust collectively and work together to ensure that hatred and inhumanity is not allowed to spread its dark shadow across Europe and the world. [...]

We are honoured to have Holocaust survivors Tomi Reichenthal and Suzi Diamond with us today, with them Kinga Paszko, whose family received the honour of Righteous Among the Nations for saving the lives of a Jewish family during the Holocaust. Their presence and words are so important in helping us to bear witness to the level to which human actions sank. On every occasion we hear them. Your personal recollections remind us of the millions of individual stories, which make up the narrative of the *Shoah*; the families torn from each other, the deaths suffered and witnessed, the lost potential, and the brutal assault on culture and identity. We recall too, of course, the courage, generosity of spirit, tenacity and great will to survive, which are also a part of the Holocaust narrative.

Three-quarters of a century ago, the 60th Army of the First Ukrainian Front arrived at Auschwitz, and when they entered the concentration camp complex, it remains hard to imagine fully the horrors they uncovered: the mass graves and the remains of the 1.1 million people systematically murdered, their possessions and personal belongings that spoke so poignantly and more powerfully than any words could possibly do, of the simplest and most basic intimacies of humanity of those who were herded into the concentration camps and gas chambers, the site of such appalling crimes. Those entering to liberate the camps discovered approximately 7000 surviving prisoners, of which 180 were children, who had been left behind in Auschwitz by the fleeing Nazis.

The vast majority of those murdered in Auschwitz were Jewish women, men and children. Others put to death in this horrible, planned way included non-Jewish Poles, members of the Roma community, Soviet prisoners of war, homosexuals, the disabled, and political and religious opponents. The sense of horror and revulsion felt by those who liberated Auschwitz has reverberated through the decades so hauntingly. For let us not forget that so little time separates us from the evil that was the Holocaust. This is not an event from the distant past.

We have to also recognize that these actions were preceded by the hate of an anti-Semitism, and the excluding stereotypes of minorities, something we must be vigilant to ensure is recognized and unequivocally opposed now and in the future.

It is important that we remember, for by doing so we respectfully and solemnly commemorate those who died or suffered at the hands of the Nazis, and we vow to do all we can to ensure that such a horror never occurs again. To quote French philosopher Paul Ricoeur, 'to be forgotten is to die twice'. As humanitarians and reflexive, responsible human beings, we have a duty to preserve the memory of the many people whose lives were taken in such an appalling way.

It is so important that our collective memory of events like the Holocaust is shared, passed on; that it remains prominent in our collective consciousness. Memory is haunted, not just by ghostly others, but by the horrors that have been done, experienced or witnessed. No wonder, then, that for Jorge Luis Borges, to remember is a 'ghostly verb'. Memory, indeed, constitutes one of the greatest sources of interrogation bequeathed to us by the twentieth century, with its cortege of pandemics, mass crimes and grotesque experimentations with totalitarianism. The ethical practice of remembering is a cornerstone in our attempts to live morally and inclusively.

Some seventy-five years on, the visible signs of World War II have largely been erased from the rebuilt cities and towns of Europe, and fewer and fewer Holocaust survivors remain to tell their stories. As time continues to pass, and as we move further away chronologically from that darkest period of history, it becomes thus even more important that we understand the obligation we have to remember events preceding that barbaric chapter, its consequences, and to learn from it. It would be a grievous error to consign the Holocaust or the lessons that should be learnt from it to a past that was assumed to be no longer relevant in our modern world.

In the eight years since I first spoke at the Holocaust Memorial Day Commemoration in Dublin, it is deeply worrying to observe an emerging trend of the rise of extremist language and politics across the streets of Europe, one that seeks to exploit what is often a loss of trust, but much more frequently informs a populism that invokes fear, exclusion and rejection of the Other.

The commitment to multilateralism that resulted from the founding moments of the United Nations in the aftermath of World War II is no longer a given. Several states, including some of the most powerful actors globally, are repudiating this multilateral order, pursuing narrow, neo-nationalist agendas. This decision is as regrettable as it is myopic, displaying a dangerous ignorance of history. Furthermore, it is eroding the respect of international standards and laws including the Geneva Conventions, the 75th anniversary of which was marked by an international conference at which I spoke last September. Refugees, immigrant communities and other minority groups are increasingly described as a threat to the rights of the majority. The many achievements by those who have fought tirelessly for human rights are in peril from new cohorts of extremists who view hard-won universal rights as somehow a threat to their own individual rights. We are witnessing the growing rise of various forms of a corrupted, distorted version of an exclusionary and often bogus, indeed mythical, type of nationalism on virtually every continent. The toxicity of anti-Semitism is not absent from this rhetoric, and it should be identified and condemned for what it is – an invitation to hatred and hate speech.

We in Ireland had been fortunate that such extremism has not gained significant support at a time when many countries in Europe, and elsewhere, have seen the rise of the Far Right. Often galvanized by the impact of austerity policy, such movements have manipulated fears and insecurities, wielding these as tools of xenophobia, seeking to excise the instincts of solidarity across the peoples of Europe, scapegoating migrants and refugees and presenting them as a threat to the job prospects of so-called 'native citizens', all of these being allegations rejected by empirical research.

However, despite the gradual economic recovery, an ugly anti-migrant sentiment is attempting to rear its head in Ireland; a corrupted form of populism has not abated across Europe; and anti-Semitism has not been eliminated from the extreme rhetoric of those seeking to scapegoat the vulnerable in order to inflame the bewildered and angry.

Those forms of misused nationalism and populism are a salutary reminder of just how fragile democracy is, how it can never be taken for granted, how easily it can be undermined when leaders and citizens not only turn away from democratic rule and its discourse of respect, but proceed to deny opposing views any legitimacy, curtail civil liberties and attempt to limit freedom of expression through undermining freedom of the press.

What a great failure it is that fewer than three generations after the catastrophe that was World War II, and given our boundless capacity for creativity and innovation, the fruits of new science and technology are being turned, not to the promotion and preservation of peace, but to the pursuit and prosecution of war, to a resile of old forms of hatred, exclusion and intolerance, to a discourse coarsened by its acceptance of aggression as the language of media and the street. We must all have the courage to ask how we have come to be losing the discourse of peace to the discourse of fear, and how the international armaments industry occupies a space that should be filled by these seeking to meet the needs of sufficiency in food, shelter, education and cooperation, and indeed how we have come to accept the allocation of ecology, society and even peace to such a narrow and limited version of economy – a chronically imbalanced approach that has served us so badly and with such destructive consequences. We must combine our efforts to achieve the alternative: the widespread adoption of a new paradigm of sustained peace and development.

I. European History and Memory

And yet, how depressing it is that the obvious parallels between the rise of fascism in the 1930s and our contemporary humanitarian and democratic crises appear to be lost on many. A 2018 survey found that 22 per cent of adult Americans had never heard of the Holocaust, while 41 per cent of Americans did not know what Auschwitz was, rising to 66 per cent of millennials.[39] We in Europe cannot be complacent either. Another 2018 survey of seven European countries found that 5 per cent had never heard of the Holocaust, with a quarter only knowing 'a little bit', and awareness levels lowest amongst young people.[40] This is precisely why it is vital that awareness of the Holocaust and the rise of fascism in Europe in the 1930s should be a core part of the history curriculum across Europe and elsewhere if we are to truly learn the lessons of history.

This also brings to mind the critical ethical questions, as Eli Wiesel, the writer and concentration-camp survivor has asked: how do we remember, how do we mourn the 6 million Jews and 5 million others who died? As anti-Semitism, xenophobia, racism and intolerance are once again on the rise across Europe and many parts of the world, we must remember the Holocaust collectively and work together to ensure that hatred and inhumanity are not allowed to spread their dark shadows across Europe and the world. We must ensure, as new generations emerge and their world becomes further removed from the horrors of the Holocaust, that we tell them that they too can learn from the actions of those who, by averting their gaze, allowed it to happen, who participated in it, who facilitated it. To quote Hannah Arendt, 'evil thrives on apathy and cannot survive without it'. We must ensure that every generation appreciates the shelter that a shared commitment to international law, its norms, practices and decisions provides for us all; the limitless possibilities that can be achieved from a shared humanity practised with responsibility and cooperation. We must preserve sites such as Auschwitz and Birkenau, where I will be tomorrow to represent the Irish people at the seventy-fifth anniversary of the camp's liberation. Such sites of genocidal acts are visible and powerful reminders of the callous, wilful annihilation of innocent people that was the fruit of hatred, racism and intolerance permitted to flourish unhindered, and from which future generations can learn of the insidious dangers of extremism.

Let us commit, as a bulwark to our democracy, on this Holocaust Memorial Day to remembering the atrocities of the *Shoah* and the bigotry, prejudice and denial of the dignity and rights of the Other, which led to it. Honouring our commitments under the Stockholm Declaration and the political declaration of the International Holocaust Remembrance Alliance, of which Ireland is a member, let us commit to ensuring that all those who lost their lives in Auschwitz-Birkenau, and in all the other concentration camps where Jews and other minority groups were confined and killed, will not be forgotten now or into the future. As we remember, let us ensure too that we do not become passive observers of prejudice or inequality in our society, but stay alert to the rise of racism and hate speech, continue to share a common obligation to value and uphold democracy, human dignity, liberty, equality and the irreducible, indivisible rights and dignity of a shared humanity.

II
TOWARDS A SOCIAL EUROPE

A New European Mind and the Need to Rejuvenate Discourse

Speech at the launch of the Jean Monnet Centre of Excellence in the New Political Economy of Europe, UCD, 28 March 2019.

It is always a pleasure, and I have always found it to be an inspiration, to return to speak in a university setting. As someone with a deep interest in the development of political economy as an academic discipline, I am particularly pleased to have been invited to launch this centre and to have the opportunity of welcoming an initiative that will assist the advancement of new thinking, new teaching and new research in European political economy. We are indeed in need of a new discourse, a discourse that will enable us to develop a new mind for Europe, a version of a European Union that can carry the best of our inherited intellectual instincts and the better instincts of our imagination for the future, one in which the citizens of a real union of European equals might find resonance and fulfilment of the self and society.

The Centre's stated mission 'to re-engage the street and advance a critical debate on the future of European integration' can be a vital part of the evolution of academic thought on many of the significant challenges which face the European Union and on the urgent need to re-engage with the European Street. This will require, I suggest, drawing upon the related disciplines of

II. Towards a Social Europe

politics, economics and, may I suggest, ethics – for is it not reasonable to ask of that which is proposed to achieve integration: what is its nature, for whom and with what consequence for lives shared?

I use the term 'discourse' very deliberately for in the present chaotic atmosphere in which we now find ourselves as we experience the consequences of decision-taking without a preceding adequate, not to speak of balanced, debate that would inform choice, the high price in institutional, even democratic terms, is so glaringly obvious. For it is surely worth bearing in mind that in the history of Europe and its member nations nearly every significant change in policy of a political-economic kind has been preceded by what Duncan Weldon has recently called 'a battle for ideas'.[1] Dare I suggest that politics had its closest connection to the street when such a battle for ideas could find a resonance in the lives and needs of those on the street? It was also, of course, a powerful version of democracy in action when the outcomes of political economy were the ground upon which political choices were cast and policy decisions made. What we need now as we reflect on the future of the European Union – and indeed our global interdependent future – is a sufficiently wide debate on such forms of political economy as can address new challenges: internal ones such as the loss of social cohesion within and between Member States of our European Union, and external ones such as responding to climate change, sustainability, new trade wars, unregulated aspects of a global financialized economy, applications of technology for other than universal benefit and a growing and deepening inequality, reflected in the concentration of wealth, and a growing application of capital for speculative rather than productive purpose.

The attraction of speaking here today is, then, not just the opportunity it offers to me for engagement with bright and enquiring minds but also the opportunity it provides to stress again the essential and urgent role which universities – as dedicated spaces of discourse – can, and must, play in assisting the understanding of the complexity of our world. UCD has a very fine tradition in European academic research and your new centre will add to that in fostering an understanding of the European Union – its origins, its ambitions – achieved and not achieved, its unity and its diversity, its strengths and its imperfections. The work you already have underway is of very practical importance for the future development of the Union and for the well-being of its peoples. I refer, for example, to Dr Aidan Regan and Dr Alison Johnston's relatively recent consideration of the capacity for integration of diverse models of capitalism in the project of integration within the European Union.[2]

However, I want, myself, to provoke a deeper question – what do we mean when we speak of a 'union'? A union of what? If we are to give consideration to that deeper question it will require of us not merely pragmatic considerations of the present but the taking into account, I suggest, of those ethical impulses that drove some of the best minds, at times of a great vulnerability, while the horror of war was still present in their consciousness, to reflect and speak of such a union as would obliterate the prospect of war. I have written elsewhere that I believe that one of the most morally compelling visions of European integration emerged in the *Ventotene Manifesto*, conceived in 1941 by members of the Italian resistance movement from their island prison, Altiero Spinelli and Ernesto Rossi. Their manifesto is a remarkable clarion call for a free and united Europe, one dedicated to disarming the worst passions of what had become a distorted European nationalism.

They pronounced, *inter alia*, that such an ideal could only be achieved and would only be preserved if it were capable of continuing, I quote, 'the historical process of the struggle against social inequalities and privileges'.[3] This document is now rightly considered one of the founding treatises of the European Union and its lasting relevance may be seen in the European Parliament building itself, which bears Spinelli's name. It is a manifesto, also, which attests to the 'permanent value of the spirit of criticism'.

It is so fitting of course that your centre will bear the name of that most distinguished of Europeans, Jean Monnet. The remarkable thing about Jean Monnet is that he is not simply a cherished curiosity of the past but rather that his thinking can be invoked as a deeply relevant beacon for the future. In the recent paper I gave at the Brexit Institute at DCU,[4] I stated that I agree with Perry Anderson that it is of no small significance that social considerations came first in Jean Monnet's thinking. In that paper I went on to recall how the International Labour Organization had been asked to appoint a group of independent experts led by the Swedish economist Bert Ohlin to prepare a report on the social effects of closer European cooperation. The 1956 Ohlin

II. Towards a Social Europe

Report recognized a fear that a reduction in tariffs and the gradual movement towards a tariff-free customs area, when combined with the free movement of capital, would lead to an agglomeration of investment in existing centres of industry to the disadvantage of those countries with higher social labour standards and that those countries would find it hard to raise such standards. In a word, many saw the danger of the existing social floor becoming a social ceiling. The Ohlin Report recommended provisions for the free movement of labour, equivalence between paid holiday schemes and the principle of equal pay for men and women to be included in the treaties.

I reference this to make the point that what are now Articles 157 and 158 of the Treaty on the Functioning of the European Union were a reflection of the politics that prevailed at the time, that held a hegemony. Politics does matter, and it is undeniable then, too, that the political context that has prevailed since the 1980s cannot be separated from our present circumstances, including a reduced role for the state, the loss of social cohesion, the alienation of the street and the loss of resonance in terms of economy with the citizens of the European Union. The summons to give prominence to social policy, as a principle of integration for the Union, is, I suggest, as appropriate today as it was when first articulated by Jean Monnet. It is inextricably linked to the aspiration of ensuring peace, stability, inclusion and sustainable economic life on the wider European continent. The remarkable achievement that is the European Union of today is also a worthy one – a union in which, to borrow Robert Schuman's phrase, war is 'not merely unthinkable but materially impossible'.[5] It serves as a reminder too that the European Union, in invoking shared possibilities, is the very antithesis of any amplification of fear within nations and peoples. This is ground we must hold.

Jean Monnet's imagination and determination made possible what must to others have seemed impossible at the time, a coming together of peoples and traditions in an unprecedented union.

The circumstances of the time, these founding thinkers felt, demanded a new mind for Europe that would go beyond the disastrous competition of anti-democratic, insatiable imperial tendencies that had called forth and delivered wars, wars that would be at the cost of the lives of the young, the poor, so much more than the affluent. The new alternative project can best be summarized, perhaps, by quoting the words of one of the founding fathers of what came to be known as the European project – Jacques Delors, who talked of the necessary alliance between 'competition that stimulates; cooperation that strengthens; and solidarity that unites'.[6] This ambition to strike a unique balance between social cohesion, economic competition and freedom (and today no doubt he would have added to it, a sensitivity to ecological issues) is what drives so many Europeans of all ages to aspire to a European Union that might reach a full and inviting potential.

However, we have entered a period when, I would say – and not for the first time in many years – the future shape of the European Union has become a matter of dispute and often ill-tempered debate. In the ongoing and lingering shadow of Brexit and of social forces which have given rise to so much doubt across Europe, the challenges of the next decade simply cannot be met with a re-issuing (and revamped version) of an invitation, to a new generation, of the old orthodoxies. The refurbishing of what has gone out of balance in failing models will be insufficient. For example the existing aspirations to integration cannot accommodate, without contradiction, such diverse mixed models of capital, not to speak of such measures as would retain cohesion as a major aim: thus they are certainly not capable of restoring a sense of authenticity, resonance or meaning to a citizenship of the European Street.

A new mind for Europe is needed, which requires a casting aside of failing assumptions within inadequate models. It requires new symmetries between the social, the economic, the cultural and the ethical. These symmetries, if they are to be achieved, will require changes in the institutional architecture of the Union. Yet if the intellectual and political contribution of the Union's members is simply one of reaction and adjustment to a wild, unregulated globalization, the prospects for such are poor. The space for the new institutional architecture and the role of intellectual work will have to be fought for.

It is also a question, which time will not allow me to deal with here in an adequate fashion, as to whether the massively increased realm of the unaccountable at global level, the forms of financialized capital, its success in defeating international accountability, may make democracy itself impossible. The starkness of my reservation as to prospects suggests the urgency of the legitimation crisis that has now begun to beckon. Social cohesion is fracturing as inequalities in wealth, power and income are deepening, as labour becomes more precarious and our societies become increasingly divided between what is often lazily described as the 'lucky' and the 'left out', those in gated communities and those on the street, those who can access highly paid employment and those left to struggle on zero-hour contracts.

Within the European Union, cohesion between the Member States has also declined, creating, I suggest again, a problem of connection and legitimacy with the European Street, as we have allowed ourselves to become divided by a common, one-size-fits-all macroeconomic policy framework, which continues to pit creditor against debtor, and those with trade surpluses against those without, those in the North against those in the South. It is difficult to see the 'sharing' a union implies in the defence of asymmetrical advantages that flowed from the impatient establishment of monetary union.

Yet there are challenges on which we could cooperate and still bring a union into existence, such as one that inspired the thinking of the visionaries of Ventotene. I refer to the opportunities to address together our responses to climate change, the forms of growth we need to change – including the imbalance between nature and an economic form that is reminding us that our planet is not insatiable; the forms of economic life and practice which assumed an unquestioned form of infinite accelerated growth, far beyond efficiency, and which, if sustainability is ever to be achieved, must be questioned. The unprecedented accumulation of greenhouse gases in the Earth's atmosphere – a legacy of a mere two centuries of industrial civilization, which now threatens a 4.5-billion-year-old planet whose human population is now most vulnerable to, and as yet unprepared for, the catastrophic consequences of climate change, with all of the devastating implications that arise for the displacement of people, involuntary migration, the degradation of the environment and the eruption of new conflicts over diminishing natural resources – must concern us all.

In those times of hubris, of uncritical pursuit of ever-accelerating growth without consideration as to consequence, of silent toleration of powerful elite opposition to regulation, the space for any pluralist discourse becomes narrow. In the boom years of the early 2000s many policymakers, shapers and takers were ensnared in a single paradigm of thought – an extreme hegemonic theory of the market, which was too readily accepted as some form of inevitability, an unavoidable achievement of modernity. It was a discourse from which the voice of the street was not merely neglected but excluded. Politics was rendered servile or near impotent in service to what was ever more abstract and unaccountable. It found its extreme expression in the assumption that there was no area of life in which the optimum circumstances could not be provided from the marketplace. Previous egalitarian discourses lost their space. The concept of the public world was now out of fashion and in so many circles could not now be heard. To speak of redistribution was to be regarded as having been stuck in the past. The models within which we have struggled favoured concentration in ownership and unregulated accumulation of wealth, both often achieved by the privatization of previously public assets. Such a version of modernity would not find any contradiction either when the socialization of private speculative debt was suggested as unavoidable – a debt that had not been the result of the action of the public but rather of private speculative investors and their institutions.

The accountability gap that has opened up between the practice, form, assumptions and demands of the economy and the experience of citizens is capable of creating a legitimacy crisis. It is much more than a defective communications problem. Of course, a rectification would be assisted by having a debate as to the ideas that should guide public policy. However, the European Union's experience at decision-making level has not been one of drawing on its intellectual or philosophical traditions, of privileging pluralist discourse, or of inviting its publics to such; the timescales of such do not appeal to those who celebrate the opportunities of transacting capital, speculatively rather than productively, in ever-shorter versions of real time. As the speed of capital transfer becomes ever more fast and mysterious, the uncomprehending publics are driven in their alienation to become 'mute' as Professor Hartmut Rosa puts it in his recent work, '"mute" in the face of what is presented to them, and sadly too easily perceived as "unknowable".[7]

If we now question why some seek solace in the simplistic or the bombastic – or, indeed, seem captured by apathy, or have even begun to speak of the death knell of participatory democracy – we must acknowledge that for too long they [the publics] have been presented with few meaningful alternatives

II. Towards a Social Europe

that would check what was unaccountable, that would challenge elite interpretation of what need not be made complex and beyond the capacity of public understanding. Many of the underlying assumptions of the dominant narrative were insufficiently contested by scholars and institutions of learning, whose own structures were now to become ever more vulnerable to the dictates and the demands of the market. Alternative perspectives from critical scholarship were disregarded or indeed sometimes ridiculed. When the most recent global financial crisis came, the street bore the brunt of the failures to pursue alternative modes of thought. The pain on the street was compounded by a sense of exclusion from the decision-making around the complex, often technical, efforts to stem the calamitous tides.

This was not, of course, a uniquely European experience, but, under severe strain, many on the street perceived a slow unravelling of the solidarity upon which they understood the European Union to have been based. This apparent privileging of a limited narrow version of an economic union, one which, unlike that which the Treaty of Lisbon might have suggested, had offered parity of esteem between competitiveness and cohesion, has had profound consequences for social cohesion, from which, I would argue, European unity is still reeling.

A dangerous vacuum has emerged among the mute and excluded, available for exploitation, for filling with old prejudices of hate, fictionalized difference, fears and abuse of media.

This image of a crisis-ridden Europe I have described is far removed from the conception of a shared union, such a union as had been conceived from the cataclysm of World War II. The union of Jean Monnet and his contemporaries, after all, drew in its time from a rich heritage of scholarship, philosophy and the most generous impulses of European tradition, as the founders sought to lay the foundations for a lasting peace. It was a peace not mentioned for rhetorical flourish, but which sought to be built not just on capital or markets, but also on the vindication of the fullness of the human experience, informed by philosophy and leading to fundamental economic, social and cultural rights. Too often, as we look to the future, we fail to adequately appreciate the rich but diverse roots of the European project. As we seek to find a new mind for Europe out of the ashes of our present threatening fragmentation, there is now a pressing need to recall the rich infusion of ideas and ideals upon which our Union was sought to be built.

The European Union offered to you now as young intellectual workers as material for not only your reflection but for achievement, completion, as students of political economy, is indeed far from perfect. Its problems too are beyond the economic, beyond what is quantifiable. There is a yearning for authenticity to which you must respond, I suggest.

As one looks to the European Street, there is an inescapable sense of disconnect between the needed fresh visionary proposals that risk being dismissed as rhetoric but are relevant and necessary if the lived experience of the most disenfranchised are to be addressed. It is, and always will be, insufficient to keep an academic distance. It may seem to those on the European Street, as Michael Longo and Philomena Murray have suggested, that 'the European Union's future no longer seems to be informed by the vision of the past'.[8] There is, therefore, an urgent need not just to re-engage with the street, but to re-engage with what it means to be European and what we want for its future. It demands a revival of the concept of social justice, of the social contract, of the common good – which for too long has been absent from our discourse.

We are seeing evidence of its gradual rediscovery in new critical theory and I welcome it. In particular, for example, in the new work of scholars such as Professor Hartmut Rosa, from the University of Jena, who has developed the concept of 'resonance' and an interdisciplinary approach to a public sociology of the common good. There are also ever-louder calls coming from civil society for 'inclusive growth' and for policies to address inequality. It is a time to seize these new opportunities for better and more sustainable living. The European Union today also faces a unique opportunity and responsibility to assert or, where necessary, reassert its founding values of democracy, human rights and the rule of law in a world in which those values are increasingly challenged. The experience of solidarity in Europe must be, I suggest, the foundation on which our Union's external action is built.

For the academic community, it demands, for example, a response that moves beyond the limited approach to the teaching of economics that has pervaded in recent decades towards new interdisciplinary and pluralist theoretical frameworks that can make connections between the lives of our citizens, the economy, society, culture, ecology and policy. Our work in education together must aim to help people make sense of the world. It must be of a quality that will withstand scrutiny. It must, as this centre offers to do, turn its attention to the difficult and often neglected questions that are contained within considerations as to the future of European integration. I believe the issues of contemporary Europe are incapable of resolution without a significant paradigm shift in intellectual work; work that will inevitably inform policy and political choice. Pessimism, sadly, is a feature of the contemporary work of some of the most distinguished scholars who have been contributing their intellectual abilities towards understanding the current dilemma of legitimacy in which the European Union now finds itself – scholars such as Jürgen Habermas and Wolfgang Streeck.

Yes, there are undoubtedly challenges, but there are opportunities too, and, while the appeal of such writers may have in recent times the aspect of an increasing desperation, even out of despair those such as Habermas continue to offer strategies that are available for cooperation between different Member States of the Union, such as a redefinition of 'subsidiarity'; new forms of assistance in reconnecting with European citizens, for renewing the European vision and thus offering hope to the most vulnerable, and in the interim there are experiments that may come from such areas of theory as New Institutional Economics.

Last year I posed a number of questions, which I believe need to be answered in any debate on the future direction of our Union. Can the macro-economic framework of the European Union sanction and protect a diversity of models, both in terms of the welfare state and alternative economic models? Can the formulation of monetary policy accommodate such difference? Can the rules of the internal market yield where they can, and surrender when they must, to the demands of labour? How do we resolve what has become an apparent clash between our fundamental values and principles – such as solidarity and a commitment to social justice – and parts of what I have said in the past might be referred to as the 'economic constitution' of the Union?

These are questions, I repeat, which cannot be answered within the frame of the old orthodoxies. Neither can they be neglected, except at great cost. Such questions are no call to despair. History is littered with the failures of

A New European Mind and the Need to Rejuvenate Discourse

certainties abandoned, resilience of peoples and the introduction and accommodation of new realities. The genius of Jean Monnet was to create institutions he knew could be mended – even bended – in the light of events, to cope with the succession of crises the Union has had to weather over the last sixty years. I remain confident that a proper, broad and inclusive discourse can help us too to find the meaningful and lasting alternatives that are much longed for in our universities, in our parliaments, across our institutions and, I believe, on the street. Respect for the search for, and articulation of, new perspectives, will produce alternatives – policy options – never inevitabilities. Behind each option will lie a series of implications for the citizen about which we must be ever vigilant. At their best, these policy options will show solidarity with the human condition. They will support human dignity; addressing issues around the future of work, seeing its significance far beyond a source of income for consumption, insecurity of housing and health, and the preservation of our increasingly fragile planet.

To create the global intellectual capacity to respond to these questions, it is clear that we must reimagine the way we teach and research economics. I have spoken many times of the international failings in the teaching of economics. In the United States some years ago I spoke of how Economics 101 [in the United States] commences its teaching of the subject at perfect competition, leaving students with a shrunken and shrivelled picture of the history of economics. If the global financial crisis has taught us anything, it is that a pluralist scholarship is required, one that students are entitled to expect and be offered; one which can more properly critique our recent and not-so-recent history and both critique and anticipate the social and economic world in which we live and which we seek to change for shared human benefit. It is not any mere normative option to be vaguely recognized. It is better economics, resonant of the finest minds in the history of political economy. The history of thought, after all, suggests that even established economic thinking, when blended with some of the more contemporary work and married to the evolution of philosophical thinking, can provide, as it were, a trail of breadcrumbs into previously unheralded spaces where we might discover the answers to some of these questions and the solutions to some of the most intractable challenges facing the world today.

II. Towards a Social Europe

Let us recall that *The Great Transformation*, written by Karl Polanyi, was first published in 1944, not long after the *Ventotene Manifesto*. The book celebrates its seventy-fifth birthday this year, but still resonates with me because it challenged the understanding of the meaning of economics, thought up to that point to be the logic of rational action and decision-making, as a rational choice between the alternative uses of scarce resources. Polanyi's theory of substantivism in its time critiqued and went beyond rational decision-making and scarcity, referring instead to the fullness of how humans make a living interacting within their social and natural environments: 'Economics is the way society meets material needs.'[9] Gunnar Myrdal's work is, of course, another seminal example of engaged research. It is such departures into new thinking that might revitalize the study of economics and, thus, help to provide new political solutions in our fractured society.

Such a new approach must, of course, in order to be relevant today, give adequate space to gender as well as equality in economics. In that regard I have been so very greatly heartened, and inspired too, by the recent work of some distinguished women in the economics field. At a recent event at Áras an Uachtaráin to celebrate International Women's Day I spoke of the new ground being broken by Irish women, paving the way for new generations of women who will use their talent and creativity in the pursuit of a better world and an enhanced future for all our citizens. We know that women engaged in research have the advantage of drawing inspiration from their experiences as women, that women frequently use that experience when choosing the area of research they wish to pursue and the questions they choose to ask. We also know that a female perspective can make a profound difference, even when researching issues that may seem entirely unrelated to gender. May I offer just two brief examples of what I see as exciting new emancipatory work.

Sylvia Walby in her book *Crisis*[10] has offered an invaluable set of linked insights in her writing of the effect on society of the financial crisis, which in turn led to the economic crisis of recession and unemployment, and caused a fiscal crisis over government deficits, and which then through the reply of austerity that was offered as policy, in turn evolved into a political crisis, one that threatens to become a democratic crisis. Borne unevenly, the effects of all of these crises have exacerbated gender and class inequalities. She identifies the hidden gendered causes and consequences of these crises and suggests, for example, that gender inequality in access to financial decision-making is to the detriment of economic development because of the inefficiencies that this creates. The conflict between democracy and capitalism, she suggests, can only be resolved through a deepening of democracy.

In *The Value of Everything: Making and Taking in the Global Economy*,[11] Mariana Mazzucato explores the concept of value today, showing how value extraction is now more highly rewarded than value creation. Mazzucato has opened a new dialogue by reminding us – and the reminder was overdue – that the creation of value is collective, that policy can be more meaningfully inclusive through the co-shaping and co-creating of social markets and that real progress requires a dynamic division of labour focused on the problems that 21st-century societies are facing. She also suggests that governments can and do play a pivotal role in creating value, despite being viewed by some ideologues as an inherently unproductive sector. Mazzucato believes that government should become an active value creator rather than just a facilitator of the real economy or simply a spender during crises.

We are on the cusp of a digital transformation. It will bring with it challenges and opportunities. It will confront us with its challenges much sooner than we expect. We need to be ready, as a policy, to offer its opportunities as widely as possible, and be prepared of course for the disruption it may offer to society as a whole. We will require policy options that can cater for and accommodate the principles and values by which we might all live together ethically, and in a manner that will ensure intergenerational fairness. Can we allow ourselves to speak again of universal provision?

In conclusion, may I repeat that there are, too, transcendent, inspiring projects that we can share. For example, the formulation of the Sustainable Development Goals and the Paris Climate Agreement hold out the hope that transformative approaches are possible. It seems to me to be so obvious that our discourses must be ones that include and empower the citizen in the fullest sense. It is my firm belief that in this century economic literacy may be as important to cohesion, citizenship and democracy as mass literacy was in previous generations to the struggles for political representation. This new and deepened literacy can help ensure that our citizens are equipped to participate in discussions and debates about the policy decisions that impinge on their daily lives; ensure respect for their dignity and their human rights. Such an inclusion and participation can be emancipatory in effect, and therefore be a source of strength to a real union of the peoples. May I suggest that our discourses of the future can only be made stronger by the integration of the principles of philosophy: these are principles that are within the reach of all, but require constant nourishing. Philosophy enables us to look beyond the obvious, beyond a perspective of reality that is bounded – or worse, still blinded – by assumption or doctrine, and nurture the creative and humane thinking necessary for truly functioning societies. Without it, we are, to paraphrase Albert Einstein, the people who see a thousand trees, but never the forest. It is not a time to be 'mute'.

Trade Unions and the European Future

Speech at the European Federation of Public Service Unions' Annual Congress, 'Trade Unions and the Future', RDS, Dublin, 4 June 2019.

The 1913 Lockout in Dublin was a seminal period in the formation of collective representation for the working classes in this country. More than 20,000 workers were either locked out of their jobs by their employers or went on strike. It marked a watershed in Irish labour history: the principle of union action and workers' solidarity had been firmly asserted.

As President, I have been privileged to be asked to speak in the past of the role of Larkin, Connolly and others, of trade unionists, and particularly of the brave and neglected women trade unionists and their importance to our history in the late nineteenth and early twentieth century. While drawing strength and courage from the exemplary bravery and determination of these individuals, and indeed from more contemporary figures like Mary Manning – the shopworker from Irish grocery chain Dunnes Stores who, in 1984, refused to handle the sale of fruit from South Africa in protest at the Apartheid regime – the labour movement draws its strength from its collectivity, from the hundreds of thousands of people willing to demonstrate solidarity in their workplace, towards their fellow citizens, and towards people all over the world. [...]

II. Towards a Social Europe

The European Federation of Public Service Unions (EPSU) works hard to deliver better working conditions, improved health and safety and enhanced rights for its members, negotiating best practice agreements that improve the working lives of European public-service workers and ensuring quality services for citizens. Of particular concern for EPSU is the issue of gender inequality, an issue to which I shall return later in my speech.

Public services, on which all citizens rely, are under increasing strain from budget cuts, liberalization, austerity, low pay and poor working conditions. Tax avoidance by multinationals impacts on the sustainability of public finances, in turn impacting on public services. The role that EPSU plays in standing up for the rights of citizens, including migrants, both in the workplace and in the services your members deliver, is also critical in ensuring that the most vulnerable citizens in our countries are protected from exploitation; I note that Congress will shortly debate a motion in relation to migrant workers.

In Ireland only one in four workers are now members of a trade union, of whom over half are public service workers. This reflects a decline in private-sector trade-union membership. In 1980 almost two-thirds of Irish workers were members of trade unions. However, there are encouraging signs that this trend is reversing, with evidence of new recruitment.

The trade-union movement, we must continually remind ourselves, emanates from a powerful, proud tradition on which, in turn, civil-rights movements, the anti-apartheid movement and equal-rights movements could call for support. It is important that we also acknowledge on all parts of this island the role of the trade-union movement, from its beginnings down to our times, in opposing sectarianism.

The trade-union movement, lest we forget, has also been an international one, and it correctly sees, as Edward Phelan did in his Harris Lecture with John Maynard Keynes in 1931, that migrating unemployment from one setting to another, effectively positioning wage levels in competition with each other in a downward spiral, could be disastrous for global economies.

An over-reliance on the economic orthodoxy of today, with limited space allowed to discover new knowledge, and adherence to what we now know to be bogus expertise, all played their part in the unfolding of, and response to, the economic and social catastrophe that was the Great Recession, which this country, with others, experienced just a decade ago. In these times, our new circumstances require a higher degree of economic literacy if such mistakes are not to occur again.

This requires, I suggest, consideration of a new eco-social paradigm, based on economic heterodoxy, such as that proposed by Professor Ian Gough and others, that recognizes the limits of the world's natural resources, as well as the role that unrestrained greed has played in creating the climate crisis. In his book *Heat, Greed and Human Need*, Gough outlines how the alternative paradigm is rooted in the concept of human need over greed. It espouses gender equality, redistribution and a reconfigured social consumption and investment strategy that transfers resources and technology from rich countries to developing countries as the key means to achieve this eco-social welfare state.[12]

The eco-social policies that underpin such an economic paradigm must simultaneously pursue both equity/social justice and sustainability/sufficiency goals within an activist innovation state, with substantial public investment and greater regulation and planning. Furthermore, socioeconomic measures are also required to offset any regressive impacts of the ecological transition for lower-income groups and to reverse growing levels of inequality.

It is apposite that the theme of your Congress is 'fighting for a union for all'. Such a title calls to mind the notion of 'inclusivity'. While Ireland has been at the forefront of truly enormous social change in recent years, which has advanced inclusivity, it has yet to achieve an acceptable level of cohesion, as is the case in much of the EU.

Results from several recently held referenda, on issues such as divorce, marriage equality and abortion rights, herald a more progressive and inclusive modern Ireland on the level of personal or identity issues, one which espouses compassion and tolerance over judgment and shame. Such progress demonstrates an increasingly liberal and secular society with an emphasis on personal freedoms. I would argue that this move towards an articulation of the desire for individual rights can be more perfectly compatible with the objectives of social cohesion, social connectedness and the move towards an eco-social model, which I advocate in this speech.

Unfortunately, however, I am struck by a growing divergence between such societal progress at the level of personal freedoms, on the one hand, and the speed with which this country and many others globally are proceeding with regard to social equity or labour policy and, in particular, workers' rights and conditions. This leads me to question the future role of the International Labour Organization (ILO) – the only surviving international institution that was created from the ashes of World War I – which, in its constitution, refers to social justice as being essential to lasting universal peace. In our present circumstances, almost a hundred years after that constitution was first proclaimed, that spirit of idealism and of vital moral purpose is more urgently required than ever, yet it is seriously undermined. This begs the question: how can the ILO rededicate itself to its founding mission in the context of an ongoing assault on workers' rights?

I believe that the founding message given expression in an achievable agenda of the ILO must be vigorously brought to the attention of the world by all of us who believe in equity and the dignity of work. How much better would it be if the necessary elements of what constituted social cohesion formed the basis of the discourse that prevailed on the streets of the world, rather than the excluded being abandoned to become the prey of xenophobes, homophobes and racists?

Being positive, I suggest that all of the prevailing ruling concepts in our present economic discourse – flexibility, globalization, productivity, innovation, social protection, decent work – are capable of being redefined, given shared moral resonance, made useful within the context of an eco-social paradigm. To these I will speak in more detail shortly.

On the subject of ecology, the most pressing issue facing us all as a global community and inhabitants of a planet that is in peril, owing to insatiable, unrestricted consumption of the earth's finite natural resources since the onset of the Anthropocene, cannot be denied. I speak, of course, of the climate crisis. Let me say first that I see the role of public servants as being transformative in acting as champions for climate action, both in terms of mitigation and adaptation. Public servants have the capacity, given a real opportunity, to shape and implement policies in these spheres that will reduce the impact of climate change and enable society to adapt to the most destructive effects of a changing climate, which we are already beginning to witness first hand – through, for instance, the increased severity and frequency of storms and extreme weather events.

There exists now a great opportunity to give leadership and for trade unions to play a strong role in pushing for fair, ambitious and binding international agreements on greenhouse gas emission-reduction targets. While the EU has a set of binding emissions targets for 2020 and 2030, we must now plan for full decarbonization of our European economies by 2050, encouraging the rest of the world to follow suit, and urging in the strongest possible terms the USA to reconsider its regressive and pernicious decision to leave the global Paris Agreement. Unions can seize the opportunity of providing a lead role in developing a strategy for a 'just transition' for workers and communities to ensure that we are all part of a sustainable, low-carbon economy and benefit from decent and green jobs. In Ireland this will mean that those impacted by the closure of unsustainable carbon-intensive electricity production, for example, must be offered reskilling opportunities to enable them to find suitable jobs in other areas, such as the green economy, or opportunities with sustainable incomes in other parts of society.

It is my strong belief that the trade-union movement can create a creative and enduring future for us members now and in the future by being a key proponent of Gough's new eco-social political economy, emphasizing responsible economics, understanding that the concept of growth *ad infinitum* is inherently flawed, recovering a discourse that has fallen prey to an uncritical embrace of neo-liberal mantras, and advocating an economic model of pluralism, which emphasizes the finite nature of the earth's natural resources and the role that rich nations must play in ameliorating the crises in which we find ourselves. As Gough puts it himself:

> Consumption and consumption-based emissions, ignored by the green growth agenda, must be given equal priority in the rich world [...] Issues of global equity, almost entirely absent from international climate negotiations so far, must be discussed and confronted [...] 'Affluence' has a class as well as a national dimension.[13]

The case that Ian Gough makes is impressive. Combining these concerns of domestic justice with both international and intergenerational justice in a global equity framework is one worthy of consideration by all partners; one worthy of support by trade unions. Such a framework, which is founded on a needs-based society, could have a conjoined positive effect on the multiple

II. Towards a Social Europe

crises in which the global community finds itself. It also implies the end of a capitalism without responsibility as to consequences as we have come to know it, moving beyond growth to a steady-state sustainable economy. This begs the question as to whether the transition route to sustainable well-being is achievable. Everything depends, as scholars such as Gough, Naomi Klein and others have identified, on the nature, variability, flexibility and reformability of capitalism.

Your trade union has correctly placed gender equality as one of its core objectives. I believe that, in order for unions to credibly fight for the promotion of gender equality in the workplace, there must first be greater gender equality within union structures themselves. I also see the inclusion of gender issues in collective bargaining as being fundamental, given the ongoing gender pay gap. Related to this is a wider objective of protecting vulnerable, marginalized workers, many of whom are women, many of whom are migrants: these groups need an ever stronger voice.

Sylvia Walby has argued in her book, *Crisis*, that the economic and fiscal crises we have lived through over the past decade, and the resulting recession (experienced severely in Ireland) have cascaded through society, and the ensuing fiscal crisis over government budget deficits and austerity has led to a political crisis which, in turn, now threatens to become a democratic crisis. Borne unevenly, the effects of the crisis are exacerbating existing class and gender inequalities:

> There is considerable under-utilized capacity in the economy as a consequence of the failure to encourage the completion of the transition in the gender regime from a domestic to a public form. This incomplete transition is, at least in part, because of the priority accorded to developing a neoliberal rather than social-democratic form.[14]

Walby argues that the future consequences of the crisis depend upon whether there is a deepening of democracy, and of democratic institutions, including within the EU. Within such considerations must be the issue of the relation of the economy to social policy and the role of the economy as instrument or determinant of public good.

Globalization is a topic to which I return frequently in my speeches as President. A key conundrum that has not been solved by most governments globally relates to how we can make globalization work for citizens, when what has been its presentation to date lacks legitimacy among much of the citizenry; in other words, is an ethical, sustainable form of globalization possible? Naomi Klein, among others, has shown how corporations have unethically exploited workers in the world's poorest countries, often those with appalling human rights records, in pursuit of greater profits. As Klein has written:

> When manufacturing is so highly devalued, it follows that the people doing the production work become highly devalued as well. The shift in corporate priorities has left factory workers and craftspeople in a precarious position. The lavish spending in the 1990s on marketing, mergers and brand extensions has been matched by (...) resistance to investing in production facilities and labour. Multinationals search the globe for factories that can make their products as cheaply as possible. And by contracting out the manufacturing work, multinationals can shed all responsibility for the working conditions inside these factories. The contracting allows multinationals to refocus on the needs of their brands, as opposed to the needs of their workers.[15]

It follows that, left unchecked, such a form of globalization will lead to a wider gap between rich and poor, with the poor getting poorer.

Globalization clearly tests values that may have been multilaterally agreed. To achieve an acceptance across borders as minimally ethical, globalization and its impact requires the management by accountable multilateral institutions so that it, for example, supports fundamental human rights and leads to long-lasting development and prosperity for citizens in general, particularly the poorest. The trade-union movement has played, and must continue to play, a leading role so that workers are not made the casualties of globalization, but rather that globalization is made to work for the world's workers.

As to the task of redefining work, we are also witnessing increases in precarious employment, contract working and an ongoing casualization of labour, as has been so well documented by Guy Standing, Noam Chomsky and others. The new emerging trends in work practices – so-called 'innovations' – are only innovations, to my mind, insofar as they maximize profits for employers and reduce employees' labour rights. I see this trend as part of an inexorable 'race to the bottom', and I believe that regulation is required in

II. Towards a Social Europe

order to protect those most vulnerable in society from being exploited as a result of the most adverse effects of these new models of work.

For example, Pádraig Carmody and Alicia Fortuin have shown in recent research how ride-sharing and 'virtual capital' have resulted in a 'hollowing out of the formal sector' and a rise in the so-called 'precariat' worker: 'Whereas many speak of the "sharing economy", a more accurate way to describe it might be the "on-demand" economy where firms divest themselves of their responsibilities to employees, reducing the structural power of labour. This represents an undermining of any social contract between the parties.'[16]

With regard to how an abuse of digitalization assists in this regard, we see online workers often are not covered by employment law or collective agreements and seldom have access to social security, paid leave or paid training owing to the fact that the platforms require workers to register as self-employed. These recent developments in the world of work are nothing less than a recurrence of some of the worst practices of the nineteenth century.

The coordination and direction of employees by an algorithm owned by a company should never be allowed to divest the employer of their responsibility any less than bogus self-employment does. After all, one of the great victories of the trade-union movement was the regulation of piecework: these old practices must not be allowed to re-emerge under the cloak of supposed innovation. It must remain an important objective of the left and of unions to reverse the systematic neglect and devaluation of working-class lives.

The ongoing displacement of secure, certain, regular employment, for which trade unions were established, by uncertain, precarious jobs and characteristic chronic insecurity is a major cause for concern. Workers are too often expected to demonstrate what is called 'flexibility', by which is meant a willingness and ability to readily respond to changing circumstances and expectations without adequate information or recompense. This flexibility is often not matched, however, with any security of tenure or appropriate income by employers, with the vista of zero-hour contracts now appearing ever more prevalent.

An uncritical globalization, pursued without consideration as to impact or social consequences, it can be shown, has had a negative impact on climate change: more goods being produced and consumed, more transport of goods across longer distances, shorter product–obsolescence cycles and a more consumerist and materially driven society. They all come at a significant price in terms of the impact on finite natural resources and greenhouse gas emissions.

I have not spoken of the so-called 'softer' impacts of globalization, such as cultural homogenization, as well as adverse effects on local communities and economies. For this is perhaps one of the greatest problems with globalization: macroeconomist exponents can all too easily evaluate the economic benefits of globalization narrowly on aggregate across countries, but fail to capture the harder-to-quantify negative 'intangibles' to which I refer.

I was heartened to read in the recent World Bank report, *Doing Business: Going Beyond Efficiency*, that even that organization – hardly a bastion of left-wing, social-democratic thinking – now believes there is justification in 'going beyond efficiency' and fostering more 'inclusive growth' globally.[17]

After decades of mainstream economic commentary espousing the virtues of privatization, deregulation and a smaller role for the state, we now appear to be at a turning point in the economics discourse thanks to the insightful contributions of economists like Mariana Mazzucato and Sylvia Walby. Mazzucato, in her books *The Entrepreneurial State* and *The Value of Everything*, effectively rebukes the austerity-fuelled world view that, in order to restore growth (after the 2008 financial crisis), all that was needed was to reduce deficits by cutting public spending, arguing instead that government investment in areas like education, research and technology is a key component of economic growth.

Even orthodox institutions such as the International Monetary Fund have slowly evolved their thinking on austerity as a strategic tool, believing that it can be self-defeating. As Keynes argued over eighty years ago, if governments cut spending during a downturn, a short-lived recession can become a fully-fledged depression. This is precisely what occurred in Ireland when the economic recession of 2008 turned into an economic depression in 2009, with an economic recovery delayed until 2014.

This prolongation and intensification of the economic bust resulted in a deepening of the experience of, as well as a widening of the exposure to, a range of attendant social ills that were a direct result of a prolonged period of constrained underinvestment by the state, many of which have not yet been resolved.

Long before Mazzucato, the spiritual fathers of creative thinking in the public sector, Keynes and Polanyi, called on policymakers not just to think

II. Towards a Social Europe

about countercyclical spending as a way to reduce the impacts of recessions and avoid overheating economies, but also to think strategically; to identify how investments can help shape citizens' long-term prospects for the better. Polanyi went so far as to argue, in *The Great Transformation*, that free markets themselves are products of state intervention, outcomes of public and private actions. This astute observation has become conveniently forgotten in much of the austerity-based neo-liberal commentary around the recent economic crisis.

Mitchell and Fazi's *Reclaiming the State* argues – in the contemporary context of Brexit Britain and Trump's America, with national sovereignty high on the agenda – that the state must be reclaimed if we are to transform societies for the people's benefit. Despite the ravages of neo-liberalism, the state still holds the capacity and much of the resources for democratic control of a nation's economy and finances. The authors advocate a new paradigm of economic heterodoxy, in which ideas are grounded in post-Keynesian, institutional, feminist, social and, importantly, ecological economics.[18]

This is an epistemological challenge to the neo-classical economic orthodoxy that espouses with rigidity the assumptions of rationality and individualism as the equilibrium nexus. As an alternative, it offers economics dealing with the institutions-history-social structure nexus. This is the form of political-economy discourse that is most promising. Young – and not so young – academics are struggling for its right to be taught in universities and institutions.

Reclaiming the State is a work that called for a drastic expansion in the state's role, while the authors include a broad renationalization of specific sectors of the economy, most notably the financial sector. Mitchell and Fazi also call for a new and updated notion of planning, one which places the commanding heights of economic policy under democratic control to enable the urgently needed socioecological transformation of production and society.

The latter project, however, needs to be presented not simply as a resile to the previous models of renationalization: this would clearly be insufficient in the context of new challenges. The role of the state needs to be defined anew, as well as the concept of sovereignty, in such a way that it is shared, can flow for the benefit of workers beyond borders, and can – because it is a transition taking place in several countries – have a regional character, one that is exemplary to global economic systems.

Any narrowly defined concept of productivity – capturing in a simplistic way merely the efficiency of production utilizing the four factors of production – while it may be important to understand in an increasingly competitive enterprise environment, is an insufficient concept when examined from a labour-productivity perspective. It is problematic because growth in labour productivity often does not lead to commensurate improvements in the incomes of workers, as evidence from studies conducted by Tony Atkinson and others suggests,[19] but is instead captured by the owners of capital, itself often speculative rather than productive. This is not only inequitable, but it places a value on the role of capital that is far higher than other factors of production, such as labour and entrepreneurship, and is inherently volatile given its speculative nature.

Such volatility has clear downstream impacts on labour markets in instances in which speculative capital does not perform in the markets as well as was envisaged, resulting inevitably in the need to cut back on other factors of production, with labour being the most easily adjusted, assisted by increasingly flexible labour markets.

I wish to revisit briefly, if I may, the concept of work itself. Andrea Komlosy, in her recent contribution, *Work – The Last 1,000 Years*, argues that the often-limited definition and classification of work has never corresponded to the historical experience of most people, whether in colonies, developing countries, or the industrialized world: 'The gap between common assumptions and reality grows even more pronounced in the case of women and other groups excluded from the labour market.'[20] I am minded to revisit the related philosophical concept of 'the dignity of labour', much advocated by Gandhi, in which all types of jobs are respected equally, no occupation is considered superior and none of the jobs should be discriminated against on any basis; is this not the ethic of work in the public service for the public good?

I believe a corollary of this concept is that a return to the fundamentals of decent, secure jobs would be a widespread increase in job satisfaction, a better sense of accomplishment and improvements in quality of life across nations. A vision in which these concepts become more embedded in the citizenry, and, in particular, employers, is perhaps provocative, even radical, as it attempts to upturn the commonly held assertion that money and wealth accumulation is the primary motivation behind humans' desire to work.

II. Towards a Social Europe

There is, in addition, a significant, growing and important body of economic research focusing on the marginal utility of income – the incremental change in satisfaction that is due to a unit change in income – which shows that satisfaction peaks at relatively modest income levels, and that steep diminishing marginal returns are evident, as people's preference for additional leisure time becomes higher than their preference for additional income. Robert and Edward Skidelsky's book, *How Much Is Enough? Money and the Good Life*, is a spirited argument against blindly accepting the 'Faustian bargain' of insatiability within contemporary capitalism: 'We need to focus much less on making money and much more on cultivating the things that matter: leisure, knowledge, friendship.'[21]

It appears that the old adage, 'money doesn't bring happiness', is a truism that even economists can now demonstrate empirically. However, the young of the world, with their proximity to each other, to nature, to the joy of shared culture, are well ahead of them, as are those who sing the anthems of their unions behind banners as they march.

Creating a society that is more equal, one in which all work is valued, and all jobs are decent and fulfilling, is not an easy task given the current milieu. However, the political-economic concept of deliberative democracy provides us with a means to engage with and promote such a vision across the citizenries of Europe.

Jürgen Habermas has written persuasively on this topic, asserting that political decisions should be the product of fair and reasonable discussion and debate among citizens. It follows, therefore, that we must become more aware as citizens about the often obscured or consciously hidden ideological assumptions that lie behind policy choices. This means that we need to foster universal political-economic literacy to deal with new and existing challenges, and a better understanding of the nature of value and what constitutes happiness.

As part of a coordinated discourse, trade unions have a crucial role in ensuring that governments' labour policies are ethically grounded, but unions also have a role in realizing this vision of a more ethically-minded citizenry and a new eco-social economic paradigm, the components of which I have elucidated in this speech.

One of the ways in which to do this is to re-establish or embed and enhance Glaucon's social contract between the citizen and the state, something which has been heavily eroded in much of Europe following decades of attack from a prevailing neo-liberal orthodoxy, eroding labour rights through laissez-faire policy and an almost fetishized embrace of unfettered globalization. Trade unions have a vital role in turning around this tide, by advocating a rights-based approach to quality work and engaging in the deliberative democratic process.

What are the lessons we have learned from the economic crisis and the 'self-regulating market'? I believe there are many – in politics, policymaking, academia, the commentariat, citizens at large – who have turned a corner, having re-evaluated often strongly held beliefs, with an appreciation that the state has an important role, that good regulation does matter, be it in the financial, construction, or healthcare sectors – all sectors in which we in Ireland have seen the catastrophic and sometimes tragic effects of under-regulation and/or lack of enforcement.

My vision is of a Europe with excellent public services at its core. Good jobs in the public sector mean quality services for citizens. Your members appreciate only too well that the services they deliver are not a cost to society, but an investment in our communities. This message must be taken to the heart of Europe.

The centrality of individualism as a source of values, with its emphasis on individual consumption, insatiable acquisitiveness, wealth accumulation and an ill-informed hostility to the state, its institutions, also those who work in them, has had a corrosive effect.

I hope that we are on a pathway of learning as peoples across Europe, that we avoid the excessive materialism that was apparent, for example, in this country during the so-called Celtic Tiger, and that we move away from narcissistic individualism and towards collective solidarity. Neither should there be a notion of any trade-union member being described as a former member. Joining, belonging, sharing the trade-union values is a life choice, anticipated by the young, cherished to the end by those who are union people.

Several global studies, such as the World Happiness Report, as well as qualitative research such as that by Esping-Andersen,[22] clearly demonstrate that those countries that manage to foster this collective solidarity, that abide by the principle of a strong social contract, that believe in the benign and even transformative possibilities of the state and its institutions, that provide universal social protection, all report the highest quality of life and life satisfaction using both objective and subjective measurements.

Mitchell and Fazi identify, as a prerequisite for the construction of a new international(ist) world order, the realization that, based on interdependent but independent sovereign states: 'The (political) right today is winning because it is capable of weaving powerful narratives of collective identity in which national sovereignty is defined in nativist, nationalist or even racist terms. Progressives must thus be able to provide equally powerful narratives [...] which recognize the human need for belonging and connectedness.'[23] That belonging, I believe, must fly over borders. Unions must work not only at home, but also in an EU context, in the better European Union they are willing to build with others.

May I conclude by stating that I believe the related battle for decent work is a defining battle of our times. I hope that your conference proves to be a fruitful and enjoyable experience, and that you will all continue to play your part in defending the hard-won rights of workers across Europe as we continue to face the challenges and obstacles to a fairer society. You have a powerful voice and one that, I know, can give leadership on the new form of economy, and that you will use wisely as you demonstrate and realize the benefits of solidarity and seek to reclaim an understanding of work as the foundation for the achievement of other human rights and a strong foundation for a life of dignity, fulfilment and flourishing.

Parliamentary Democracy in the European Union

Speech at a reception for the European Association of Former Members of Parliament, Áras an Uachtaráin, 9 June 2017.

As a former parliamentarian myself, honoured to have spent over three decades serving in the Irish national parliament, I have the greatest respect for the work that parliamentarians perform, for their practice of debating, differing, and reaching accommodation on the important issues that shape our public world. I am delighted, therefore, to have this opportunity to meet you. I understand that this is the first biannual meeting of the Bureau of the European Association of Former Members of Parliament to be held in Ireland, and the theme you discussed this morning in the Seanad Chamber – i.e. the Future of Europe – is one that is of fundamental importance to the shared future of all the countries you represent. Indeed, it is one of the central political questions of our time.

Your visit to Ireland comes, of course, at a moment of unprecedented internal and external challenges for Europe. That which seemed inconceivable only yesterday, the unravelling of the European Union, has become thinkable, brought home to us by the thunderbolt of the British decision to exit the Union. Communication, and more alarmingly still, trust, between the peoples

II. Towards a Social Europe

of Europe and their institutions is endangered. We know that, unless decisive political action is taken, unless we create the conditions for a thorough moral and intellectual awakening, the European Union might well perish, and with it a certain idea of Europe: one that is rooted in a spirit of peace, cooperation and solidarity beyond national borders.

For all the gravity of the multiple crises currently facing our union, it remains my profound conviction, however, that, provided it recaptures the affection and trust of its peoples, a strong and united Europe continues to be the best answer we have to offer to the great challenges of this century, from unfettered financial speculation to climate change or indeed security threats, of which the horrendous attack on London Bridge[24] last week was but the latest demonstration. Yes indeed, European unity is the best chance we have of shaping the global agenda on all of those new realities that touch and disrupt the daily lives of our citizens. That is the demonstration which all of us who call ourselves Europeans need to make, in practice and in public discourse. That is the great collective task we must tackle, without delay, without getting bogged down in political and economic fire-fighting, but with long-term vision, and having at heart, throughout, the hopes, the fears, the vulnerabilities and the immense potential of the millions of women, men and children whom our Union of European nations is here to serve.

Parliamentarians, as the elected representatives of those women, men and children, have a crucial role to play in that process. I would go so far as saying that the challenges we face call for a reassertion of the relevance of parliaments, their discourse, and their role in policy formation. This holds true in all matters of public interest, from foreign policy to economic and fiscal policy.

As for the first realm, I strongly believe, as I argued in my address to the Parliamentary Assembly of the Council of Europe two years ago, that parliaments can and must hold governments accountable for what is said and done, or not said and not done, in the wider world, in the name of their citizens. Economic and social matters must, similarly, be reclaimed as another essential area for proactive parliamentary activity and discourse. It is not enough to respond to the contemporary crisis of democracy, in Europe and beyond, by resorting simply to formal measures and procedures aimed at increasing transparency and the probity of the political personnel. Those issues of transparency and probity are very important, of course, but we must go further. Genuine accountability can never be reduced to a procedural matter: it also has to do with power, its distribution and the effectivity of its exercise by the people and their elected representatives.

Is European democracy not endangered when, for example, that power is leeched from parliaments to unaccountable global financial markets and rating agencies, whose orthodoxy and modes of action are predicated on abstract, de-peopled principles? In the highly complex, fast-changing and globalized world of this early twenty-first century, the challenge facing our national and European parliaments is, I believe, that of finding new ways of claiming back competence, legitimacy and political traction over realities that largely exceed national boundaries and jurisdictions. That is, indeed, a highly complex, if not daunting, challenge. Yet, it is an ambition that cannot be surrendered.

Parliaments matter hugely and they must continue to matter. Centuries of effort have been invested by European citizens in securing the vote. It is to their elected representatives that citizens look for accountability, for opening up new collective possibilities lodged in a variety of policy options, and for connecting them to wider horizons through their work in regional fora such as the European Parliament, or in international, multilateral institutions. Can we let go of these hard-won advances? Have we considered the consequences?

As Jürgen Habermas, the eminent German philosopher, has reminded us, without the constant exercise of public deliberation, and without citizens being enabled to submit their arguments to rational disputation, democracy itself will not survive. Parliaments must continue to play a central role in preserving and enlivening the public world that lies at the heart of European democracy – that essential space shared by citizens who must be free to debate in an open and pluralist manner, whose children must be enabled to imagine alternatives to the ideas and practices that govern our present circumstances, in Europe and in the wider world.

Parliamentarians have a most valuable perspective to offer to any holistic response to the contemporary crisis of democracy. Every day, on the streets, in their clinics, they encounter the hopes, the achievements, but also the feelings of insecurity and precariousness experienced by their fellow citizens.

II. Towards a Social Europe

Those are the voices [...] that must be at the centre of any discussion on the future of Europe. And your voices, too, your experience and your perspective, as former parliamentarians, must be a part of that debate.

The voices of the European Street are loud. We must listen to them, and respond not by adjusting what is failing, but by offering a vision based on the solidarity of all citizens in all Member States going forward together. Let us, then, approach the multiple crises currently facing our European Union with creativity, political courage and a renewed commitment to the demands of representative democracy. Let us acknowledge the current loss of trust on the European Street by rebuilding the democratic pact between European citizens and their institutions, with a positive regional invitation that is in step with future global realities and necessary reforms.

Indeed, what better solution than a united Europe do we have to offer in responding to the great collective issues currently facing us? Which alternative means of cooperation do we have at our disposal that would enable us to meet effectively the global environmental challenge, the challenge of development, the challenge of demography and large-scale migration and, also, yes, the challenge of democracy, in a context where we are witnessing the rise of so-called 'illiberal democracies' and increasingly emboldened transgressions of the rule of law both inside and outside the EU? What better response do we have to offer than a stronger European Parliament, and closer coordination between our national parliaments, to voice the aspirations of the peoples of Europe and give shape to our shared future?

We are [...] at a moment when a new departure is required for our European Union – when a new departure is possible. The time has come to craft new policies, grounded in new connections between ethics, ecology and economy. The time has come to gather our strength and unite our efforts, not to break up the edifice painstakingly built by generations before us. The uncertainty of our global environment will not disappear through the wave of a magic retreat behind national borders. No border, no great wall, has ever stopped the spread of pandemics, the flow of migrations, or indeed global warming. Neither should we, Europeans – who represented a quarter of the world population in 1900, and will account for a mere 5 per cent of it by 2060 – mistake the end of *our* world for the end of *the* world.

Let us, if I may invert the words used by Pope Francis in his address to European leaders in Rome last March, learn to use our wings again and elevate our gaze.[25] Let us recognize those new realities that will shape our future and respond to them in concert, in a spirit of intellectual honesty and openness to contradictory debate. Let us continue to build on the shared experience we have garnered through decades of shared institutional and legislative practice. Let us take further the tools of cooperation and solidarity we have created together, and the ability we have developed, in the transnational forum that is the European Parliament, to look at any issue of common interest from different angles, through the eyes of other nations.

Caithfimid comhoibriú seachas scoilteadh. An bealach is fearr atá againn leis an clár oibre domhanda a mhúnlú ná trí Eoraip aontaithe, seachas trí mhíbhinneas guthanna éagsúla in iomaíocht le chéile, le go mbeidh muid in ann na luachanna ar mór againn iad a fhuáil tríd an gclár oibre sin, agus cearta agus dínit an duine a chothú, agus do gach cineál beatha.[26]

Solidarity in Europe: Achieving Authenticity on the European Street

Lecture at the European University Institute, Florence, Italy, 10 May 2018.

It is always enriching for the human spirit to visit Italy, this most beautiful country, the origin of so much of the world's culture and creativity; all the more so to be in Florence, a city forever associated with names like Dante, Michelangelo and Galileo. It is always a particular pleasure to speak at a university, especially when the invitation comes from such a distinguished one and one which has the capacity for an interface with policy. The attraction of speaking here today at the European University Institute is not just the opportunity it offers for engagement with bright and enquiring minds but also because of the essential role – I would even say urgent role, which universities can and must play in understanding the complexity of our world and in addressing its challenges, empowered with adequate scholarly reflection and commitment to humanity in the fullness of its possibility and capacity.

I'm pleased, of course, to have been given the opportunity to participate in this timely, and indeed urgent, conference on 'The State of the Union'; and because the theme of the conference is perhaps the most important one facing our continent, namely 'Solidarity in Europe'.

Solidarity in Europe: Achieving Authenticity on the European Street

Allow me, if I may, to say a word about the two venues in Florence for this conference. Today we meet in Fiesole, where much of *The Decameron* is set. Giovanni Boccaccio might almost have been thinking of the role of universities and of the importance of fresh and creative thinking in Europe when he wrote: 'You must read, you must persevere, you must sit up nights, and exert the utmost power of your mind. If one way does not lead to the desired meaning, take another; if obstacles arise, then still another; until, if your strength holds out, you will find that clear which once looked dark.'[27]

This captures well the importance, this week and always, of moving beyond received wisdom towards the honest, open reflection and original thought which the European debate requires. Above all we need, in the European Union, a pluralism of scholarship. It is something we may be losing. It was John Henry Newman who wrote, 'in a higher world it is otherwise, but here below to live is to change, and to be perfect is to have changed often.'[28]

Tomorrow the conference meets at Palazzo Vecchio, which has been the seat of civic government for much of the period since it was built more than half a millennium ago. Michelangelo's *David*, which arguably celebrates human beauty more wonderfully than any other statue, stands outside the Palazzo quietly dominating the piazza, even if the original statue is, of course, now in safekeeping elsewhere. Michelangelo's *David* should remind us of three things which are essential for the European Union as we consider its future: first, that respect for culture, in its diversity, must be at the heart of our public discourse and our public space, of our common enterprise; second, that the impact of our policy decisions on human beings must be foremost in our thoughts and in all our endeavours; and finally, in a contest as to future direction there is no inevitability that the Goliaths of this world will come out on top; no certainty that might will be proved right.

Despite the many historic achievements in the history of our continent, many centuries of which were tarnished by war, suffering, expropriation of resources and exploitation of colonized peoples, the European Union today faces a unique opportunity and responsibility to assert – indeed, where necessary reassert – its founding values of democracy, human rights and the rule of law in a world in which those values are increasingly challenged. Solidarity in Europe, the timely theme of this conference, must be, I suggest,

II. Towards a Social Europe

the foundation on which our Union's action is built. It must be the star which guides our action at home and in the wider world. We have entered a period when, for the first time in many years, the future shape of the European Union has become a matter of contestation and debate. In the shadow of Brexit and of social forces which have given rise to so much doubt across Europe, we Europeans are invited to define, through deliberation, the outlines of the European Union that we seek.

Political and institutional leaders across the Union are making their contributions to that debate. The so-called Future of Europe debate has been launched because we must together identify the significant reforms which are needed to reconnect the European Union with its citizens. If we fail in that aim, the debate would serve little purpose. In contributing to that debate, I strongly share President Macron's view that our Union must be renewed and rebuilt from below. We may differ, however, in terms of the degree to which our assumptions about the connection between economy and society must also be changed, from the top, and down through the institutional architecture. Business as usual cannot address the challenges we face. May I suggest that we have an obligation to Europe's history, to our people and to the wider world, to examine and address those challenges, and the conversation on these issues must involve us all.

Our first obligation to Europe is to understand and affirm the nature of the European project, the nature, form and aspirations for the Union we seek to make and to explain not only what is but what might be better to our citizens. While reform should be our driving aim, if we fail to understand or recognize what is failing, the fullness of what is in need of reform, we will likely set our course in the wrong direction. We must understand Europe in all its complexity if we are to preserve and strengthen it. We must, above all, avoid being trapped in any single paradigm of thought. We can, for example, achieve a reworking of economic strategies by relocating economics within culture, within a political economy. Centres of learning, such as the European University Institute, can play a necessary and valued role in developing that understanding. While many doctoral theses are written to help us to understand the European Union, I would like today to mention briefly just three points, which seem to me fundamental to understanding our Union.

First, we must understand the diverse roots of the European project. One of the most morally compelling visions of European internationalism – considered as one of the founding documents of European integration – emerged from the Italian resistance movement, in the manifesto composed in 1941 on the island of Ventotene by Altiero Spinelli, a member of the Italian Communist Party, and his colleagues. That is not, of course, to say that the European Union did not have other important roots reflecting other political persuasions, but it is to give the lie to any idea that in its conception the European project was simply and exclusively about capital and markets. Indeed, while the seminal Schuman Declaration, drawn up in 1950 by the visionary Christian Democrat who gave the document its name,[29] spoke of production, it also spoke of peace, and while it spoke of modernization and markets, it also spoke of equalizing and improving living conditions for workers.

This is a breadth of vision we need today. [...] It is a breadth of vision so many of our European citizens see us as having lost. The objectives to which the Union commits itself, which are now contained in Article 3 of the Treaty on European Union, reflect *inter alia* the inheritance of some of the most egalitarian and humane traditions which, although their origin is by no means confined to Europe, saw an important flourishing in Europe. The rich scholarship, philosophy, moral instinct and generous impulse that contributed to and drew on an enriched European thought yielded an impulse towards the promotion of social justice and protection, equality between men and women, solidarity between generations, economic and social cohesion and solidarity between Member States. These principles lie at the very root of the European project and reach their fullest European expression today in the Charter of Fundamental Rights.

The second point I would like to underline, with a view to our understanding of our Union, concerns our way of doing business. The European Union's culture of accommodation, respect and compromise has been with us so long that perhaps we now take it for granted. The decision-making process of the European Union is complex, painstaking and can be frustrating. Like every human construct, it is imperfect. It makes mistakes, sometimes big mistakes. But our calm, respectful and, when we are at our best, rational way of doing business, underpinned crucially by the rule of law, should never be taken for granted on a continent which has been the scene and the source of so much suffering. It should never be taken for granted by countries which, even recently, have known dictatorship. It cannot be taken for granted by small countries which know all too well the realities of power when it is unconstrained by institutions in which all are represented and by the binding rule of law. And equally it should not be ignored by large countries, which may be tempted by the illusion that in a modern world of globalized trade and finance they can go it alone. We should always strive to improve the way we work in the European Union, and be vigilant when its principles are called into question, but we should also celebrate it by giving authentic credence to its values and their sources. We must not allow those values which citizens need to be drowned out by a disconnected set of discourses from different silos, as it were, giving us 'silo speak' rather than 'citizen speak'.

My third point about understanding the Union goes back to what I said at the outset, namely that people – our citizens, and the citizens of the planet – must always be foremost in our thoughts and in our endeavours. It is thus imperative that we not only find better ways of explaining to people how our Union works but also better ways of learning from people what form of European Union they want. The opportunity of the current debate about the future of Europe must not be squandered. I am pleased that public debate about the future is being encouraged across so many of the Member States of the Union and that, in that context, the Irish government has been conducting a citizens' dialogue. We cannot – and should not – wish away the complexity of the European Union, but we cannot be lazy as to how we present and respect that complexity. Spectacle constructed for the media must not be allowed to replace the necessary discourse upon which our and our citizens' future depends. Language matters. It must not impede the new economic literacy that we need. Media management cannot substitute for in-depth discussion informed by scholarship and commitment to future generations.

I would like to touch briefly on one issue, which has in a sense been delivered to us by special delivery rather than one we would have chosen to address, namely Brexit. I am conscious that much of the work by our diplomats on the agenda of the Union necessarily concerns managing current challenges rather than looking ahead to reshaping our shared future. Of course, like so many of you, I regret the decision of our nearest neighbour. Although I am conscious of the ongoing debate in the UK about some of the circumstances around the conduct of the referendum, we must accept the decision of the British people, as indeed we should accept any other democratic decision they may choose to take. I would like to pay warm tribute to the support of our European partners and of the European institutions for Ireland's concerns in the Brexit negotiations and, in particular, for the unqualified support we have received for the maintenance of the Good Friday Agreement in all its aspects. The European Union has for several decades provided generous political and financial support for peace on our small island. It has also, over time, provided much of the wider context in which peace was possible. Few could have predicted the central and necessary role that the European Commission, with support from all our partners, would be playing today in seeking to ensure the full protection of what has been achieved in our peace process, in effect the maintenance of the status quo in the application of the agreement on the island of Ireland. There could be no better example of the solidarity which is the theme of this week's conference.

Jacques Delors once said that 'Europe does not just need fire-fighters, it needs architects too.'[30] It is important, therefore, as Delors implied, to take opportunities; to raise our eyes above the road immediately ahead and shift our gaze towards the horizon; to look beyond the immediate roadblocks to consider where we are heading and whether we need to adjust our direction.

There could not be a more important guiding theme for our reflections on the future of the Union this week than the theme chosen for this conference, namely solidarity. Solidarity was in the DNA of the founders of the European Union, so when our solidarity is inadequate or lacking we call into question our very nature. Solidarity is not a possession to be stored away. It is a living impulse. It must be no mere aspiration but something of concrete achievement and policy decision to which we can point.

Internal and external solidarity are necessarily linked. One of the great tasks of the next decade will be to achieve cohesiveness within the communities and between the communities of our common European home. It is only by achieving that goal – by rebuilding our capacity and willingness to work together to lead fulfilling lives in all spheres of human activity – that the

II. Towards a Social Europe

Union can play the full leadership role of which it is capable in confronting the global challenges common to all humanity: the pressing demand for just and sustainable development; the imperative of vindicating the human rights of those fleeing war, persecution and famine; and above all, the urgent necessity to address the causes of climate change and to mitigate its consequences.

The most urgent task is to rebuild its internal cohesion on the principle of solidarity. I have no doubt that the European Union has within it the capacity to bring into being a new discourse that leads to a fairer, more inclusive union. To achieve that we must, as a first step, be ready to challenge failed and failing paradigms. Let us not forget, as we meet in Florence, which provides Galileo's final resting place, that more than 400 years ago the Roman inquisition described Galileo's belief that the earth revolves around the sun as 'foolish and absurd in philosophy and formally heretical'. Surely all of us who seek a union capable of accomplishing these great tasks in this century cannot rely on any failed orthodoxies, whether in thought or action. The intersection of all of these matters – climate change, migration, the role of the state and the future of our economy – has been considered in depth by scholars such as Professor Ian Gough, a former Jean Monnet Fellow at this institution. If we are ready to challenge old and unconvincing certainties, to have the open minds which real scholarship requires, then we can preserve and even strengthen the vision of the European Union. In doing that we can re-energize a model in which the peoples of other continents have placed, perhaps increasingly place, their hopes.

As we consider the strengthening of European solidarity, it is essential to recognize that the Founding Treaty of the European Union, while some might wish it were so, was far from being a neo-liberal charter. The Union, properly interpreted, was not envisaged to consecrate private profit over public purpose. Rather, the Union was to be a bedrock of profound values and overarching rules. Above all it should be seen as a process – a context for creative and open debate between our elected governments; a structure for framing and evolving policy through democratic and open discussion in our institutions and parliaments. It is vital that that debate and discussion be enriched by contributions from wider society, including academia. The emphasis must be on a courageous questioning untrammelled by preconceptions.

In strengthening internal solidarity, it is important to recognize that the challenges we face are not just economic. They are social, political and cultural. The form of the market calls for redefinition. The market must not be accepted as an unregulated market, as end point rather than instrument. Human beings, all of our citizens, must be at the heart of our endeavours. We are, after all, the best of our moral social scholarship tells us, social beings, not simply consumers, targets, to be treated as commodities within a totalizing version of an unregulated and insatiable market.

The dignity of work, therefore, in all its facets and in its essence as a shared human activity, must be at the centre of the values by which we want to live. A first and urgent task must be to restore sustainable and fulfilling employment to the citizens of the European Union. There is nothing more corrosive to society and more crushing to the individual than endemic unemployment, or the insecurity and uncertainty of the vulnerability of a precariat. Unemployment in the EU has come down and we should welcome that. Yet there are still nearly 18 million men and women without work. More shockingly, nearly 18 per cent of our young people are unemployed, with the figure being much higher in some Member States. Where short term work has been created it is too often precarious work. We must define and create work in a way that can provide the necessary self-fulfilment and protections of the worker.

We must be cautious, too, when we use words such as 'populism'. Populism must not be confused with popular will. However, we must at the same time be forthright in condemning the rise of those populists who, through the fomenting of fear, relentlessly exploit the anxieties of the vulnerable and the frustration of those who are left behind. Nothing would give more succour to abuses of such populism than for us to fail to create just and equal societies with real opportunities for participation. The European Union, given the political will, and its strong legal framework and tradition, could – if it demonstrates imagination and determination in addressing its own challenges – make a significant contribution in confronting the excessive deregulation and erosion of rights that is emerging at global level.

However, to do that we need to revisit the relationship between economic and social policy in a fundamental way. While I therefore warmly welcome the convening of the Social Summit for Fair Jobs and Growth in Gothenburg in

II. Towards a Social Europe

November last year, which aimed at boosting growth, creating fair jobs and fostering equal opportunities, and see it as a step towards creating a strong and tangible social dimension, obviously much further progress is needed. The Summit's recognition of the need to put people first and that employment and social progress are first and foremost created on the ground was a good starting point. It was an attempt, I would suggest, to reconnect with the project of the European social model, which is rooted in our recent history and which recognizes that solidarity among citizens and social cohesion are values that must be fostered and maintained – not as mere by-products of, or compensations for, or as residual of a successful economy, but as foundational elements of economy in their own right. Our leadership, our authenticity in terms of concern for our citizens is tested by our willingness, or lack of it, to embrace new paradigms of practice and theory, including in the economy, to emerge; our willingness to allow what is failing to be discarded, to make way for what needs to be born.

The twenty principles set out in the European Pillar of Social Rights, which was proclaimed by the Gothenburg Summit, are a step forward, and many of them point generally in the right direction. But the Union needs to go further and to start by delivering on the commitments it has made. The principles agreed in Gothenburg indicate, for example, that everyone has a right to quality and inclusive education, training and life-long learning; that employment relationships leading to precarious working conditions shall be prevented; and that workers have the right to fair wages that provide for a decent standard of living. Such principles cannot be allowed to remain aspirational: if they do, they will merely feed into the disillusion that is evident in so much of our society. The agreed principles must now, urgently, be transformed into principles of practice supported by Member States. Pending social legislation should be driven forward and the further necessary legislation should be tabled. This is essential if the social principles are to achieve authenticity where it matters most: on the European Street.

There are, of course, other priorities on the European agenda: the completion of the single market, including the digital single market, and of the Banking Union as well as the next steps towards Economic and Monetary Union (EMU). A sufficient basis for the legitimization of such developments depends on a prior achievement of social cohesion, and such developments must be subordinated to that aim. These priorities can only deliver their intended benefit to our citizens if located within a social vision. If they are put forward in the right way they will be greatly beneficial to our citizens. It is not for me to be prescriptive as regards the details of how to take these dossiers forward. However, it is my strong conviction that unless solidarity within societies and between Member States is demonstrated – a very great deal more solidarity than has been demonstrated in the past – our efforts, and any short term or superficial success, will be hollow. Solidarity should also characterize the Union's approach to the wider world. The stronger and more cohesive we can be internally the more effective a role we can play externally to that end.

In speaking of the external role of the Union, we should acknowledge that the role of this continent over the centuries, as seen by much of the world, has often not been a glorious one. There is nothing essentially moral in the varying practices of Europeans or the role our members have played in history; even if, needless to say, many Europeans have made very positive contributions to our world. We need to transcend our past if we are to remove the capacity of a past wrong to limit our present, curtail our future. The warm East–West relations that have been created between Ireland and its neighbours required a facing of the past on both of our parts. Surely it would be positive, let us take the relationship between European nations and Africa, that a similar clearing of the past take place, with the aim of not losing the opportunity for dialogue in the present and our joint hopes for the future.

In all humility but with every confidence, our Union should take as its starting point the urgent and growing need to defend multilateralism. Multilateralism is an important form of solidarity. It provides a context in which solidarity makes sense and can have maximum effect. In a world in which insularity often seems to be taking hold, in which for some patriotism and selfishness are increasingly intertwined, in which there are those who would even beat their ploughshares back into swords, the European Union has both an opportunity and a responsibility to provide leadership on the importance of working together through agreed institutions. Resiling to the inevitability of war, abandoning the prospect of peace, reviving the literacy of democracy, bringing a new literacy of economics into being – these are choices that will, in how they are made, define the very future of multilateral institutions.

II. Towards a Social Europe

Recently I spoke at the United Nations as to the importance of not allowing the strut of the most powerful, and the arms industry, to drown out the whispers from the gallery of the UN that yearn for peace, the elimination of poverty, freedom for minorities, respect for indigeneity. The United Nations lies at the very heart of the multilateral system. Like all human organizations, it can lay no claim to perfection. To cite just one example, the UN Security Council should become more representative of the wider international community, in particular the Global South. The UN's weaknesses, however, are no reason to talk it down. Rather they constitute every reason for building it up. The UN remains the essential framework for the assertion of global values and provides the only global context for aspiring to the solidarity of all humanity. The European Union and its Member States must continue to work strongly in support of the United Nations with which they share not only important values but also a fundamental commitment to multilateralism as a way of doing business. The Union has an important role, through the UN and elsewhere. By working with others to defend human rights, democracy and the rule of law while avoiding hubris, and in no sense claiming perfection for ourselves, the European Union now finds itself in a context that offers leadership, a role which we should take forward, obviously with full respect for others on the one hand, but with determination on the other, offering a strong diplomacy, new mechanisms for achieving peace, avoiding the lure of the international arms industry and its advocates.

The Sustainable Development Goals can be seen as a charter for global solidarity. They challenge all of us to deal with trade, debt, the environment, intellectual and spiritual freedom, as well as cultural diversity, in a spirit of justice, partnership and mutual solidarity. I am proud of the leadership role that Ireland played in the negotiation of those goals. The international community must now commit to the implementation of the Sustainable Development Goals and to realizing their full potential. The European Union carries in a sense three separate responsibilities in taking forward those goals: the responsibility of history; the responsibility of an inclusive and sustainable prosperity; and the responsibility which flows from our values, including notably the principle of solidarity.

Africa offers the European Union both a particular challenge and an opportunity to bring new models of connection between economy, ethics, and sustainable ecology into being. The Union itself and its Member States constitute the largest aid donors to the African continent. However, the Union should collectively do much more on a continent where so many still suffer from hunger but which at the same time has so much potential for the future. While the Union should continue to help to build resilient and accountable states in Africa, states which will deliver for their young populations and which in future can be strong partners with us in achieving sustainability. Europe's willingness to transact the previous relationship with Africa with the new scholarship of contemporary Africa would be of immense assistance. The European Union should give a lead in removing the impediments to the transfer of the science and technology which Africa needs to achieve sustainability and respond to climate change.

Climate change is not only an environmental challenge but also a challenge of security, development and justice – it is an existential threat to our planet. The Paris Agreement in 2015, of course, left very significant challenges ahead. However, when compared with the disappointing failures of the past, the acceptance of the scientific reality of climate change and the reflection of that reality in a universal, legally-binding agreement remains of immense significance. What is required now, first and foremost, is that all of those who made commitments must stand by them and deliver on them. The Secretary General of the United Nations, António Guterres, rightly insisted at last year's Climate Conference in Bonn that our duty to future generations also requires us to raise our level of ambition. The contribution of the European Union is central to what has been achieved on climate change and European leadership is now required more than ever in taking forward that achievement. In this area also, the Union's approach must rediscover fully its founding value of solidarity. Climate justice demands that those countries and peoples who have least contributed to the problem of climate change should not be expected to pay the highest price to resolve it. Priority should therefore be given to accelerating support to the Least Developed Countries including the mobilization of the necessary resources.

Perhaps the greatest current challenge which the Union faces in terms of solidarity relates to migrants. As Pope Francis has reminded us, 'migrants and refugees are not pawns on the chessboard of humanity'. The New York Declaration for Refugees and Migrants delivered a strong message of solidarity and contains detailed commitments which, if implemented, would ensure a more humane, dignified and compassionate response by the international community to the plight of refugees and migrants. I am pleased that Ireland played an important role as co-facilitator of that Declaration. However, the consequences of the continued failure to transform into effective action the promises which have been made are often evident and sometimes tragic. I would like, as others have done, to pay strong tribute to Italy for the leadership role it has played in recent years in saving the lives of migrants crossing the Mediterranean to escape extreme poverty, hunger, conflict, and ethnic cleansing; people seeking in Europe a better life for themselves and for their families, as Europeans have sought a better life abroad in centuries past. I am pleased that the Irish Naval Service has been able to provide some support to Italy's efforts. Clearly the issue of migration in the Union is complex and sensitive, not least because of the threat of significant forces in our societies today which seek to exploit people's fears and to use opportunities to direct those fears against those whom they portray as different from ourselves. This should not make us hesitate from providing the new institutional, including financial, arrangements appropriate for a collective response.

Let me say in conclusion that I believe we should remain committed to the European vision and to the potential for the founding principles of the European Union to provide the foundations of a renewed and strengthened union. To make that possible, we need a creative and courageous vision at this crucial moment in the history of our continent. I believe that what is required, as the timely theme of this week's conference so rightly implies, is for us to rediscover the enabling and inspiring principle of solidarity, solidarity within the Union and solidarity with the wider world.

If I may, I will conclude by returning to Michelangelo who once observed that: 'every block of stone has a statue inside it and it is the task of the sculptor to discover it'. We are in a sense the sculptors of this European generation, still working on a block of valuable marble which has been passed down to us from the founding fathers of the European Union. If solidarity remains our guiding principle, I have no doubt that our European future, the outlines of which we can see but much of which remains to be discovered by our own chisels, will be a source of pride for ourselves and an object of admiration for others.

III
THINKING ABOUT EUROPE

On the State of Democracy in Our Changing World

The Aristotle Address 2019, the Stoa of Attalos at the Ancient Agora of Athens, 10 October 2019.

It is a great pleasure indeed to return to Athens following our State Visit last year [...] Reflecting on this visit to the *agora*, I was aware of course of its significance in the history of ancient Athens, and for democracy itself, as a particular gathering place for discourse here in the heart of the capital. To speak at this site is a moving experience for anybody aware of the debt we all, in generation after generation, owe to that founding exchange of ideas, that pursuit of truth and beauty in its wholeness of mind and body, that was the Greek contribution, and let us be grateful too to those who saved it for us, leaving after their expulsion from Europe a legacy of translation of thought that was not confined by borders.

The Stoa, as we know, served not only as a vital point of new dialogue and ideas, but also as a place of shelter. Perhaps, therefore, as we face the many challenges for democracy today and concerned for all of our European family, it is especially fitting that we gather here this evening, in advance of our meeting of the Arraiolos Group [...], which coincides with the broader dialogue and debate taking place under the aegis of the Athens Democracy Forum.

III. Thinking About Europe

All of the Irish playwrights, from John Millington Synge, William Butler Yeats, George Bernard Shaw and on to Brian Friel, Tom Murphy and Marina Carr in the modern period; the major poets including Seamus Heaney, one of our Nobel Laureates, Brendan Kennelly, Tom Paulin, and Michael Longley have all published work based on the Athenian tragedies. As with many Irish poets, Seamus Heaney, in particular, was drawn to Greece time and again over the years.

Then too in the contemporary period a critical literature is rich with work such as Professor Brian Arkins' *Irish Appropriation of Greek Tragedy* and *Hellenizing Ireland*, a major work of scholarship,[1] and Professor Fran O'Rourke's *Aristotelian Interpretations*,[2] to which I will refer.

It has been, is and will always be, a pleasure, a moral renewal in intellectual terms through the resonances it suggests, to visit Greece, a country and a people that has given, and continues to give, so much to Europe, indeed to the world, by way of its contribution to civilization, both ancient and contemporary, to culture, aesthetics and philosophy including founding discourses on democracy itself. For this is the very reason we are all gathered here today in the *agora* where Athenians, dating back to the sixth century BC of Cleisthenes, gathered to host their assemblies. All adults, male citizens at birth, were members of the Assembly 'Ecclesia', with regular attendances of 6000, thus making that discourse on this hill one of the earliest and most important wellsprings of democracy.

It is a discourse that found its way into the creative work of all the nations of Europe and beyond. In our own Gaelic language, the mythical stories of Greece have always been present, and some of our modern plays recall the specific use that was made of the classical sources of Greek myths in the Gaelic hedge schools that preceded the founding of primary education institutions that would promote the widespread use of the English language in Ireland.

Indeed, the distinguished Professor, and Scholar of Classics, George Thomson who in the early 1930s taught at University College Galway, an institution in which I taught myself for decades, in discussing his translation of Homer's *Odyssey* into Gaelic – a task he undertook on the Irish-speaking Blasket Islands off the Kerry coast in the west of Ireland – in opening what was a seminal contribution on oral culture, stressed the role of oral culture in the genesis of Homer's great work.

The lessons of that period and its discourses remain for us. Yes, they include the price paid for imperial tendency, the price of war, the ethics that might or might not be present in the relationship of victor and vanquished, but it also includes, let us never forget, the importance of the performative – taking an idea and making it happen for the people beyond the *agora*. Accepting the responsibility of extending the understanding and the discourse to amplification by the performative is also something for which we are indebted to Greece.

A constant in the Greek emphasis is wholeness, of life, the body community, it informs the architecture of that early period, and on through centuries it privileges the indivisibility of culture. We should never forget that for the Festival of Dionysus a comedy had to be submitted for consideration, together with the tragedy, thus recognizing that all of life was also in the comedy, the movement in the tragedy being towards an emancipatory catharsis.

In both there was the privileging of the performance. From this let us take perhaps just two lessons: the achievement of authenticity was sought to be delivered through words to the collective, and thus in the movement from monologue through dialogue we can make our way to the lodgment of the wisdom that is in the words given to the chorus, with the message that engaged the audience. What an empowering analogy this can be for our own times – engaging with the European Street as our *agora*, turning our words into the discernible shape of proposed resolution in action.

A further lesson is that through the privileging of the performative the contribution of the heart in the achievement of truth was necessary. Aristotelian reason would not suffice on its own to offer a glimpse of the fullness of life's wonder, hope or grief.

Our nations, Ireland and Greece, may stand at different corners of this beautiful, fascinating and varied continent, yet it is easily recognized what connections we have had from earliest times and, even more importantly, how those values that invoke reason and culture, in performances that we might share in common in the future, may assist us as we work together in the crafting and making of a union of European publics that will have the capacity to acknowledge, respect and celebrate Europe in all its diversity – a European Union which we might offer as not only a regional achievement, but, because of its far-seeing humanity, a global, intergenerational exemplar.

III. Thinking About Europe

Such a union, I suggest, must be built on the production and preservation of pluralist interdisciplinary intellectual work by citizens who have the courage to make an interrogation of how life is to be lived. It can draw on the memory and experience of our various but shared historical struggles for independence, experience that includes a large and valuable migratory component. Both Greece and Ireland will mark important anniversaries, of 1821 and 1921, on our respective paths to independence and I am sure that over the coming period we will find ways of reflecting on that shared history. Drawing on all of this, but also on the imaginative, humanistic values in our peoples and their culture, surely we are capable of giving an ethical, inclusive dimension to life and the structures on which our shared future on a vulnerable planet might be based.

For all of our peoples, our experience is a rich one, one that contains moments of emancipation as well as anguish, experiences that equip us well for the challenge of envisioning and constructing a European Union of humanity, shaped to meet the needs of all of our citizens. We must, to achieve this, become ever closer, become better listeners to each other and others beyond our vision, in our discourse-sharing, our hopes, our shared challenges, and it is through a recognition of the healing and life-enhancing power of culture we can call up again that indomitable courage that is needed to be different, to take a stand, to endure.

What we are seeking is not omniscience but rather the materials and instruments for achieving, or restoring, trust, and in doing that we will always have to acknowledge fallibility and an inexhaustible wonder. Professor Fran O'Rourke has told us that the Irish, who valued Aristotle as a treasure, did not regard him as omniscient. Professor O'Rourke refers to James Joyce's 'scribbledehobble', his workbook for *Finnegans Wake*, where he wrote of 'three things Aristotle didn't know: labour of bees, flow of tide, mind of women'.

We in the European Union have resources of mind and heart, performances of agony and shared joy, and compassion to call upon. For despite its mixed historical experience, including the numerous historic achievements of our continent, many centuries of which were tarnished by war and suffering, the European Union today still retains a capacity from its legacy of thought, importantly from its Greek contribution on the rational, from its historic commitment to intellectual discourse that led to the undoing of the trammels of empire and that informed the struggle against imperialism.

We in our time have been given a unique opportunity and indeed responsibility to assert, deepen, and where necessary, reassert, those founding values of democracy, cohesion, shared prospects, human rights and the rule of law in an increasingly interdependent world of vulnerabilities in which those values are challenged.

These values are neither abstract, nor are they optional extras, nor are they ever confined by borders. They go to the very core of our humanity, and such values should be respected and upheld by all Member States. Central to these values, and their vindication, is the concept of the constitution, respect for, treatment of the Other; of meeting the Other with what the cultures and belief systems of the world have called 'hospitality'; the concept of acknowledging the importance of recognizing and understanding the circumstance of the movement of people, who in the exercise of their hopes are bringing with them their stories and their cultural endowments. For we Europeans are, all of us, the product of migratory beings ourselves, sometimes forced, other times voluntary. That is the evidence of millennia.

Paul Valéry wrote in 1919 of how, after the needless catastrophe of World War I that was the collision of empires, 'an extraordinary shudder ran through the marrow of Europe'.[3] We, too, in our times have felt a similar shudder. Nowhere more so than during the recent financial crisis, the subsequent sovereign debt crisis, and the so-called Great Recession that affected much of the Western World, including Europe. I am aware of the high price that was paid and most acutely by those most vulnerable peoples who were at a far distance from the speculative forces that were its source. If this is the country of Aristotle, Plato, Homer, Hesiod, Aeschylus, Euripides, Herodotus, Xenophon, it is above all, let us never forget, the country of our fellow citizens of Greece, who in the modern period, too, have given us a world-class cultural contribution. The recession impacted greatest in the communities of the peripheral Member States of the EU.

Today, we find ourselves confronted by the challenge of a keen and growing awareness that, in some critical respects, in institutional terms, and in the quality of our responses, we have been failing to live up to the needs, ideas

III. Thinking About Europe

and expectations of citizens of the European Union. It is clear now that, as a direct result of the somewhat blunt and often insensitive handling of the crisis, social cohesion has been significantly damaged. This has had a consequence in fuelling the rise of euro-scepticism, exclusionary forms of neo-nationalism and austerity-sourced populism, nativism, reactions that are built on negative invocations of fear and ignorance, including a fear and exploitation of ignorance that scapegoats the stranger, the Other.

These manifestations, however, are not the root causes of the discontent on the European Street. They are symptoms only. To come to grips with their source, we must delve deeper into structures, drill down to the assumptions on which policy is based, its processes utilized. We must ask how did a single hegemonic role come to prevail for four decades, for a market theory that was extreme, and that was accompanied with the exclusion of a role for the state?

To answer such a question, we are called to engage in mind work and, beyond that, to reassert the right and space for mind work, critical scholarship, examine the assumption of the paradigm that has failed, allow for a new inclusive paradigm to come to prevail.

It is only when we take the necessary steps to address the underlying sources of anxiety – including social insecurity, uncertainty as to the future of work, the yawning equality gap, and the crisis of democratic unaccountability in global economics, that we can recapture the desire for cohesion originally envisaged in the best instincts of our founders. We are, after all, not inventing the concept of the 'social' when we speak of 'social Europe'. Was it not there as a principle in all of the better language of our heritage, including the founding moments of the European Union, for example, in the words of such as Altieri Spinelli in the *Ventotene Manifesto*? But is it a social Europe we seek?

The future of the European Union must be discussed in ethical and inclusive terms, I suggest, taking account above all else of the anxieties from below. The future must be crafted from connections to the European Street. This requires a process that is open, honest and genuinely inclusive, one that does not recoil from asking difficult, challenging questions. It requires an honest critique as to the distribution of life choices, one that constitutes an attempt to reimagine and rebuild, involves recognizing how we look at each other in our vulnerabilities, and recognizing that we will be judged by future generations as to whether we averted our gaze from the vulnerabilities of our planet, our continent, or humanity itself or had the empathy necessary to celebrate our interdependency.

The prevailing political economy discourse for almost four decades now has not been sufficiently challenged intellectually, or scrutinized with sufficient courage, by the body politic, even if there have been cracks that have occasionally let in the light. The recent embrace by many institutions of 'behavioural economics', such as that by the World Bank, constitutes an overdue recognition of what is failing, but that recognition is simply insufficient to the challenge we now face. Neither is any simplistic, often facile, placing of new lenses over the orthodox neo-liberal paradigm sufficient to the task at hand. We cannot continue with a paradigm that has not merely failed, but that has imprisoned intellectually so many policymakers and their supporting intellectuals and commentators.

Such an approach would simply mask the manner in which context was abandoned in the hegemonic policies of recent decades and how, in doing that, the critical care and emancipatory potential of disciplines such as sociology and political science were eschewed in a narrow practice that had no tolerance for discussion as to the adequacy of theoretical insight, methodological rigour, or empirical validation.

We have, as a result, had a lesser economics; one that, at best, is descriptive of a set of measures that sought to satisfy an ideological position rather than assist in creating policy options that could be social and emancipatory in their reach. The moving of economics away from philosophy, the contraction of philosophy to an internal scholasticizing, has left social studies as a form that is, at best, one of description, rather than analysis or narrative suggestion.

It is heart-breaking, too, to me as a former university teacher, to realize how, with a diminished role for the state being pursued, those institutions gifted with the responsibility for independent, critical thought, having been made fragile as to funding, bowed to pressure and became colluders in a neo-utilitarian myth that substituted uncritical description, and thus rationalization of what is failing, for creative collective scholarly thought.

With neo-liberalism as the dominant ideology that has been shaping our world today, notions such as democracy, social justice, equality and humanitarianism have been replaced at the personal level by a crude and forceful individualism which is driven by an insatiable consumerism, social indifference and an aggressive self-aggrandizement, thus further reinforcing the decline of ethically inspired political advocacy that results so often in the divorce of the purpose of intellectual practice from the pursuit of universal values like truth, justice and peace.

Those who benefit from such a flawed model are never the public, now or in the future. It is a minority who benefit and who, in the defence of an unregulated accumulation, can ignore the consequences of their model, be it in ecological or social terms. This minority is often footloose, existing beyond the reach of regulation, of accountability, by state or parliament, out of democratic reach itself. Data indicate that this minority is getting wealthier at the expense of the poorest. The growth of an unaccountable form of speculative capital activity can dislodge even the efforts of governments. This must change. The survival of democracy itself requires it.

However, there is a growing light. Because of the work of brave scholars, some who endured, others with new work, I believe we are now at the cusp of a paradigm shift in the political-economy discourse, a shift that has the potential, if lodged among the body politic, and should it gain widespread institutional legitimacy, to be transformative, to assist in the great challenges we face to deepen democracy, achieve accountability over a growing and threatening global realm of unaccountable corporations, and turn the tide on yawning inequality.

Paradigm shifts do happen, even in economic theory or practice. We last saw such a paradigm shift in economic thinking in the early 1980s, as Keynesian thinking gave way to the neo-liberal paradigm, advocated by Friedrich von Hayek and Milton Friedman, which much of Western society embraced with what was a determined, unfettered abandon.

A new paradigm of economy is now urgently required, one that might steer us back towards what will be a long but essential road of societal and ecological reparation, one that will address and reduce inequality whilst simultaneously operating within an ecological awareness of the planet's natural systems and their constraints, not easy, but necessary for survival itself, and our best prospect for an enduring form of cohesion as we live together.

Such a new form of economic heterodoxy is an eco-social paradigm, and it has been so well advanced by engaged public intellectuals such as Professor Ian Gough and others. Professor Gough, in his book, *Heat, Greed and Human Need*, outlines how the alternative paradigm is rooted in the concept of human need over insatiability. It promotes notions of gender equality, redistribution of income, wealth and resources, and a reconfigured social consumption and investment strategy that transfers resources and capital from developed countries to developing countries in such a way as to achieve this eco-social welfare state.

The eco-social policies that underpin such a paradigm must concurrently pursue both equity as well as wider social justice, through sustainability and sufficiency goals within an activist innovation state, yes working with partners, but with substantial state investment and transparent and robust regulation and planning.

Socio-economic measures are also required to negate any adverse impacts of the ecological transition for the poorest in society and to ameliorate, rather than threaten to deepen, growing levels of inequality. The approach that scholars such as Professor Gough offer is an approach that is garnering support as one that represents our best response towards intergenerational justice.

This is a responsible economics. It accepts that the concept of accelerated economic growth *ad infinitum* is inherently flawed. Scholars such as Ian Gough are, I suggest, recovering a discourse and a political-economy discipline that has fallen prey to an uncritical embrace of neo-liberal refrains. They advocate for an economic model of pluralism which emphasizes the finite nature of the Earth's natural resources and the role that rich nations must play in ameliorating the crises in which we find ourselves. As Gough puts it himself:

> Consumption and consumption-based emissions, ignored by the green growth agenda, must be given equal priority in the rich world. [...] Issues of global equity, almost entirely absent from international climate negotiations so far, must be discussed and confronted. [...] 'Affluence' has a class as well as a national dimension.

Such work as that of Gough, Kate Raworth[4], Mariana Mazzucato, Sylvia Walby and others offers hope by showing us how we can, as a global community, ensure that no one falls short on life's essentials (from food and housing to healthcare and political voice), while ensuring that collectively we do not overshoot our pressure on Earth's life-supporting systems, on which we fundamentally depend – such as a stable climate, fertile soils, and a protective ozone layer. Such ideas of balancing outcomes were, of course, at the heart of discourse here in the Stoa.

Public intellectuals in Western democracies have, historically, vociferously denounced war and imperialism, oppression and the violation of universal values such as truth, social justice, freedom whenever and wherever they occurred. I am concerned that this is not now the case as the deployment of human, scientific, and technological capacities are once again being delivered to preparations for war, exploitation of conflict, a diplomacy surrendered to fear, and livelihoods made fragile in a trade war provoked by the strong for their unique and sole benefit, ignoring all consequences.

I believe public intellectuals have a particular ethical obligation, as an educated elite, to take a stand against the increasingly aggressive orthodoxies of the marketplace, of extreme individualism, that have permeated all aspects of life, including academia. Is it not as important to experience the development of the social self through others, and one's connection to citizenship and history as it is to accept one's role as a useful unit in a consuming culture? Universities function within a culture, and how they negotiate that relationship defines their atmosphere. Their ethos establishes, too, whether they are contributing to the culture, or surrendering to its excesses.

The challenge for us all now is to achieve, for all of our citizens in their different generations, a capacity and an institutional space to debate and seek a version of eco-social political economy that meets our demands for a deepening of democracy. We must not despair even if, at present, that capacity at so many institutional levels is not so much in evidence. We must encourage and support the growing body of academic thought that is advocating for an alternative.

There is work to be done. There is no clear evidence in European thinking that collective welfare is replacing the aggregation of individual property-based wealth as an aspiration. The prevailing narrative seems to be trapped intellectually in a structure of thought which it appears unable to challenge, from which it seems unable, or at times even unwilling, to escape or exit. This being rendered 'mute', as Professor Hartmut Rosa puts it in his recent work *Resonance: A Sociology of Our Relationship to the World*, presents a fundamental challenge for those of us wishing for a renaissance of democracy and cohesion in Europe and elsewhere.[5]

I believe that the transformation that is required must seek to extend and deepen democracy and initiate changes in our political structures, our institutions, our language of discourse, our way of dealing with each other, and in our consciousness. Such a programme requires not just intellectual work, but its delivery with moral courage. It needs a commitment to dialogical thought, and the patience to listen to the assumptions of the Other is essential, observing the essential courtesies of discourse.

Sylvia Walby has argued in her book, *Crisis*, that the economic and fiscal crises which we have lived through over the past decade, and the resulting recession (experienced severely in Ireland and Greece) has cascaded through society, and the ensuing fiscal crisis over government budget deficits and austerity has led to a political crisis which, in turn, now threatens to become a democratic crisis and a wider crisis of legitimacy for the European Union.

Parliaments matter. Centuries of effort have been invested by European citizens in securing the vote, indeed in extending the vote. It is to parliament that citizens look for accountability, for strategic alternatives. If national parliaments, if the European Parliament, lose the capacity to deliver accountability, where else might it be found?

The political-economic concept of deliberative democracy provides us with a means with which we may engage and promote our vision across the citizenries of Europe, actively encouraging societal participation. Jürgen Habermas has contributed persuasively on this topic, asserting that political decisions should be the product of fair and reasonable discussion and debate among citizens.

It follows that we must become more aware as citizens about the often obscured, or consciously hidden, ideological assumptions that lie behind policy decisions. We must, thus, foster universal political-economic literacy to deal with new and existing challenges, and a better understanding of the nature of value and what constitutes happiness and well-being.

Habermas is critical of the technocratic policies advocated by several Member States that continue to be imposed on the populations of the economically weaker, crisis-stricken Member States, and which have had the effect of undermining solidarity across the EU. He argues for an alternative to the technocratic, austerity-centric approach, that it be replaced by a deeper democratization of European institutions, through which the EU might have the possibility of fulfilling its core founding principles and thus ensuring that, as he puts it: 'rampant market capitalism can once more be brought under political control at the supranational level'.[6] He argues for more profound political integration in Europe so as to create a shift in the imbalance between politics and the market, which is continuing to the present day in the wake of the neo-liberal self-disempowerment of politics.

This disempowerment of politics was evidenced during the 2008 financial crisis and subsequent economic recessions across the EU as pressure being exerted by the financial markets on politically fragmented national budgets, which quite scandalously fostered a collectivizing, pejorative self-perception of those populations afflicted by the crisis.

Habermas asserts that the response by markets, lead governments, key international organizations and the mainstream neo-liberal commentariat all contributed greatly to the punitive character and grounds on which assistance was offered to 'programme' countries by, 'turning the "donor" and the "beneficiary" countries against each other and fomenting nationalism'.

Are there any lessons we have learnt from the economic crisis, the 'self-regulating market' and the long, devastating period of austerity imposed on millions of European citizens?

I believe there are many – in politics, policymaking, academia, the commentariat, citizens at large – who have reassessed what were sometimes strongly held beliefs, with a new-found appreciation that the state does, and should, have an important role to play across all spheres of public policy, that good regulation does matter. The legitimation crisis is not, of course, confined to the European Union, or its members. The role of the state at a global level will be crucial in approaching issues such as climate change and sustainability.

As to the growing realm lacking in accountability, there is a serious problem. What of institutions not answerable to parliament, people, or their laws? It is an issue that was addressed by His Excellency the President of Greece, in the Aristotle Lecture in 2016. He spoke of those non-state entities of international scope devoid of democratic legitimacy – financial markets, credit-rating agencies – and the President spoke of the declining discourse on social welfare and the rule of law.

The European Union was born with an invocation for solidarity. What does solidarity demand of us now? That is the challenge to us all. I suggest its focus must be intergenerational, be defined as a multi-dimensional concept embracing ecosystem, society, culture and economy. There must be a collective approach in bringing what is unaccountable into accountability, for it is this combined with lack of institutional transparency that is contributing to an undermining public trust in democracy.

Where do we go from here? I believe the impressive setting of today's address carries weight and begs a number of important questions:

- Can we make such a similar space as the agora of the past was available to us today, an agora whose participants will help us keep traditions such as the Socratic tradition alive, allow for the questioning of assumptions and methods?
- Can we move society away from the current trajectory of unrestrained concentration and accumulation, deepening inequality, ever-falling social cohesion and ecological chaos, to a civilization of simplicity and equality?
- Can the music of our hearts send a new beat to our mind, one from which ideas, in a Hellenic way, become truthful words, and actions follow that might be remembered by future generations as having been informed by both rationality and soul?

Of course, it is possible.

If it is radical reform that is necessary, let us be courageous. Let us remember that in the energetic pursuit of new thought that characterized the European Enlightenment, there were some powerful European examples within it of dissident and radical thought, such as Diderot, Kant and Herder. They, in their times, identified that flaw in the Enlightenment thinking that had led to support for empire, with its insatiable drive, which they courageously challenged. They, in their time, sought to dislodge the paradigm of unaccountable imperialism, domination and cultural extinction.

III. Thinking About Europe

We should collectively support the concept of an ambitious new European social dimension in which a binding and effective pillar of European social rights is not just enshrined but delivered; one that should be achieved with the involvement and cooperation of the International Labour Organization, one that will not only support decent minimum wages and improve workers' rights across the EU, but facilitate participation in all areas of life, of the public space. Above all, we need to offer the European social model in a gendered eco-social form, and move on from – escape from – the blinkered neo-liberal agenda.

I believe that the often radical institutional reforms to which I have referred could yield a deepening of deliberative democracy, address the growing alienation from the EU felt by so many of its citizens, offer an alternative to, for example, austerity populism, provide the European institutions with greater legitimacy; it is by fostering deeper political-economic literacy among our peoples that we bring about the necessary eco-social paradigm shift of which I speak. Democracy demands it, and the world requires it. We should all help, and in doing so we will be invoking and benefiting from the power of reason and the grace of thought that is the Greek gift to humanity. A gift that endures.

Overcoming Disciplinary Boundaries

Speech to the European Research Council, Iveagh House, Dublin, 12 October 2016.

The work of the European Research Council [ERC] is faced with great challenges. Indeed, we are challenged, not just to secure understanding and support for a science appropriate to the great issues of our time, such as climate change and sustainable development, but also to protect the long vision and the atmosphere needed for the freedom of fundamental science to wonder and discover. The ERC's commitment to long-term, exploratory research has become of even more fundamental importance in a context marked, across Europe, by significant pressures on governments' funding of basic research in the aftermath of the recent financial crisis, towards the analysis and understanding of which such little intellectual effort has been directed. We live at a time when ever more spheres of human activity are required to adjust to quantifiable objectives and short-term productivity, criteria which ignore scientific ethos at its best or wider social responsibility. Indeed, the language of the market has been leaning on academic culture and educational institutions in a way that is not simply making the case for the utility of an instrument of science but rather that of an ideology.

Research and science have moved, at least rhetorically, from the periphery to the centre of government agendas throughout Europe. However, debates about the role of knowledge and research are often taking place in a very narrow political and untested ideological space. What might we come to know? With which aspects of research might policymakers concern themselves, with what consequences or benefits, and for whom? These are important questions for all European citizens.

In a recent address to the European Universities Association, I critiqued what I called an unquestioning and narrowly defined utilitarianism which, I suggested, is profoundly harmful to research. If we want to continue to nurture, in Europe, independent thinkers, adventurous and questioning scholars, it is vital, I believe, that our research and educational institutions preserve themselves from any excessive emphasis on short-term outcomes and that which is measurable. It is vital that they are sheltered from quantification solely in terms of consumption patterns – models which are so unsustainable and inadequate for the future as well as the present.

Intellectual creativity is not quantifiable. It can never be fully or appropriately described in statistics – in the number of patents, publications, or even in the number of jobs, so very important to our citizens, that it might generate. Nor should knowledge acquisition and research training ever be assessed exclusively in terms of their effects on the wider economy and the labour market, however important such a focus may be. Science, education, training – these are processes and practices that have an intrinsic value, fostering as they do the development of such intangible life-enhancing skills as empathy, imagination, analytical thinking, patience, clarity in reasoning, as well as sheer curiosity.

Research with intended and tangible applications is, of course, immensely worthwhile. Yet public funding for the applied research we need should never be at the expense of investment in basic research. So many of the inventions that have revolutionized our daily lives (for the better or the worse) are the product of basic research, even serendipitous discovery, with no direct application. As all of you here know very well, cutting-edge innovation is rarely neatly foreseeable, and researchers must be allowed to journey into the false avenues as well as the fruitful ones. They must be free to take the gaits of serendipity that arduous professional training, collegial work, and appropriate funding have made possible. If we truly want Europe to be a cradle of innovation, it is vital, therefore, that we continue to support exploratory research at, and beyond, the frontiers of understanding. This means sustaining firmly, in all of our respective countries, that bedrock of basic research from which all scientific breakthroughs spring.

The case for 'frontier research' was eloquently made by the President of the ERC, Professor Jean-Pierre Bourguignon, during his visit to Dublin in November 2014.[7] In the address he delivered at the Royal Irish Academy, Professor Bourguignon argued that diminishing public support for what is sometimes called by the beautiful name of 'blue-skies research' endangers the very research base of our European countries, as well as pushing our most promising scientists to seek opportunities abroad. Professor Bourguignon also pointed out how basic research foundations are very difficult to recover once they have been disengaged for a period. May I say that I fully share your concern at how failing support for pioneering research can damage Europe's research capacity in the long term.

I also share your views as to the need to protect our research infrastructure from the dependency that the incursions of commercial interests can so often represent. The damage that vested private interests can cause to scientific integrity is illustrated most vividly, I believe, by the false science that has been produced in some countries to bolster arguments that deny the reality of climate change. Such bogus science is not just harmful to the ideal of truth upheld by the profession, but also to the welfare of all those who dwell on this fragile planet.

We are fortunate, in Europe, to have a body like the ERC to sustain the standards of research excellence. Indeed, since its creation by the European Commission in 2007, the ERC has supported so many promising ideas and some of the most talented researchers across the European Union. May its reach become ever more extended and inclusive, avoiding the lure of the strong, so that the weak may become equal.

Importantly, as pointed out by Professor Bourguignon in his interviews to the Irish media two years ago, the ERC's work is by no means a substitute for ambitious national research policies. It remains the primary responsibility of each government to ensure the flourishing of the great intellectual potential, the genius, that there is at the heart of every European people.

III. Thinking About Europe

Here in Ireland, recent decades have witnessed significant advancements in the fields of science and research. And there are probably no better-suited hosts for the discussions of the ERC's Scientific Council, on their meeting in Ireland, than the Irish Research Council and the Royal Irish Academy – two institutions that have been amongst our most passionate and consistent advocates for frontier research.

The older of these two distinguished institutions, the Academy, has, over its long history, been home to many pioneering scientists such as, for example, Ernest Walton, who was awarded the Nobel Prize in Physics in 1951 for his work on the artificial splitting of the nucleus of the atom. And one of the Academy's past presidents was, of course, William Rowan Hamilton, whose discovery of quaternions made a significant contribution to algebraic theory.

Surprisingly perhaps, Ireland's contribution to the development of European science is not always appropriately acknowledged, even amongst Irish people. This is possibly because the power of imagination has, in this country, found such remarkable incarnations in the realm of literature and in the words of such as Swift, Wilde, Yeats, Joyce, Shaw and Beckett. Yet, alongside Hamilton and Walton, it seems only right that we also remember the names of, for example, Robert Boyle, who, in the seventeenth century, was instrumental in demonstrating the virtues of observation and experimentation as a means to apprehend the natural world; of John Tyndall, who explained why the sky is blue and was the first scientist to prove the greenhouse effect; of Nicholas Callan, who invented the induction coil; of William Parsons, who built the world's largest telescope and enabled astronomers to locate new structures in the heavens; of George Gabriel Stokes, who investigated the phenomenon of fluorescence and advanced the wave theory of light; or of John Lighton Synge, who pioneered the study of black holes.

It would be a mistake, though, to view science as somehow strange or beyond the boundless imagination of our great writers. It was an Irish scientist – George Johnstone Stoney, Professor of Natural Philosophy at Queen's College Galway – who coined the term 'electron'. But it was an Irish writer, James Joyce, who gave the word 'quark' its spelling, in a line of *Finnegans Wake*.[8] This may have been an unintentional contribution to the development of particle physics, but it illustrates well the wealth of sources that shape the way we see, understand and talk about science. James Joyce was endlessly curious about science and knew what he was about when Adam and Eve became atoms and ifs in *Finnegans Wake*. As Walter Isaacson said: 'Science gives us the empirical data and the theories to tie them together, but humans turn them into narratives with moral, emotional and historical meaning.'⁹

Indeed, not through its physical properties alone can our universe or any of our lives together, or in lonely isolation, be understood. The humanities have something essential to contribute – alongside biology and neuroscience – to, for example, our comprehension of the nature of human consciousness or what it means to be human. It is through leaping the boundaries that divide discipline from discipline, science from the arts and humanities, and by marshalling the diverse influences from our intellectual heritage that we can best meet the complex challenges of the future, learn to live, and try to love.

May I conclude [...] by suggesting that the contemporary European challenge of recovering social Europe, of building cohesion and legitimacy, of eliminating fear, is not merely about connecting the currency, the economy and the people in a new and different way: it is, I am profoundly convinced, about forging a new humanism – an atmosphere of ethical intellectual venture that will enable new generations of scholars to explore possibilities yet unknown.

May I invite you, then, to seek to make a new discourse with fellow Europeans, and lodge within it an invocation of the emancipatory possibilities of intellectual curiosity, the joy of empathetic science and the sharing of insight, a collective openness to serendipity, and above all, not just the defence but the celebration of pluralist scholarship and kindness in teaching.

Ethical Challenges for the European Union

Address at the Pontifical Irish College, Rome, 22 May 2017.

The hospitality that generates our gathering here today reflects that which has been the role of this venerable institution over the centuries of its existence: the Irish College is not just a distinguished place of teaching and scholarship; it is also, for Irish visitors and for Irish people in Rome, a house of welcome and conviviality, an open door – a home from home.

Next year it will be exactly four hundred years since the founder of this college, the distinguished Franciscan friar and scholar, Luke Wadding, arrived in Rome at the age of thirty. Like so many others before and after him, he left the shores of Ireland in the hope of contributing something to the wider world and to the great conversations of his time, driven by a deep-seated sense of his spiritual mission.

This morning I had the great honour of meeting with a man who exemplifies in the most striking and moving of manners this extraordinary importance of the spiritual as a powerful wellspring of global ethics, coupled with an ardent commitment to placing what is the essence of humanity at the heart and centre of the global conversations of our time. Pope Francis is a man who touches us all by his unique courage in identifying the crippling contradictions of our age and the need to engage with the assumptions that sustain them. He does this with words that are infused with both humility and passion. He has been, since his elevation, a compelling voice tirelessly awakening us to the web of interdependencies that weaves humanity together, as well as weaving us all, humans and non-humans, to our shared and fragile planet.

Indeed from the first moments of his papacy, Pope Francis has been an indispensable voice of humanity and clarity. He has journeyed to places of discord, where he has sought to sow the seeds of peace. He has been a voice for those most vulnerable – calling for housing for the homeless, land for the landless and the native peoples, dignified employment for those excluded from the labour market and the fundamental right that all of them have to question 'macro-relations' of power and inequality.[10] He has called upon us all to respond with compassion and justice to the people and families across the globe who are migrating in desperation and hope. He has spoken up for 'Mother Earth' itself, not just in his encyclical letter, *Laudato Si': On Care for our Common Home*, but in many of his public speeches including, most memorably, in his gripping address to the Third World Meeting of Popular Movements last November.

I was delighted, this morning, to have the opportunity to discuss some of these themes with Pope Francis. Both of us share a conviction that new connections between ethics, economy and ecology must be at the core of all work of social and intellectual reconstruction in this new century. This is indeed a discussion to which I have sought to bring my own contribution, using the medium of the presidency of Ireland to encourage a debate on ethics across all sectors of Irish society. I fully share Pope Francis's observation that, I quote, 'Ethics has come to be viewed with a certain scornful derision. It is seen as counterproductive, too human, because it makes money and power relative. It is felt to be a threat, since it condemns the manipulation and debasement of the person.'[11]

I believe that an ethic of human dignity, a holistic approach to human life, is precisely what must be established as the informing principle and practice of the new, integral approach to development that our times demand – a conception of development that would serve the human person in his or her integrity, never reducible to criteria of efficiency, or production, or indeed self-absorbed consumption.

III. Thinking About Europe

This is a challenge, dear friends, shared by all of us, from north and south, east and west – and not just a challenge that concerns primarily the poorer nations of the world. Indeed, it is a challenge that must be at the heart of our collective efforts at rebuilding a positive and ambitious vision for the future of the European Union.

In my conversations this morning with Pope Francis, and with Cardinal Parolin and Archbishop Gallagher, we spoke of the challenges posed to Europe as a whole, and of course to Ireland and Northern Ireland more particularly, by the decision of Britain to leave the European Union; but we also spoke of the need to tackle the urgent and wider task of building new paths of hope and renewal for European citizens.

That is the great collective task, which all of us Europeans must undertake in concert, without delay, addressing issues of reconnection between the citizens on the European Street, their governments and their institutions. We need to do so with clarity of mind, vision, and having at heart, throughout, the hopes, the fears, the vulnerabilities and the immense potential of the millions of women, men and children whom our union of European nations is here to serve. The particularities of the Brexit negotiations are very important, but a concentration on a part of what challenges us must not be at the cost of the greater issues we cannot neglect – issues of democratic reengagement, redefined subsidiarity and a re-articulation of solidarity and cohesion.

As with the great task of building peace and reconciliation in Northern Ireland, there are those who will say that the challenges currently facing Europe are too deep and complex to solve. And as with Northern Ireland, it is important that we do not evade difficulties; that we face them in a spirit of truth and honesty, while keeping our eyes firmly set on the ideal and the greater human values guiding our actions.

In this, all of us are invited to act together, in our different capacities, and according to our own means. The project of building peace in Northern Ireland offers us an example. It involved governments, diplomats, political parties, community groups, as well as spiritual leaders and ordinary members of all religious denominations. It was local and personal and international all at once. It was both urgent and generational in its nature. Defining the future of our European Union must similarly be an exercise in inclusion. All of us – elected representatives, diplomats, members of the laity and of the clergy, and simply concerned citizens – are called upon to play our part in the construction of that future. We are invited to contribute to building a European Union where new connections between ethics, economy, society and ecology will have been established, new policies been forged that will preserve social cohesion and environmental harmony. That is the vision of the European Union we need to offer as exemplar to the global community, as we face together a world of rapid change and inescapable interdependency.

We Europeans are challenged, in other words, to rebuild a socially accountable and sustainable version of the productive economy. We are challenged to restore a hierarchy of purpose, whereby economic objectives, tools and measures are designed to serve the fundamental objective of human development – challenged to restore an ethical vision of the social as the foundation of our union of European peoples. My view is that we must accept, too, the implications of treating work as a fundamental human experience – work in all its aspects: producing, caring, work of the hand, work of the heart and work of the imagination, beyond and above any reification. The worker should never be stripped of this essential dignity; her dreams, energy and toil never reduced to an adjustable unit of labour.

We must prepare the future, dear friends, not await it in fear. Let us, if I may invert the words used by Pope Francis in his address to European leaders gathered in Rome last March, learn to use our wings again and elevate our gaze. Let us recognize the new realities – demographic, cultural, environmental – that will shape our future and respond to them with wisdom, openness, creative innovation, and with confidence, exploring the connections of science, technology and, yes, ethics and philosophy too. The simplistic solutions put forward by the voices of fear and cultural entrenchment are ones that are not fit for a world that requires more, not less, understanding of complexity; more, not less, cooperation; and more, not less, concerted action on the common issues that concern all those who dwell on this earth. Is it not the case that our own reluctance to critique models of connection between economy and society that are failing our people has allowed the space of discourse to be dominated by such predators of anxiety?

III. Thinking About Europe

I look forward, dear friends, to joining with others in welcoming Pope Francis to Ireland next year. As you all know, it is his hope and intention to attend the World Meeting of Families in Dublin in August 2018. For him as well, it will be a return visit. I know that for a great many people in Ireland, Pope Francis's visit will be a moment when they will be inspired, and strengthened, and indeed challenged. It will be another important moment in the global dialogue we so pressingly need about the kind of society we want to build for this and for future generations. It will also be a demonstration of that very special gesture of warmth and hospitality that is an Irish welcome to a visitor.

The Idea of Home

Speech at the Galway International Arts Festival, NUI Galway, 21 July 2018.

Today I have returned to what are most familiar surroundings. I have fond memories of delivering lectures in this university, though some of those lectures were given in very different circumstances. I can recall being handed that most dreaded of university time slots – 9 o'clock in the morning – for one of the courses I had prepared. Fortunately, this was Ireland in the 1970s so when I entitled the course 'Deviance, Crime and Punishment' I was ensured a lecture hall full of students, many of whom I was later informed were in fact auditing the course.

I introduced them to Michel Foucault – then considered an avant-garde thinker – and to many an exciting source of the new sociological ideas on the role and nature of gender, incarceration and crime in modern societies – perhaps not what they were expecting or, indeed, hoping for. I remember hearing from the chair of the Department of Political Science and Sociology, Professor Edmond Dougan, fellow sociologist, head of department, and a Franciscan, that our students had told him how, in introducing the concept of society, I had taken it all apart for them. 'Yes, Michael,' he said, 'but did you put it back together for them at the end?'

The sheer breadth of the theme of the 'First Thought Talks' strand of the Arts Festival – 'home' – provides me with an opportunity to return to, and to reflect on, some of the matters with which I have sought to engage, as a university lecturer and as a citizen. It would be too great an impertinence to hope that I can put everything back together for you at the end of my reflection on the concept of 'home', and I am not promising anything!

Today, unlike my lectures all those years ago, I do not wish to begin with Foucault but with a reference to the work of two very different philosophers that Foucault himself nonetheless considered as formative intellectual influences, even if his own thinking developed in radically different directions: Martin Heidegger, whose legacy continues to be haunted by his monstrous moral failings in the 1930s and 1940s, and Gaston Bachelard, a French philosopher who transformed the philosophy of science in the 1950s. Though neither share much in terms of perspective or trajectory, they both offered meditations on the manifold meanings of 'home'.

In an essay entitled 'Building Dwelling Thinking', published in the collection *Poetry, Language, Thought*,[12] Heidegger asked two questions, 'What is it to dwell?' and 'How does building belong to dwelling?' He writes that 'dwelling is the basic character of Being in keeping with which mortals exist'. Dwelling and the processes of building, making and shaping thus emerge almost as circular phenomena – even as people create a place, they forge a relationship between themselves and that place, such that they begin to dwell. In Heidegger's words, 'the relationship between man and space is none other than dwelling, strictly thought and spoken'.

As a student of migration, I am particularly struck by the implication of this last sentence, expressing as it does an underlying assumption in favour of the universality of a fixed relationship with a specific space, and indeed perhaps a specific time. It displays a disposition so intrinsic to much of modern social science – one that finds it difficult to encompass the experience of movement or of the interstices, the space between spaces.

Migration and movement have always been a part of the human experience – indeed, for some historic peoples they constituted the very foundation of their social and economic lives. An obvious example are nomadic peoples. The life of all migrants, seasonal and settled, cannot be handled by such formulation. That is not to say they did not dwell, nor that they did not form relationships between themselves and a particular space, such that it became a treasured place in which a home could be made, but they were never sedentary, nor bound to one place, or even one identity, often being people of split identities. 'Transience' requires a near continuous redefinition of 'home'. This is something caught in literature, as it is missed by a privileging of the sedentary in the social sciences.

In 1958, a number of years after Heidegger first delivered the lecture that would become 'Building Dwelling Thinking', Gaston Bachelard completed a short volume entitled *The Poetics of Space*.[13] Though better known for his epistemological work, he turned his attention to what he termed the 'phenomenology of the imagination', the study of the poetic meaning of the house and of the intimacy imbued within everyday household places, such as the attic, the cellar or the drawers. In *The Poetics of Space*, he writes, '[the house] is our first universe, a real cosmos in every sense of the word', that it is 'the topography of our intimate being'. Think of the positioning of the chair near the fire in Arensberg and Kimball's study of Lough and Raymona in Clare in the 1930s.[14]

The house, Bachelard reasoned, emerges as the home by becoming a site of intimacy and creativity, of memories and dreams. What is remarkable is the degree to which, in the work of Gaston Bachelard, concerned as it is on the face of it with the evocation of the architecture of spaces, home is presented not only as a physical space, but as an immaterial reality, not a defined place of retreat but a series of relationships and intimacies with places and between people, and indeed I would add that between people the estimation of the form of the house, the status it indicates takes on a role as an indicator of position in the class system, even of respectability, or assumed lack of it.

Is this definition of 'home' then to be a function of residence, simply occupying space with security, a space from which one moves to participate, circulate; and how and when does a condition of ownership arise? Is it as a guarantee of security, occupation being an insufficient criterion of what is 'home'?

Going beyond the theme of 'home' as a set of balances, perhaps between security and freedom, it may be useful to consider briefly the evolution of our planetary 'home' from earliest times through to the Anthropocene. Time restricts a deep consideration of 'home' in terms of our shared planet, our loss of symmetry between nature and habitation. Yet I believe that this is a perspective that we must seek to recover and uncover anew as we try to wrestle with

III. Thinking About Europe

the consequences of the changes that humanity has wrought upon our shared and vulnerable planet, a planet home now to over 7.6 billion human beings and innumerable other animals and plants.

These changes that we live with and suffer from in today's world, are themselves a product of a very particular type of human civilization, one formed by two great revolutions in economic and social organization, the Neolithic and the Industrial Revolutions. Both produced and reproduced very particular ideas and ideals of 'home', ones which in their assumptions are our contemporary legacy but are not open to critique and evaluation as they should be in responsible scholarship and citizens' debate, and perhaps this constrains our capacity to reimagine our collective future today.

The Industrial Revolution, usually situated within the second half of the eighteenth century, is now understood to have inaugurated what the Nobel Prize-winning atmospheric chemist, Paul Crutzen, has categorized as the Anthropocene, a new geological epoch in world history marked by the influence of a single species – our own – on the global environment.[15]

The term Anthropocene has its own distinguished genealogy. It was first used by the Italian geologist Father Antonio Stoppani, in 1873,[16] who was in turn influenced by the American diplomat George Perkins Marsh, whose 1863 book *Man and Nature: Or, Physical Geography as Modified by Human Action*, was foundational for the environmental movement in the United States. At the core of Marsh's work lay an imaginative analysis of the acute crises of the sedentary civilizations the ancient Mediterranean world brought about by soil degradation occasioned by the intensive farming techniques of the Neolithic Revolution, an early example of surplus seeking affluence provoking an environmental crisis.

We can discern in the rise and fall of these ancient cultures a presaging of the Anthropocene. Though not yet cursed with the capacity to radically transform the carbon or nitrogen cycle, these older peoples were still able to degrade the environment enough to doom themselves, to lose their 'home' in nature. Theirs was a radically different culture than that which had gone before. It was based not on migration, hunting and foraging, but upon the cultivation of the soil and the domestication of animals, upon settlement, whether in isolated homesteads, clusters of dwellings, or densely populated cities, and, above all, upon the capacity to transform the muscle and sinew of humans into energy.

For the first time since our ancestors, the *Homo habilis*, emerged two million years ago, human beings created cultures focused on a single, sedentary space in which buildings, such as the temple, rather than nature, became the locus of spirituality, and hierarchical social relations emerged to coordinate production in Neolithic societies, overseen as they were by a new administrative/managerial class, often claiming divine sanction, driven by a new, highly gendered division of labour.

It is not a coincidence that slavery, the most abhorrent of human institutions, arose in those years – in a recent work, the anthropologist James C. Scott made the chilling observation that the walls erected around settlements in the slave societies may have been built not to exclude those without, but to imprison those within.[17] I do not necessarily subscribe to the thesis hinted at by such speculations, namely that the foundation of a state, whether historical or in the present day, has rested and can only rest on violence. After all, the city-states of the ancient world would create, over time, protean republics, albeit ones marred by systemic and profound injustices.

We find, in ancient Rome, even in the works of conservative members of the senatorial class such as Cicero, a commitment to the ideal of political community founded upon solidarity, with a shared commitment to an ideal of justice, however hypocritical the exclusion of slaves, women and even other Italian men from citizenship would later appear. This ideal also suffused the civic life of Athens, finding its expression in Aristotle's *Politics* and the orations of Demosthenes.

It provided a basis for an ideal of 'home' as a set of relationships and shared commitments, rather than a settled place – as important as place was. This is represented above all by the success of the Athenian statesman Themistocles, who persuaded his fellow citizens to evacuate their beloved city to facilitate a unified Greek response to the invading Persian empire. Even though Athens was burnt to the ground, the Athenian city-state continued anew in a neighbouring fishing village. Yet this was an ideal of immaterial home and homeland that was exclusive and profoundly unjust, available only to the small pool of men eligible for citizenship. How much can we consider the Greek household, the *oikos*, from which we derive the word economics, or household management, as a home in the physical sense, as the site of intimacy and belonging imagined by Gaston Bachelard? It was more likely that it was a place of alienation and loneliness for many members of the household, excluded as women and slaves were from any participation in public life.

Even as the concept of the public realm was given form by city-states, so too arose a new vision of the private household, dictated, managed and controlled by the aristocratic patriarch, a social construction later given juridical form within Roman law. We might recall the image of the Roman senator controlling households with thousands of slaves in addition to his wife, sons and daughters. The social construction of the patriarch was to prove the most durable, if lamentable, foundation of the Roman world, weathering the disintegration of the sedentary Roman civilization under pressure of countless migrations by nomadic peoples, who would in turn lay the groundworks for the feudal order of the medieval world. The political imaginary of that new world was one entirely dominated by ideas of hierarchy, represented by the great Chain of Being imagined by the Neoplatonists connecting the lowliest plants and animals to the heavens, and by the gradual sacralization of the figure of the monarch.

Despite all the distance in time and space between medieval France and ancient Mesopotamia, they were both still Neolithic civilizations, impelled to produce energy through human effort alone. The peasant, the labourer bound to the land, was the archetypal producer in all Neolithic cultures. Tied to his homestead, subject to the often-arbitrary power of his superiors, whether a feudal lord or a municipal administrator, he and his family provided, through a lifetime of back-breaking toil, the material basis for the entire civilization. The Roman republic was one of the rare ancient or medieval policies that, for a time, professed to be a confederation of independent farmers, a community of households and families, each with their own small stake in their country.

The house of the peasant was clearly a place of work, one with its own gendered division of labour, as women and children carried their own burden of the labour, not only in ensuring the survival of the family through the historically feminized tasks of caring and cleaning but through work in the field and then, as the insatiable Atlantic empires of north-west Europe began to inexorably expand their economic capacity through conquest, the concept of the 'workshop' emerges. A recent article in the *Economic History Review* by Jane Humphries and Benjamin Schneider has detailed the massive extent of hand-spinning in eighteenth-century England.[18] In the 1750s it was the single largest category of employment, with nearly a million women and children engaged in yarn production, their work constituting over a third of a poor household's income. Such labour was overwhelming, carried out in workshops in the home, and it was exploitative, as employers owned the materials and simply 'put it out' to their employees to work on and return.

Then came the mechanization of production, which Humphries and Schneider speculate was a response not to high wages, as previously hypothesized, but to the availability for employment of still more impoverished women and children. This moved the world of paid work from the house to the factory. Social constructions of time, of behaviour, social and even sexual, were changed by this. The split between factory time, without the allowance of discretion, and home time, where the family could be reproduced. Inventions such as the spinning jenny still required energy produced by the human, and animal energy. For all the sophistication of Neolithic civilizations, whether in medieval Ethiopia or early modern England, they were ultimately constrained by nature and relied on plant life to sustain both people and livestock.

That constraint was eliminated in time by the discovery of the ability to convert energy released by the combustion of carbon into mechanical energy. This gave rise to a new relationship between economy, ecology, ethics, culture and society, one that rested upon a narrow and distorted vision of political economy. A vision of accumulation that sanctioned poverty amidst plenty, and internationally an imperialist ideology that integrated the new science and technology of the era in an ideology that asserted a hubris of superiority that regarded the conquered and the dispossessed as, at best, backward, inferior.

In the industrialized heartland of western Europe, this new industrial civilization required not peasants but workers, and a new working class emerged in the towns and cities. By the end of the nineteenth century, skilled workers would be enabled, in a mimetic sense, to replicate the domesticity of a growing professional and mercantile middle class, with women carrying out domestic unpaid labour and men undertaking paid work in the new factory system. The product of work and the worker were distanced from each other.

This is the era in which Émile Durkheim first began his work which, *inter alia*, offered us the concept of 'anomie' arising from his study of suicide; and of course, it is also the era in which Karl Marx wrote, to whom the idea of 'alienation' was central. Changes in the mode of production forced deep changes in the wider context of personal, family and social relations. The writings from literature have a theme of a world in which one could not be 'at home'.

It is perhaps not surprising then that it was also the era in which there occurred, in legal scholarship as much as in everyday practice, a separation of the idea of home and house, of property and dwelling. For the conflict between ideas of home and property, between dwelling and belonging, was never greater than in the industrial and imperial era. The clash in the assumptions of differing civilizations in conflict would lay the seeds of a harvest that took a century to ripen.

We need only think of the native peoples of North America and Australia, whose ideals of life and what was envisaged as 'home' were very different from those developed in north-west Europe. When I visited Australia last year I did so in the knowledge that such ideas were still a matter of contestation, not least in the aftermath of the Mabo judgment, which finally recognized the interests of the Aboriginal people to the land, at least within the ambit of the common law. The conception of land, and of 'home' – of 'country' – held by the first Australians, the oldest surviving human culture, was that the people belonged to the land as much as the land belonged to the people. The Mabo judgment overturned the doctrine of *terra nullius*, a hubristic, monstrous, imperialistic fiction that the peoples of Australia had no claim, at least under English common law, to the land they had inhabited and shaped for 60,000 years.

The vast confiscation of tracts of land, not only in Australia but also in North America, were justified and consecrated by the theories of John Locke, sometimes heralded as a father of modern liberal thought and toleration, although his categories were constructed by exclusion.

If his *An Essay Concerning Toleration*[19] excluded the Catholic Irish with the memorable phrase that 'papists are like serpents', thus did he exclude those who did not farm the land from his theory of the right of property as a natural right. The native Americans were, Locke wrote, 'savage beasts'.

As the Italian philosopher Domenico Losurdo rightly reminds us, the idea that land becomes property by virtue of being mixed with labour was used to exclude an entire continent of people who did not share such a conception of property, and whose natural resource management was not considered 'labour' by those who considered themselves settlers.[20] Such a theory of property was then the basis for what we should call the 'great dispossession of home' inflicted on the peoples of America and Australia. David Hume in 1767 in his *History of England* wrote: 'The Irish, from the beginning of time, have been buried in the most profound barbarism and ignorance and as they were never conquered, never invaded by the Romans from whom all the Western world derives its civility, they continued still in the most rude state of society and were distinguished only by those vices to which human nature not tamed by education, nor restrained by laws, is forever subject.[21]

Our own national history is indeed marked by its own great dispossession and the sustaining prejudices of the project of colonization. Even as the conquest and creation of the imperial settler states reached its zenith and its conclusion in the late nineteenth century, the conception of 'home' in this country, and its relationship to property ownership, was undergoing its own transformation under pressure from one of the greatest movements of thought and action ever seen on this island – the land movement.

Irish society in the 1870s was a product of the conflicts of the seventeenth century, of an Act of Union that would lead to the impositions of a single paradigm of economic thinking as to trade and productivity, and of the catastrophe represented by the Great Hunger. Ireland was a largely rural society, characterized by a large number of fragmented smallholdings, though not as many were farmed on a subsistence basis as on the eve of the Famine. At the height of economic and legal relations sat a small number of landlords, operating through estate managers or middle men, with intermediate landlords and sub-letters.

The common-sense political economy of property ownership had changed in content but not in form, as the Lockean idea of property as a natural right had given way to the Benthamite idea of secure property rights as the most efficient means to ensure that the owners of capital would maximize the utility of capital. Do we not hear an echo of this in present circumstances? In 1848, in the depth of the Famine, James Fintan Lalor raged against the idea that property should be inviolable, writing:

> I acknowledge no right of property in eight thousand persons, be they noble or ignoble, which takes away all right of property, security, independence, and existence itself, from a population of eight millions, and stands in bar to all the political rights of this island and all the social rights of its inhabitants. I acknowledge no right of property which takes the food of millions and gives them a famine, which denies to the peasant the right of a home and concedes, in exchange, the right of a workhouse.[22]

Against that individual right, Fintan Lalor asserted a still greater right, the right, in his words, 'to live in [this land] in security, comfort and independence'. His statue now stands in his native Portlaoise. Despite his acknowledgment by and great influence on Davitt, Connolly and Pearse, he perhaps still remains something of a lost prophet, his democratic radicalism unjustly paling beside the more easily managed romanticism of his friends in the Young Ireland movement.

Yet it was his idea of 'home' as an inalienable social right, and its association with the idea of the nation, of the wider national community as 'home', that was invoked, whether knowingly or not, by Charles Stewart Parnell when, at a public meeting in Limerick on 31 August 1879, he implored the tenants of Ireland to 'ke[ep] a firm grip on their homestead' and to join the Land War, which had then taken the form of a nationwide rent strike to secure the historic demands of fixity of tenure, fair rents and free sale.[23]

Beyond the intimacies of home there is the longing for the security of the dependents to whom it constitutes shelter. It is still somewhat forgotten today that when the male leaders of the Irish National Land League were imprisoned, it was the women who took up the fight, bringing a level of organization and discipline hitherto unseen in the conduct of the Land War – Parnell's sister, Anna, being the most prominent amongst them. They brought a new and renewed energy and vigour to protests against evictions, and, where they failed to prevent families being removed from their homes, they erected temporary shelters and buildings for them in anticipation, it was hoped, of a return to their homes following victory in the Land War. Security of the home and homestead was not, as far as they were concerned, to be subordinated, as it might have been by others, to the prospect of Home Rule. It is significant that the Ladies' Land League, the 'first national organisation of Irishwomen led and organised by women', as Jennie Wyse Power would later remember,[24] sought no small or partial objective but a transformative set of demands, oriented around the protection, and indeed creation, of 'home' – home as a physical dwelling and shelter, home as a place of security and safety. In doing so, they redefined the very vision of what the wider national home could be, and what it should seek to be.

I do not wish to necessarily revisit the history of the Land War or the manner in which vast amounts of land were redistributed, through successive Land Acts, to those who were in many respects the most powerful of the tenant farmers, even as those in marginal lands or landless labourers continued what had become a familiar pattern of emigration.

Political economy does matter, the assumptions of differing versions of political economy feed policy. I would like to reiterate a point I made during a lecture I gave at the University of Melbourne last October, when I reflected upon the influence of Irish political economists in Australia and Ireland. It illustrates how an instrument can have different outcomes and be defined by historical setting. In the 1840s an Irish disciple of the economist David Ricardo named Robert Torrens emigrated to the infant colony of South Australia, hoping to establish a 'New Hibernia' in the Southern Ocean, populated by independent Irish farmers tilling small plots of land.

That plan failed as South Australia was instead caught up in a huge wave of land speculation as land grants issued by the colonial government were rapidly resold to such an extent that title disputes were endemic in the new colony. That crisis of ownership was resolved by Torrens' eldest son, Robert Richard, through the introduction of the principle of registration by title, the defining feature of which is the indefeasibility of title given to the registered proprietor.

There is a moral and ethical point here – the Torrens system did not only constitute a means to resolve a temporary crisis of colonial speculation, it also constituted a legal technology of empire by which to extirpate any claim to

III. Thinking About Europe

title held by the first occupants of the land, who, in turn, did not share any of the assumptions inherent in either common-law ideas of property, whether legal or philosophical, or in the Torrens system. Land grants had been issued to colonial speculators on lands inhabited by the first peoples of Australia, and the Torrens system guaranteed their expropriation, despite the pledge to respect the 'rights and enjoyments' of the first occupants outlined in the Letters Patent authorizing the colonization of South Australia.

The great irony is that the Torrens system, when extended to Ireland in 1891 in the context of the Land Acts of 1885, 1891, 1903 and 1909, successively financed the purchase and transfer of the landlords' interest in the land to their tenants. Even as the principle of title by registration was used to dispossess the first peoples of the colony of South Australia, it was used to reconstitute the property relations built over the long centuries of conquest in Ireland, severing the old ties to the land and delivering to Irish tenants unencumbered freehold title.

In Ireland, this represented a partial liberation from the past to enable something of the making of home, albeit one gradually in much part dominated by a new hegemonic grazier class. In Australia it heralded a total suppression of the past, marking a subjugation of a concept of home to the new demands of industrial-era imperialism.

To return to the idea of the home as an immaterial reality – as that set of relationships between people and with place – we might gain an understanding of just how traumatic such a rupture and confiscation was not just in Australia, but for all indigenous people.

In what areas are markets the appropriate mechanism? On what terms should their presence be regulated? If housing is to be a right, in what circumstances does it call for protection, vindication, by the state? These are unavoidable moral questions. Standing behind our present debate on housing are all of those assumptions as to the role of the state, the status of essential needs versus property rights. For citizen choice, policy options have to be transparent and evaluated in terms of the assumptions they make as to the role of the market and the state.

We are also forced to look once again at our own efforts in this country to utilize the idea of 'home'. Those of you attending Catherine Corless' talk later will recognize that for those placed in mother-and-baby homes, the 'home' constituted a place of incarceration, of loss, of retribution, even of invoked revenge for the breaking of an authoritarian version of birth, life, the family and society.

Returning to Gaston Bachelard's idea of home as the site of intimacy and of safety, we must ask: has the 'private home', the household – that concept so prominent in the inheritance of Roman law – not also been a place of oppressive gender relations, the most terrible manifestation of which is domestic abuse?

As to work itself, the more quotidian example is, of course, the distribution of domestic labour, and the double burden of working in the market economy and in the household still placed on women. In this present moment, it feels as if the women's movement has been infused with a renewed vigour and authority, and so I am confident that we will continue to make progress by acknowledging the past and continuing to build a better future.

This university is fortunate, I believe, to host the Centre for Housing Law, Rights and Policy Research, whose work is so critical to enhancing our understanding of the housing system here in Ireland, and its complex relationship with international and European financial and monetary policy developments. The Centre is home to scholars who provide a comprehensive understanding of the role of housing, so may I quote Dr Padraic Kenna: 'housing addresses the basic need for human shelter, but also facilitates the essential human requirement for home'.[25] I am obliged not to stray any further into the detail of housing policy in Ireland, not only for constitutional reasons but also because I am aware that Catríona Crowe has assembled an excellent panel to discuss housing this evening. I do, however, wish to make two more general observations at the level of principle.

First, that Dr Kenna's observation is absolutely vital – indeed, it is a moral truth that reflects the struggles in our history. Even as a residual or minimum response, the Land Acts were, after all, accompanied by a series of Labourers Acts, which were passed, after concerted activism, to provide Exchequer subsidies to local authorities to construct new housing at fair rents for landless rural labourers in Ireland. Between 1883, the year of the first Labourers Act, and 1914, nearly 50,000 rural cottages were built by local authorities in Ireland, housing over a quarter of a million people. We should

III. Thinking About Europe

not underestimate what a remarkable deviation from the *laissez-faire* verities of the day this represented, nor what a partial victory, however belated it was, for the more emancipatory elements of the Land League; even if the purpose of the costs of losing social cohesion was to be the driving motive, that and the need for labour. In Irish cities, local authorities were rather slower to make use of the Housing of Working Classes Acts, the urban counterpart of the Labourers Acts.

There was, of course, no legal right to 'home' recognized, but a moral right was asserted, and it was partially recognized. It was a recognition that home is something greater than shelter, not merely any temporary expedient. It is about the acquisition of the means to belong in community and to participate in society without shame, as the philosopher-economist Amartya Sen might put it. There is not, as yet, a justiciable right to 'home' as housing in the Irish legal order, though I welcome previous discussions of the convention on the possible incorporation of economic and social rights in our Constitution. This is a debate that we urgently need not only to continue but also to deepen by taking into account the work of Professor P. J. Drudy, Des Collins, and others, as well as Dr Kenna. Can and should we integrate the idea of the right to a home into our law and policymaking in a serious way?

Second, if we recognize that housing is necessary for the creation of home in our society, we need to think seriously about all the constituent parts of our housing system. I use the term 'system' deliberately, for the term 'housing market' can obscure the massive and necessary role played by the state through fiscal, monetary or other policy areas, in all the various parts of the system, from planning to the financing of construction, to the design and regulation of construction itself, and to the various mechanisms by which occupation of a home is financed, whether it is through rent or by home purchase.

How many homes should be constructed every year? How should construction be financed? How should living spaces be designed? What mix of housing tenure do we collectively believe is appropriate? What kind of ownership structures, whether they be municipal, private or collective? Let us widen the debate and engage seriously with a full range of the policy answers to these questions, being willing to eschew any ideological obstacles to the widest possible range of policies.

Rereading the *White Paper on Housing* published in 1964 is instructive – its historical review outlines how the state decided to embark on a massive house-building programme in 1933, in the midst of the Great Depression. As a consequence, local-authority homes constructed exceeded private construction for the fifteen years between 1933 to 1948. That was a public-policy choice, and the state was clear about it, and clear and open in its objectives.

It was during that same period that the Swedish Social Democrats enunciated a remarkable political ideal: the *folkhemmet*, or 'people's home'. It is a phrase that contains within it the idea of a home as a political community and as a set of solidary-based relationships, not unlike in their period and setting the Irish *clochán* or *baile*; and it is one that, in its policy implementation, demanded, and continues to demand, the provision of homes as a matter of right for all the people.

In this age of the Anthropocene I believe that not only this ideal of home as a political community committed to a rights-based vision of justice can be sustained, but that it *must* be sustained. To do so, however, our horizons cannot simply be confined to a single territorially-defined political community. We, all of us on this planet, share what Pope Francis has termed 'our common home', and, if we are to meet the challenges presented to this common home we are obliged to widen our perspective of home to encompass all the people of this earth.

For in the twenty-first century there can be no partial solidarity, whether national solidarity or European solidarity. We require now an international solidarity, shorn of national antagonisms, open and willing to cooperate where we can and sacrifice where we must. For Europe, this may well be another century of the immigrant, a reversal of the great outflow to the New World and colonies experienced in the nineteenth century.

This is not only a moral or political argument, but a practical one. After all, birth rates are far below replacement levels across the European Union, and an ongoing necessity for immigration to support our economies in the global north will continue to draw people to our shores.

Then too, given the current trajectory of greenhouse gas emissions, despite all the promises of the Paris Climate Agreement, there will also be millions of people seeking refuge from environmental degradation and the depletion

III. Thinking About Europe

of natural resources. Our capacity for solidarity will be tested, and it will be measured by our willingness to welcome those fleeing climate disaster, war, and persecution.

Many of the challenges we confront are those which test our capacity for, and willingness to engage in, collective deliberation to discern the common good, and collective action to achieve it. The history of the indigenous peoples of the world is their testament to our human ability to forge collective conceptions of home; conceptions upon which collective institutions of government and governance can be built. Let us recall and draw on the best ideals available to us from our collective past, and let us imagine together a shared future for all the peoples of our common home.

IV
CONNECTING EUROPEAN CULTURES

Of Greece and Ireland: An Ancient and Enduring Relationship Full of New Possibilities

Lecture at the University of Athens, 23 February 2018.

As President Pavlopoulos[1] and I stood together during our national anthems yesterday, I felt deeply moved as I reflected on the rich history which we share. Our two nations stand at opposite corners of this continent, yet it is easily recognized what connections we have had from earliest [times] and, even more important, what we might share in common in the future. As we participate in the making of a union of European publics that can acknowledge, respect and celebrate diversity, what we both bring is a valuable experience. It includes the production and preservation of intellectual work, an interrogation of how life is to be lived, an historical struggle for independence and a national family that includes a large and valuable migratory component. We are not either of us backward countries, incapable of giving a moral, inclusive dimension to life or the *oikonomia* on which it might be based.

As to ancient times: ever since the Greek explorer Pytheas of Massalia recorded the first encounter between the Hellenic and Irish worlds, our connections have grown in scale and complexity. It is an encounter that has continuously enriched the Irish mind and expanded our experience. My native landscape – bounded by Galway Bay to the north and the River Shannon to the south – was first described and mapped by a Greek geographer, Claudius Ptolemy, writing in Alexandria in the second century AD. Among the first and perhaps among the greatest of Irish navigators, St Brendan most likely used Ptolemy's maps and navigational aids some 400 years later when he became the first European to reach the North American continent. Both of our peoples have been travellers. For the journeys we have attempted we have constructed myths of gods made human in their weakness, and told stories of humans who, in their aspirations to be godlike, have fallen into being merely heroic. We share the sea, the importance of the interpretation and symbolism of a journey, migration, island life, land, possession and dispossession. Navigation and exploration have been at the centre of our experience as migratory peoples. They have defined our intellectual development too: the journeys undertaken, and not just over water to new places but within, a soul journey that tests and extends the frontiers of human understanding. The Irish poet Paula Meehan captures this sense of journeying and the daring that so often characterizes it:

> I've always loved thresholds
> the stepping over
> the shape changing that can happen
> when you jump off the edge into pure breath
> and then the passage between the inner and outer.[2]

Paula Meehan's lines are a distant echo of words spoken by Socrates to Meno just a short distance from where we are today: 'That we shall be better and braver and less helpless if we think that we ought to enquire [...] that is a theme upon which I am ready to fight, in word and deed, to the utmost of my power.'

When the learning of classical Greece was receding from memory in western Europe an enquiring Irishman, schooled in Greek, John Scotus Eriugena, translated the work of Dionysius the Areopagite, patron saint of Athens. Eriugena championed the primacy of reason and upheld the Greek tradition of bold philosophical speculation in the ninth-century Carolingian

Court. May I suggest, however, that perhaps a hubris came with such a privileging of the rational above all possible sources of truth, wisdom, knowledge or insight.

Returning to the influence of Greek learning, on the more educated and fortunate in Ireland: it was profound. For example, around five thousand editions of Greek and Latin authors appeared in Dublin between 1700 and 1791. Indeed, it was an Irish scholar, Robert Wood, who first proposed that Homer's was an oral rather than a literary voice. It was another Irishman, James Joyce, who gave Homer's voice a twentieth-century inflection. It is rightly said that the Joyce we know could never have existed without Homer and Aristotle. Professor Fran O'Rourke said, 'It is arguable that Aristotle – next to Homer – was Joyce's greatest master,'[3] but Joyce was also influenced by his encounter with contemporary Greece. He arranged for the cover of *Ulysses* to be printed in the colours of the Greek flag – white letters on a blue field; the wall of his apartment in Paris was decorated with a Greek flag obtained while in Trieste; he sought out and enjoyed the company of Greek expatriates in wartime Zurich; he learnt a repertoire of Greek songs from his friend Paul Ruggiero; and when he died in 1941, a Greek lexicon was found on his desk. There is significance too in the fact that, while not competent in speaking the ancient language, he spoke the contemporary vernacular Greek of his time.

The first holder of the Chair of Ancient History at Trinity College, J.P. Mahaffy, epitomized this engagement with the contemporary Greece of his times. Mahaffy approached his subject through its people and communicated this love of travel, discovery and collection to, among others, his celebrated pupil Oscar Wilde, whom he sought to save from what he saw as 'increasing Popish influences'.[4] Over 140 years after it was written, his love for Greece and its people is palpable in his *Rambles and Studies in Greece*, recently reissued, with a fine commentary from my former colleague Professor Brian Arkins. Mahaffy is, however, also guilty on occasion of that imperialist mind that was, and still can be, dismissive of cultures other than its own – an example might be his remarks on the futility of achieving the standards of the British Constitution by peoples such as the Greek people, at the time of his travels.

What is closest to my own memory, as a child, is an oft-recalled feature of Irish rural life as to the place of Greek. I am referring to the place which

IV. Connecting European Cultures

the classical tradition long held on the popular mind through the teaching in informal, rural 'hedge schools', of Greek and Latin, and the foundation myths of both. I believe this was unparalleled elsewhere in Europe. In my own county of Clare, there were 275 such hedge schools in 1824. Their literary expression is found, for example, in the character of the rural hedge-school-master Hugh Mór O'Donnell in Brian Friel's play *Translations*, set in 1834.[5] Though O'Donnell is forced to concede that English may be the language of the future, he must persist in teaching Greek and Latin to his pupils. 'We feel closer to the warm Mediterranean,' he tells the English officer whose job it is to give an English form to Irish place names.

I am conscious that for many engaging with the Greek people, the Greek world of lived experience, the contemporary lived space of urban and rural Greece with all its contemporary challenges sometimes gets neglected, and I hope that my visit is interpreted as a wish to engage with the present and future of the Greek people as well as it being an obvious acknowledgment of the source of those foundational concepts of politics, discourse and democracy which have been gifted to humanity.

In making and deepening connections between Irish and Greek peoples it is important, however, to remember that Greece is not simply a philosophical archive rich in reward for ransacking. It is a people, a land of olives, of ships, of migrants, of villages, of science, technology, a people with a reconstructed language and a music that represents a fusion between tradition, the body and modernity. This is something we should be able to understand from within our own experience.

While the cultural affinity between Ireland and Greece is beyond doubt, it is rooted not only in our culture but also in our mutual historical experience. Within that is a mutual experience of migration. While this is, of course, a common historical and sociological experience across Europe, it is proportionately of larger scale, and given more importance in our experiences.

Though rarely voluntary in the past, the impact of migration can be for the person immensely enriching, conferring a capacity, in the words of Seamus Heaney 'to live in two places at the one time and in two times at the one place, a capacity to acknowledge the claims of contradictory truths without having to choose between them'.[6]

This is an insight, of course, given more centrality in literature than in politics. There is no better example of this capacity, in any literature, than Constantine Cavafy, whose work was wholly unconstrained by time or space. A man who on his short walk to his desk at the Ministry of Public Works in Alexandria could traverse two thousand years of history, passing the site of a Byzantine church, of Hadrian's Egyptian palace and of the spot where Alexander the Great's body was once displayed, encased in a gold sarcophagus – landmarks of three great eras in the experience of the Greek diaspora. E.M. Forster's description of the poet 'standing ... at a slight angle to the universe'[7] could aptly be applied to any migrant in our history or refugee on our shores.

In Ireland, as in Greece, the scale of our dispersal, over time and space, has been exceptional – to the point where, for each of us, our sense of self must draw on the experience of our diaspora. This is reflected in our citizenship laws in both of our countries, which afford citizenship rights to the grandchildren of those born in Ireland or Greece. Migration in our current period has been described as morally, politically and economically the defining issue of the twenty-first century. As the Irishman who headed the Global Forum on Migration and Development put it in a number of passionate statements on migration and the defence of the most vulnerable, the way we respond to the challenge 'reveals a great deal about the state of our society, the integrity of our communities, and the prospects for our collective future'.[8] He was referring to the global response, but he might equally have been referring to the response of individual states.

In this regard the word empathy (from ἐμπάθεια, *empatheia*) is Greek in origin but was reclaimed and given affirmation by Greece in the eyes of the world through the reception shown to those fleeing from crisis on Europe's borders. Viewed this way, the hospitality shown by Greece to today's victims of war, expulsion, dispossession and nationalism is by any measure extraordinary. Ireland's response to the migration crisis has involved sustained participation in rescue operations in the Mediterranean and leadership at UN level where we helped secure agreement on the 2017 New York declaration, described by the UN High Commissioner for Refugees as a 'political commitment of unprecedented force and resonance' filling 'what has been a perennial gap in the international protection system – that of truly

IV. Connecting European Cultures

sharing responsibility for refugees'.[9] I believe that our response – in Greece as in Ireland – is, and will be, best informed when it draws on our respective historical experiences.

This university was founded just years before a devastating famine killed upwards of a million Irish and forced another million to flee their homes for safer shores. In the same period, Greece has suffered multiple upheavals and refugee flows, including the devastation of the Greek community in Asia Minor in the 1920s. The challenge of displacement and responding to refugee flows is one of several challenges now confronting our global community – challenges that require an agreed global response. [...]

In terms of multilateral involvement, Ireland and Greece have been partners in peacekeeping, have worked together on the UN Human Rights Council and each has served with distinction on the UN Security Council. Indeed, we each have ambitions to serve again in the coming years. Ireland and Greece, because of such multilateral commitments, are well equipped to play a disproportionate role – this time in Europe, but also well equipped because of many other factors. One is our journey to independence, each conscious of a distinct cultural identity and a cultural influence disproportionate to our size, yet each dominated into the near historical period by a major power. In short, we each know something of the process involved in achieving sovereignty and attempting to use it in a new way. We have not always been successful, and when it comes to equality in terms of life chance, we both can recognize what a weak flame within nationalism equality of economic life or gender can become. Our attempts, in both cases, however, had to be made on the foundations left as the detritus of empires.

In the past I have written of 'clientelism', in the Irish case, as Nicos Mouzelis among others has written in the case of Greece, but I believe it is important to place such a usage in context.[10] After all, the abuse of the privileges of power from abroad, or through the agency of native elites, preceded any native inclination to search for either patrons or brokers. It cannot be explained simply as an indigenous feature of political culture. If the field beneath the goose has been taken, it is for survival the mass of the people must scratch. That is why corruption at the top and clientelism near the bottom, or at the local level, are of the same coinage.

Jürgen Habermas (b. 1929). © Wolfram Huke, Wikimedia Commons.

Hannah Arendt (1906–1975), c. 1963. © Jewish Chronicle Archive/Heritage-Images.

The Manifesto of Ventotene, August 1941. Source: Reteccp.org.

Altiero Spinelli and Ernesto Rossi, authors of the Manifesto of Ventotene. Source: Artribune.

President Higgins speaking at the Holocaust memorial event, Mansion House, Dublin, 27 January 2019. © Maxwell Photography.

Monument to the victims of the extermination camp at Treblinka, Poland. © Adrian Grycuk.

*Exhibition on the history of the 1918–19 flu pandemic, Áras an Uachtaráin.
© Maxwell Photography.*

President Higgins with Professor Federico Fabbrini, Director of the DCU Brexit Institute, at the inaugural event of the Brexit Institute, Dublin City University, 'Brexit, Ireland and the Future of Europe', on 25 January 2018. © Maxwell Photography.

President Higgins receives members of the Bureau of the European Association of former members of Parliament at Áras an Uachtaráin, 9 June 2017. © Maxwell Photography.

President Higgins marks the installation of Pangur Bán with sculptor Imogen Stuart at Áras an Uachtaráin, 21 January 2020. © Maxwell Photography.

President Higgins with the President of the Federal Republic of Germany, Dr Frank-Walter Steinmeier, at Schloss Bellevue, Berlin, after a welcoming ceremony on the first day of his state visit to the Federal Republic of Germany, 3–5 July 2019. © Maxwell Photography.

President Higgins speaking at the Paulinum, University of Leipzig, 4 July 2019. © Maxwell Photography.

King Willem-Alexander and Queen Máxima of the Netherlands with President and Ms Sabina Higgins, Áras an Uachtaráin, 12 June 2019. © Maxwell Photography.

At the Palazzo Corsini in Florence in May 2018. From left: President of the Hellenic Republic H.E. Mr Prokopis Pavlopoulos, President of Italy H.E. Mr Sergio Mattarella, President of Ireland Michael D. Higgins, President of the Portuguese Republic H.E. Mr Marcelo Rebelo de Sousa. Earlier in the day President Higgins delivered an address at the European University Institute titled 'Solidarity in Europe – Achieving Authenticity in the European Street'. © Maxwell Photography.

President Higgins at the Conferral of an Honorary Doctorate at Vytautas Magnus University, Kaunas, Lithuania, 20 June 2018. © Maxwell Photography.

President Higgins with the President of Croatia H.E. Ms Kolinda Grabar-Kitarović, Mr Jakov Kitarović and Ms Sabina Higgins at Áras an Uachtaráin, 3 April 2017. © Maxwell Photography.

The President's Study, Áras an Uachtaráin.
© Maxwell Photography.

President Higgins, Ms Sabina Higgins and their dog Síoda, Áras an Uachtaráin.
© Maxwell Photography.

As to the struggle for independence, the Greek independence movement exerted an emotional pull on many Irish: Irish writers of the nineteenth century, Thomas Moore and Lady Morgan among them, wrote – with empathy – of the oppression of the Greek people under Turkish rule. Nineteenth-century Irish awareness explains the involvement of Irishmen in the Greek independence movement. One of the most notable of these is buried close to here and depicted in the beautiful stained-glass windows of St Paul's Anglican Church. Richard Church, born into a Quaker family in Cork, became commander of the Greek land forces in 1827, assisted the coup in 1843, which secured a form of constitutional government, argued at the Congress of Vienna for an independent sovereign Greek state, and became a Greek citizen and lived out his later years in Athens.

In both of our cases the long fingers of dying empire were stretched and can be discerned in the origins of both of our civil wars. The struggles of the twentieth century, including the Greek lives lost in the struggle against fascism, are there as part of the history of a century that claimed so many young lives in war.

For each of our peoples our experience is a rich one, which contains moments of emancipation as well as grief; experiences that equip us well for the challenge of envisioning and constructing a European Union of humanity shaped to meet the needs of our citizens. We must become close again in our discourse-sharing, on a people-to-people basis, our hopes, our challenges and our indomitable courage to be different, to endure.

Pangur Bán

Reception for Imogen Stuart to mark the installation of the sculpture Pangur Bán, Áras an Uachtaráin, 21 January 2020.

May I commence by expressing my gratitude to Imogen Stuart, one of Ireland's most respected artists, whose creative vision will so enhance this shared space here in the Áras.

Pangur Bán was, of course, inspired by the ninth-century poem believed to have been written by an Irish monk, somewhere in the vicinity of Reichenau Abbey in Austria, where the Benedictines, to this day, care for the original manuscript and continue this monastic tradition that has had such a profound influence on the history and civilization of Europe. Indeed, this poem and this sculpture tell us much of our European story: an Irish monk, living in Austria over a thousand years ago, has his poem translated by an Englishman, Robin Flower, which in turn sparks the creative fires of a gifted sculptor, born in Germany and living in Ireland.

This is the human condition. Our stories have always been intertwined. We have always travelled and lived amongst each other, sometimes returning, sometimes not, reinterpreting and reframing each other's experiences, as understood through our own perspectives; creating a shared narrative that in turn is to be reworked and reshaped by arrivals and departures and by the passage of time. I am glad that the ambassadors of both Germany and Austria could join us today. This is, of course, our shared heritage.

Imogen has so beautifully reflected on the work of this monk whose name is now lost to us, and whose words have been represented by Robin Flower. The text incorporated into the sculpture reminds us of how words and art so emotionally and instinctively interact with each other. At the heart of both the words and the sculpture is the concept of living and working in harmony. The writer tells us that 'So it goes. To each his own. No vying. No vexation,' while the artist makes her own aesthetic journey into that congruent space. It is, of course, a shared and enduring space; a creative collaboration between two artists separated by time and place and form, who speak quietly and harmoniously to each other across a distance of so many centuries.

Indeed, it is greatly inspiring to see how the work of one artist can renew itself through the imagination of another, reimagined in a different age and reshaped through the prism of a different experience and a different time. Is féidir le splanc inspioráide gach teorainn a shárú. Is féidir le healaíontóirí a bheith ina n-anamchairde gan aird ar chonstaic ama nó cultúir.[11]

It is also uplifting to witness how intuitively visual art and words can interact, relating instinctively to each other; kindred spirits. Through the great talent of Imogen Stuart, a poem written over a thousand years ago has been brought visually to life in this modern age, remaining relevant to a new and very different audience to that which prevailed when it was first created.

Imogen is, of course, one of Ireland's foremost sculptors and has been a much-valued member of Ireland's arts community for a very long time. Indeed, some years ago, I had the privilege of conferring on Imogen the Torc that signified her election as a Saoi of Aosdána,[12] and on that occasion I remarked that I am always struck by how often, when Imogen Stuart's sculpture comes up for mention in conversation among the many artists I have had the pleasure of knowing as friends, praise for her work goes hand in hand with a profound and moving affection for the artist herself.

That is a great tribute, but also a very well-deserved one that reflects the generosity of spirit that defines Imogen Stuart the artist. Imogen has always demonstrated a sincere will to place her art, not in separate spaces for the elite, but right into the heart of society and community, to be enjoyed and appreciated by everyone.

Much of her art has been created for the Catholic Church – works such as the penal cross in Lough Derg, the water fonts at the shrine at Knock, the stations of the cross at Ballintubber Abbey and the carved altar in the chapel of

IV. Connecting European Cultures

University College Cork, offering a quiet but uplifting backdrop to the spiritual lives of those who come to worship, seek succour or sit in silent contemplation.

Several generations of children have played around *The Fiddler of Dooney* statue in Stillorgan Shopping Centre, while *Pangur Bán* was for many years a natural part of the daily lives of shoppers in Dún Laoghaire and then later of the students who congregated around it in the Arts Block at University College Dublin. Imogen's sculptures are also displayed in schools, hospitals and other public buildings, enjoyed in a spirit of community and togetherness while also, I have no doubt, speaking quietly to the imagination of many and inspiring other aesthetic journeys into reimagined worlds.

Closer to our home, even before the arrival of *Pangur Bán*, Imogen had left her mark on Áras an Uachtaráin with her own superb work on the portrait bust of Mary Robinson in the Francini Corridor, and also through her participation in the selection committee for the sculpture we had commissioned for the centenary of the 1916 Rising. Imogen's experience as a sculptor was such an important element of that committee's inspired choice of *Dearcán na nDaoine – The People's Acorn* by Rachel Joynt.

The inclusive nature of Imogen's art is greatly evident in *Pangur Bán* through the careful placing of the integral benches, which invite the public to become active participants in her work, rather than passive observers. Indeed, as we have seen in the video we compiled for today's event, it was greatly impressive, when *Pangur Bán* was being installed downstairs, to witness just how much attention Imogen and her daughter Aisling paid to the positioning of each element, including the benches, and to realize what an important component they are of this great creative expression.

It is a creative expression that we are so fortunate to have here in Áras an Uachtaráin, and I would so like to thank the President of UCD, Professor Andrew Deeks, and Ruth Ferguson, UCD's Art Curator, for facilitating its relocation to the home of the President of Ireland. For over a thousand years, the story of the little white cat and his monk companion have entertained and instructed, each devoted to his craft, each acting out their instinctive and schooled natures in perfect harmony.

Now, through Imogen's vision and generosity, Sabina and I, the staff of the Áras, and the thousands of people who visit here every year can enjoy the vivid detail of this sculpture that brings the written material so sharply alive.

We can be prompted to thought and reflection, and appreciate this unique opportunity to experience how a gifted creative in a contemporary age can interpret artistic works written in the past.

So many moments in time slip quietly past, unrecorded and forgotten. We are, however, greatly fortunate to have the writers, the painters, the poets, the sculptors, who capture those singular incidents or images that clarify and define an important moment of epiphany. To those imaginative and creative people, we owe a great debt of gratitude. Not only do they create something that is aesthetically beautiful and uplifting, but they also assist us in understanding our world and our place in that world.

It is also worth remembering the developer and patron of the arts Mr Kish Kennedy, who developed some of Ireland's earliest shopping centres including Stillorgan and Dún Laoghaire. It was he who saw the value in including public art in his developments and a man for whom Imogen, I know, had the highest regard.

The poem 'Pangur Bán' has captured the imagination of so many artists. Translations of the poem into English have been undertaken by such literary giants as Robin Flower, Frank O'Connor, W.H. Auden and, of course, Seamus Heaney. In more recent years, Pangur has been introduced to new generations through several illustrated books for children and his appearance in the animated film *The Secret of Kells*, where his owner, Brother Aidan, was famously voiced by Mick Lally. [...]

Let me also thank especially the enthusiastic work of our Office of Public Works [OPW] colleagues who have embraced this project so enthusiastically and who have Pangur looking his best for display, and also the staff from Áras an Uachtaráin who have prepared for our celebrations today.

But most importantly, today I am delighted to express such gratitude to Imogen Stuart. *Pangur Bán*, like all of Imogen's work, speaks to us silently but profoundly, imbued as it is with a deep humanity and the life-enhancing spirit that makes her creations such a joy to experience. It is such a pleasure and a privilege to provide a new home for *Pangur Bán*, a home in which I can assure you it will continue to be enjoyed in a spirit of shared community and friendship.

We are honoured to receive this work today, and honoured all the more by the presence of Imogen who has made such a distinguished contribution to the cultural life of our nation.

Ireland and Germany

Toast on the occasion of the state dinner hosted by Frank-Walter Steinmeier, President of the Federal Republic of Germany, and Ms Elke Büdenbender, Schloss Bellevue, Berlin, 3 July 2019.

I have greatly enjoyed this first day of the visit in Berlin. I appreciated the wide-ranging and important discussions we had as well as my dialogue with Chancellor Merkel and with the Governing Mayor of Berlin.

Ireland and Germany are bound together through long historical, cultural, and economic ties and through our shared membership of the European Union. These enduring ties are of importance to both of us.

There are many great names in our past and in our present stretching from well more than a thousand years ago down to the present day. All are part of the rich material through which we know one another as countries and as people, and today we are closer than at any time in our history. A random selection from the many personalities that have been part of our relationship reveals a wonderful richness and variety:

I think of Kilian, Patron Saint of Franconia, who came from Co. Cavan in the seventh century; Georg Friedrich Händel, who premiered his *Messiah* in Dublin in 1742; the colourful and controversial Lola Montez, the Sligo woman, dancer and king's mistress who caused mayhem in the Bavarian court in the 1840s; the writer, pacifist and 'First Lady of Munich', Annette Kolb, whose 1912 novel *The Specimen* was partly set in Ireland; sculptor Imogen Stuart, Berlin-born but based in Ireland since 1951, and whose work has become an integral part of our island's built environment; Heinrich Böll whose *Irisches Tagebuch* (Irish Journal) of 1957 has had an unparalleled impact on German perspectives on Ireland; Elizabeth Shaw, the Irishwoman whose children's classic, *Der kleine Angsthase* (The Timid Rabbit), published in 1963, was beloved bedtime reading by children in the former East Germany; and not forgetting U2 who, inspired by German reunification, recorded the classic *Achtung Baby* album in Berlin in 1990.

Today we are reminded that, as before, it is through our people and our culture that we have come to understand, and will understand, one another best.

The year 2019 is the ninetieth anniversary of Irish–German diplomatic relations. Over the decades we have forged a relationship which has grown stronger and deeper with each passing year.

While we speak a different language, we share values and principles which allow us to speak with a resonance and respect, not only on the fundamentals we agree on, but on the nuanced differences we can equally discuss. We stand together as active and proud members of the European Union.

While I do not wish this evening to focus on the decision of the United Kingdom to leave the European Union – a decision with profound consequences for Ireland – it should not be either avoided or evaded. I would like to acknowledge the very strong EU solidarity which has been shown to Ireland at this difficult moment. It has been a very tangible reminder of the value of us being together and staying together in Europe to continue to defend, maintain, improve and promote the core values on which the Union is founded: democracy, cohesion, shared prospects, human rights and the rule of law.

Our shared commitment is present in our approach to the multilateral institutions. We are deeply committed to the United Nations and the values of multilateralism, which we are determined to uphold in its institutions in what are challenging times.

I look forward to us working together to achieve cohesion within and between the members of our European Union and, if it will bolster efforts, having an exemplary role in responding to global issues, such as responding to climate change and achieving sustainability.

IV. Connecting European Cultures

We share a belief in protecting the vulnerable, in the essential nature of human rights, in the peaceful resolution of conflicts, and in the need to build a better world.

The desire to be part of the effort for a better world is shared by the young people of both our countries. They seek to be part of the solution to the many conflicts and challenges in our crisis-stricken globe, to experience hope, a path forward.

Of these challenges and crises we face, and which I have mentioned, perhaps the greatest in terms of its existential impact, relates to climate change. I know that Germany has taken steps to address anthropogenic climate change since the mid-1980s, starting with your participation in the international negotiations of the Montreal Protocol. Just two weeks ago, the Irish government launched a comprehensive whole-of-government *Climate Action Plan to Tackle Climate Breakdown*, demonstrating Ireland's commitment to tackling the climate crisis.

While the EU has imposed binding emissions targets for 2020 and 2030 on all its Member States, I suggest we must now go further in Europe and plan for full decarbonization of our economies by 2050, encouraging the rest of the world to follow suit, and urging in the strongest possible terms those who have not signed the Paris Accord on Climate Change, or indeed those, such as the USA, who have decided to exit from the agreement, to reconsider their decision.

A radical shift to a new economic paradigm in a decarbonized world, an eco-social political-economy perspective, is required to achieve what we have agreed as principles. In dealing with the socioeconomic consequences of climate change, we must be conscious of the need for a 'just transition' for workers and communities to ensure that we are all part of a sustainable, low-carbon economy and benefit from decent and green jobs.

In Ireland and Germany this will mean that those impacted by the closure of unsustainable electricity-generation stations, for example, must be offered reskilling opportunities to enable them to find suitable jobs in other areas, such as the green economy, or opportunities with sustainable incomes in other parts of society.

I know that you recently celebrated the seventieth anniversary of your Basic Law. It is a constitution grounded in respect for human dignity and the inviolability and inalienability of human rights. I salute your continued adherence to and celebration of a constitution, which, to quote its preamble, takes its inspiration from, 'the determination to promote world peace as an equal partner in a united Europe'.

President Steinmeier, I want to acknowledge the crucial role you have played in fostering a continuing commitment to multilateralism and the peaceful resolution of conflict. As Foreign Minister you worked actively towards a vision of a better world. And as President, I know you have placed a high priority on understanding and highlighting our values as Europeans. I want to acknowledge your contribution – as both a philosophical thinker and as a politician – to the ongoing debate on the changing world order, and to the importance of values in international relations and cohesion in society. At a time when core values are under threat, Ireland and Germany stand together, side by side, in defence of our shared values and our way of life.

I am pleased that during this visit I will have engagements in four different German states. I know that in Berlin I am only seeing a sliver of the true diversity of this country. It is a particular honour that tomorrow I will travel to Saxony, the first Irish president to do so in an official capacity – indeed the first Irish president to officially visit any part of the former East Germany outside of Berlin. This visit will be an opportunity for me to reflect on the Leipzig protests some thirty years ago and on the enormous achievement that is the process of German reunification. We in Ireland understand the removal of borders and the challenges and complexity of overcoming old divisions; this is a task which does not end, and there is much we can continue to learn from one another.

This evening we celebrate our existing links, but I hope that this visit will be the start of an ever more diverse, ever stronger and ever-growing Irish–German relationship.

Ireland and the Netherlands

Speech at a state dinner in honour of Their Majesties King Willem-Alexander and Queen Máxima of the Netherlands, Áras an Uachtaráin, 12 June 2019.

May I first of all extend a *céad míle fáilte* on behalf of the people of Ireland to Their Majesties King Willem-Alexander and Queen Máxima of the Netherlands on this the occasion of their first state visit to Ireland. I hope that this state visit will rekindle memories of His Majesty's childhood holidays in Sneem in Co. Kerry.

The people of the Netherlands and Ireland have much in common and share strong values on a broad range of issues, among them social inclusion, tolerance and respect for human rights, and a strong history of scholarship in a wide range of disciplines. Our outward-looking foreign policy, human-rights emphasis, economic and trade policies facilitate our ties, and our common European Union membership underpins and supports our strong bilateral relationship.

Our country has traditionally been referred to as the 'land of saints and scholars' and one of the earliest links between our two peoples was indeed a scholar from across the water who studied in a monastery in Ireland in the seventh century before departing for what is now the Netherlands. Willibrord became the first bishop of Utrecht and was later canonized. His legacy is still remembered by historians in Carlow who travelled to Utrecht just last year to celebrate the connection.

The Irish language has been influenced by ancient Dutch, demonstrating the powerful effect of other nations' tongues on the words we use and the fluidity of language. It was recently reported that a new word of Old Dutch had been discovered in an ancient Irish manuscript, dated to the seventh century, which is quite remarkable for historians of that language given that only one other Dutch text survives from that period. This represents one of the earliest milestones in the study of the Irish language and the beginnings of Celtic linguistics, and it suggests that some early Dutch speakers may have come to Ireland as exchange students to study in our famous monastic schools.

Our peoples share a thirst for knowledge and have a great respect for scholars. That Your Majesty's illustrious predecessor, Stadhouder Willem the Silent, chose to found a university in Leiden during the earliest days of the Dutch republic is the tangible demonstration of this belief in the importance of education and of providing an environment where critical thinking is welcomed and nurtured.

The critical thinking by those first scholars in Leiden started a tradition of asking questions to which there was as yet no answer. Within a relatively short period, Your Majesty's *alma mater* provided a forum for leading thinkers from the seventeenth century right up to the present day. I am delighted that in 2019, many Irish students make the decision to broaden their education through graduate and postgraduate study in Leiden and other great universities in the Netherlands.

It is fitting that the EU programme which has enabled young people pursuing university studies to live and experience life in other Member States, is named after the great Dutch humanist Erasmus. These exchanges and opportunities have offered the young people of our Union, and many Irish amongst them, the chance to explore cities, cultures and identities.

Programmes such as the joint Masters in Food Science run between universities in France, Ireland, Sweden and the Netherlands are striking demonstrations of the different skills and attitudes that each of our countries bring, and how the European Union is at its best in allowing each of the Member States to combine perspectives, values and skills for the common good.

The ERASMUS programme is just one tangible expression of the benefits that the European Union offers to our peoples. At a time of great threats to multilateral cooperation, we must not ignore the importance of the European project, nor take it for granted.

Our shared European Union has brought enormous benefits for both our peoples, especially in terms of its impact on the democratic, environmental and social standards, living conditions and expectations.

The threats posed by Brexit and the challenges to the core values of our Union, which are posed from within and without by populism. The exploitation of the gap that has been allowed to grow between our European Union and the European Street, by an invocation of old hatreds and divisions embedded in a narrow uncritical manner. These have drawn a heavy price from the peoples of Europe. We must ensure, by our joint efforts, that intolerance and illiberalism are not allowed to once again take root on our continent.

In the Netherlands we see a consistent thread of striving for the better regulation of interaction between states through law – from Hugo Grotius, the father of international law, source of the contemporary human rights discourse and distinguished alumnus of Leiden, to the Hague Conventions in the late nineteenth and early twentieth centuries.

This continues right unto the present day whereby The Hague is rightly known as the International City of Peace and Justice, as the seat of the International Court of Justice, the International Criminal Court and the Organisation for the Prohibition of Chemical Weapons. In the fight against impunity and the fight to rid the world of the scourge of chemical weapons, the Netherlands will find in Ireland a strong partner.

Our cooperation on the multilateral stage is not, however, limited to The Hague or Brussels. We work closely in the United Nations, in Geneva and New York where our representatives collaborate on the most critical issues of our time – on the protection of human rights, the promotion of sustainable development and the promotion of peace and security.

We hope to build on the recent solid performance of the Netherlands on the UN Security Council if we are elected next year,[13] and we greatly appreciate the political, technical and moral support that the Netherlands has offered us in our campaign for membership. The Dutch are famous for being direct and we are confident that this trait will be brought by the Netherlands to the Human Rights Council because challenges to and breaches of human rights must be challenged in the most direct manner.

As Your Majesties visit Trinity College tomorrow, you will see a statue of Oliver Goldsmith, yet another Irish alumnus of Leiden University, though records of his attendance have been lost to history. There you will also have the opportunity to see the Fagel Collection and to hear of the work being undertaken between Trinity College and the Royal Library to make this wonderful resource available to a much wider audience.

Linkages in the arts between our two countries have been long and varied – from Nathaniel Hone the Elder, the son of a Dutch immigrant, to his Irish descendant Evie Hone, one of our most cherished artists whose captivating use of the medium of stained glass teaches us how to look at light.

If our present generations have a special feeling and respect for the world of nature it owes much to the creativity and passion for nature of another Dutch artist – Gerrit van Gelderen who, through his nature film work, showed Ireland to the Irish in a new light. His partnership with the late Éamon de Buitléir on the series *Amuigh Faoin Spéir* – in the earliest days of broadcasting on Raidió Teilifís Éireann – showed Irish people the wonders of our own country. Later on, his own series *To the Waters and the Wild* helped to inspire a generation with respect for our own natural heritage.

Another Dutchman who has been a wonderful friend to Ireland is Professor Matthijs Schouten and I am very pleased that he is in a position to be with us tonight. A younger Matthijs, a student of wetlands ecology, came to Ireland in the 1970s to study Ireland's raised bogs. His observations of the ongoing damage being caused to our bogs at that time left him profoundly worried that Ireland would follow the Dutch experience, which had led to the almost complete destruction of its peatlands. In 1978 a determined Professor Schouten was instrumental in saving Mongan bog in Westmeath, a bog that was earmarked for peat harvesting. Instead, with the cooperation of Bord na Móna, a state agency, and An Taisce, a conservation organization, the bog was saved. Professor Schouten did not stop there – soon after, the Dutch Foundation for the Conservation of Irish Bogs was formed, which gathered funds and garnered support to acquire a number of our threatened Irish bogs for conservation purposes. In 1987, as a member of parliament, I was privileged to have been invited by Dr Schouten to Baarn to be present when Prince Bernhard officially handed to an Irish government minister the deeds of three Irish bogs

IV. Connecting European Cultures

that had been saved through Professor Schouten's work and the work of his colleagues in the Netherlands and in Ireland. We owe him a great debt.

While the sea has served as the highway which has connected us since the earliest of times, it also poses a threat: not just to those who make their living from it but for those living in coastal communities with the threat of rising sea levels from global warming. Just as the people of the Netherlands are famous for coming together to build defences against the sea, the global community must also come together and adopt that *Poldermentalitet* to face that common threat together.

One area where both our countries have much to learn from and share with each other is in making our agriculture even more sustainable and I hope that Your Majesties will find the visit to our National Botanic Gardens tomorrow stimulating. Making our agriculture ever more sustainable is good for our own communities and is a way in which we can contribute to help rid the world of the scourge of hunger. Though due to very different causes and separated by almost a century, both our countries have experienced the horrors of famine and this has driven both of us to prioritize nutrition in our development cooperation policies.

The Netherlands is the world leader in the development of the 'Fair Trade' movement. The independent certification enabled customers and distributors alike to track the origin of the goods to confirm that the products were genuinely benefiting the producers, allowing goods from peripheral developing economies to be sold into mainstream markets. Importantly, disadvantaged producers are offered a fair price for their crop, often significantly above the market price once they adhere to various social and environmental standards. This initiative reaches a large consumer segment while raising awareness among the citizenry about ethical trading. Fair Trade commands a significant market share across several product lines in Ireland today. This socially-grounded economic model, based on the principles of equity and ethics, is sadly all too lacking in modern trade and globalized supply chains with their narrow focus on profit maximization, often to the detriment of labour rights and working conditions.

Whereas relations between our countries stretch back over many centuries, formal diplomatic relations were not established until 1949 and it is a matter of pride that the first ever woman appointed as head of an Irish diplomatic mission, Josephine MacNeill, was appointed as Minister to the Netherlands in 1950.

Now, almost seventy years later, more than ten thousand Irish people call the Netherlands home, with nearly a thousand of those being students. Serving as ambassadors for our country, they have brought their passion for our culture, music and traditional sports with them and shared it with people of many other nationalities. It may interest you to know that the Netherlands is home to one of the oldest Gaelic Athletics Association (GAA) clubs in Europe – Den Haag – which was founded in 1984 and also one of the youngest – Groningen – which was founded in 2018. Assisted by this visit we celebrate all that we have been sharing, and will share, in friendship and ever closer relations.

Ireland and Sweden

Speech at a state dinner in honour of Their Majesties King Carl XVI Gustaf and Queen Silvia of Sweden, Áras an Uachtaráin, 22 May 2019.

I have had the pleasure of meeting King Gustaf previously on a very special occasion when I was honoured to be Seamus Heaney's guest at his Nobel Prize award ceremony in 1995, a prize awarded 'for works of lyrical beauty and ethical depth, which exalt everyday miracles and the living past'.

Our cultures share much in common. The Viking period and the clear influence of the Norse-Gaels in our culture and language is manifest. We credit the Vikings with establishing our principal urban settlements, including our capital city. Our love affair with the written word ensures that the Irish Annals – a series of manuscripts compiled by Irish monks over a millennium – comprise one of our richest sources of knowledge about Viking sites.

The importance of mythology in the history of our two cultures is one form of Seamus Heaney's 'exalting of the living past' – and the scholarship of both our peoples shares a deep and extensive interest in this subject. Norse mythology consists of tales of various deities, beings and heroes derived from numerous sources from both before and after the pagan period, including what is suggested from medieval manuscripts, archaeological representations and folk traditions. Central to both Irish and Norse mythology are the plights of the gods and their interactions with various other beings, both their benign and malignant touching of the earth and earthlings.

Our shared interest has also had an institutional expression. Sweden has long had links with the Irish National Folklore Collection, held in University College Dublin. This archive – which owes so much to the work of the late Séamus Ó Duilearga, the former Professor of Folklore at University College Dublin and Director of the Irish Folklore Commission – has performed and continues to perform an essential function, I suggest, in ensuring access to our forbearers' intensity of vision and imagination, to the diversity of their beliefs and practices, and their extraordinary inventiveness. It enables us to approach that unique combination between the particular and the universal that is characteristic of vernacular culture.

The late Bo Gunnar Almqvist, former professor of Irish Folklore at University College Dublin, who was born in Alster, western Sweden, and who studied at Uppsala University, a university I have had the privilege of visiting when I served as Minister for Culture, is perhaps one of the best-known Swedes among academics in Ireland. He made a remarkable contribution to the study of Irish folklore, including more than ninety articles and numerous books on Irish and international folklore. Among the innovative courses Professor Almqvist instituted during his career in University College Dublin was a module on 'The Folktale and Medieval Literature'. I am delighted that we are joined this evening by other distinguished scholars from the world of Irish folklore, including Professor Séamas Ó Catháin, former Head of the Department of Irish Folklore in University College Dublin.

Another shared, near-contemporary interest of our two countries is the area of film and indeed the arts more generally. For two countries with relatively small populations, Ireland and Sweden can be proud of the significant contributions that the creative citizens of both our nations have made to the world of arts.

When one thinks of Swedish film, of course, the work of the great Ingmar Bergman immediately comes to mind. Bergman was, without doubt, one of the greatest artists of the twentieth century. He made, through literature and film, a unique and seminal contribution to our understanding of the human condition. Working often in a symbolic and emotional language that was deep

IV. Connecting European Cultures

to the very core, yet accessible, his influence on modern-day directors remains immense, including on Irish directors.

There are myriads of variable connections. Tomorrow at the National Library we will hear of the influence of August Strindberg to James Joyce's work. Indeed, my wife Sabina, in the past, has acted in two plays, *Miss Julie* and *The Father* from that great prolific Swedish playwright and author.

Turning, briefly, to contemporary issues – we must all now be concerned for the future of our shared European Union. We must not forget the importance of the European project, and the enormous benefits that have resulted for both of our peoples from its existence and particularly its impact on social and environmental conditions. In this regard, Sweden has often played a central role.

Developments such as the European Pillar of Social Rights were signed in Gothenburg in November 2017. The Pillar was aimed at delivering new and more effective rights for citizens through a set of twenty principles and rights – from the right to fair wages, to the right to health care, from lifelong learning, a better work–life balance and gender equality, to minimum income.

The EU continues to have the capacity to be an area where the rights of citizens in a fast-changing world can be secured and advanced.

For example, inward migration continues to be an important and, I suggest in parts of the discourse for malignant purposes, an abused issue in Europe. Sweden and Ireland have on this issue some common experience. May I suggest that our experience of managing inward migration into our two countries is something, at our different levels, of which we can both be proud. Future historians will acknowledge the humanitarian and practical example of Sweden in this regard. Historically, of course, our countries can both claim to have similar experiences of outward migration during the nineteenth century, especially to the United States.

We all are now living in the world of a new economic order where productive capital is so much lesser than new speculative flows, a development that has exacerbated the conflict of ecological, social and business models, leaving us a challenging legacy that threatens human survival itself. We need to discuss a new path to symmetry between those dimensions of our lives. We might, with benefit, recall the pivotal role that certain Swedish figures played in attempting to shape a socially responsible economic order that secured peace. Figures such as Olof Palme, whom I had the fortune to meet many years ago and who played a hugely significant role in international politics from the 1960s with his policy of non-alignment towards the superpowers, accompanied by support for numerous Third-World liberation movements following decolonization, including an informed, idealistic yet practical economic and vocal support for a number of developing country governments.

Of course, when one speaks of a morally inclined political economy there are so many Swedish scholars, including Gunnar Myrdal and Göran Therborn.

In so many global challenges Sweden has given a lead. Sweden has been at the forefront of climate change policy and sustainable development since the 1980s when it was one of the first countries to apply economic instruments, such as carbon taxes, and other policy measures aimed at climate-change mitigation. A Swedish Climate Act in 2018 established targets for net zero greenhouse gas emissions by 2045. Ireland's government has announced that we will be following such Swedish example with an ambitious climate change plan in the coming months to ensure we are on a path of decarbonization across the economy.

May I also pay tribute to Sweden's contribution to human rights legislation. In 1766 Sweden became the first country to introduce freedom of the press and today, human rights are central to Swedish foreign policy – and our own foreign policy.

In 2008 Sweden chose eight prioritized areas to be advanced in its foreign policy work for international human rights, including: building democracies, strengthening freedom of expression, abolishing the death penalty, combating torture, combating summary executions and arbitrary detention, protecting the rule of law, protecting human rights and international humanitarian law, and fighting discrimination.

At the United Nations we share leadership on disarmament issues. Ireland and Sweden have a shared vision of a world where the production, storage and use of all nuclear weapons would be banned. This aspiration is given tangible form in our consistent support for multilateral institutions, and through them for disarmament and non-proliferation, and in the determination of our peacekeepers to prevent conflict.

IV. Connecting European Cultures

Ireland's peacekeeping has always been strongly predicated on our neutrality. As members of the UN we are committed to maintaining international peace and security, and in honouring that commitment our position as an independent and neutral state has been greatly valuable. For over sixty years, United Nations peacekeeping has served as the standard-bearer of the world's shared commitment to international peace and security. Membership of the United Nations has, for both our countries, been a central pillar of our foreign policy.

We have worked together within that framework to promote global peace and security, and both our countries have sought to be neutral mediators in the pursuit of international justice and peace and the promotion of global welfare.

Our history of serving together as UN peacekeepers has created a profound connection between our two nations. Today we continue to serve on a number of UN missions – including in the Middle East, Western Sahara and the Democratic Republic of the Congo, and we are proud of our record of six decades of unbroken UN service in peace-support missions all over the world, and of the Irish men and women who make it possible.

I know that you share with your cousin Prince Charles a concern for nature. During your time here, you will visit the Burren, an area of outstanding natural beauty on our western Atlantic coastline. The Burren is renowned for its gentians but also for its unique agricultural traditions, and considerable thought and effort has been expended on ensuring that our farming tradition can continue in that region with simultaneous protection for priority habitats for conservation. The Burren Farming for Conservation Programme we regard as an exemplary project, which shows a great understanding of the role that must be taken by local farmers if we are to merge the urgent demands of environmental concerns with sustainable economic and social factors.

You will also be undertaking a visit to the Marine Institute, whose research is so important to us in developing policies which will support the sustainable development of Ireland's marine resources. The connection between Ireland and the ocean is, as in the case of Sweden, as old as time itself. The sea has played a fundamental part in both of our social and economic histories and it is to be recalled that, as an island nation, Irish people and, in particular, our coastal communities have always depended to some degree on the bounty that our seas provide. The fishing sector plays an important role in some regions and communities across Sweden, and I know we share a common concern for the conservation and sustainable use of the oceans and their resources, and an understanding that the world can no longer continue testing them to their limits.

Ireland and Lithuania: Towards a Shared Future Within the European Union

Speech at the Vytautas Magnus University, Kaunas, 20 June 2018.

It is a great honour for me to receive this award[14] from a university whose history so closely parallels that of modern Lithuania – tracing as it does its origins to the early days of the Republic, abolished during the dark days of Soviet occupation, and revived again as you reasserted your independence. The distinguished list of past recipients is truly humbling and I am profoundly moved to be placed amongst them.

I am conscious that I accept this award under the watchful gaze of this portrait of St Thomas Aquinas. With the passage both of time and of his works into doctrine, it is perhaps easy to forget what a truly radical thinker Aquinas was. He was a man who looked at the world around him, a world in flux, and found the prevailing orthodoxy lacking. His voice was at its best a dissenting voice. With great courage and intellectual vigour, he enkindled a new and compelling paradigm of thought, accommodating both the demands of orthodoxy in a theology that not only nursed certainty but sought to impose it, and of a theology and philosophy which had retained some categories of both wonder and experience – faith and reason – in ways which influenced Western thought for centuries.

Perhaps it was too heavy, that burden of injustices with which he struggled. I do not suggest he was the first, or indeed the only person, to explore these particular avenues of thought. But, in bequeathing us an almost unparalleled legacy of commitment to scholarship – a commitment he shared with such as Albertus Magnus and Bonaventure – he has left an indelible footprint on the landscape of human thought. Whether his works provide solace or provoke rebuttal, his intellectual legacy is proof that paradigms of thought are not eternal; they can and do change.

Today, we are so desperately in need of that kind of scholarly rigour and independence of thought: that capacity to question, to listen, to critically evaluate. To dissent without descending into demagoguery and retain the necessary elements of discourse. To dare to suggest novel ways of meeting the great challenges of our time. These are emancipatory skills; they are necessary for participatory citizenship; they are skills which can be taught; and they are essential in protecting the citizens of now and of the future from the hubris of the strong.

As Aquinas said: 'It is better to illuminate than merely to shine, to deliver to others contemplated truths, than merely to contemplate.'[15] It is vital therefore that we, the academic community and public representatives alike, labour to ensure that our young people receive the fullest possible education, one that prepares them for life, as well as work. The value that this university places on the teaching of liberal arts is another of the many reasons that I prize the honour you have given me this afternoon.

One of the great rewards of the study of history is to learn to reflect on our past, to identify common threads, and, in so doing, to find keys to unlock pathways to our future. For Ireland and Lithuania, when we look to our pasts, we see nations with deep historical roots and treasured cultural identities; both of which helped to sustain our sense of self in our long struggles for statehood. Thus I am particularly honoured to be in Lithuania in this the year of the centenary of your independence.

As you charted your course to national freedom, so too was my country making its own arduous journey to self-determination. In Ireland, we are in

IV. Connecting European Cultures

the midst of a Decade of Centenaries – a series of commemorations marking the momentous, revolutionary and, at times, very different approaches taken in the years leading to, and following, the foundation of our state. As President of Ireland, I have endeavoured to encourage a process of ethical remembrance – reflecting on those seminal events in a way that is sensitive to and accepting of the manifold, sometimes competing, sometimes absent, perspectives on our history. In doing so I have drawn on the work of writers such as Paul Ricoeur, Richard Kearney, Hannah Arendt and David Rieff.

Re-engaging with the past as a project that is ethically driven, seeking to understand and build a bridge to the Other, creates a need to remember, to forgive; sometimes in the interest of ethics to park or forget and, ultimately, to release us from the confines of past events, so that we can be free to imagine a more fulfilling future. Conscious that I speak in a university, I would ask that, as citizens and academics, we must all value, deepen and extend what space there might be for such an inclusive discourse, all over Europe, and between previous European colonial powers and continents such as Africa and Latin America. History, with other categories in its historiography, open to real evidence, re-evaluation and indeed revision, is a vital part of citizenship and history belongs to all of our people.

In 1919, a year after you gained your independence, one of the early acts of the first Dáil Éireann, the parliament of Ireland, was to issue a 'Message to the Free Nations of the World'. It was issued in three languages: Irish, French and English. It sought to establish the abiding principles upon which our foreign policy would rest. It stated that Ireland

> believes in freedom and justice as the fundamental principles of international law, because she believes in a frank cooperation between the peoples for equal rights against the vested privileges of ancient tyrannies, because the permanent peace of Europe can never be secured by perpetuating military dominion for the profit of empire but only by establishing the control of government in every land upon the basis of the free will of a free people.

We demonstrated our commitment to such fundamental principles by being one of only three states to have never, in any way, recognized the occupation of Lithuania by the Soviet Union. It is why on 23 August 1989 we marvelled at that somatic act of solidarity – when some two million people from this country, from Latvia and from Estonia held hands to form a human chain over 600 kilometres long – an act of extraordinary peaceful defiance to reclaim your place amongst the free and independent nations of the world.

It is a matter of great pride to the people of Ireland that, less than fifteen years later, you took your place amongst the Member States of the European Union in Dublin. The 1st of May 2004, at a reception at Áras an Uachtaráin, the home of the President of Ireland – The Day of Welcomes, as we christened it – was a truly remarkable moment in the history of our Union. The late Seamus Heaney, who had such a great respect for, and whose work drew so heavily from, the rich tapestry of European culture, recited a poem written for the occasion:

> So on a day when newcomers appear
> Let it be a homecoming and let us speak
> The unstrung word, as it behoves us
> Move lips, move minds and make new meanings flare
> Like ancient beacons signalling, peak to peak.[16]

As ever, indicating the power of a poet to distil meaning and emotion, in just a few words he captured the essence of the occasion. This arrival of new members was a moment of healing and of hope – hope for the founding ideals upon which the Union was built. Our shared institutions and our shared values, it was felt, had a capacity for building bridges across a common space divided, that might have been at a time at the mercy of an imperialist tendency in the past and so recently and artificially divided by a wall, but that now had the capacity to make a new future, different from the old.

At a time when these founding ideals seem increasingly maligned, and the living memory of the great catastrophe that stands as background to the birth to our Union fades, it is critical that we remember that the European Union is first and foremost a union founded upon the invocation of fundamental values. Forged from the embers of World War II, ours is a union that seeks to be based on peace, freedom and democracy; a union based on the rule of law, respect for human rights, equality and human dignity; a union with the capacity to leave the dark colonizing past behind and to demonstrate cooperation and solidarity throughout the world, with all of humankind. These are values that

IV. Connecting European Cultures

can never be taken for granted or assumed to be unchallenged, particularly by those who know only too well the pain and isolation that their absence causes.

As small, fledgling independent states, Ireland and Lithuania committed our people to these ideals and to each other. Our sovereignty, so long fought for, would be neither impinged nor extinguished – as it had been so often in our past – but would be shared, and in that sharing it would be expanded to create a common space, one that we share to this day, one in which our citizens travel, study and work, encountering one another in a spirit of friendship and solidarity.

In the years since, our European destinies have been ever more intertwined, not least through the tens of thousands of your sons and daughters who now call Ireland home. They add so much to the vibrancy and texture of Irish life, but we Irish know only too well the gnawing ache that migrants, in their leaving, can carry with them, and the void that they leave behind at the point of origin, their home and community. After all, these feelings are at the centre of our literary and musical inheritance in both of our cases.

To borrow again from the words of my friend Seamus Heaney, they know what it is 'to live in two places at the one time and in two times at the one place'.[17] Yet through them, and through our joint work in the European Union, we have come to know each other better. I am here today to celebrate that deepening friendship and to look to its future. I greatly welcome our increased opportunities for engagement within the European Union, which connects us across a vast range of areas: social, cultural, political and economic.

In a union that urgently needs to address the challenges of sustainability and climate change – our last great gesture of hope internationally – ensuring that there are opportunities for our young people, to rebuild economic and social cohesion, to reconnect with the European Street, and to advocate for a more just international order, it is essential that we – Ireland and Lithuania – work together to build shared perspectives and to amplify our voices.

We may be nations with small populations on opposite sides of the continent, but it is clear that we share our responsibilities. We are committed to being at the heart of European policymaking. Indeed, it is a responsibility and a right. In so being, we must be cognizant that the policy choices we make have far-reaching implications for human beings, for the most vulnerable amongst us, and for our increasingly fragile planet.

Ireland and Lithuania: Towards a Shared Future Within the European Union

We must, all of us as members of the European Union, therefore look beyond the immediate policy challenges and towards the vista of our shared European future. When I visited Greece earlier this year I emphasized that the future of Europe cannot rest on a limited conversation between the strongest, nor, I should add, the most proximate.

The United Kingdom's departure will have significant implications for all Member States, but nowhere will it be felt more keenly than in Ireland. The history of that which many refer to as 'the Troubles' on our island is well known, but perhaps less appreciated is the crucial role the European Union has played in the pursuit and maintenance of the cherished peace which eluded us for so long.

The European Union has over the decades provided generous and timely political and financial support for peace and reconciliation on our island helping to foster new cross-border and cross-community relationships and linkages. More intangibly, but no less crucially, it has provided much of the wider context and framework for peace – a framework in which barriers melted away and cooperation in areas from tourism to agriculture, from education to civic society became not just possible but the norm.

I want to thank Lithuania, and all of our European partners, for the understanding they have demonstrated for Ireland's unique concerns in the Brexit negotiations, and, in particular, for the resolute support you have shown in protecting the gains of the peace process and the Northern Ireland Peace Agreement. There could be no more meaningful expression of European solidarity.

At the same time, we recognize that in a palpable sense, European solidarity is fraying. Solidarity is the cornerstone of our Union. Like the peace on our island, it must be fostered and cherished. There is an undeniable discord on the European Street, a sense that social and economic cohesion has fractured. When he visited Ireland in February, Foreign Minister Linkevičius kindly participated in a debate in University College Cork on the theme of 'Ireland and Lithuania in the European Union'. He described what we are experiencing as a 'stress test'; a stress test of our European unity, our values and our leadership. I very much agree. The strength we must demonstrate together must, I believe, be value-based, with a capacity to endure, one that will also have the capacity to defend multilateralism and resist any intimidation to resile to a privileging of militarism rather than diplomacy.

I am a firm believer that Ireland's, and indeed Lithuania's, destiny lies at the heart of a European Union that lives up to the very best ambitions of its founders, and to the aspirations of its citizens. The founders of European integration would have been amongst the first to call for us to embrace the plural debate needed to overcome our current – as I am in a school of theology, let me call it – crisis of European faith.

Yet, as Pope Francis reminded the leaders of the Union when he addressed them on the occasion of the sixtieth anniversary of the signing of the Treaty of Rome, a crisis is not only a dark moment of confusion and fear, but also a conjuncture at which we see errors in full light, enabling us to see more clearly all the possibilities for a more hopeful future: 'The word "crisis", Pope Francis stated, 'has its origin in the Greek verb *kríno*, which means to discern, to weigh, to assess. Ours is a time of discernment, one that invites us to determine what is essential and to build on it.'[18]

Ireland, and many of the nation states of Europe, have experienced profound and prolonged economic and social crises over the past ten years, some generated internally and some as a consequence of the global financial crisis. That larger global crisis revealed the weaknesses of the prevailing ideas and orthodoxies that preceded, and in some respects created, the conditions for the crisis itself. For far too much time a single economic discourse has dominated in our Union and across the world, one that was, and perhaps still remains, inadequately challenged and contested, and it has too often been presented as inevitable, rather than as a policy choice among many, which should be made by democratically elected governments. Our Union has been, at times, riven and divided by the multiple crises that we confront, and solidarity between Member States has been strained. We have too often reduced the term 'European Union' to the level of an oxymoron. We must stand up for the social Europe that we know to be possible.

Now is indeed the time for discernment, and to all of us who believe not just in the best of our Union, but in democracy itself, the wide debate about the future nature of our Union should be affirming, not disheartening. We need to hear from the highest to the lowest level of the institutions of the

European Union that a discourse on Social Europe is welcome, that critical and pluralist scholarship is welcome in that discourse. The evidence for such a willingness is weak. As that distinguished German philosopher Jürgen Habermas has reminded us, without the constant exercise of public deliberation, without citizens being enabled to submit their arguments to rational disputation, democracy itself will not survive.

Our Union can no longer be constructed and reconstructed from above. If it is to survive in this new century, it must be also renewed and rebuilt from below. This is a project that must not become the preserve of the strong and powerful, whether in the form of a conversation between the larger states of our Union or the unaccountable and non-transparent economic actors which increasingly dominate the organization of consumption, production and distribution. Those Member States, such as Ireland and Lithuania, that have endured long and unremitting struggles for national independence seek a union of equals, one that acts for the benefit of all European citizens.

We have an egalitarian and humane European inheritance upon which to draw, one that encompasses the vast expanse in times and space that characterizes our continent, from the *Summa Theologica* of Thomas Aquinas to the samizdat poetry of Tomas Venclova. We often speak of the founders of the contemporary European Union, and, while we should recognize the vision of those statesmen sixty years ago, we should also acknowledge the moral patrimony that was available to them and is available to us as we seek to reshape our shared Union.

In its founding moments, the European Union was not a project dedicated solely to the freedom of the markets or of capital. It drew on the rich patrimony I have mentioned. It envisioned a larger freedom, one that can only be achieved through the vindication of the fundamental social, economic and cultural rights. One of the most morally compelling visions of European internationalism – considered one of the founding documents of European integration – emerged from the Italian resistance movement. I speak of the manifesto composed in captivity by Altiero Spinelli and Ernesto Rossi, one of the founders of the anti-fascist Giustizia e Libertà, on the island of Ventotene in 1941. That manifesto was remarkable for articulating the demand for a federation of European states dedicated to disarming the worst passions of European nationalisms, and in asserting that such a federation could only be achieved, and would only be preserved, if it was capable of continuing 'the historical process of the struggle against social inequalities and privileges'.[19]

We might ask whether our Union is today capable, intellectually and institutionally, of giving co-equal representation to the spirit of Ventotene and to the spirit of Frankfurt embodied by the European Central Bank. For in this new century, we shall confront both new and old challenges: the pressing need for just and sustainable development; the necessity of protecting the human rights of those fleeing war, persecution and famine; the growing inequalities in income, opportunity and wealth both within and between countries; and above all, the urgent need to address the causes of climate change and to mitigate its consequences. We cannot continue to privilege economic models that only serve to widen inequalities, to create rather than mitigate instability, and to degrade rather than protect our environment.

These are not only European, but global, challenges, and they require global solutions. Three years ago, Pope Francis wrote of our duties to the other peoples of our planet: 'in the present state of global society, where injustices abound and growing numbers of people are deprived of basic human rights and considered expendable, the principle of the common good immediately becomes, logically and inevitably, a summons to solidarity and a preferential option for the poorest of our brothers and sisters'.[20]

Our solidarity must extend beyond our borders. In this precarious world, global solidarity is the most important contribution we can make to peace and stability. In our shared commitment to undertake international peace support missions to prevent and resolve conflict in the support of the United Nations, Lithuania and Ireland give shape to that solidarity.

These commitments also demonstrate the important role that small nations can play in securing peace. As a small state, Ireland believes that the multilateralism to which I have referred as being now under so much serious threat is the best platform for projecting our values and our voice on the global stage. As we experience a worrying retreat from multilateralism, the European Union and its Member States must continue to work strongly in support of the United Nations with which we share not only important values, but that fundamental commitment to multilateralism in which so many of the peoples of the world place their hopes.

Peace cannot be built, nor can it be sustained, by any narrow diplomacy, defined by transaction, in service of a national advantage at the cost of other nations. Peace rests but upon a diplomacy of the common good, one built on mutual respect and understanding, one that is open to the possibilities of the future, one that rejects any invocation of fear. A European Union recoiling to a diplomacy reliant on fear, a European Union which defines security in terms of military preparedness alone, will be unable to meet the challenges of our century, nor will it be capable of demonstrating the solidarity demanded by the Paris Climate Accords and the 2030 Agenda for Sustainable Development. We must craft a European Union based on hope and resolve as to values that can be shared, one that unequivocally asserts that it is through deliberation that a community of nations can discern and give shape to a common good. [...]

As I draw my remarks to a close I am reminded of the words of one of the distinguished recipients of the honour you have bestowed on me today and a native son of Lithuania, Czeław Miłosz:

> Human reason is beautiful and invincible.
> No bars, no barbed wire, no pulping of books,
> No sentence of banishment can prevail against it.
> It establishes the universal ideas in language,
> And guides our hand so we write Truth and Justice
> With capital letters, lie and oppression with small.
> It puts what should be above things as they are,
> Is an enemy of despair and a friend of hope.
> It does not know Jew from Greek or slave from master,
> Giving us the estate of the world to manage.[21]

At this critical juncture in history, we have indeed been given the estate of the world to manage: we have available to us not only the valuable instruments of reason, but also the music of the heart. We must allow both to give us hope. Let us do it well, let us do it ethically, with humanity, humility and compassion in our hearts, and, most of all, let us do it together, *le chéile*.

Ireland and Croatia

Speech at a state dinner in honour of Kolinda Grabar-Kitarović, President of Croatia, Áras an Uachtaráin, 3 April 2017.

I am delighted to have this occasion to celebrate the friendship that unites our two peoples – a friendship that your visit acknowledges and deepens; and a friendship which Sabina and I experienced at first hand in your beautiful country in early June 2013. This was our very first state visit since my election as President of Ireland, and it took place at a time when Croatia was getting ready to become the twenty-eighth Member State of the European Union. I recall the atmosphere of excitement and optimism that surrounded this historic event, an event which coincided with the last day of Ireland's presidency of the Council of the EU.

Your visit now comes at a time [...] when the European Union is facing the exit of a member. It is a time, too, of much confusion and turbulence on the European Street – a confusion that is amenable to political exploitation in an atmosphere of fear, ignorance and some righteous anger at economic and social exclusion.

These appeals from the European Street are ones that concern both of us, as directly elected presidents, and I believe, Madam President, that in facing these challenges we can both be encouraged by the warm bilateral relations that exist between Croatia and Ireland. These warm relations are ones that have

Ireland and Croatia

grown in part from our shared experiences. We are two nations who have had inflicted on us the experience of imperialism, two peoples who cherish their hard-won national independence; we have similar population and territorial sizes; both our peoples have emigration at the heart of their history, which gifts us an intimate understanding of the propriety and richness of hospitality for the migrant and the visitor. Then too, our two states can also learn and share so much from their respective relations with borders, and their consequences, ours with Northern Ireland, and yours with Bosnia-Herzegovina.

Croatia and Ireland are also renowned as two lands of astonishing natural beauty, although, admittedly, the beautiful Croatian landscapes and coasts bask in a distinctively warmer climate. The attractions of the Adriatic are ones that had a spectacular influence on one of our greatest Irish writers, James Joyce, who was to spend a year teaching English to the Austro-Hungarian naval officers stationed at Pula, today renowned, amongst other things, for its film festival. According to one of his early biographers, Richard Ellman, it was in Pula that James Joyce 'felt the first stirrings of dandyism': he rented an upright piano, put on weight, grew a moustache, 'had some teeth fixed', bought a new suit, and, 'with [his wife] Nora's help in curling began to wear his hair *en brosse*'.[22] Some Joycean scholars have also emphasized how James Joyce's craft as a writer was informed by the 'Babylon of languages' he found in Pula, a place where *Mitteleuropa*, the Mediterranean and the Balkans meet, and where the Italian, German, Serbo-Croatian, Slovenian and even Istro-Romanian languages could be heard on the streets.

During my 2013 state visit to Croatia I had the opportunity of recalling the memory of another Irishman, Laval Nugent, who, in the nineteenth century, left his native Co. Westmeath in Ireland and became a field marshal in the Austrian army. The journey of Laval Nugent connects us to an important chapter in Irish history, which saw so many sons of Ireland leave this island after the fateful defeat of the Boyne and offer their services to the Catholic monarchies of continental Europe.

I know that Laval Nugent is remembered as a patriot by many Croats, and I was pleased to learn that one of his former properties – Trsat Castle in Rijeka – was part of this year's Global Greening initiative, in celebration of Ireland's national St Patrick's Day. I was equally delighted to learn of a deepening cooperation between Rijeka, your home city, Madam President, and Galway, the place which I have come to call home in Ireland. The two cities are getting ready to become our European Capitals of Culture in 2020. I know that you intend to visit Galway this Wednesday and I assure you that you have chosen wisely! [...]

As you are well aware, Croatia joined the other members of the European Union at a very critical juncture in its sixty-year history. Now all of us Member States are called upon to respond to unprecedented challenges, both external and internal. Indeed, we are confronted simultaneously with the need for institutional, political, economic and financial measures that are inclusive. In parts of the Union there have been alarming security threats. We frankly face a very grave institutional and political crisis at European level.

We in Ireland are required to respond, not only to Brexit, but also to the wider challenge of political legitimacy. European citizens must be enabled to empower themselves with a vision for Europe as a global exemplar in sustainability, human rights, inclusion and accountable policy, rather than allowing themselves to be the pawns of xenophobic populisms across the continent – populisms that are threatening the very future of the European project, and which also have the capacity to lose the peace the European Community was founded to make possible.

We must approach these multiple crises with hope, courage and renewed political will. We need [...] to acknowledge the current loss of trust on the European Street by rebuilding the democratic pact between European citizens and their institutions, with a positive regional invitation that is coherent with future global realities and necessary reforms. The Union, after all, let us remind ourselves, draws its legitimacy from the support of its people – and for this legitimacy to endure, it is important to recall that European democracy is endangered whenever decisions that are the legitimate object of political debate in national and European elected fora are leaked, or ceded by default, either to the outcomes of speculative markets, or to the automaticity of rigid, and, although their assumptions are rarely stated, essentially ideological, fiscal rules.

Democracy is endangered whenever a hegemonic, empirically unaccountable version of abstract economics, perhaps based on a narrow theory of interests, prevails, at the expense of the fundamental objectives of social cohesion and democratic vigour. We are reaping the consequences of this neglect of social cohesion. The voices of the European Street are loud. We must listen to them, and respond not by adjusting what is failing, but by offering a vision based on the solidarity of all citizens in all Member States going forward together. Indeed, as the distinguished German philosopher Jürgen Habermas has reminded us, without the constant exercise of public deliberation, and without citizens being enabled to submit their arguments to rational disputation, democracy itself will not survive. The public presentation of accommodations reached at European level, the policy instruments used to fend off our recent financial crisis, have, too often, had the effect of separating European institutions from the people they are meant to represent. The European public discourse has not been sufficiently informed, for example, in terms of the macroeconomic assumptions, justification and consequences of fiscal measures or so-called 'austerity measures', in such a way as would have enabled genuine moral-political choice. The discourse must change, become more permeable to the concerns, the fears, the hopes, of European citizens. The choice, then, as I see it, is between recovering a flexibility in decision-making that will be democratically accountable, or remaining transfixed, waiting for the system to be overturned.

In this regard, I must confess disappointment at the outcome and statement from the recent Rome Conference. We must go further and foster a new democratic moment in Europe, by inviting and enabling our citizens to deliberate, not only on European issues, but also on the great global issues that are at the root of much of their current malaise. We must allow citizens to gain informed political understanding of the immense transformations at play in the wider world, not just in the geopolitical realm, but also in relation to such matters as demography, ecology and climate, sustainable development and the landslide changes in international production, finance and trade. We must also, importantly, reclaim the public discourse on Europe from those who distort and undermine it, so as to reaffirm forcefully the vital relevance of the European Union to the great challenges of this new century.

Indeed, what better solution than a united Europe do we have to offer in responding to the great collective issues currently facing us? Issues including the global environmental crisis, development, migration and the challenge of democracy, in a context where we are witnessing the rise of so-called 'illiberal democracies' and the transgressions of the rule of law both inside and outside the EU?

It is important to remember [...] that Europe has always strengthened, not weakened, its identity through a courageous engagement with the great challenges of history. This is a lesson particularly worth recalling as Europeans are challenged, today, to respond in accordance to their founding values to the needs of thousands of migrants and refugees who are fleeing to their territory. Can our collective answers to them be predicated upon restrictions of the rule of law, or an encroachment of the human rights and core liberties proclaimed in our treaties? We should never forget, nor neglect, be it only temporarily, the values that are the very heart of the European project; values that were invoked after a nadir had been reached in terms of atrocity and violation of human dignity in so many settings of detention in Europe.

The founders of Europe recognized both the fragility and the fundamental value of the concept of human dignity; they understood the crucial importance of having shared institutions of peaceful cooperation. These are, of course, values that are acutely understood by the people of Croatia, for whom the memory of fratricidal war is a fresh one, as it is indeed for us on this island. We face the challenge of remembering actions that are not now, and indeed never were, defensible.

The framework and the values offered by the European Union are important, then, not only in that they have served, and continue to serve, to strengthen our respective journeys towards peace and reconciliation, but also because they are, at a deep level, propitious to what I call 'ethical remembering', or what the French philosopher Paul Ricoeur has called 'narrative hospitality':[23] that is, a critical perspective on one's own narratives, as well as an openness to the memories, the stories, the grievances of the Other, the neighbour, the enemy of yesterday – the partner in new possibilities and the friend of today. This is an *acquis* – an immensely valuable historical and ethical *acquis* – which must serve to attach us all very firmly to that great enterprise that is the project of unification in peace and sustainable prosperity of the European continent.

It is a great project; it is a project to be consolidated, not unravelled; and it is also, as we all know very well, an unfinished project. All of us in the European Union are grateful to be able to rely on you, President Grabar-Kitarović, on the Croatian government and on the Croatian people as goodwill ambassadors for your former sister-republics within the Yugoslav federation, whose peoples are today awaiting to share in the promise of peace, stability and prosperity offered by the Union.

We are [...] at a moment when a new departure is required for our European Union – when a new departure is possible. We can, together, breathe new life in the European vision. In doing so, we will also be saving a model of cooperation and cohesion on which the peoples of other continents have placed their gaze, and a model on which Croatia's neighbours from the western Balkans have placed their hopes.

V
THE FUTURE OF THE EUROPEAN UNION

Giving the European Union a Future That Will Engage Citizens: A Shared Challenge

Speech at the inaugural event of the Brexit Institute,
Dublin City University, 25 January 2018.

'We, civilizations, now know ourselves to be mortal.'

When these words were written by Paul Valéry in 1919, he was reflecting on the devastation that the empires of Europe had inflicted upon themselves, upon their subjects and upon others, through the devotion of their formidable industrial power and scientific knowledge to total war and mutual destruction. 'Everything has not been lost,' Valéry continued, 'but everything has sensed that it might perish. An extraordinary shudder ran through the marrow of Europe.'[1]

A similar great shudder, reinforced perhaps by the further slaughter of World War II, must have been felt by the leaders of the six European nation states who met in Rome sixty-one years ago, on 25 March 1957, to lay the foundations of the European Union. Aware that Europe had, for the second time in the century, come to the brink of total moral and material collapse and reached a nadir in relation to respect for human life, freedom and dignity, the founders of European integration were seeking to invoke a new shape to their relationships – a shape that would give longevity to what might be a potential

V. The Future of the European Union

European solidarity of peoples and, in the process, give as instruments to achieve this their nations' shared institutions of peaceful cooperation.

Valéry's 'shudder' reminds us of the importance of context and how we must in our reflection be aware of changes in context, whether stated or hidden. The commitment given to each other by the six founding states in Rome stood in contrast to that imperial impulse, which had subjected Europe to decades, if not centuries, of warfare, and certainly for many of the peoples of the world was the insatiable source of centuries of oppression.

Only five months before that fateful meeting in Rome in 1957, Konrad Adenauer, the Chancellor of West Germany, and Guy Mollet, the Prime Minister of France, while conducting negotiations in Paris on the shape of the future Common Market, were interrupted by a phone call from the British Prime Minister, Anthony Eden, who informed a shocked French leader that Britain was unilaterally withdrawing from the Anglo-French attack on Egypt as the military adventure had incurred the displeasure of the United States. It was a salutary lesson for all three leaders. They were learning that European nations could no longer continue to subject large swathes of the planet to imperial rule without international implications.

At that time, the majority of the peoples of the global south of course still faced a long and unremitting struggle for independence, self-determination and national freedom. That struggle is one that we must never forget as Europeans: its hurt carries the imprint of a legacy of empire, part of the European legacy that must be acknowledged. It is a legacy that requires to be transacted in an adequate ethical exercise of remembering. The consequences of it being perceived as continuing to exist in alternative forms in the collective memories, without acknowledgment, and without being confronted, erodes mutual trust. However, let us in Ireland not forget either that while the imperial project was one under which this country suffered, it was also one in the administration and defence of which many of our people partook in the past.

The best aspirations for European integration then gave an expression to a very different logic to that which had plunged the continent and world into war twice in a century. These aspirations represented much more than a yearning for idealism, and still represent today the triumph of idealism over cynicism, of hope over fear, and of the promise of international solidarity and new collective achievements over the lure of any seduction to the abuse of national power. Sovereignty, in the new circumstances envisioned, it was suggested, would be neither imposed nor extinguished, as it had been so often in the European past. It would be shared, and thus in its sharing be enabled to create not an exclusive and demarcated zone of control, but a common space, one which endures today, one in which our citizens might travel, study and work freely, encountering each other in a spirit of friendship and amity. Aspects of it have come to be, as over three million students have crossed borders to study. Over one million babies have been born to couples who studied under the ERASMUS Programme.

It is important to recall that the objectives of the Union, now contained in Article 3 of the Treaty on European Union, reflect, *inter alia*, the inheritance of some of Europe's most egalitarian and humane traditions. Those were traditions that, in their source, were not confined to Europe. They included traditions that had in many instances been often brought to Europe from afar. That rich scholarship, philosophy, moral instinct and generous impulse that contributed to and drew on an enriched European thought would yield an impulse towards the promotion of social justice and protection, equality between men and women, solidarity between generations, economic and social cohesion and solidarity between Member States. These principles reach their fullest expression through the rights enumerated in the Charter of Fundamental Rights, which has had legal effect throughout the Union since 2009.

May I suggest that the past ten years have severely tested our collective commitment to such a rich and enabling moral patrimony. The trajectory towards increasing inequalities of income, wealth, power and opportunities within societies and between nation states, evident since the early 1980s, has continued, and continues to be presented in an arrogant abjection of empirical test or consideration as to social consequence, as some natural order of things, rather than the outcome of a policy paradigm sourced in a narrow version of political economy, which has yielded so painfully slowly, if at all, to critique, and still more slowly to change.

We have had a tacit and, in recent decades, accommodating, narrowing of intellectual work, an intolerance of critique and a blind acceptance of a unilinear vision of growth, the components of which, I repeat, are neither made

V. The Future of the European Union

matters of empirical critique, or social test. As a consequence, economic and social cohesion has fractured; and political policies resiling to, and deploying, rhetoric once thought banished from the continent of Europe, have seized their moment and begun to re-emerge.

In the absence of an adequate and inclusive discourse, and emboldened by those who seek to mimic the language of the far right for short-term electoral advantage, these political forces – exploiting and drawing on the despair, alienation and anomie of so many citizens – seek to divide us against one another on the grounds of ethnicity, religion and nationality. While not succeeding in recent electoral contests to achieve majorities in the short term, their gains represent a formidable challenge to any future social cohesion.

In responding to these developments, it is important that we use words such as 'populist', 'nationalist' and 'ethnic' with care. These words as concepts have, after all, in history been used for emancipatory purposes on occasion. We must instead engage with the factors that facilitate the abuse of such terms in current circumstances.

We are entering a time when, for the first time in many years, the future shape of the European Union has become a matter of contestation and everyday debate. This conference today reflects that realization. In the shadow of the UK referendum result, and of those social forces which have given rise to so much doubt across Europe, we are invited to imagine and define, through deliberation, and with regard to the necessary courtesies of discourse, the outlines of the European Union that we seek.

The European Commission, under the leadership of President Juncker, issued a very welcome *White Paper on the Future of Europe* last March, and has issued a number of reflection papers on globalization, on deepening economic and monetary union, on the future of European defence, the future of the Union's financial framework, and on what the Commission has referred to since the 1980s as the 'social dimension'. This of course complements the report issued by the Presidents of the Commission, European Central Bank, European Parliament, Eurogroup and the European Council on proposals for the completion of economic and monetary union.

Political leaders across the Union have begun to make their own contributions. Some seem to seek, or envisage as adequate, a renewal in the existing institutional arrangements and practise what some have called a methodological revision. I do not share their optimism. May I take the opportunity therefore to welcome in particular the interventions by President Macron in Athens and Paris in favour of recognizing and acknowledging the depth of the crisis of social connection that threatens any version of a strong, efficient and inclusive Europe. Some of us may not agree with the totality of his argument, but I would like to recognize the courage, the vigour and the spirit in which it has been offered in those speeches.

In enunciating his vision and his programme – and it is refreshing to see a leading politician outline a programme for Europe – he has enriched and enlivened what has been for some time a moribund debate. However, it is important, too, that it be clearly understood that from the outset any Franco-German agreement on the future of the Union will not suffice to answer the deep and sincerely held concerns of those who have sought as their hopes for the European Union the vindication of their aspirations for it to be a union of equals for the benefit of all European citizens.

Above all, I would like to agree with President Macron – in the strongest terms – that we are at a moment when we must recognize that the Union cannot, as in the past, be reconstructed from above, but can only, if it is to survive in this new century, be renewed and rebuilt from below. This is necessary if we are to recover any sense of authenticity in our pursuit of the democratic ideals invoked at the founding of the Union – so recently recapitulated by the leaders of the Twenty-Seven in Rome last March – and used to legitimate every successive treaty change since that time. For so many citizens in the Union these ideals cannot be recognized in the social outcomes of policies that often indeed seem to contradict such language and its principles. Public spectacles replete with rhetorical flourishes have come to be perceived by European citizens as simply an abuse of the symbolic, an inadequate disguise for the absence of authenticity in the transition from policy exposition to practice.

As an imbalance between competitiveness and cohesion, in European Union aspirations and rhetoric, has deepened, it has become clear that the great challenge that confronts the Union – and one of the great tasks of the next decade – will be to achieve cohesion within the communities and between the communities of our common European home – and I include the tasks

V. The Future of the European Union

facing the Irish state. Such a cohesion might enable us as a union to practise social responsibility abroad. It is only by achieving this goal – by rebuilding our capacity and our willingness to work together to lead fulfilling lives in all spheres of human activity – that we can confront the global challenges that will be common to all humanity in this century: the pressing demand for a just and sustainable development; the imperative of welcoming those fleeing war, persecution, famine and natural disasters; and above all, the urgent necessity to address the causes of climate change and mitigate its consequences.

Our common European institutions must be adequate and sufficient to enable the restoration and protection of social cohesion. This is not simply a matter of the 'social dimension' of the Union being addressed by the recasting of those existing directives relating to the social *acquis*, as important as they may be. Restoring social cohesion requires something far more searching: nothing less than a critical examination of the institutional framework of economic and monetary union, of the assumptions on which both operate, and of the manner in which we understand globalization, by which I mean, *inter alia*, the liberalization of capital and goods markets, and the consequential rise of the economic and largely non-transparent power and authority of the multinational corporation. Neglecting this critique, advocating for 'business as usual', while failing to take on these challenges is to allow this century to emerge as an authoritarian one, one in which the opposing extremes in the European Street will come not from any mediating institutions already weakened, often denied support. In the atmosphere of a single version of economic theory many of the mediating institutions have been damaged, often, and unfairly, presented as part of the colluding apparatus of an imposed austerity.

There is nothing inevitable in any of this. We should have by now not only rejected the hubristic and fallacious prognostications of such as Professor Fukuyama.[2] There is an alternative vision available to be offered for an emancipatory rights-based European international vision. It is in our heritage. There is a scholarship and a practice that sustains such an option.

For example, one of the most morally compelling visions of European internationalism – considered by the European institutions as one of the founding documents of European integration – emerged from the Italian resistance movement, in that remarkable manifesto composed in 1941 on the island of

Ventotene by Altiero Spinelli, a member of the Italian Communist Party, and Ernesto Rossi, one of the founders of the anti-fascist Giustizia e Libertà. The *Ventotene Manifesto*, in its emphasis on the peopled economy, the shared prospect of humanity, composed in captivity as it was, is remarkable for containing a demand for a federation of European states dedicated to disarming the worst passions of European nationalisms. These demands were not modest, and they required – in the eyes of the authors of the manifesto – the social regulation of private property, the nationalization of utilities, an egalitarian distribution of both urban and rural land, equality of educational opportunities, and the displacement of charity by the provision of 'food, lodging, clothing and that minimum of comfort needed to preserve a sense of human dignity'. The home of the European Parliament, which gives democratic voice to the emerging European *demos*, is now named after Altiero Spinelli.

Let us not forget that the democratic nation states, which emerged after World War II in western Europe, were influenced by those who had led the Resistance. The constitutions adapted at the end of World War II contained social and economic rights, which were given a material reality through the construction of national welfare states. These constitutional initiatives represented distinctive national traditions, reflecting historical contingency, dependency, structure and agency. They were not merely idealistic. They were pragmatic in the best sense and they sought support – and got it – in the European Street. Neither were they in any technical sense, because of this, perceived as lesser.

In fact, their proposals had an empirically-based scholarship as sources of policy. The British Labour Government of 1945–51 pursued its 'New Jerusalem' – something Harold Laski called a 'revolution by consent'[3] – through a commitment to full employment, nationalization of major industries, the construction of the National Health Service, and the reform and strict control of the financial sector. The French Fourth Republic created a technical public body composed of economists, le Commissariat général du Plan, to coordinate and plan (on an indicative basis) the post-war economy. In Germany, the post-war Federal Government was heavily influenced by the economic philosophy of 'ordoliberalism', first promulgated by leading economists in the 1920s, which envisioned the role of the state as the creator and regulator of the competitive market economy. The origin of the term 'social-market economy' can be found in the writings of Alfred Müller-Armack,[4] though the Germany which developed may have been somewhat more social than the ordoliberals were comfortable with, and Germany's corporatist model reflected the traditions and strengths of Europe's most powerful and influential labour and trade movement. Taken together, while they did not reflect all of the most fervent hopes of the leading elements of the wartime anti-fascist movement (particularly its communist and socialist components), these developments did reflect a post-war mind of Europe that recognized a role for the state, and they constituted a great advance in the recognition of social rights and of the responsibility of the democratic state to regulate, govern and manage the economy in the interests of all the people.

I have outlined these admittedly stylized and necessarily exaggerated portraits – even while omitting four of the original six, the social democracies of Northern Europe, the nations of the Communist Bloc, the Iberian countries then under the rule of dictators, and of course the Irish state – to provide an illustration of the diversity of institutions in the leading industrial countries in post-war Europe.

Students of comparative political economy and comparative social policy will be very aware of the construction of typologies of European states by reference to a constellation of historically determined economic, social and political arrangements. For example, the political economists Peter Hall and David Soskice have used the term 'varieties of capitalism'[5] to refer to analytically distinct models of capitalism, while the Danish sociologist Gøsta Esping-Andersen identified, in his 1990 work *The Three Worlds of Welfare Capitalism*, three distinct welfare regimes.[6] While there is an argument that all states can be shown to have begun, under the influence of a hegemonic economic discourse, to converge towards a turbocharged version of the liberal model, we can still identify strikingly different economic and social institutions whether in the labour market, in the financing and ownership of, and relations between firms, or in the degree to which states meet the most basic needs of their citizens.

Scholars of comparative economic and social institutions can of course construct any number of typologies to classify and compare nation states, and the Member States of the European Union. What matters now is whether the project of European integration is capable of drawing, or willing to draw, on this diverse array of institutions, and in its project of integration be sustained and enhanced by recognizing diversity, and whether such an integration can meet the demand for social justice and social cohesion. There is a nightmare possibility – that diversity will not be taken into account, that the adjustment to an un-empirically tested market without the need for popular assent will prevail. Asserting that diversity has been recognized will not be sufficient. The European Street will seek evidence in their lives that it has.

The demand for social cohesion was, we should not forget, recognized at the beginning of the Union. The institutional origins of the Union lie in the Schuman Declaration, given legal form through the Treaty of Paris, which established the European Coal and Steel Community. The Coal and Steel Community contained the embryonic components of the future Europe: a technocratic executive in the form of a High Authority; a parliamentary assembly; a court of justice; a council of national ministers; and a common regulated market in coal and steel. That Community reflected a *mélange* of the social-market and *dirigisme* models: the High Authority had significant powers to fund and direct investments yet it was also committed to combating excess concentrations or abuse of dominant market positions. The latter is now, of course, a battle lost and we are left with flimsy rationalizations of its inevitability and its occasional hubristic flourishes as to its ultimate universal benefit. This is an ideological position that eschews empirical test.

Though one would not say the early institutional forms of the European Union were infused with the spirit of Ventotene, it was significant that the High Authority of the Coal and Steel Community was empowered to direct enterprises to raise wages, to instruct states to compensate workers for wage reductions, and to direct financial aid to offset the negative effects of technological advances in the industry on the workforce, including programmes of early retirement, transitional allowances, mobility grants and retraining. Let us recall, too, that these features were felt to be required to give the Community legitimacy in the eyes of the workers, particularly those German workers in the Rhineland who would be most directly affected by a shared approach to coal and steel. The Social Democratic Party of Germany, refounded in 1946

V. The Future of the European Union

on the principle of 'a socialist Germany in a socialist Europe', was profoundly suspicious of any project of European integration led by its domestic opponents. Its leader, Kurt Schumacher, feared what he saw as a Europe constructed on the foundations of, in his words, 'capitalism, clericalism, conservatism, cartels'. Schumacher, a politician of immense moral courage – imprisoned in Buchenwald by the Nazis for ten years – was an early exemplar of the truth that one can be a passionate advocate of European unity, and at the same time be a trenchant critic and opponent of defective institutional design, and the absence of ethical intent in the specific projects of union.

When the European Economic Community was formed in 1957, it took the form of a political commitment to create a common market. In retrospect, of course, all things can take on the appearance of inevitability, but we should recall that for Jean Monnet, the intellectual architect of the Coal and Steel Community, the common market was a scheme considered too vague and – to a man who was, after all, the leading technician within le Commissariat général du Plan – too economically liberal to succeed in ensuring European integration. In 1955 Jean Monnet posed the question: 'Is it possible to have a Common Market without federal social, monetary and macro-economic policies?'[7]

As to the first point, that of a common social policy – and I here would concur with Perry Anderson that it is of no small significance that social considerations came first in Jean Monnet's thinking – the International Labour Organization was asked to appoint a group of independent experts, led by the Swedish economist Bert Ohlin, to prepare a report on the social effects of closer European cooperation. There was a considerable fear, recognized in the 1956 Ohlin Report, that a reduction in tariffs, and the gradual movement towards a tariff-free common customs area, when combined with the free movement of capital, would lead to an agglomeration of investment in existing centres of industry, to the disadvantage of those countries with higher social and labour standards, and that those countries would find it hard to raise such standards. In a word, many saw the danger of the existing social floor, so hard-fought for in the six, becoming a social ceiling.

The Ohlin Report recommended provisions for the free movement of labour, equivalence between paid holiday schemes and the principle of equal pay for men and women be included in the treaties. The enumeration of a requirement of equal pay for equal work (now Articles 157 and 158 of the Treaty on the Functioning of the European Union) reflected the social provisions of the constitution of the French Fourth Republic. They themselves were adaptations of the great legislative victories of the Popular Front in France in the 1930s – and would prove to be of immense importance in this country when Ireland acceded to the European Economic Community. One of my predecessors in the presidency, Dr Patrick Hillery, as the first European Commissioner appointed by Ireland, ensured that these treaty obligations were reflected in a directive, and furthermore courageously refused to grant Ireland a derogation from its provisions despite significant pressure to do so.

The Ohlin Report reflected the assumptions of what we might now call the Bretton Woods era, that period between 1945 and 1973 in which the international policy regime for capital and finance dramatically suppressed, restricted and regulated the role of the financial markets in allocating resources through the control of capital movements, state ownership of banks and other market interventions. The international monetary system revolved around a system of fixed but flexible currencies pegged to the dollar, which acted as the anchor and international reserve currency. This era has been termed one of 'embedded liberalism', in which governments were enabled to pursue domestic policy goals such as full employment and the building of the welfare state. When faced by balance of payments crises governments could restrict capital mobility or adjust their exchange rates, rather than reducing government expenditure.

In this context, Ohlin and his colleagues assumed that members of the Common Market would use the traditional Bretton Woods policies at their disposal to protect their desired social and labour standards. We should also recall that the Member States had retained a large degree of autonomy under the *acquis*, at least before the Single European Act, that enabled them to intervene in their own economies. Social Europe was not then deemed to be in danger, or even something that was necessary to articulate in 1957. It was generally believed that domestic autonomy would be protected, and that social policy did not need to be Europeanized to be enhanced. It was not until a summit in Paris in April 1972 that the social objectives of the Community were recognized as being as important as its economic objectives and it is

V. The Future of the European Union

from them that the term 'Social Europe' first became widespread. The resultant Social Action Programme of 1974 in many respects bears the hallmark, and carries the spirit of the student and worker protests of '68. It represents what, in retrospect, appears to be a high point of ambition, both in terms of its analytic content and its programmatic intent. If I may quote from the second paragraph of the programme submitted by the then Commission to the Council:

> There are continuing, and in some cases worsening, problems over the distribution of income and wealth within the Community, and over worker participation within industry. There are problems caused by the failure of the infrastructure in some sectors to keep pace with the demands on it. And then there are the problems caused by growth itself – problems of industrial pollution, of a deteriorating environment, of a conflict of values in some cases between industry and society, disruptions to the pattern of life, and a growing dependence on migrant workers whom society is not always ready to accept as citizens while it continues to require their services to maintain its standard of living.[8]

May I suggest that such an analysis is now, unfortunately, more apposite than ever. The solutions proposed were nothing less than a harmonization of labour standards, worker participation and industrial democracy towards the highest level then extant in the Community, which at that time meant West German standards, and the preparation of the directive on equal pay between men and women, to which I have already alluded. Can we imagine the European Commission of today making such proposals and in such terms? May we anticipate it as an agreed statement from Davos?

Jean Monnet, reflecting in 1978 on the events of '68 in France, and of the brief alliance of radical students and workers, wrote that, 'the cause for which they had fought still remained: it was the cause of humanity. And I believe that we have still not adequately responded, either before or after that salutary warning.' Can we imagine a *fonctionnaire* of that stature today speaking with such acuity and with such sympathy with the European Street? Our times are reflective, I suggest, of a lost discourse. A vacuum has emerged that must be filled by public discourse, a vacuum that cannot be met by competing rationalizations from the silos of the European institutions.

Giving the European Union a Future That Will Engage Citizens: A Shared Challenge

That very moment – when social Europe was proposed as a solution to many of the challenges with which we still struggle today, and which, may I suggest, have grown in severity to this day – coincided with the beginning of a radical shift in the manner in which the relationship between the economy and society was understood, or construed, with implication for the role of the state. I am speaking, of course, of the ideology that dares not speak its name, that political theory of economic governance known as neo-liberalism. We know its structures all too well – the market, neo-liberals suggested, could and should allocate resources. The pursuit of private profit was suggested as being more efficient than public provision for public purposes. The laws of the market – though drafted and enforced by the state – now carried the new logic and were elevated to the status of immutable and unchangeable laws of nature.

It would be a mistake, may I suggest, to read the Treaty of Rome as a *sui generis* legal text, devoid of institutional and social context, and to imply that it was a neo-liberal charter. That would be to ignore the context I have outlined. The collapse of the Bretton Woods regime in the 1970s and the transition to an international monetary system based on international capital mobility and financial deregulation in the 1980s significantly undermined the capacity of states to rely on such mechanisms as were identified in the Ohlin Report. I believe it is important for us, if we wish to be authentic in our discourse, to recognize that this was a policy choice – reflective of new intellectual and above all political orientations – on the part of states and international institutions. Institutions, just like political parties, have an identifiable intellectual history, even with the best of rhetorical cover.

'Globalization' – and here I refer specifically to the liberalization of finance and capital markets – is far too often spoken of as if it is some kind of phenomenon that is external to the political process, one which cannot be managed. International cooperation to manage such flows has been painfully slow to develop, and in truth a *laissez-faire* philosophy still prevails. As a result, a significant minority of capital accumulators have benefited. From such lassitude it is publics who have been the losers.

Within the European Economic Community, the response to the monetary instability of the 1970s was a suspension of plans for economic and monetary union. Instead, a number of attempts were made to establish an

V. The Future of the European Union

intra-European fixed currency regime, the most durable of which proved to be the European Monetary System. A commitment to maintain fixed rates within a narrow band without frequent revaluations within the Monetary System required, for some countries, policies that constituted the abandonment of full employment as a policy. Monetary policy, a key part of the Bretton Woods policy mix, was subordinated to the necessity to retain fixed rates. A more advanced form of monetary cooperation was considered desirable following the Single European Act, which advanced the completion of the internal market and provided for the removal of all capital controls by 1990. Tommaso Padoa-Schioppa, one of the architects of monetary union, has argued that this capital liberalization within the Community inevitably led to monetary union itself. It was Padoa-Schioppa who used the phrase the 'inconsistent quartet' to refer to the impossibility of simultaneously pursuing free trade, free capital mobility, fixed exchange rates and an autonomous national monetary policy.[9]

By the late 1980s a political commitment to the internal market required free trade and free capital mobility, while the functioning of the common agricultural price level of the EEC's Common Agricultural Policy required stable exchange rates. The creation of a shared currency governed by a single monetary policy under the influence of all Member States was then, unsurprisingly, a preferred option for most Member States, rather than the maintenance of a fixed exchange-rate regime, fidelity to which would determine each state's monetary policy.

This familiar sequencing of integration was not inevitable. In the late 1960s the six members of the European Economic Community had advanced plans to create an economic and monetary union, which would have facilitated the removal of capital controls and further liberalization of trade. I refer to the Werner Plan, presented to the Council and the Commission in 1970, which seems out of time when compared to the European Monetary System and the monetary union many of the Member States of the European Union are members of today. Let me make two observations: first, the Werner Plan envisioned a 'centre of economic decision-making', answerable to a European Parliament elected by universal suffrage, responsible for coordinating national budgets and utilizing both fiscal deficits and surpluses to maintain, amongst other objectives, full employment; and second, that the proposed 'centre of economic decision-making' and the proposed community system of central banks should pursue the same economic objectives. We might speculate how differently such a version of institutions or their role, being underpinned by such different assumptions, might approach the economic policy of the European Union today.

Instead of such a set of proposals as the Werner Plan might suggest, economic and monetary union has followed those precepts agreed at Maastricht: an independent central bank, which is solely devoted to achieving price stability and national fiscal policies constrained by the Growth and Stability Pact and now by the Fiscal Stability Treaty. The agreement of the Fiscal Compact, that which many have seen as a quasi-constitutionalism of anti-Keynesian macroeconomic policy, and the administrative schema which complements it – the European Semester, the Macroeconomic Imbalance Procedure, the renewed Stability and Growth Pact and so on – have embedded another level of economic coordination. For many of us – and I do not just speak of those whose political careers have been spent on the left, for I think there may be some sympathy within the European institutions for a similar view – the recommendations directed to countries in the European Semester reflect a partial, limited, and very particular view of economic and social policy, whether it be in the demand for flexible labour-market policies or neo-liberal reforms of social protection, all of course advanced under the rubric of 'structural adjustment'.

From the European Street it might be asked where are we to discuss – see justified and empirically tested – the assumptions that are made in those 'structural adjustment' proposals, or the bases for the calculated possible outcomes in relation to economic growth or efficiency, not to speak of social consequences or further loss of cohesion. The five presidents have suggested, as part of their prospectus for an Economic Union, a stronger focus on employment and social protection as part of the Semester process. Will that be accompanied by a willingness to debate and dispute fundamental assumptions of what constitutes an 'efficient' economic model, on the part of both the Commission and Council members? How is this to be made fit with movements for a European Union of the future that seeks to build a movement for reform from below?

V. The Future of the European Union

The interpretation of the *acquis communautaire* by the Court of Justice of the European Union has also developed on a very particular trajectory since the mid-1970s, and that direction has had troubling implications for Member States' domestic commitments to social and labour law. As Fritz Scharpf and others[10] have so convincingly detailed, integration has occurred through case-law and between the Luxembourg Compromise of 1966 and the re-emergence of qualified majority voting in the late 1980s. In early landmark judgments, the European Court of Justice declared that it saw itself as being at the centre of a new supranational legal order and through the doctrines of the supremacy and direct effect of European Union law became a key driver of integration. The construction of this legal order took place through the referral of cases by national courts to the Court of Justice. By its nature, this form of integration was negative, taking the form of the striking down of what were considered barriers to the free movement of goods, services, capital and workers.

While there may have been disquiet regarding the closing of the scope for Member States to regulate business on grounds that it violates the 'rules of the market' embedded in the treaties, few expected that the Court of Justice would elevate those economic freedoms above what we consider fundamental rights, such as the right to strike. Yet, for example, the so-called Laval quartet of cases in the late 2000s raised the prospect that the court would do just that, and it has. Furthermore, they raised the prospect that the social *acquis* would operate as a ceiling, rather than a floor. These judgments were reached before the incorporation of the Charter of Fundamental Rights into the *acquis*, and I hope – as I know that many of us who advocated for the Treaty of Lisbon in this country do – that the charter will have an appreciative effect on judicial reasoning when fundamental rights seem to conflict with the economic freedoms. History would not suggest that we can be optimistic.

However, may I suggest that these judgments reflect the confluence of a number of very specific logics: first, that the treaties reflect, above all, a European Economic Constitution, which establishes a framework for a very specific model of the market economy; second, the continuing influence of neo-liberal philosophy; and finally, that until social and labour rights are categorically given the same priority – if not a higher one – as economic freedoms in the treaties, the latter will prevail. These issues must be clarified by public debate and through engagement with the European Street.

This latter point – the delicate balance between the economy and society – was implicit in the work of the Commission in the 1980s. The Single European Act was above all, as the legal scholar Christian Joerges has suggested,[11] a project of integration through market building: it represented a re-regulation of an expanded new market, as evidenced by European legislation on consumer protection, health and safety, and protection of the environment. The President of the Commission, Jacques Delors, as we know so well, recognized that the creation of this new market demanded a form of regulation at least equal in scope and effect. Yet we also know that his vision was not fulfilled, and that the social chapter, as welcome and hard-fought as it was, has proved inadequate. Indeed, in this time of declining trade-union membership, the voice of the representatives of labour has never seemed weaker.

We have not yet reckoned with the consequences of the profound collision of the social and the economic represented by the Single European Act and the Maastricht Treaty. National social policies, and national economic policies designed to ensure social protection, must now comply with the exigencies and demands of an internal market whose intrinsic logic is ever more informed by neo-liberalism. The traditional policies of the Bretton Woods era are no longer possible within the confines of economic and monetary union. Yes, the Treaty of Amsterdam was a very welcome, if partial, attempt to regulate this new European market and to coordinate the action of Member States through the inclusion of the Employment Charter, and yes, the Treaty of Lisbon, by enumerating the values and objectives of the Union and settling the question of whether the Charter of Fundamental Rights was part of the *acquis*, represented an advance.

The five presidents have suggested that economic and monetary union will ultimately lead to a banking, fiscal and political union. As the political negotiations on the shape of the banking union – most importantly of course the future financing of the Single Resolution Fund for failed banks – are ongoing, I do not wish to comment directly on that issue. I do, however, wish to suggest that the European Street will not give their consent to the creation of what they correctly see as an enduring austerity union. The internal market cannot be the *ne plus ultra* of the European legal order – we must recall that for the European Street, indeed for all democrats in the Union, the laws of the market are seen as, and must be experienced as, instrumental and not intrinsic.

The economy, as the *Ventotene Manifesto* reminds us, must be subordinated and subject to the democratic will of the people. I have spoken of the diversity of our economic and social models in Europe: let us take, I suggest, this observed diversity not as a negative, but as a medley of opportunities, which we should celebrate and from which we should extract the very best materials for the future. I do not wish to be too prescriptive on the kind of institutional change required in the coming years but let me suggest a number of questions that I see as crucial: can the macroeconomic framework of the European Union sanction and protect a diversity of models, both in terms of welfare states and alternative models of capitalism? Can the formulation of monetary policy be accommodative of such difference? Can the rules of the internal market yield where they can and surrender when they must to the demands of the dignity of labour?

May I suggest that to the European Street the very project of European integration at its best was and is itself instrumental, as post-war Europeans were invited only to vindicate those values and objectives for which the Union came into existence and to which, indeed, it is now constitutionally committed, even if they are contradicted by social outcomes. They supported European Union values, which they saw as necessary and which, above all, could bring an end to centuries of internecine war and imperial domination. Rosa Luxemburg once stated that the foundation of socialism must be 'not European solidarity, but international solidarity, embracing every region, race and people on Earth [...] Every partial solidarity is not a stage towards the realization of genuine internationality, but its opposite, its enemy, an ambiguity under which lurks the cloven hoof of national antagonism.'[12]

World War I should have taught us that peace does not rest on common markets or globalization: that war occurred at a high point of the interconnection of free capital and goods markets. No, peace depends on a shared commitment to one another, on our capacity for compassion, empathy and sympathy, and to institutions that do not divide or harm society, but rather institutions that unite and protect it.

Let us therefore, in the European Union, lift our gaze to encompass the needs of all humanity, all of their history, their possible futures, and let us do so with recognition of all of our cultural diversity. After all, the challenges which will test the European Union in this century – climate change, global migration, the future of work – are common to us all on our fragile and shared planet. Our best aspirations, our sustainable future, can only be met by restoring social cohesion and promoting social justice within our institutions here at home, within the institutions of the European Union, and within our global institutions. Our horizons must be limitless, for we, all of us, owe each other an imprescriptible moral duty. We need a new mind for our times, a mind informed by hope rather than fear, not only for Europe but for humanity itself on our shared and vulnerable planet.

The Future of Europe: Re-Balancing Ecology, Economics and Ethics

Speech at the University of Leipzig, 4 July 2019.

All good universities share a commitment to learning, to building from past achievements into future thinking. Many boast of grand halls and prestigious, historic buildings. Few, however, have the courage and vision to create a space such as this Paulinum.[13] It is a magnificent achievement, and I salute the university, the city and the state of Saxony for creating this space, which so harmoniously marries the ancient and the modern, the religious and the secular.

I am told that in his Leipzig years, the great composer Johann Sebastian Bach – with his respect for the long reach of time and with a concern for what might endure and be universal – lost interest in preparing new music for the then Paulinum Church, which stood on this site, one of four churches for which he was responsible. He was frustrated, we are told, by the fact that the city would not make more resources available to him. I certainly appreciate Bach's lament! However, I am sure that the gifted composer himself would approve of this space.

As evidenced by the Paulinum, creating the new in the shadow of the past, building for the future while recognizing all that has gone before, and using the materials available in present time, is a challenge well known and well understood in Leipzig. An ethical engagement with the past in all its complexity is an unavoidable moral, but, I believe, enabling task, which allows the light to illuminate the present, enables us to see the imagined forms of what could be better, and invites us to a more harmonious existence, helps surely in seeking a future of fulfilment. This is an issue that I, as President of Ireland, have sought to address on several occasions in the past. It is an ongoing challenge for all of us as citizens, and must also be an issue that is properly addressed and given due consideration by Member States, and indeed with the European Union itself, in the unfolding architecture of its institutions, asking of their relationship to their aspirations and concerns, how decisions echo, fail to echo, or are dissonant on the European Street.

I have visited Leipzig in the past and am aware of its cultural heritage. The city of Leipzig has played a significant role, not only in German history but also in European history. This visit I make today is the first ever state or official visit by an Irish president to Saxony, or indeed anywhere in the eastern part of Germany other than Berlin. I truly hope that my visit will initiate a renewed and deeper relationship both with you and with your neighbouring states. My visit, as President of Ireland, reflects Ireland's commitment to the deepening and widening of the Irish presence throughout Germany. Our wish is to forge new friendships.

May I acknowledge, too, the special role of this university in promoting and protecting minority languages. I know that this is an important seat of Sorbian studies, and I am delighted that it has also become a centre for the study of the Irish language in Germany. Our individual languages enrich the tapestry of European life, each in their own unique manner. We have a duty of care to them that is intergenerational, ensuring that they remain alive and vibrant for future generations. That we have the Irish language in use and on the curriculum today is due to the assistance given by a number of German scholars to Dr Douglas de Híde, among whom was Dr Kuno Meyer, who died in Leipzig in 1919. May I acknowledge Professor Sabine Asmus and her students who are with us today for all their efforts in this regard. Gabhaim buíochas libh agus treaslaím libh as bhur n-iarrachtaí.[14]

I am honoured also that [...] I will have the opportunity to visit the St Nicholas Church and pay tribute to the courage of those civilian protestors

V. The Future of the European Union

thirty years ago, whose courage and determination paved the way for what would become a seismic geopolitical shift across our continent, with their peaceful actions leading to the reunification of Germany and to a new era of partnership in Europe. Now, once again, we are at a significant moment in the European Union. We are called upon in the face of new challenges, some within, others external. We are challenged to renew our commitment to be together as a union, to embrace an adequate discourse on the changes we urgently need to make, changes that will require courage if we are to defend the space of intellectual rigour, allow freedom of discourse, allow policy change. [...]

May I suggest some radical changes we need to make in our thinking and our policies. It is my belief that there is an urgent need to make new connections between ecology, economics and ethics, and not only for the sake of the European Union, but for the sake of our shared fragile planet, that we must seek to forge a new path on which we can travel together in the interests of all our citizens. My critique and proposals go beyond adjustment, or the mere placing of an ecological or humanitarian lens on existing public policies or even on existing economic development paradigms. Such an exercise has been tried, given rhetorical expression, and has not succeeded. No authentic structuring of such an approach, by way of delivery, has happened or has been experienced in the formal or institutional discourse, and most importantly it has not found its way to the European Street where trust in words and actions needs urgently to be recovered to achieve a convincing authenticity of policy. We have, as a global community, to respond to the consequences of climate change, the need to achieve sustainability, to achieve a radical shift to a new economic paradigm in a decarbonized world. An eco-social political-economy perspective is required to achieve what we may have agreed as principles.

As I am speaking in a university, may I stress that the required paradigm shift needs a space of epistemological freedom in our institutes of learning, by which I mean staff and students being allowed to think, university teachers given freedom to teach at least pluralistically, and fundamentally, free to critique a current orthodox capitalist system that is unregulated and unaccountable in its consequences for society and social policy. Change is not possible if its outline is not allowed to be considered in a deliberative way and its principles taught. However, necessary change is being resisted by a combination of those frightened, rendered mute or stricken with intellectual lethargy, by wielders of corporate power, opponents of state regulation, and a minority of citizens who are happy to have gained access to an ever more insatiable accumulation process.

The scale of the change that is required is, to my mind, similar to that which occurred in the late 1980s and early 1990s in Central and Eastern Europe, an invocation of a moral future of peace similar perhaps in scale, scope and significance to that advocated in the *Ventotene Manifesto* in its day by Altiero Spinelli and Ernesto Rossi. That statement, written by Altiero Spinelli and Ernesto Rossi in 1941, became the programme of the (Italian-based) European Federalist Movement. Its extraordinary vision spoke of human needs and purpose beyond borders: it had, as its core objective, the creation of a solid international state. European Federalism and World Federalism are presented in the *Ventotene Manifesto* as a means to prevent future wars. The manifesto is widely regarded as the birth of European federalism.

Then too, in its turn, the much-quoted Schuman Declaration reminded us that 'Europe will not be made all at once, or according to a single plan.' I am well aware that there is a tendency among some of the dispirited to look with nostalgia at such statements and recall the days of the pioneers of the European Union: Robert Schuman, Konrad Adenauer, Jean Monnet and others, as moments of inspiration when such suggested new ideas could catch the mood and became a reality. Yes, it is important to recall how they came together to share a purpose that was drawn from and transcends a diversity of interests and sought to plant the seeds for peaceful cooperation and political union. However, we need to consider nostalgia with care. Nostalgia is often our response when we feel inadequate in the face of new challenges; a prelude to a confession of failure or desperation, thinking we might, in the absence of any perceived or earned hope from present intellectual work, deal with the future by reaching back into the past, as though the tools of yesterday might equip us for the needs of tomorrow. The onus is on each generation to invent, even to re-invent, the tools for its analysis and existence in the complexity of its time. That is one of the achievements of Jürgen Habermas as he breaks away from the pessimism that could be seen in Theodor W. Adorno's work.

V. The Future of the European Union

We are neither at the end of history nor of ideas. That was a hubristic construct of Francis Fukuyama[15] scandalously shared by too many, and insufficiently withdrawn. There is a further danger, of course, of our present being imparted with a rationalization, by a distorted or limited vision of the past; in other words, origins that were mixed in motivational terms. However one looks at such texts as the Schuman Declaration, they stand as examples as well as a challenge to all future generations to anticipate and adapt to changing circumstances and to meet new demands, as needed. Our challenges now must draw forth a shared perspective because of our interdependency, an interdependency that goes beyond issues of trade. They are shared challenges requiring a shared response that goes beyond borders. Resiling to any narrow view of nationalism speaks, not as it may have in the past, of a nation's demand of freedom for its people, but rather, now, often in desperation as a defence of narrow interests. Interests that facilitate inequality and the unrestrained accumulation by the few at the cost of the many.

Nor in international relations can we accept the rhetoric or indeed renewed preparations for war between the most heavily armed as a substitute for engaged and authoritative diplomacy. Sustaining peace, achieving peace, is why the United Nations was formed. Like Germany, Ireland is a staunch supporter of the United Nations, and membership of the UN has played an important role in our development. Both of us, through the United Nations, not only support a fair, rules-based order in international affairs; we exist, survive and prosper because of it. Together, in peacekeeping, disarmament, sustainable development, climate, nutrition, human rights and humanitarian assistance, we have striven to match our words with actions and funding, offering support to multilateral structures. While the UN system has flaws, Ireland and Germany share a conviction that there is no better way to meaningfully address the common opportunities and threats that face us. It is our best available space and we must defend and support it.

I chose to come to Leipzig to present these ideas because I firmly believe that the task of envisioning, of renewing Europe, of future-proofing the Union, cannot take place exclusively in meetings organized in the capitals of Member States. There must be a European conversation that is widely diverse and inclusive, and it must be supported by those institutions and citizens given the privileged space of intellectual work. Europe is not in any exclusive way a union of capital cities, but of all the people in our cities, towns, villages and rural hinterlands. Between our peoples we may have achieved a capacity to communicate, but in current conditions it is an individualized, privatized experience of communication, often ephemeral, trivial, one that cannot replace the previous and now fragile shared world of public-service broadcasting, pluralism in media, public speech in the *agora*. We are made to discuss our present circumstance and possible shared futures in these new conditions, but we should not be pessimistic. We have a resource that we share, a respect for intellectual work and in addition to the benefits of reason, the music of the heart. Germany and Ireland's sharing of a respect for ideas is as important as sharing innovation and trade, and they go together. What better place to discuss the future of Europe than in Leipzig, where the great German poet Friedrich Schiller first composed his wonderful lyric 'Ode To Joy',[16] a version of some of his words put to music by Beethoven for the fourth movement of his masterful Ninth Symphony, that beautiful, rousing expression of musical brilliance, which was adopted as the anthem of our shared European Union.

Drawing on that spirit, may I suggest a fundamental reflection on what is meant when we use in our discourse the words 'Europe' and 'European'. Are we merely talking about the geographical coordinates of the continent and peripheral island states that comprise Europe as it is known in its physical sense? Are we talking of a block of consumers, or a trade bloc? How often, when we speak of a European Union, are we speaking of a social Europe? In other words, what does it mean to those of us living now, and to generations yet to live in what we call a union, to be 'European' in the early twenty-first century? What set of shared values and ethics do we, as Europeans, aspire to uphold, defend, build upon and promote across our Member States and indeed out into the world?

Despite the many historic achievements of our continent, many centuries of which were tarnished by war and suffering, the European Union today still retains – through its legacy of thought, its commitment to intellectual discourse, its openness to undo the trammels of Empire and struggle against imperialism – a unique opportunity and responsibility to assert and, where

V. The Future of the European Union

necessary, reassert, its founding values of democracy, cohesion, shared prospects, human rights and the rule of law in an increasingly interdependent world in which those values are challenged. These values are neither abstract, nor are they optional extras, nor are they confined by borders. They go to our very core and should be respected and upheld by all Member States. Central to these values and their vindication is the concept and circumstance of free movement of people, exercising their hopes, bringing with them their stories and their cultural endowments. Indeed, migration, inwards and outwards, has been a key aspect of European history for centuries. Migration was taking place long before the origins of the Common Market and the European Economic Community. Migration, inwards and outwards, has shaped who we are as Europeans – our influences, our values, our sensibilities; indeed, it has been part of the basis of our prosperity.

However, this prosperity, fuelled by assumptions of unlimited ever-accelerated growth and of an infinite source or resources, cannot avoid the consequences it has helped occasion, including the impact of climate change. It is instructive perhaps to stand back and look at the features of the period that has had such an impact on our planet and ourselves. The Anthropocene era in which we now live has created a new set of existential challenges that threaten humankind's survival on the planet. If we consider the onset of the most recent consequences of the Anthropocene to have commenced at the start of the Industrial Revolution, sometime in the 1760s, we can trace how this period was the genesis of a cycle of events that has resulted in the ecological crisis we now face. The Industrial Revolution, which began in Great Britain, resulted in that country controlling a global trading empire with colonies in North America and the Caribbean, and with political influence on the Indian subcontinent. The development of trade and the rise of commerce were among the major contributors to the Industrial Revolution. It marks a major turning point in history: almost every aspect of daily life was influenced in some way. In particular, average income and population began to exhibit unprecedented and sustained growth. It is in this period, too, that we see the rise of the industrial city, such as Manchester. Every aspect of life was changed, not just the connection between home and work. Time and space were redefined, colonized, as Michel Foucault might have put it.

The Industrial Revolution in continental Europe came a little later than in Great Britain. Based on its leadership in chemical research in the universities and industrial laboratories, Germany, which was unified in 1871, became dominant in the world's chemical industry in the late nineteenth century. The focus in Germany was the support of industrialization, and so heavy lines criss-crossed the Ruhr and other industrial districts, providing good connections to the major ports of Hamburg and Bremen.

Why did the Industrial Revolution originate in Europe? Economic historian Joel Mokyr has argued that political fragmentation (the presence of a large number of European states) made it possible for heterodox ideas to thrive, as entrepreneurs, innovators, ideologues and heretics could easily flee to a neighbouring state in the event that any one state would try to suppress their ideas and activities. This flux is what set Europe apart from the technologically advanced, large unitary empires such as China and India: providing, through such migration, innovation and renewal of intellect, insatiable curiosity and *technos*, served as 'an insurance against economic and technological stagnation' as Mokyr puts it.[17] China had both a printing press and movable type, and India had similar levels of scientific and technological achievement to Europe in 1700, yet the Industrial Revolution would occur in Europe, not China or India. In Europe, political fragmentation was coupled with 'an integrated market for ideas' where Europe's intellectuals used the *lingua franca* of Latin, had a shared intellectual basis in Europe's classical heritage and the pan-European institution of the Republic of Letters.

Historian Peter Stearns has suggested that 'Europe's Industrial Revolution stemmed in great part from Europe's ability to draw disproportionately on world resources'.[18] The new world of industry was inextricably linked to colonization, empire domination and an ideology that saw certain differences of culture as, at best, backwardness. It would be a great error, surely, to fail to take account of the immense body of philosophical work which was appearing in print.

I must leave to another occasion the combination of dispossession, conquest, exploitation, domination and cultural extinction that made this possible. The consequences of this acquisition and exploitation of resources, of course, are now all too apparent, as we see the ecological and social impacts of the exploitation of the world's finite natural endowments.

V. The Future of the European Union

Just as there were a few Enlightenment voices against empires – for example Denis Diderot, Immanuel Kant and Johann Gottfried Herder – there were dissenting voices during this period that are usually presented as being 'mostly from the arts'. During the Industrial Revolution an intellectual and artistic hostility towards the new industrialization developed, associated with the Romantic Movement. Its critique was of what was emerging as a version of what life was to be, rather than what it might be, a life that included the search for beauty in form, and a beauty to be celebrated in nature and rural intimacies. Romanticism privileged the traditionalism of rural life and recoiled against the upheavals caused by industrialization, urbanization and the wretchedness of the working classes. Its major exponents in English included the artist and poet William Blake and poets William Wordsworth, John Keats, Lord Byron and Percy Bysshe Shelley. The movement stressed the importance of nature in art and language, in contrast to 'monstrous' machines and factories; the 'dark satanic mills' of Blake's poem 'And Did Those Feet in Ancient Time'. Mary Shelley's novel *Frankenstein* reflected concerns that scientific progress might be double-edged. French Romanticism, likewise, was highly critical of industry. In a later period, it would move further from a realism of rural existence towards an anti-urban myth of an idealized rural existence, creating what Raymond Williams called a 'false pastoral'.[19] In its most reactionary form, it would be used to fuel an anti-urban ideology. As Josiah Strong put it, 'God created man in a garden. The city is a result of The Fall.'[20]

It is interesting that in the current debate on the future of the European Union, the resource of those ideas that are available in literary imagination, culture in general, are rarely articulated, even recognized, a neglect for which the Union has paid a heavy price. Ideas matter. For example, it would be impossible to teach social or political theory and its connection to economics and policy without reference to the Frankfurt School in all its periods.[21] Its scholars have produced some of our best critiques of economy, self and society.

As Empires were formed and bolstered during the Industrial Revolution, Europe then witnessed the rise of nationalism. In the nineteenth century, a wave of romantic nationalism swept the European continent, transforming its countries and its peoples. The invention of a symbolic national identity became the concern of racial, ethnic or linguistic groups throughout Europe as they struggled to come to terms with the rise of mass politics, the decline of the traditional and, most often, exploitative, social elites, popular discrimination and xenophobia. By the end of the period, the ideals of European nationalism had been exported worldwide and were now beginning to develop in – and compete with and threaten – the empires ruled by colonial European nation states. The period that followed on from the detritus of competing irrational empires, namely the rise of extreme nationalism and fascism and Europe's descent into two catastrophic world wars, should alert us to the insidious dangers that can result from narrow nationalist movements, uninformed by democratic or utopian ideals, especially when there is a confluence of economic and social turmoil.

This brief review of European history over the past two-and-a-half centuries reminds us that there was a mind of Europe before its industrial evolution, a Europe of life and the spirit of letters, of music and philosophy, before the Europe of coal and steel; a Europe that flourished without the overzealous and insatiable exploitation of natural resources. The Commercial Revolution that preceded the Industrial Revolution, for instance, was marked by an increase in general commerce, and the growth of financial services such as banking, insurance and investment. There was even a morally informed literature on the ethics of transactions and commerce. History leads us to believe that there can, indeed, be a Europe beyond coal and steel as we continue in the Anthropocene era. A change giving us hope for a green Europe is possible without damaging irrevocably the fine ecological balance of the planet and its 7.5 billion human inhabitants and 8.7 million diverse species. This is a version of society that combines ecology, economy and culture, that is rooted in social justice, humanitarianism and ethics.

To achieve this vision of Europe, I suggest again little less than a paradigm shift in social theory, policy and practice. In new emerging literature, consideration of a new eco-social paradigm, based on economic heterodoxy, is available to us in scholarly work such as that of Professor Ian Gough and others, work that recognizes the limits of the world's natural resources, as well as the role that unrestrained greed has played in creating the climate crisis. In *Heat, Greed and Human Need*[22] – I wish it were in the hands of all students of the social sciences – Professor Gough outlines how our alternative paradigm can be rooted in the concept of human need over insatiability. The paradigm he outlines champions principles of gender equality, income, wealth and resource redistribution, and a reconfigured social consumption and investment strategy that transfers resources and technology from developed countries to developing countries as the key means to achieve this eco-social welfare state. The eco-social policies that underpin such an economic paradigm must concurrently pursue both equity and social justice, as well as sustainability and sufficiency goals and they require an activist innovation state, with substantial state investment and an acceptance of greater regulation and planning. Furthermore, socioeconomic measures are also required to negate any adverse impacts of the ecological transition for the poorest in society and to ameliorate, rather than threaten to deepen, growing levels of inequality. Difficult the transition may be, but it offers an approach that is garnering support as our best gesture towards intergenerational justice.

Gough's eco-social political economy emphasizes responsible economics, understanding that the concept of accelerated economic growth *ad infinitum* is inherently flawed. In doing this scholars such as Ian Gough are recovering a discourse and a political-economy discipline that had fallen prey to an uncritical embrace of neo-liberal refrains. It advocates for an economic model of pluralism, which emphasizes the finite nature of the earth's natural resources and obviously the role that rich nations must play in ameliorating the crises in which we find ourselves. As Gough puts it:

> Consumption and consumption-based emissions, ignored by the green growth agenda, must be given equal priority in the rich world. [...] Issues of global equity, almost entirely absent from international climate negotiations so far, must be discussed and confronted. [...] 'Affluence' has a class as well as a national dimension.

Kate Raworth's book *Doughnut Economics*[23] is yet another example of the works that provide a powerful conceptual framework emphasizing social and ecological boundaries in humanity's 21st-century challenge to meet the needs of all within the means of the planet.

In other words, this scholarship offers hope by showing us how we can, as a global community, ensure that no one needs to do without life's essentials (from food and housing to healthcare and the political voice), while ensuring that collectively we do not overshoot our pressure on earth's life-supporting systems, on which we fundamentally depend – such as a stable climate, fertile soils and a protective ozone layer.

As to our current position and returning to the European Union and our shared future, while the EU has imposed binding emissions targets for 2020 and 2030 on all its Member States, we must now go further in Europe and plan for full decarbonization of our economies by 2050, encouraging the rest of the world to follow suit, and urging in the strongest possible terms the USA to reconsider its decision to leave the international Paris Agreement on climate change, a decision which, to my mind, is inexcusable, ill-informed, profoundly myopic and threatens future generations with catastrophic climate consequences. In dealing with socioeconomic impacts of climate change, we must be conscious of the need for a 'just transition' for workers and communities to ensure that we are all part of a sustainable, low-carbon economy and benefit from decent and green jobs. In Ireland and Germany this will mean that those impacted by the closure of unsustainable carbon-intensive electricity production, for example, must be offered reskilling opportunities to enable them to find suitable jobs in other areas, such as the green economy, or opportunities with sustainable incomes in other parts of society. Beyond that, there must be good social policies that ensure no loss of citizen participation rights.

Globalization as we have experienced it, pursued without consideration as to social impact or consequences, I suggest, has had an accelerated negative impact on climate change: more goods being produced and consumed, more transport of goods across longer distances, shorter product obsolescence cycles, and a more consumerist and materially driven society. All of these aspects of globalization have come at a significant cost in terms of the impact on finite natural resources and related carbon emissions. Those who benefit from such a flawed model are certainly not the public, now or in the future. It is a minority who will benefit and who, in the defence of an insatiable, unregulated accumulation, will ignore the consequences of their model, be it in climate or social terms; a minority that often is footloose, existing beyond the reach of regulation by state or parliament. The growth of an unaccountable form of speculative capital activity can dislodge even the efforts of governments. This must change. Democracy itself requires it. The growth of what is unaccountable is not an exercise in freedom. It is a threat to democracy.

V. The Future of the European Union

It is a source of encouragement that, after decades of mainstream economic commentary championing the belief in the inevitable and often extreme unregulated versions of the market, privatization, and a smaller role for the state, we now appear to be experiencing a turning point in the economics discourse thanks to the insightful contributions of economists such as those whose works were already mentioned, and also Mariana Mazzucato and Sylvia Walby. Mazzucato, in her books *The Entrepreneurial State* and *The Value of Everything*[24] effectively rebukes the austerity-fuelled world view that, in order to restore growth (after the 2008 financial crisis), reducing deficits by cutting public spending is fundamental, arguing instead that government spending in key investment areas such as education and research and development is a key driver of economic growth. Thankfully orthodox institutions such as the International Monetary Fund have slowly evolved their thinking on austerity as a strategic tool, believing that such policies can cause harm, and be self-defeating. John Maynard Keynes argued over eighty years ago that if governments cut spending during an economic slump, a short-lived recession can become a fully-fledged depression. This is precisely what occurred in Ireland when the economic recession of 2008 turned into an economic depression in 2009, with an economic recovery delayed until 2014.

Bulmer and Paterson, in their book, *Germany and the European Union: Europe's Reluctant Hegemon*,[25] argue that Germany – given its modern institutional contracts, export performance and influence, as well as its long record of fiscal solidity and the attractiveness of its social market economy model – had, and continues to have, the capacity to be a natural European leader on economic matters, in giving leadership in achieving a new paradigm.

Many decades before the emergence of contemporary political economists I have mentioned, the spiritual fathers of creative thinking in the public sector, Keynes and Polanyi, called on policymakers not just to think in terms of economic policy exclusively about countercyclical spending as a way to reduce the impacts of recessions and avoid overheating economies, but also to think strategically; to identify which investments can help shape citizens' long-term prospects for the better. Polanyi went so far as to argue, in *The Great Transformation*, that far from being in the grip of any inevitabilities, free markets are indeed the products of government interventions, outcomes of public and private actions. This astute observation has been conveniently cast aside in much of the austerity-based neo-liberal commentary analysing the recent economic crisis. The instrument that is the state must be repossessed by its citizens if we are to transform societies for the benefit of the citizenry, for the state still holds the capacity and much of the resources for democratic control of a nation's economy and finances. This is but one form of an epistemological challenge to the neo-classical economic orthodoxy that espouses with rigidity the assumptions of rationality and individualism as the equilibrium nexus.

The role of the state, as well as the concept of sovereignty, therefore, needs to be defined anew in such a way that both are shared and can flow for the benefit of citizens beyond borders, while still retaining – because there is a transition taking place in several countries – a relative and regional character, one that is exemplary to global economic systems. The concept of sovereignty, defined with responsibility beyond national borders, could be even more powerfully defined as one requiring a *consciousness* beyond borders in order to avoid falling into the trap of a de-peopled technocracy, or of ignoring human feeling. Nations, after all, live by and share sentiments of the heart as much as by what is perceived as rational. It is this sensibility and capacity that obstructs the ambition of technocracy. We must have the courage to examine the structural basis of the issues which face us.

The Brexit vote in the United Kingdom, the election of Donald Trump in the United States, the growth of nationalist and anti-immigration parties in Europe and, most recently, the 'yellow vest' insurrection in France have all been represented as at source a populist reaction to the rising inequality, stagnant incomes and economic insecurity that have become the dominant trends in many industrialized countries, as has been keenly noted by John Evans in *Social Europe*:

> They reflect a growth of relative deprivation, where significant segments of populations feel that, whereas others have gained from economic and social change, they and their families have lost out – and they fear a future of even greater insecurity. Sharpening divisions appear after decades of the weakening of intermediary institutions, notably trade unions, whose economic role was to act as a brake on rising inequality

and whose political role was to provide voice to those feeling unjustly treated and to negotiate solutions to their grievances.[26]

Brexit, Trump, nationalism and street violence all represent answers that we may perceive as inimical to an important question: how to reforge agreement on redistributive justice for those who have lost out, either objectively or subjectively, from globalization, technological innovation (including digitalization), so-called innovation (including the casualization of labour) or responses to climate change. How then might we regain trust? What are the consequences of a legacy of dismissed or weakened mediatory institutions? Evans asserts that

> a new social accord is essential, in workplaces and communities, to rebuild trust in fractured societies. It must reduce income inequality, support purchasing power and median incomes, address job quality, and counter the spatial concentration of discontent. Above all, it will entail reconstructing and reinforcing intermediary institutions, such as unions, which can provide voice and collective solutions.

Jürgen Habermas has made a seminal contribution in his fine collection of essays on the EU including 'The Lure of Technocracy'. Habermas articulates a coherent and wide-ranging defence of the project of European unification and of possible parallel developments towards a politically integrated world and society. In developing his key concepts of the trans-nationalization of democracy and the constitutionalization of international law, Habermas has offered some valuable suggestions as to how we might respond to circumstances such as the current impasse in which we find ourselves. Habermas is harshly critical of the incremental, technocratic policies advocated by several Member States that have been, and continue to be, imposed on the populations of the economically weaker, crisis-stricken Member States, and which have had the effect of undermining solidarity across the EU. He argues that if the technocratic, austerity-centric approach is replaced by a deeper democratization of European institutions, the EU has the possibility of fulfilling its core founding principles and ensuring that 'rampant market capitalism can once more be brought under political control at the supranational level'.[27] Habermas defines a continuum in which capitalism and democracy are presented, if not at opposing ends of the spectrum, as very much in conflict with each other, and he discusses with frightening accuracy the abject spectacle of a capitalist world society fragmented along national lines.

Does this mean, then, that there is emerging, or perhaps has already formed, a fundamental incompatibility of democracy and capitalism, especially a capitalism that is so heavily enmeshed with an unfettered globalization, which itself lacks legitimacy among much of the citizenry? Unlike Wolfgang Streeck, who articulates a more pessimistic conclusion, Habermas asserts that two interventions would improve the democratic basis of the Union: joint political framework planning, and revisions to the Treaty of Lisbon to democratically legitimize the corresponding competencies, 'in particular, equal involvement by Parliament and Council in the law-making process and equal accountability of the Commission to both institutions'. This is because, as Habermas puts it, 'a generalisation of interests that cuts across national borders is only possible in a European Parliament organised by parliamentary functions'. He argues for more profound political integration in Europe so as to create a shift in the imbalance between politics and the market, which is continuing to the present day in the wake of the neo-liberal self-disempowerment of politics.

This disempowerment of politics manifested itself during the 2008 financial crisis and subsequent economic recessions across the EU as pressure being exerted by the financial markets on the politically fragmented national budgets, which fostered a collectivizing pejorative self-perception of the populations affected by the crisis. Habermas asserts that the response by markets, lead governments, key international organizations and the mainstream neo-liberal commentariat all contributed greatly to the punitive grounds on which assistance was offered to 'programme' countries by 'turning the "donor" and the "beneficiary" countries against each other and fomenting nationalism'. Such an impasse repeating itself could be overcome if pro-European parties conduct joint-transnational campaigns against the falsifying representation of social questions as national questions. It also requires, he argues, 'extending the monetary union into a supranational democracy', which could provide the institutional platform for reversing the neo-liberal trend of recent decades. Above all, Habermas has argued (in *Europe: The Faltering Project*) for a policy

V. The Future of the European Union

of gradual European integration in which key decisions about Europe's future are put in the hands of its peoples, rather than the 'neo-liberal orthodoxy'.[28]

Are there any lessons we have learnt from the economic crisis, the 'self-regulating market' and the long, devastating period of austerity imposed on millions of European citizens? I believe there are many – in politics, policy-making, academia, the commentariat, citizens at large – who have reassessed what were sometimes strongly held beliefs, with a new-found appreciation that the state has important roles to play across all spheres of public policy, that good regulation does matter, be it in the financial, construction, or healthcare sectors – all sectors in which we in Ireland have seen the catastrophic and sometimes tragic effects of under-regulation and/or lack of enforcement.

The legitimation crisis is not confined to the European Union, or its members. The role of the state will be crucial in approaching issues such as climate change and sustainability. There is a serious gap: what of institutions not answerable to parliament, people, or their laws? It is an issue that was addressed by the President of Greece, Prokopios Pavlopoulos, in the Aristotle Lecture in 2016. He spoke of non-state entities of international scope devoid of democratic legitimacy – so-called financial markets, credit-rating agencies – and the declining course of social welfare and the rule of law.

Looking ahead, my vision is of a Europe with excellent public services at its core. Good jobs in the public sector means quality services for citizens. We must remember that the services the public sector delivers are not a cost to society, but an investment in our communities. This message must be taken to the heart of Europe. I suggest that what is actually unaccountable is the speculative flows of insatiable capital; a global, unregulated, financialized version of economy represents the greatest threat to democracy, the greatest source of an inevitable conflict, and the greatest obstacle to us achieving an end to global poverty or achieving sustainability.

In conclusion, I return to where I began, to Schiller's 'Ode to Joy'. Rereading the poem before my journey here, I was struck again by its powerful messages of freedom and solidarity. Schiller's first stanza concludes with the lines: 'Every man becomes a brother, / Where thy gentle wings abide.' This expression of solidarity and tolerance reminds us forcefully of the purpose, the guiding principle of the European Union: solidarity between our nations and solidarity with others. What does solidarity demand of us now? I suggest it must be intergenerational, be defined as a multidimensional concept embracing ecosystem, society, culture and economy (both trade and fiscal). There must be a joint approach to making accountable what is unaccountable, a joint approach to what is undermining public trust in democracy, to what has no concept of citizens, but one of insatiable consumers.

But solidarity is not the only message we can take from Schiller's poem, for it is a lengthy work, and only the first stanzas were put to music by Beethoven. The composer was himself, perhaps, aware that not all of the stanzas may have been appreciated by his then masters, for these stanzas reflect idealistic calls for what must be done to create a better world. The poem after all in its fullness appeals for the millions to strive for a better world: for help for the innocent, for speaking truth to friend and foe and alike, for honour only to those who merit it, and for an end to those who lie.

It was a call in its day for rescue from tyrants, mercy to villains, and hope until the dying hours. The poem expresses the essence of European values – idealistic values, undoubtedly, but values which we must continue to strive to fulfil. 'Ode to Joy' represents values that must be given concrete, tangible reality in Europe, offered to and experienced on the European Street.

Responding to the necessary transformation of this relationship between economy and society, on which I have reflected in this address, is an urgent priority, in times that are marked, in the absence of an adequate and inclusive discourse, and I believe as a consequence, by the rise of an ever more rancorous rhetoric, one which is frequently founded in despair, alienation, anomie, exclusion, and one which produces statements from the unaccountable that seek to divide us against one another on the grounds of ethnicity, religion and nationality. This Europe we seek must be one in which such hateful squabbles are replaced with openness, inclusivity, cohesion, solidarity and a recognition that the shift to a new gendered eco-social paradigm of wealth creation and distribution is pursued together and without delay, and not just for our benefit in the European Union, but for the future generations whom we would wish to inhabit a peaceful, harmonious world that is supported by a sustainable vision of economy and society, and enriched by a diversity of cultures.

Europe and Africa: Towards a New Relationship

Webinar address to the Institute of International and European Affairs, Áras an Uachtaráin, 10 June 2020.

I am delighted to be with you all today, even if it is to be in a virtual sense, to address the important topic of how we might pursue the most fruitful relations between Africa and the EU; how Europe might release itself from the narrative of the past and be part of a narrative of hope, by engaging as equals with our planet's neighbouring continent of the young.

This is a topic on which I, as President of Ireland, have spoken on several occasions, a topic about which I feel passionately, for the quality of the European Union's relationship with the continent of Africa and its people is a subject of such great importance, a topic which carries hope in its transformative potential for so many, yes, for Africa, but also for all of us as we seek to address the issues of our time, including the dysfunctional balance of economy, society, culture and, most importantly, ecology and the loss of biodiversity.

MISCONCEPTIONS OF AFRICA

We have now the gift of new, empirically-based research published on Africa. For Europeans the issue is: do we read it, respond to it, allow it to influence policy and our EU–Africa relationships and agreements?

For example, the subtitle Carlos Lopes and George Kararach gave to their recent valuable work, *Structural Change in Africa*, is *Misperceptions, New Narratives and Development in the 21st Century*.[29] I was struck by something most basic when I first read the book. It was how the Mercator projection has suggested to generations of Europeans that the continent of Africa is about the same size as Greenland. Greenland is, in fact, fourteen times smaller. 'Mercator's 1569 cartographic definition of the world became one of the most influential and widely circulated world map projections throughout the nineteenth and twentieth centuries,'[30] the authors write. They go on to point out that indeed the landmass of Africa is, 'the size of India, China, the United States and most of Europe combined', and that 'Africa's blue or maritime economy is even bigger than its landmass'.[31] The Democratic Republic of the Congo is about half the size of the European Union.

When it comes to the continent of Africa, we have so many misperceptions, however, to undo. 'Misperceptions' is perhaps misleading, for indeed the distortion of African realities has a long spectrum that includes, for example, the racist language of David Hume in his essay 'Of National Characters' in 1748, to the annual reports of certain extraction companies in contemporary times, and of course if we are to undo misperceptions, we must reconceptualize, redo development theory and practice, international trade, architectures of debt and dependency. It is significant, too, that anthropology is missing as a tool in the contemporary accounts. That great intellectual and moral impulse to understand culture seems to have been consigned to nineteenth-century history shelves with the decline of the Empire, a project it served so well. Yet of course, it could yield, in contemporary times, valuable insights if utilized as alternative to some World Bank reviews.

Today Africa is the continent of the young, accounting for 20 per cent of the young people of the world, a continent of over 1.3 billion people in 2018. It constitutes 16 per cent of the world's human population. It is, therefore, a continent on which the hopes of so much of our shared future rests. It is on this continent we might perhaps see the playing out to fruition of our efforts at achieving the United Nations Sustainable Development Goals, provide an adequate anticipation and response to climate change – in short, achieving that connection between economy, society, ecology and culture that we so urgently need and cannot postpone, involving, as it does, the future of the planet itself as a habitable space.

For Africans there is the urgent need for reducing poverty, for good security in the basic necessities of life, for delivering healthy living conditions, for universal basic services including education and healthcare, for peace and reconciliation and an end to conflict, and for an enduring, sustainable future built on prosperity in its widest, most fulfilling, inclusive sense.

For the achievement of a fruitful dialogue between the European Union and Africa, there are preliminary tasks to be accomplished at European level, one of the most important being abandoning any affected amnesia as to the brutal colonization of previous times, acknowledging the detritus of imperial subjugations, which surfaces too often, stirred by fingers of hands that are carrying the old intent.

For while Europeans choose to forget, Africans rightly remember. We in the European Union must transact that painful memory if we are, as Hannah Arendt might put it, to stop the events of the past crippling us in the present and obstructing us in the future. I worry that we have not reached the point of critical sophistication that will do that. I recall the dismissive response I received to a quotation I made in one of my papers from one of Sankar Muthu's books. I think it was *Enlightenment Against Empire*.[32] We do really need to be free and courageous in critiquing empire in the same way as we have been willing to set about critiquing the extremes and possible abuses of nationalism past and present.

IRELAND AND AFRICA

Ireland's relationship with Africa is quite a unique one, from the work of Roger Casement to contemporary non-governmental organizations and Irish Aid. It has, unlike the historical relationship of former empires, been largely one of identifying with the aspirations of Africans for lives of freedom from hunger, access to education and achievement of inclusive rights, including the full rights of women to participation in all aspects of life. These are powerful foundations upon which to emphasize, within the European Union, the need to develop a future relationship with the continent of Africa that will be one of African agency in a transformed Africa.

Ireland brings to the African table its own experience, not only of an economic, social and political domination, but also the experience of a suppressed culture, forced exile and, frankly, of racism; as Hume put it in the specific case of the Irish, they having missed out on the civilization that he thought a Roman occupation might have brought them, thus were uncivilized, but, above all else, 'lesser'.[33] Ireland welcomes the centrality of African agency in the new work on the transformation of Africa, and sees it as being an immensely valuable contribution, having a global significance as we redefine economics and its connection to ecology and culture.

Ireland has, due to its missionaries as much as to its aid and development workers, developed a special connection with African nations resulting from its contribution to education. We can, as a result, be looked to as a source of leadership in other areas, such as addressing those unfair and imbalanced terms of trade that currently prevail, which confine African produce to the lower end of the value chain: Africa's benefit from its coffee trade, for example, is a paltry 10 per cent, while the appalling trade conditions imposed on coffee products from Africa limit any gains in the value of finished products.

Not only as President of Ireland, but through a lifetime in Parliament, I have often stressed that Ireland needs to continue to deepen its diplomacy with the continent that will, after all, be the birthplace of over 2 billion people by 2050; a continent of such population that, quite scandalously, continues to be under-represented on the Security Council of the United Nations, not allowed to adequately present its own version of African needs and possibilities. Ireland's deepening of diplomatic representation in Africa is currently underway, I am glad to hear.

It is not only in addressing the under-representation of the people of Africa that Ireland can give a lead. At the United Nations, Ireland can show leadership in calling for an urgent review and redesign of the architecture of the global financial institutions: an architecture for so long now past purpose; an architecture that has not succeeded in preventing our planet, in ecological terms, of being brought to the brink of survival itself; that has failed to eliminate global poverty; that has deepened inequality; that has lost cohesion between and within north and south and has left a world where conflict is endemic and never short of armaments produced in countries including those who speak of a peaceful world.

Given all of this and what Africa now faces, in conditions of pandemic, an offer such as a suspension of six months' interest on debt, as proposed by the G7, should be seen for what it is – a grossly inadequate gesture offered from a distance by those not sufficiently engaged with the human dimension of their proposals in a financialized global economy that eschews any notion of a moral compass.

Last month Ireland became the twenty-seventh non-regional member of the African Development Bank. This is an important addition to the deepening ties that will inform Ireland's relationship to Africa and its people. The African Development Bank, and the African Development Fund it administers, can play a significant role in fostering sustainable and inclusive social and economic growth and prosperity, helping the African continent to achieve its potential in a sustainable way as the continent of promise and opportunity. For Africa it is just that, a continent where transformation is already underway. In that we can be partners.

The African Development Bank is currently implementing a ten-year strategy to 2022, focused on two objectives: inclusive growth and green growth for Africa, aiming for a prosperity that is more equally shared and meets the needs of present generations without compromising the well-being of future generations. This also involves the taking into consideration of the differing social, economic and environmental aspects that arise in the sustainable development of countries which have differences that must be recognized.

To achieve these objectives, the bank has set five operational priorities, including infrastructure development, regional economic integration, private sector development, governance and accountability strengthening and upscaling skills and technology training, together with three areas of special emphasis, namely fragile states, gender, and agriculture and food security. A disbursement of $6.6 billion occurred in 2018 to successful projects in these priority areas.

There have been many great achievements already resulting from such funding. For example, 100 per cent of new lending from the African Development Bank on energy projects in 2017 was on renewables, up from 14 per cent in 2015. Just last week, a new solar farm on the outskirts of Mogadishu should, according to its owners, quadruple power generation for the Somalian capital while also cutting costs. It has provided eight megawatts of clean electricity since March, and is predicted to provide one hundred megawatts by 2022.

Technology has also given other benefits, contributing significantly to the enabling of democratic processes. In line with the freedoms that characterize democracy, today more Africans can access the Internet, use mobile phones and share information with the world at large. The total sub-Saharan African population with Internet access has almost tripled, from 7 per cent in 2010 to nearly 22 per cent in 2017. Likewise, the number of mobile-phone subscriptions in sub-Saharan Africa has almost doubled to 764 million in the same period, according to Daniel F. Runde's analysis, 'The Role of the AfDB and the Future of Africa', published by the Centre for Strategic and International Studies in October last year.[34]

Our membership of the African Development Bank and its trust fund is an investment in Africa's potential, and Ireland's partnership with these important regional multilateral institutions will advance our shared, but redefined, development priorities. Membership and investment will open future opportunities for Irish science and technology in the region, as well as support projects that spur food security, sufficiency, poverty reduction and sustainable economic development at different levels across Africa. Africa, 'the smart continent' of the future, with a civilization of sufficiency and inclusion, can be an exemplar and, I believe, a leader in the better and inclusive use of technology.

COVID-19 AND AFRICA

As our world, in all its different circumstances, continues to respond to the threat to individuals, families, communities, societies and economies, it is difficult to overstate the toll that the COVID-19 pandemic has taken – the lives cut short, the space and time for the expression of grief curtailed for those who have lost loved ones, lack of access, denial of liberty to those experiencing severe illness or who are vulnerable, livelihoods made insecure or lost for millions of families.

Coronavirus, being a global problem, necessitates a global response. Yet it is so plainly evident that societies differ in their capacity to respond, with those

V. The Future of the European Union

in Africa in a profoundly exposed position in terms of resources – given, for example, the proportion of the population reliant on the informal economy that prevails and the consequent limitation of any measures that may be utilized in responding to COVID-19. While the pandemic is a global threat, our global vulnerability differs greatly. These differences test both our global solidarity and the architecture of our multilateralism now so much under threat.

COVID-19 is a reality in all countries of Africa. We should therefore remind ourselves that there is now an unprecedented opportunity for Europe to begin its journey towards a new contemporary and future shared ethical relationship, and do so not only as good regionalism, but also as an exercise in multilateralism, forging a new approach in its relationship with Africa, this time based on solidarity – a relationship that will include a fundamental re-examination of how unfair trade and existing debt structures are impeding not only Africa's capacity to respond to COVID-19, but also the necessary transformations that continent is getting underway, with an African agency that seeks a new form of partnership with its most proximate neighbour, the European Union.

May I suggest that now is not a time for retreating behind borders. In the African countries where COVID-19 has arrived in greatest numbers, there are immense problems and inequalities in terms of healthcare provision. The same is true of Latin and Central America.

Given such inadequacies of equipment and personnel, where it is most needed, there is a real risk that the pandemic could be difficult to contain across Africa and Latin America, and could result in mass fatalities and wider socioeconomic problems, particularly in the possible event of a second wave of the virus. The prospect of a future vaccine does not come guaranteed, despite multilateral requests, as to its widespread availability in impoverished nations. There is a need for a global response as to the freedom and capacity of access of all to a vaccine that will have been probably developed with shared global research, state and private.

United Nations Secretary General Guterres has correctly underscored how, if COVID-19 is to be countered, richer countries must assist those less resourced, or potentially, as he put it, 'face the nightmare of the disease spreading like wildfire in the global south with millions of deaths and the prospect of the disease re-emerging where it was previously suppressed'.[35]

The unresolved issues of hunger are now, in 2020, all exacerbated. According to recent research published by Oxfam, coronavirus could double chronic hunger in Africa. Both the virus and the restrictions imposed to curb its spread are disrupting planting, harvesting, the movement of farm labour and the scale and distribution of produce across Africa. There are urgent calls for borders to remain open for essential agri-food trade.

In this context, it is necessary to recognize how dangerously fragile, often shallow, at times contradictory, multilateralism has become; how some conflicts are being continued even as the United Nations recently called for a ceasefire to enable citizens and their governments to respond to the challenges posed by the coronavirus.

In addition to the threat posed by the COVID-19 pandemic, many African countries, particularly those in the east of the continent, are now in the throes of a second wave of desert locusts, many times worse than the plague that descended a number of months ago. The locusts present 'an extremely alarming and unprecedented threat'[36] to food security and livelihoods, according to the United Nations. A swarm of just half a square kilometre can eat the same amount of food in one day as 35,000 people.

STRUCTURAL PROBLEMS

Yet, we must be cognizant that, once the COVID-19 crisis is over, all of the inherited and acquired structural impediments to Africa's sustainable development remain. Perhaps the largest of these impediments remains debt. The continuing failure to achieve the will of the members of the United Nations – which is making debt, and credit flows, serve as instrument rather than stranglehold, be it in relation to the sustainable development goals, climate change, migration or pandemics – is surely one of the greatest global failures. Responding adequately to structural global inequalities can, by *inter alia* recognizing African agency, provide the continent with the prospect of carving out a path of recovery of its deep and diverse cultures, a shared prosperity, an enduring peace, and a hopeful future, not only for all its citizens, but for us all, for the achievement, I repeat, of a sustainable connection between economy, society and ecology.

I use the term 'agency' very deliberately, as I agree with development economist and High Representative of the Commission of the African Union,

V. The Future of the European Union

Carlos Lopes, that it is through the creation of African agency – that capacity to act autonomously and independently, which has been denied to Africa at so many points during its colonial and post-colonial periods – that Africans will be enabled to undertake the necessary structural reforms so as to create a brighter, shared future.

There are some basics that it is necessary to repeat. The health of the populations of the planet must take precedence over any abstract version of global debt. Statistics illustrate how, for instance, in 2016, Angola spent nearly six times as much servicing external debt as it did on public health care. Fifteen countries in sub-Saharan Africa spent more paying creditors abroad than on doctors and clinics at home. This is morally outrageous. Furthermore, sub-Saharan Africa spends less than 5 per cent of its total government expenditure on public health, a consequence, in part at least, of the debt-ridden nature of its economies. There is now an unanswerable case for a global campaign for universal basic services.

When it comes to trade and the economy, recent low commodity prices have led to decreased revenues, with African exports having declined by approximately a third in recent months. The Chinese economic slowdown has impacted severely on African exports given the high dependency of many African countries on the Chinese market. Furthermore, many African countries collect relatively low levels of taxation revenue by international standards, with estimates indicating that as much as 89 per cent of people, in some states, and even regions, work in the informal economy, compounding the economic challenges facing the continent.

Sub-Saharan Africa remains one of the least industrialized regions in the world, and the modern industry that is currently in place struggles to keep pace with what are usually referenced as international productivity metrics. If labour productivity has stagnated or declined in many African countries over the past sixty years, only to recover modestly since 2000, and GDP has tripled in the same period, serious wealth and income distribution questions are raised. Jobs distribute income, even if in some parts of our planet industrialization has been irresponsible in ecological and human terms. Yet there is an industrialization, as Lopes and Kararach point out, that can be appropriate for Africa on best use of resources, natural and human. Critical, too, is the transfer of science and technology on new terms.

The external shocks I referred to earlier, including China's slowdown and falling commodity prices, as well as the widespread drought in eastern and southern Africa, have led some industries to become a drag on their economies rather than being engines of growth or available for structural transformation.

This is all the more worrying because Africa is still predominantly specialized in relatively low-technology industries with a huge dependence on agriculture. Findings from some of the better work in the development economics field suggest Africa's long-term development would entail a diversified move away from exporting raw materials and the attendant reliance on high commodity prices, entry into more complex, advanced activities that yield higher-value goods and services for export, thereby increasing the share of GDP derived from advanced manufacturing, and improving competitiveness *vis-à-vis* other world markets. What, then, are the prospects for these developments? Let me quote, if I may, from Lopes and Kararach's book, *Structural Change in Africa*:

> Five decades of development planning have not yielded the 7 percent, which is the minimum required to double average incomes in a decade. Instead, there are a range of highly unequal and vulnerable economies that remain entrenched in poverty. The evolution of industrial policy in Africa mirrors the evolution of development planning. These include the import substitution policies that took root after the independence era, then planning was enthusiastically driven in the 1960s through to the 1970s; the structural adjustment programmes of the 1980s when planning waned and the state was rolled back; and then this was followed by poverty reduction strategy papers in the 1990s when liberalisation, deregulation, and privatisation were entrenched as methods of economic management. The weaknesses in understanding Africa as well as its misrepresentation during these periods has a lot to do with the deficits in industrial production and the incidences of de-industrialisation. This is ironic since most governments implemented various industrial policy strategies and interventions to promote industrial development.
>
> Manufacturing as a share of output and employment decreased or remained low over most of these periods. As African countries prepare to take their rightful places in the future global economy, they have a real opportunity to promote economic transformation through the industrialisation process by capitalising on the continent's abundant natural

resources, adding value to them, while also supporting the development of infant industries. The manufacturing sector in particular has been the engine of economic development for the majority of developed countries, and very few countries have developed their economies without a strong manufacturing base, so much so that the terms 'industrialised' and 'developed' are often used interchangeably when referring to such countries.[37]

As with many other global issues, establishing the root cause of Africa's political and economic challenges is fundamental for understanding the dynamics of the African continent which, as Lopes and Kararach correctly identify, requires an understanding of how the issues of geography, economy and demography have influenced, and will continue to influence, Africa's development.

COLONIZATION AND ITS LEGACY

Returning, if I may, to the ethics of transformation and a meaningful multilateralism, it is critical to recall that, between the 1870s and 1900, Africa suffered European imperialist adventurism and aggression, diplomatic pressures, military invasions and eventual conquest and colonization. Despite many African societies' brave resistance, foreign domination was successfully imposed, and by the early twentieth century much of Africa, except Ethiopia and Liberia, had been colonized by European powers.

The European imperialist push into Africa was motivated by factors that were not just economic, but also political, social, cultural and racist. The colonial drive followed the collapse of the profitability of the slave trade, its abolition and suppression, as well as the expansion of the European industrial revolution.

An interplay of economic factors – the imperatives of capitalist industrialization including the demand for assured sources of raw materials, the search for guaranteed markets and profitable investment outlets – as well as political factors, including inter-European power struggles and competition for pre-eminence, together with social factors such as rising unemployment and poverty in Europe, all led to this 'scramble for Africa'.

The colonization was characterized by frantic attempts by European commercial, military and political agents to declare and establish a stake in different parts of the continent through inter-imperialist commercial competition, the declaration of exclusive claims to particular territories for trade, the imposition of tariffs against other European traders, and claims to sole control of waterways and commercial routes across Africa.

The arbitrary national boundaries that followed have been largely responsible as sources for ethnic conflicts on the continent due to the forced separation of ethnic groups across states and the forced assimilation of others within states. Colonialism also replaced the pre-colonial governance structures with western ones, creating a system of kleptocracy in some nations through the formation of hierarchical ruling structures. Economic rewards given to African elites created a dominant leading class at the expense of other Africans and the continent's natural resources.

Despite the demise of colonialism, some elites have remained and maintained their relationships with former colonialists as part of a shared corruption in parts of Africa. Such elites are being continually rewarded for draining their states' natural resources and thereby reinforcing inequality.

Colonialism, furthermore, created single-crop economies in societies that relied overwhelmingly on agriculture, sentencing African economies to the volatile whims of markets and market-based fluctuations, and exposure to crop failure. Forced integration of developing states into the international trading arena augmented the already widespread inequality between developed and developing states.

Central to colonization was indirect rule and assimilation, and a consistent theme propagated by the imperialists was the portrayal of the indigenous Africans as uncivilized and uneducated. This racist notion, widely promulgated, legitimized the ill-treatment and exploitation of those who were colonized, including their relegation to the status of second-class citizens in their own countries.

FORGING A NEW RELATIONSHIP BETWEEN EUROPE AND AFRICA FOR AN 'AFRICAN ENLIGHTENMENT'

As to the future then, the basic physical conditions for economic transformation are challenging and apply to different degrees in many (but not all) African countries: small, often fragmented markets, poor infrastructure, remoteness and sometimes a scarcity of relevant natural resources all play their part in the continued poor trade and wider economic performance of many African countries. Even when these factors are taken into account, however, there remains a large unexplained 'residual'.

It is good, therefore, that a new generation of scholars, which includes professors Lopes and Kararach, is examining those structural features of the African economy that account for its past record and are serving to impose limitations on its future development. I am not sure, however – may I mischievously suggest – that they have departed sufficiently from the notorious modernization theory, with its linear assumptions. Yet what is most important is their suggestion as to what is possible, and that will include an appropriate form of industrialization that can be ecologically well fitted and adjusted to local capacity.

If Europe is sincere about its wish to be a partner in enabling Africa to achieve an inclusive, sustainable and prosperous future, debt cancellation must be an intrinsic element of a new, authentic European-led response. It is my strong view that a temporary cancellation of debt interest would not suffice as an effective response. Rather, a much more radical approach is required to effectively relieve Africa's debt burden, by restructuring, redefining and, in some cases, forgoing the bulk of outstanding debt. Such an approach would be a fitting demonstration of genuine European solidarity with our neighbours to the south. It could help to consign to the category of transacted painful memory so much of the horrendous consequences of hundreds of years of colonial and post-colonial hubris, exploitation and abuse. There is such strong evidence that our current development models are in disarray or producing dysfunctional consequences. A new model must come from a genuinely inclusive dialogue. Enabling Africa to become self-sufficient and to develop sustainably will require giving agency to Africans to build a sustainable future for all Africans.

Why debt cancellation will help in this regard is by allowing strategic commodities that are held by the state to be used for economic advancement for all, rather than serving debt repayments. Improving agency may also require alterations to the forms of bureaucratic and governmental systems in place in some African nations so as to achieve inclusivity and accountability. It will also necessitate a willingness on the part of the state to work inclusively with civil society in its engagements with external partners.

African agency is not about the freedom to imitate failing paradigms: neither should African agency be solely seen as emanating from, and being exerted solely by, governmental elites. Rather, it can be a by-product of independent civil society and progressive movements across Africa at individual and societal levels, working with entrepreneurial versions of the state towards shared goals.

Agency also relates importantly to the multilateral level. The ongoing under-representation of African nations in international organizations, including the United Nations, is a major cause for concern. We should all be concerned at this under-representation. We continue to witness an historic, unjust under-representation of an Africa which was still ruled by colonial powers when the United Nations came into existence and the Security Council established. Africans must be allowed to have influence in Council decisions affecting their own continent. The increasing effect of climate change on international peace and security gives this proposal even greater urgency.

A 21st-century 'African Enlightenment' is underway and, may I suggest, it can draw on sources deeper and richer than any limited European eighteenth-century rationalism. For example, it can draw on a diversity of pre-imperialist sources of wisdom, as well as the vigour and energy that comes from being the continent of the young on our planet.

To enable such a transformation requires us Europeans to reconceptualize development models in relation to Africa and indeed elsewhere, to emphasize the need to seize the possibilities of transformational change, to be partners; partners with a listening capacity, as we offer our help in the efforts to build a sustainable future for the planet.

As to what is already underway in Africa, we have examples available to us. We can build on excellent initiatives already receiving assistance from the European Union, such as the Great Green Wall, a project led by the African Union, which aims to transform the lives of millions of people by creating a mosaic of green and productive landscapes across North Africa, combating the effects of desertification.

The key structural changes that are required in relation to Africa have been identified by Lopes, Kararach and many others. These include changing politics, respecting Africa's diversity, embracing a deeper understanding of the policy and historical context, not defeated by it or its consequences, a move to sustainable industrialization, increasing agricultural productivity and diversity, building a new social contract, adjusting to climate change and inserting agency in the relationship with Africa's key partners, especially China.

As Lopes and Kararach have written, an effective European input into an African 21st-century Enlightenment requires an agreed and appropriate definition of what is meant by 'structural transformation'. It requires an understanding that, while Africa seeks transformation, it is not alone, and that any such transformation must be grounded in eco-social sustainable policies. It requires, too, a proper understanding of the role of new forms of sustainable industrialization in any transformation, as well as other key enablers such as innovative development financing.

CONCLUSION

Whatever policy proposals that are made now and in the future must accept that it is past time that the residues of the imperialist mindset, succeeded as it was by 'the idea of Progress' of modernization theory with its ethnocentric linearities, must be eschewed from informing assumptions in policies, diplomacy and scholarship. I agree with Carlos Lopes that such residues continue to permeate modern-day misconceptions of Africa, often propagated in ignorance by the media; misconceptions, misreadings that are not only cartographic, but also pervade work on risk perceptions, levels of conflict, problems of political stability and other spheres of human existence.

Such misconceptions too often portray a continent in continual crisis, despite that continent having made significant progress in recent years. Such accounts usually form the basis of an unhelpful and inauthentic African narrative that portrays a gap between perception and reality with relation to its transformative potential. I am not for an instant discounting the need for institutional change. Of course, an overall commitment to good governance and state well-being is needed in many African states as a prerequisite, but this cannot be used as an excuse for shirking Europe's moral and ethical obligation to progressing and being partners in Africa's overdue economic and wider social transformation.

We need now, all of us, to move beyond our prescriptive approach to dealing with African challenges; an approach that often resulted in programmes of aid in the past that were externally imposed, conceived and applied without proper understanding of the crucial need for African agency, that were offered, delivered, even imposed without due cognizance of history and the context of Africa as a diverse, fast-changing continent. Perhaps it is even an appropriate time to return to using old tools in our task such as anthropology. I agree with Carlos Lopes that a paradigm shift in African Union–European Union relations is now urgently needed. Our challenge as Europeans must, therefore, be to forge that new relationship with Africa, by arriving at a new place founded on real multilateralism and solidarity, so that we can be ethical partners in the necessary structural change that can deliver universal basic services and transformational prosperity in Africa, and an enduring, sustainable future for the continent of the young, on which those of us who believe in global social justice and solidarity place so much collective hope.

VI
A MULTILINGUAL EUROPE – TRANSLATIONS INTO IRISH, FRENCH AND GERMAN

Pangur Bán

Fáilte roimh Imogen Stuart chun suiteáil na deilbhe, Pangur Bán, *in Áras an Uachtaráin, 21 Eanáir 2020 a chomóradh.*

I dtús báire ba mhaith liom mo bhuíochas a ghabháil le hImogen Stuart, duine d'ealaíontóirí céimiúla na hÉireann, a gcuirfidh a fís chruthaitheach go mór leis an spás roinnte seo san Áras. Ba é an dán a chreidtear a scríobh manach Éireannachsa naoú haois áit éigin i gcóngar Mhainistir Reichenau san Ostair, ar ndóigh, a spreag cruthú na deilbhe, *Pangur Bán*; go dtí an lá atá inniu ann tá an bhun-lámhscríbhinn faoi chúram na mBeinidicteach agus iad ag leanúint leis an traidisiún manachúil sin a raibh tionchar chomh mór sin aige ar stair agus ar shibhialtacht na hEorpa. Go deimhin, insíonn an dán sin agus an dealbh sin go leor dúinn faoinár scéal Eorpach: manach Éireannach, é ina chónaí san Ostair níos mó ná míle bliain ó shin agus a dhán aistrithe ag Sasanach, Robin Flower, gníomh ba chúis le racht cruthaíochta i ndealbhóir tallannach, a rugadh sa Ghearmáin agus atá ina cónaí in Éirinn.

Sin í an staid dhaonna. Bhí ár scéalta fite fuaite ina chéile riamh. Bhíomar riamh ag taisteal agus inár gcónaí i dteannta a chéile, ag filleadh uaireanta, ag fanacht uaireanta eile, ag léirmhíniú an athuair agus ag athmhúnlú taithí a chéile, mar a thuigeamar iad trínar bpeirspictíochtaí féin; insint roinnte á cruthú againn a ndéantar í a athshaothrú agus a athmhúnlú dá réir ag daoine ag teacht agus ag imeacht agus ag imeacht aimsire chomh maith. Tá áthas orm

VI. A Multilingual Europe – Translations into Irish, French and German

go bhfuil ambasadóirí na Gearmáine agus na hOstaire araon ábalta a bheith inár gcuideachta inniu. Is é sin, ar ndóigh, ár n-oidhreacht roinnte.

Tá machnamh déanta ag Imogen ar bhealach álainn ar shaothar an mhanaigh sin, nach bhfuil aon rian dá ainm fanta againn, agus a bhfuil a chuid focal curtha ag Robin Flower romhainn an athuair. Cuireann an téacs atá cuimsithe sa dealbh i gcuimhne dúinn an tslí ar féidir le focail agus leis an an ealaíon idirghníomhú lena chéile ar shlí atá chomh mothúchánach agus chomh hinstinneach sin. I gcroílár na bhfocal agus na deilbhe araon tá coincheap an chónaithe agus an tsaothraithe le chéile go síochánta. Deir an scríbhneoir linn: 'So it goes. To each his own. / No vying. No vexation,' agus tugann an t-ealaíontóir faoina turas aeistéitiúil isteach sa spás comhchosúil sin. Ar ndóigh, is spás comhroinnte agus buan atá ann, comhiarracht chruthaitheach idir beirt ealaíontóirí atá scartha óna chéile ó thaobh ama agus áite agus cineáil de, a labhraíonn go ciúin agus go réidh lena chéile trasna achar ama na gcéadta bliain.

Go deimhin, is ábhar mór inspioráide a fheiceáil conas is féidir le saothar ealaíontóra amháin é féin a athnuachan trí shamhlaíocht ealaíontóra eile, athshamhlaithe in aois éagsúil agus athmhúnlaithe trí phriosma taithí eile agus ama eile. Is féidir le splanc inspioráide gach teorainn a shárú. Is féidir le healaíontóirí a bheith ina n-anamchairde gan aird ar chonstaic ama nó cultúir.

Is ábhar spreagtha atá ann, freisin, a fheiceáil cén chaoi ar féidir leis an ealaín agus leis na focail idirghníomhú a dhéanamh, caidreamh á dhéanamh acu go nádúrtha lena chéile, mar spioraid den chineál céanna. Trí thallann iontach Imogen Stuart, tá dán a scríobhadh os cionn míle bliain ó shin tugtha chun beochta go físiúil san aois nua-aimseartha seo, agus é fós ábhartha do phobal an lae inniu, atá an-éagsúil ó na léitheoirí ar cruthaíodh ar dtús dóibh é.

Ar ndóigh, tá Imogen ar dhuine de dhealbhóirí mór le rá na hÉireann agus í ina ball luachmhar de phobalealaíontóirí na hÉireann leis na blianta fada. Go deimhin, roinnt blianta ó shin, bhí sé de phribhléid agam an Torc a bhronnadh ar Imogen, comhartha gur toghadh í ina Saoi de chuid Aosdána[1], agus ar an ócáid sin luaigh mé gur dhíol suntais a mhinice a thug mé faoi deara, nuair a bhíonn dealbhóireacht Imogen Stuart á plé, go moltar í as a saothar agus go dtaispeántar, ag an am céanna, gean tochtmhar, domhain don ealaíontóir féin.

Is ábhar mór ómóis atá ansin, agus ómós atá tuillte go maith aici agus a léiríonn an dea-chroí a shainíonn Imogen Stuart, an t-ealaíontóir. Léirigh

Imogen i gcónaí a toil mhacánta chun a saothar ealaíne a chur i gcroílár na sochaí agus an phobail ionas go mbainfeadh an uile dhuine taitneamh agus tuiscint as, seachas é a chur i spáis ar leith don scothaicme.

Is ar son na hEaglaise Caitlicí a chruthaigh sí cuid mhaith dá healaín – saothair amhail an Chros ó aimsir na bpéindlíthe i Loch Dearg, na humair uisce ag an scrín i gCnoc Mhuire, Turas na Croise i Mainistir Bhaile an Tobair, agus an altóir snoite i séipéal Choláiste na hOllscoile, Corcaigh, a sholáthraíonn cúlra ciúin ach spreagúil do shaol spioradálta na ndaoine a thagann chun adhradh a dhéanamh, chun fóirithint a fháil nó chun suí go ciúin ag déanamh a marana.

Tá roinnt glún tar éis súgradh a dhéanamh thart timpeall ar dhealbh Fhidléir Dhúna in Ionad Siopadóireachta Stigh Lorgan, agus ar feadh na mblianta ba chuid nádúrtha de ghnáthshaol shiopadóirí Dhún Laoghaire *Pangur Bán*, agus ina dhiaidh sin de shaol na mac léinn a bhíodh ag cruinniú thart timpeall air i mBloc na nDán sa Choláiste Ollscoile, Baile Átha Cliath. Tá dealbha Imogen ar taispeáint, freisin, i scoileanna, ospidéil agus foirgnimh phoiblí eile, agus taitneamh á bhaint astu i spiorad an phobail agus an dlúthchaidrimh, agus ag an am céanna, táim cinnte de, tá siad ag dul i gcion ar bhealach réidh ar shamhlaíocht cuid mhaith daoine agus ag spreagadh turas aeistéitiúil go dtí domhain athshamhlaithe.

Níos gaire dár mbaile, fiú sular tháinig *Pangur Bán*, bhí a lorg fágtha ag Imogen ar Áras an Uachtaráin, lena saothar iontach ar dhealbh bhrád phortráide de Mary Robinson i nDorchla Francini, agus lena rannpháirtíocht sa choiste roghnaithe i gcomhair na deilbhe a bhí coimisiúnaithe againn le haghaidh chomóradh céad bliain Éirí Amach 1916.

Leagadh an oiread tábhachta ar thaithí saoil Imogen mar dhealbhóir go ndearna an coiste rogha inspioráideach agus an coimisiún á thabhairt do Rachel Joynt as *Dearcán na nDaoine – The People's Acorn*.

Tá gné chuimsitheach ealaín Imogen le brath go follasach in *Pangur Bán* tríd an tslí a suiteáiltear na binsí go cúramach ar shlí chomhtháite, rud a thugann cuireadh don phobal a bheith rannpháirteach ina saothar seachas a bheith ina mbreathnóirí géilliúla. Go deimhin, mar atá feicthe againn san fhíseán atá curtha i dtoll a chéile againn i gcomhair imeacht an lae inniu, b'ábhar mór suntais an aird a thug Imogen agus a hiníon Aisling ar shuiteáil gach aon ghné den saothar, na binsí san áireamh, agus *Pangur Bán* á shuiteáil thíos staighre, agus a thuiscint cé chomh tábhachtach is atá siad sa léiriú mór cruthaitheach sin.

Is léiriú ealaíonta atá ann a bhfuil sé d'ádh orainn é a bheith againn anseo in Áras an Uachtaráin, agus ba mhaith liom buíochas a ghlacadh le hUachtarán an Choláiste Ollscoile, Baile Átha Cliath (UCD), an tOllamh Andrew Deeks agus le Ruth Ferguson, Coimeádaí Ealaíne UCD, as a athlonnú go Teach Uachtarán na hÉireann a éascú. Ar feadh os cionn míle bliain, tá taitneamh agus foghlaim á mbaint as scéal an chait bhig bháin agus a chompánaigh, an manach, gach aon duine díobh tiomanta dá cheird, gach aon duine ag léiriú a nádúir instinnigh agus fhoghlamtha go síochánta lena chéile.

Anois, trí fhís agus trí fhéile Imogen, is féidir liom féin agus Saidhbhín, foireann an Árais, agus na mílte duine a thugann cuairt ar an áit seo gach bliain, taitneamh a bhaint as mionghnéithe soiléire na deilbhe sin a chuireann beocht san ábhar scríofa. Is féidir sinn a spreagadh le machnamh a dhéanamh agus le meas a bheith againn ar an deis ar leith seo chun tuiscint a fháil ar an gcaoi ar féidir le duine cruthaitheach sa saol comhaimseartha saothar ealaíne a scríobhadh san am atá caite a léirmhíniú.

Scaoiltear tharainn an oiread sin deiseanna go ciúin, gan taifead agus gan chuimhne. Tá an t-ádh dearg orainn, mar sin féin, go bhfuil scríbhneoirí, péintéirí, filí agus dealbhóirí inár measc a chuireann in iúl na heachtraí nó na híomhánna ar leith sin a shoiléiríonn agus a shainíonn splanc léargais thábhachtach. Táimid go mór faoi chomaoin ag na daoine samhlaíocha agus cruthaitheacha sin. Ní hamháin go gcruthaíonn siad rud éigin atá álainn agus spreagúil ar bhun aeistéitiúil, ach cuidíonn siad linn ár ndomhan agus ár n-áit sa domhan sin a thuiscint.

Is fiú, freisin, smaoineamh ar an bhforbróir agus pátrún na n-ealaíon, an tUasal Kish Kennedy, a thóg cuid de na hionaid siopaí is luaithe in Éirinn, Stigh Lorgan agus Dún Laoghaire ina measc. Ba é a thuig an luach a bhain le healaín phobail a chuimsiú ina chuid forbraíochtaí, agus tá a fhios agam gur dhuine é a raibh ard-mheas ag Imogen air.

Tá cuid mhaith ealaíontóirí ann a ndeachaigh an dán 'Pangur Bán' i bhfeidhm go mór orthu. Is mór le rá na scríbhneoirí litríochta a d'aistrigh an dán go Béarla, amhail Robin Flower, Frank O'Connor, W.H. Auden agus, ar ndóigh, Seamus Heaney. Le blianta beaga anuas, cuireadh Pangur in aithne do ghlúine nua trí roinnt leabhar maisithe do pháistí agus trína chur i láthair sa scannán beochana *The Secret of Kells,* ina ndearna an t-aisteoir cáiliúil Mick Lally guthú a úinéara, 'Brother Aidan'. [...]

Ba mhaith liom, freisin, buíochas ar leith a ghlacadh lenár gcomhghleacaithe as an OOP[2] as a gcuid oibre díograisí; tá an tionscadal seo glactha go díograiseach acu chucu féin agus Pangur dea-réitithe acu don taispeántas, agus glacaim buíochas le foireann Áras an Uachtaráin a réitigh ár gceiliúradh inniu.

Ach is tábhachtaí ar fad a bheith ábalta mo bhuíochas ó chroí a chur in iúl do Imogen Stuart inniu. Téann *Pangur Bán,* ach an oiread le saothar iomlán Imogen, i gcion orainn ar shlí chiúin agus dhomhain, é lán leis an daonnacht agus leis an spiorad a fheabhsaíonn an saol, rud is cúis leis an taitneamh a bhaintear as a cuid saothair chruthaithigh. Is pribhléid mhór agus ábhar pléisiúir áit chónaithe nua a sholáthar do *Phangur Bán,* áit a mbainfear taitneamh as i spiorad an phobail agus an chairdis roinnte.

Is mór an onóir dúinn glacadh leis an saothar seo inniu, agus onóir speisialta dúinn go bhfuil Imogen i láthair, bean a bhfuil cion mná den scoth déanta aici i saol cultúrtha ár náisiúin.

Aistrithe le Pádraic de Bhaldraithe

Une certaine idée de « la maison »

Discours prononcé au Festival international des Arts de Galway (Galway International Arts Festival), NUI Galway, le 21 juillet 2018.

Aujourd'hui, je suis de retour dans un environnement qui m'est très familier. J'ai d'excellents souvenirs de cours donnés au sein de cette université, dans des circonstances cependant bien différentes. Je me souviens que l'une de mes classes avait été fixée au plus redoutable des horaires, à savoir neuf heures le matin. Fort heureusement, nous étions dans l'Irlande des années 70 et le choix d'intituler ma série de cours « Déviance, crime et châtiment »[3] m'a garanti un amphithéâtre bondé. J'ai d'ailleurs appris plus tard qu'une bonne partie des étudiants présents y avait en fait assisté en auditeur libre.

Je les ai sensibilisés aux travaux de Michel Foucault, alors considéré comme un penseur avant-gardiste. Pour beaucoup, le philosophe offrait une source passionnante de nouvelles perspectives sociologiques sur le rôle et la nature du genre, les notions d'enfermement et de crime dans nos sociétés modernes, même si cela ne correspondait pas forcément aux attentes ou aux espérances de mon auditoire. J'ai encore en mémoire ce que m'a un jour confié le professeur Edmond Dougan, Président du Département de science politique et sociologie, également collègue sociologue, directeur de département et franciscain. Nos étudiants lui avaient raconté qu'en leur présentant

Une certaine idée de « la maison »

le concept de société, j'en avais ce faisant démonté un à un tous les aspects. « Tout cela est authentique, Michael. » Puis il m'a demandé : « Mais au fait, est-ce qu'à la fin, vous avez bien pensé à tout remettre en place pour eux ? »

L'étendue du thème de ce volet du festival intitulé « Échanges autour des pensées premières » (*First Thought Talks*) me donne l'occasion de revenir – et de mener une réflexion – sur certains des sujets qui ont suscité mon intérêt, à la fois comme professeur d'université et simple citoyen. Il serait cependant bien prétentieux de ma part d'espérer remettre tout en place pour vous à la fin de ma réflexion autour du concept de « maison » et c'est pourquoi je ne puis rien vous promettre !

Contrairement aux premières minutes de mes cours durant toutes ces années, je ne souhaite pas aujourd'hui débuter en citant Foucault, mais plutôt en faisant référence aux travaux de deux philosophes très différents, que Foucault lui-même, bien que sa propre pensée ait suivi des directions radicalement opposées, considérait comme source d'influences intellectuellement formatrices. Je veux parler de Martin Heidegger, dont l'héritage philosophique restera toujours entaché par des prises de positions d'une moralité abjecte dans les années trente et quarante, et du philosophe français Gaston Bachelard, dont les recherches ont transformé la philosophie des sciences à partir des années cinquante. Quoique différents dans leurs perspectives philosophiques et leur parcours, tous deux nous invitent néanmoins à méditer sur les nombreuses formes que peut prendre le concept de « maison ».

Dans un essai intitulé « Bâtir habiter penser »,[4] Heidegger pose deux questions : « Qu'est-ce que l'habitation ? » et « Comment le bâtir fait-il partie de l'habitation ? » Il écrit « qu'habiter est le trait fondamental de l'être (Sein) en conformité duquel les mortels sont ». Le lieu où l'on habite et l'ensemble du processus qui vise à construire, fabriquer, donner forme, constitue de ce fait un phénomène qu'on pourrait qualifier de presque circulaire. Même quand les gens créent un espace de vie, ils forgent entre eux-mêmes et ce lieu une relation au point de commencer à habiter ce lieu. Heidegger écrit que « la relation de l'homme et de l'espace n'est rien d'autre que l'habitation pensée dans son être ».

En tant qu'observateur des migrations, je ne manque pas d'être frappé par les implications de cette dernière phrase. En effet, elle sous-tend l'hypothèse qu'il existe une universalité dans une relation établie avec un espace spécifique et peut-être même une période spécifique. Cela démontre une disposition intrinsèque qui occupe la plupart des sciences sociales modernes. Elle confirme la difficulté à englober l'expérience du mouvement ou celles des interstices, l'espace entre les espaces.

Migration et mouvement ont toujours fait partie de l'expérience humaine. C'est un fait que, pour les peuples anciens, ces phénomènes constituaient le fondement même de leur vie sociale et économique. Si nous prenons l'exemple des peuples nomades, il est clair que la vie de tous ces migrants, saisonniers ou permanents, ne saurait être réduite à une telle formulation. Cela ne signifie en rien qu'ils ne se sont pas fixés à un endroit, ni qu'ils n'ont formé de liens entre eux et un lieu de vie particulier, assez fort pour qu'il devienne un endroit privilégié et idéal où construire sa maison. Ils n'ont cependant jamais été sédentaires, pas plus qu'ils ne se sont attachés à un lieu, ni encore à une identité, étant eux-mêmes issus d'identités diverses. L'éphémère demande une perpétuelle redéfinition de ce que l'on entend par « maison ». Cela relève plus du domaine de la littérature car les sciences sociales ont souvent eu tendance à ignorer cet aspect pour concentrer leurs recherches sur les sédentaires.

En 1958, quelques années après qu'Heidegger ait donné sa première conférence qui allait devenir « Bâtir habiter penser », Gaston Bachelard terminait un bref ouvrage intitulé *La poétique de l'espace*.[5] Plus connu pour son travail épistémologique, il s'est cependant aussi intéressé à ce qu'il appelait « la phénoménologie de l'imaginaire », l'étude du sens poétique de la maison, de l'intimité qui imprègne tous les endroits de la vie quotidienne, comme le grenier, la cave ou les tiroirs. Dans *La poétique de l'espace*, il écrit que « [la maison] est notre premier univers. Elle est vraiment un cosmos. Un cosmos dans toute l'acception du terme, c'est-à-dire la topographie de notre être intime. » Songeons au positionnement de la chaise près de la cheminée dans l'étude d'Arensberg et Kimball[6] menée dans les communautés rurales de Luogh et Rynamona du comté de Clare dans les années 30.

Dans le raisonnement de Bachelard, la maison prend consistance de foyer en devenant un lieu d'intimité et de créativité, de souvenirs et de rêves. Une chose est remarquable dans l'œuvre de Gaston Bachelard, manifestement intrigué par l'organisation de l'espace. Le foyer y est en fait présenté, non seulement comme espace physique, mais également comme réalité immatérielle, non comme un lieu de réconfort, mais comme un lieu où se tissent une série de liens et de relations intimes avec les lieux et entre les gens. J'ajouterais que la perception de la configuration de la maison, et le statut qui lui est ainsi conféré, joue un rôle d'indicateur sur la place occupée dans la société, confirmant la respectabilité ou, au contraire le manque supposé de celle-ci.

Cette définition signifie-t-elle que « la maison » ne revêt alors qu'une fonction de résidence, un endroit occupé fournissant un espace sécurisé, un espace d'où on sort pour participer à la vie quotidienne, se déplacer ? Dans ces conditions, comment et quand la notion de propriété apparaît-elle ? Celle-ci doit-elle être comprise comme une garantie de sécurité, partant alors du fait que l'occupation d'un espace serait un critère insuffisant pour appréhender ce qu'est le concept de « maison » ?

Au-delà du thème de « la maison » définie comme, disons, une série d'équilibres entre sécurité et liberté, il semble utile d'examiner brièvement l'évolution de notre « maison planète » depuis les temps les plus anciens jusqu'à « l'Anthropocène ». L'échelle du temps humain ne permet pas une considération approfondie de « la maison » au regard de notre planète, et de la perte de symétrie entre nature et habitat. Je crois pourtant que c'est une perspective que nous devons nous efforcer de retrouver voire de redécouvrir dans notre effort pour saisir les conséquences des changements que l'humanité a infligé à la terre, planète vulnérable que nous avons en partage. Une planète qui abrite plus de 7,7 milliards d'humains et un nombre incalculable d'animaux et de plantes.

Ces changements et les souffrances de notre monde actuel, sont eux-mêmes le fruit d'un type particulier de civilisation humaine, basée sur deux grandes révolutions dans l'organisation économique et sociale, la révolution néolithique et la révolution industrielle. Ces dernières ont développé, puis reproduit des idées et des idéaux très singuliers autour du concept de « maison ». Ces principes ont constitué notre héritage contemporain. Pour autant, ils ne semblent pas ouverts à la critique ni à l'évaluation, comme cela devrait être le cas dans le cadre d'une recherche responsable et d'un débat citoyen. Il est d'ailleurs envisageable de penser que cela entrave notre capacité à réinventer aujourd'hui notre avenir collectif.

On situe habituellement la révolution industrielle dans la seconde moitié du XVIIIe siècle. Il est toutefois désormais admis que cette période est aussi le point de départ de ce que le chimiste spécialiste de l'atmosphère Paul Crutzen, colauréat du prix Nobel de chimie, a baptisé « l'Anthropocène », à savoir une nouvelle ère géologique dans l'histoire du monde, marquée notamment par l'influence d'une seule espèce, en l'occurrence la nôtre, sur l'environnement global.

Le terme Anthropocène possède sa propre et éminente généalogie. Il a été utilisé pour la première fois en 1873 par le Père Antonio Stoppani, géologue italien lui-même influencé par John Perkins Marsh, dont le livre *L'Homme et la nature ; ou, la géographie physique modifiée par l'action humaine* paru en 1863, a été fondamental pour le développement du mouvement environnemental aux États-Unis. Au cœur des travaux de Marsh se trouve une analyse novatrice des situations de crises aigües traversées par les civilisations sédentaires. En utilisant des techniques agricoles intensives, héritées de la révolution néolithique, le monde méditerranéen ancien a provoqué une dégradation des sols. Nous avons ici l'un des premiers exemples d'un système d'abondance, toujours en quête de surplus qui a mené à une crise environnementale.

Nous pouvons entrevoir, dans la splendeur et la décadence de ces civilisations anciennes, le prélude à l'Anthropocène. Même s'ils n'avaient pas encore été accablés par le pouvoir de transformer radicalement le cycle du carbone ou de l'azote, ces anciennes peuplades étaient pourtant déjà en mesure de dégrader l'environnement au point de se condamner eux-mêmes et de compromettre leur « maison » dans la nature. Leur civilisation était totalement différente de celles qui les avaient précédées. Leur développement n'avait pas pour fondement la migration, la chasse et la cueillette, mais bel et bien la culture des sols et la domestication des animaux, l'implantation dans un lieu, que ce soit par le biais de propriétés isolées, de groupes d'habitations ou de villes densément peuplées, et par-dessus tout, la capacité de transformer les ressources physiques du corps humain en énergie.

Pour la première fois depuis nos ancêtres *Homo habilis*, apparus il y a 20 millions d'années, des êtres humains ont inventé des cultures dans un espace unique et sédentaire où des bâtiments tels les temples, sont devenus, en remplacement de la nature, le centre de la spiritualité. Au sein des sociétés néolithiques, une forme de relations sociales hiérarchisées s'est peu à peu imposée qui a rendu possible une production coordonnée sous le contrôle d'une nouvelle classe dirigeante, se réclamant souvent de l'approbation divine. L'un des effets de ce phénomène a été le développement d'une division du travail fortement axée sur la différence entre les sexes.

Ce n'est donc pas un hasard si l'esclavage, la plus ignoble des institutions humaines, a commencé à cette période. Au cours de ses récentes recherches, l'anthropologue James C. Scott a fait ce constat glaçant que les murs érigés autour des camps dans les sociétés esclavagistes avaient probablement été construits non pour exclure ceux au dehors, mais pour emprisonner ceux restés à l'intérieur. Je ne souscris pas pour autant à la thèse laissant entrevoir de telles spéculations. Quelle que soit l'époque, les fondements d'un état, ne pouvaient et ne peuvent pas reposer uniquement sur la violence. Force est de constater que les villes-états du monde antique ont créé au fil du temps des républiques instables, certaines caractérisées par un degré d'injustices systémiques et profondes.

Nous trouvons dans la Rome antique, et dans les travaux de membres conservateurs de la classe sénatoriale, comme par exemple Cicéron, d'une part un engagement en faveur d'un idéal de communauté politique construite sur la solidarité, et d'autre part une volonté partagée pour un idéal de justice, aussi hypocrite que soit l'exclusion du droit à la citoyenneté touchant les esclaves, les femmes et mêmes d'autres Italiens, qui est apparue plus tard. Cet idéal a également imprégné la vie civile d'Athènes et a trouvé son expression dans l'ouvrage *Les politiques* d'Aristote et dans les oraisons de Démosthène.

Cela a fourni le socle d'un concept de « maison » perçue en tant qu'ensemble de relations et d'engagements partagés plutôt que comme un lieu de sédentarité, aussi important que le lieu ait pu être. Thémistocle, homme d'état athénien, est celui qui incarne le mieux ce concept. En effet, il est parvenu à persuader ses concitoyens d'évacuer leur cité tant aimé pour permettre aux Grecs de répondre avec un front uni à l'invasion de l'Empire persan. Et même si Athènes a été complètement détruite par les flammes, la cité-état d'Athènes s'est bientôt reconstituée dans un village de pêcheurs voisin. Cependant, cet idéal de maison et de patrie immatériels, caractérisé par l'exclusion et la profonde injustice, n'était réservé qu'à un petit nombre d'hommes jugés dignes d'être citoyens. Dans quelle mesure peut-on alors considérer le concept de maison chez les Grecs, le *oikos*, d'où viennent les termes « économie » ou

« organisation du foyer », comme une maison au sens physique du terme, comme le lieu intime, peuplé de biens divers imaginé par Gaston Bachelard ? N'était-ce pas au contraire un lieu d'aliénation et de solitude pour beaucoup de membres du foyer, exclus, au même titre que les femmes et les esclaves, de toute participation à la vie publique ?

En même temps que les cités-états donnaient forme au domaine public, se mettait en place une nouvelle vision du foyer privé, dirigé, organisé et contrôlé par le patriarche aristocratique, une construction sociale qui a trouvé plus tard une traduction dans le cadre du droit romain. L'image du sénateur romain avec femme et enfants, menant son foyer entouré de milliers d'esclaves, ne manque de nous revenir à l'esprit. Fondement bien regrettable de l'Empire romain, la construction sociale dans le cadre d'un patriarcat s'est en même temps avérée la plus durable, permettant de résister à la désintégration de la civilisation sédentaire romaine, sous la pression d'innombrables migrations de peuples nomades. Ces derniers ont jeté les bases de ce qui allait devenir l'ordre féodal du monde médiéval. L'imaginaire politique de ce nouveau monde était entièrement dominé par l'idée de hiérarchie, représentée par la grande chaîne de l'être conçue par les néo-platoniciens, chaîne reliant aux cieux les plantes et les animaux les plus minuscules, ainsi que par la sacralisation progressive de la figure du monarque.

Malgré la distance temporelle et spatiale qui sépare la France médiévale de la Mésopotamie antique, les deux étaient en fait des représentations de civilisations néolithiques, forcées de produire de l'énergie en ayant exclusivement recours à la force humaine. L'image du paysan, du travailleur fidèle à la terre, représentait l'archétype du producteur agricole dans toutes les sociétés néolithiques. Attaché à son bien, soumis au pouvoir exercé de manière souvent arbitraire par une autorité supérieure, un seigneur féodal ou un membre de l'administration communale, le paysan et sa famille, fournissaient tout au long d'une vie de labeur éreintant, la base matérielle de toute une civilisation. La République romaine a été l'un des rares régimes antiques ou féodaux qui, pour un temps au moins, a prétendu être une confédération de fermiers indépendants, une communauté de foyers et de familles, chacun avec ses modestes fonctions.

La maison du paysan était sans conteste un lieu de travail avec des tâches divisées en fonction du genre. Les femmes et les enfants faisaient leur part de labeur, assurant non seulement la survie de la famille à travers des besognes de tout temps relevant de la compétence des femmes, comme assurer le bien-être des membres de la famille ou effectuer les corvées de nettoyage, mais également grâce à leur participation aux travaux des champs. Les empires atlantiques du nord-ouest de l'Europe ont ensuite peu à peu imposé par la conquête une expansion inexorable et insatiable de leur pouvoir économique. Le concept d'atelier était né. Un récent article de Jane Humphries et Benjamin Schneider, publié dans la revue scientifique *Economic History Review*, a par exemple décrit en détail l'extension massive du filage artisanal dans l'Angleterre du XVIIIe siècle. Dans les années 1750, cet artisanat représentait la plus large source d'emploi avec près d'un million de femmes et d'enfants actifs dans la production de fil. Leur travail constituait plus d'un tiers du revenu d'un foyer vivant dans la pauvreté. Ce type de travail était principalement effectué dans des ateliers à l'intérieur des maisons, et relevait d'un système d'exploitation dans la mesure où les patrons étaient propriétaires de l'outil. Ils leur mettaient ainsi le marché en main leur demandant simplement de travailler et de faire du rendement.

La mécanisation de la production constituera plus tard une nouvelle étape. Humphries et Schneider avance la théorie selon laquelle cette nouvelle dynamique était une réponse, non aux salaires élevés, comme certains en avaient auparavant émis l'hypothèse, mais un appel au travail des femmes et des enfants de plus en plus en situation de pauvreté. Ce modèle a fait passer le travail rémunéré de la maison à l'usine. La construction sociale du temps, des comportements sociaux voire sexuels, en a été transformée tout comme la répartition du temps passé à l'usine avec ses cadences infernales, et le temps à la maison où la famille pouvait se perpétuer. Des inventions comme la machine à filer dépendaient encore de l'énergie produite par les humains et les animaux. L'ensemble du progrès des civilisations néolithiques, qu'elles se situent dans l'Éthiopie médiévale ou à l'aube de l'Angleterre moderne, restait en fin de compte tributaire de la nature et reposait encore sur la vie végétale pour nourrir les hommes et le bétail.

Cette contrainte a finalement été éliminée lorsqu'on a découvert qu'il était possible de transformer l'énergie provenant de la combustion de carbone en énergie mécanique. Cela a eu pour conséquence le développement d'un nouveau type de relation entre économie, éthique, culture et société. Une vision étriquée et déformée de l'économie politique. Une vision favorisant l'accumulation qui fustigeait la pauvreté au milieu de l'abondance. Au niveau international, une idéologie impérialiste prenant en compte les nouvelles sciences et technologies de l'époque revendiquait une supériorité arrogante considérant les dominés et les dépossédés au mieux comme retardés, voire inférieurs.

Au cœur de l'Europe occidentale industrialisée, cette nouvelle civilisation ne réclamait pas de paysans, mais des ouvriers. Dans les villes moyennes et les grandes villes, une nouvelle classe ouvrière était en train d'émerger. A la fin du XIXe siècle, les ouvriers qualifiés étaient en mesure, dans une sorte de mimétisme, de reproduire le modèle domestique de la classe moyenne professionnelle et mercantile, alors en plein essor. Les femmes accomplissaient les tâches ménagères sans rémunération et les hommes, eux, avaient un travail rémunéré dans ce nouveau système industriel. L'écart se creusait entre l'ouvrier producteur et le produit de son travail.

C'est à cette époque qu'Émile Durkheim a commencé ses travaux qui, entre autres choses, nous ont familiarisés à « l'anomie », concept résultant de son étude sur le suicide. Cette époque est également marquée par les écrits de Karl Marx pour qui l'idée d'aliénation était centrale. Les transformations des modes de production ont entraîné des changements profonds dans le contexte plus vaste des relations à la fois personnelles, familiales et sociales. La littérature allait désormais pouvoir explorer un nouveau thème, celui d'un monde où régnerait l'impossibilité de n'être jamais « chez soi ».

Il est donc à peine surprenant de constater que, durant cette période, s'est opérée une séparation entre l'idée de foyer et de maison, de propriété et d'habitation, à la fois dans la doctrine juridique et dans la vie quotidienne. En fait, le conflit entre foyer et propriété, entre habitation et possessions n'a jamais été plus criant que durant l'époque industrielle et impériale et allait semer les graines d'une récolte qui a mis un siècle à mûrir.

Les peuples indigènes en Amérique du Nord et en Australie avaient un idéal de vie et une perception du mot « maison » et « foyer » qui différaient notablement de l'acception qu'on s'en faisait dans l'Europe du Nord-ouest. Lors de mon voyage en Australie l'an passé, j'ai gardé à l'esprit que de telles idées étaient toujours contestées, surtout après le jugement de Mabo, reconnaissant enfin les droits fonciers du peuple aborigène, du moins dans le cadre du droit commun. La conception de terre et de « maison » – de « pays » – développée par les premiers aborigènes australiens, la plus ancienne culture encore existante, avait pour postulat que le peuple appartenait à la terre autant que la terre appartenait au peuple. Le jugement de Mabo a renversé cette doctrine de *terra nullius*, une fiction juridique, arrogante, monstrueuse et impérialiste selon laquelle les peuples d'Australie ne pouvaient revendiquer, en vertu du droit commun anglais, les terres sur lesquelles ils avaient habités et qu'ils avaient façonnées par leur travail pendant soixante mille ans.

Les théories de John Locke ont justifié voire consacré la vaste confiscation des terres en Australie et en Amérique du nord. Ce dernier a parfois été décrit comme le père de la pensée libérale moderne et de la tolérance alors même que ses axes de réflexion se construisaient à partir de l'exclusion. Si son *Essai sur la tolérance* excluait de sa théorie sur le droit à la propriété comme droit naturel les catholiques irlandais, usant de cette phrase mémorable selon laquelle « les papistes sont comme des serpents », il en allait de même pour ceux qui ne cultivaient pas la terre. Selon John Locke, les Amérindiens étaient assimilés à des « bêtes sauvages ».

Comme le rappelle à juste titre le philosophe italien Domenico Losurdo, l'idée que la terre devienne propriété en vertu du principe qu'elle doit être associée au travail a été utilisée afin d'exclure un continent entier de personnes qui ne partageaient pas une telle conception de la propriété. En clair, ceux qui se revendiquaient comme colons ne considéraient pas la gestion des ressources naturelles comme un travail. Cette théorie de la propriété a ensuite constitué la base de ce que nous appellerons « la grande dépossession des territoires » qui s'est abattue sur les peuples d'Amérique et d'Australie. Dans son *Histoire d'Angleterre*, David Hume écrit :

> Dès le commencement, les Irlandais avaient été ensevelis dans les ténèbres les plus profondes de la barbarie et de l'ignorance. Comme les Romains par qui toutes les nations occidentales avaient été civilisées ne les avaient ni conquis, ni même attaqués, ils restèrent dans l'état de société le plus grossier et le plus informe, et ne se distinguèrent que par les vices auxquels la nature humaine est sujette, tant que l'éducation ne l'adoucit pas ou qu'elle n'est pas réprimée par les lois.[7]

VI. A Multilingual Europe – Translations into Irish, French and German

Cette grande dépossession et ses préjugés durables, moteur du projet de colonisation, font également partie de notre Histoire nationale. Lorsque la conquête et la création des états par les empires impériaux ont atteint leur apogée et leur terme à la fin du XIXe siècle, la conception de « maison » dans notre pays ainsi que son rapport au concept de propriété foncière a subi sa propre transformation sous la pression de l'un des plus grands mouvements de pensée et d'action qu'ait connu cette île, à savoir l'agitation agraire.

La société irlandaise des années 1870 était le produit des conflits du XVIIe siècle, notamment de l'Acte d'Union, qui a imposé un seul paradigme de pensée économique en matière de commerce et de productivité et mené à la tragédie qu'a représentée la Grande Famine. L'Irlande était un pays essentiellement rural, caractérisé par un nombre important de petites exploitations. Cependant, celles qui pratiquaient une agriculture de subsistance n'étaient pas en aussi grand nombre, comme c'était le cas peu avant la famine. Tout ce qui pouvait concerner l'économie et le droit était l'apanage d'un petit nombre de propriétaires qui agissaient par l'entremise de maîtres de domaine et d'intermédiaires, d'aristocrates terriens et de sous-locataires.

L'acception commune en termes d'économie politique du sens de la propriété foncière avait changé dans son contenu, mais pas dans sa forme. En effet, la notion de propriété définie par Locke, avait cédé la place à l'idée développée par le philosophe anglais Jeremy Bentham, selon laquelle le droit à la propriété assuré était le moyen le plus efficace, pour les détenteurs de capitaux, de maximiser l'utilité de leur capital. Cela ne fait-il pas écho à ce que nous vivons aujourd'hui ? En 1848, au plus fort de la Famine, James Fintan Lalor fustigeait l'idée de propriété inviolable :

> Je ne reconnais aucun droit de propriété à huit mille personnes, qu'elles soient nobles ou non. Huit mille personnes qui confisquent à une population de huit millions tout droit à la propriété, à la sécurité, à l'indépendance et jusqu'à son existence même. Huit mille qui se dressent contre tous les droits politiques et sociaux de l'île et de ses habitants. Je ne reconnais aucun droit de propriété à ceux qui retirent la nourriture de la bouche de toute une population et la condamne à la famine, qui refusent aux paysans, le droit à une maison, mais qui en échange leur octroient le droit à un atelier domestique.[8]

Pour aller à l'encontre de ce droit individuel, Fintan Lalor a été encore plus loin et a fait valoir un autre droit, le droit, je cite, « de vivre [sur sa terre] en sécurité, dans le confort et l'indépendance ».[9] Aujourd'hui, sa statue trône à Portlaoise, sa ville natale. Malgré la reconnaissance dont il a bénéficié et sa grande influence sur Davitt, Connolly et Pearse, il demeure une sorte de prophète méconnu. Il est dommage que son concept de démocratie radicale soit resté dans l'ombre du romantisme, plus facile à exploiter, de ses amis du mouvement Jeune Irlande.

Il n'en reste pas moins que sa vision de « maison » en tant que droit social inaliénable, associée à l'idée de nation, de communauté nationale au sens large, a été mise en avant, intentionnellement ou non d'ailleurs, par Charles Stewart Parnell lors d'un meeting à Limerick, le 31 août 1879. Parnell a appelé les fermiers locataires d'Irlande à « défendre fermement leur terre »[10] et à rejoindre le mouvement d'agitation agraire. En fait, les fermiers locataires du pays étaient invités à ne plus payer leur loyer. Cela a ouvert la voie à des revendications qui ont fait date, à savoir un contrat de fermage entre le tenancier et le propriétaire, un loyer raisonnable et la possibilité de cessation du bail.

Au-delà de la maison comme lieu d'intimité, se manifeste le désir de sécurité de ses occupants pour qui la maison constitue également un abri. On a aujourd'hui tendance à oublier que les leaders masculins de La ligue pour un territoire national irlandais (*Irish National Land League*) ont été emprisonnés. Les femmes ont alors dû continuer la lutte à un niveau d'organisation et de discipline jamais atteint auparavant dans la conduite de la guerre agraire. Anna, la sœur de Parnell, en est le meilleur exemple. Ces femmes ont apporté une énergie et une vigueur nouvelles pour s'opposer aux évictions. Lorsqu'elles ne pouvaient éviter l'expulsion des familles, elles les installaient dans des abris temporaires en espérant qu'il leur serait possible de retrouver leur foyer une fois la guerre agraire gagnée. En ce qui les concernait, la sécurité du foyer et de la propriété ne devait pas, comme cela aurait pu être le cas pour d'autres, être subordonnée à la perspective du Home Rule.[11] Il est important de noter que la Ligue agraire féminine (*Ladies' Land League*), « première organisation de femmes irlandaises dirigées par des femmes »[12] comme le rappellera plus tard Jennie Wyse Power, ne s'est jamais limitée à des objectifs mineurs ou de portée réduite. Au contraire, la Ligue se mobilisait pour un ensemble de revendications en vue de proposer des transformations dans le domaine de la protection et de la création d'une maison, une maison en tant qu'habitation et abri physique, une maison en tant que lieu de sécurité. Elles ont ainsi redéfini la perception même du concept de foyer national élargi, soulignant ce qu'il pourrait être et ce qu'il devrait s'efforcer d'être.

Je ne reviendrai pas sur l'histoire de la guerre agraire, ni sur la manière dont de nombreux hectares de terre ont été redistribués, au fil des différentes lois agraires, à ceux qui, à maints égards, étaient les plus puissants des fermiers locataires, même lorsque les paysans sans terre ou cultivant des terres marginales, ont quitté le pays perpétuant ainsi un motif d'émigration désormais familier.

L'économie politique est essentielle. Les différentes appréciations des politiques économiques alimentent la politique en général. Je voudrais réitérer ici un point mentionné dans une conférence que j'ai donnée en octobre dernier à l'université de Melbourne. Je parlais de l'influence des économistes politiques irlandais en Australie et en Irlande et souhaitais montrer comment certaines techniques pouvaient produire des résultats différents selon le contexte historique. Dans les années 1840, Robert Torrens, un disciple irlandais de l'économiste David Ricardo, a émigré dans la toute nouvelle colonie d'Australie méridionale dans l'espoir d'y fonder une *New Hibernia*, une nouvelle Irlande, au bord de l'océan austral, où s'étaient déjà établis des fermiers irlandais indépendants, cultivant des parcelles de terre de petite taille.

Cette initiative a échoué. En effet, L'Australie méridionale se trouvait alors au cœur d'une vague spéculative. Les prêts octroyés par le gouvernement colonial étaient rapidement revendus, ce qui ne manquait pas de provoquer des conflits durables autour des titres de propriété dans cette nouvelle colonie. C'est Robert Richard, le fils aîné de Torrens, qui a mis un terme à cette crise. Il a eu en effet l'idée d'introduire un principe d'immatriculation des titres fonciers rendant ainsi irrévocable le titre du propriétaire inscrit.

Il y a ici un point moral et éthique. Le système mis en place par Torrens constituait non seulement un moyen de résoudre la crise temporaire due à la spéculation coloniale, mais instituait également un outil juridique dans l'empire qui permettait d'éradiquer toute prétention au titre détenu par les premiers occupants d'une terre. En conséquence, ces derniers ne partageaient aucun des a priori implicites des deux régimes de propriété dans la Loi commune (*Common Law*), qu'ils soient juridiques ou philosophiques ou même dans le cadre du système prôné par Torrens. Les concessions de terre avaient été accordées à des spéculateurs coloniaux pour des terres occupées par les premiers peuples d'Australie et le système Torrens devenait le gage de leur expropriation malgré l'engagement de respecter les droits et leur plein exercice pour les occupants d'origine, comme énoncé dans les lettres patentes autorisant la colonisation de l'Australie australe.

La grande ironie de cette histoire est que, lorsque le système Torrens a été appliqué en Irlande dans le contexte des Lois agraires de 1885, 1891, 1903 et 1909, il a servi à financer l'achat et le transfert de terres du propriétaire au fermier locataire. Même si le principe d'immatriculation des titres fonciers a conduit à déposséder les premiers peuples des colonies de l'Australie méridionale, cela a permis la reconstitution des rapports de propriété construits au fil des siècles qui ont vu la conquête de l'Irlande. Les anciens liens à la terre étaient rompus et assuraient aux locataires irlandais un titre de propriété plein et sans contrainte.

En Irlande, cela représentait une libération partielle du passé permettant un éventuel projet de construction de sa maison, bien que progressive dans des endroits largement dominés par une nouvelle classe d'éleveurs tout-puissants. En Australie, cela a marqué une rupture avec le passé. Le concept de « maison » se trouvait assujetti aux nouvelles exigences de l'impérialisme de l'ère industrielle.

Pour revenir à l'idée de maison en tant que réalité immatérielle, c'est-à-dire de relations entre les personnes et le lieu, on appréhende mieux le choc représenté par la rupture et la confiscation, en Australie certes, mais également pour l'ensemble des peuples indigènes.

Dans quels domaines le marché devient-il l'outil approprié ? A quels types de règles devrait-il être soumis ? Si l'on part du principe qu'avoir une maison est un droit, dans quels cas, dans la mesure où c'est un droit, peut-on faire appel à l'état pour que ce droit soit protégé ou défendu ? Immanquablement, des questions morales se posent. En toile de fond de notre débat d'aujourd'hui, se profilent toutes ces hypothèses concernant le rôle de l'état, la place des besoins essentiels par rapport aux droits à la propriété. Pour le citoyen, toute option politique se doit d'être transparente et évaluée dans le cadre du rôle prétendu qu'il donne au marché et à l'état.

VI. A Multilingual Europe – Translations into Irish, French and German

Cela nous oblige de nouveau à analyser les efforts que nous déployons dans notre pays pour réaliser l'idée de maison, de foyer. Ceux d'entre vous qui tout à l'heure assisteront à la communication de Catherine Corless, comprendront que pour les enfants ou les mères placés en foyer, ces endroits s'apparentaient plus à un lieu d'enfermement, de perte, de châtiment voire de vengeance annoncée dans la remise en cause de la vision autoritaire de la naissance, de la vie, de la famille et de la société.

L'idée de maison comme lieu d'intimité et de sécurité exprimée par Gaston Bachelard nous amène à nous poser un certain nombre de questions. Le domicile privé, le foyer, concepts si importants dans la loi romaine, n'ont-ils pas été un lieu d'oppression dans les relations entre personnes, dont la violence domestique en est l'expression la plus horrible ?

Concernant le travail, l'exemple le plus quotidien est assurément la répartition des tâches ménagères et le double fardeau de l'activité dans l'économie de marché et à la maison qui, le plus souvent, incombe aux femmes. Aujourd'hui, il semble que le mouvement féministe connaisse une vigueur et une autorité renouvelées et je suis convaincu que nous continuerons à progresser si nous prenons en compte le passé, tout en poursuivant nos efforts pour un avenir meilleur.

Cette université a la chance, je le crois, de disposer d'un Centre de recherche sur les législations, les droits et les politiques concernant le logement (*Centre for Housing Law, Rights and Policy*) dont le travail est capital pour améliorer notre compréhension du système de logement en Irlande et le lien complexe avec le développement en matière de politique monétaire et financière au niveau européen et international. Le Centre accueille des universitaires qui nous aident à comprendre précisément le rôle du logement. Je me permets de citer Dr Padraic Kenna: « Le logement répond au besoin de base pour les humains d'avoir un abri ; il facilite aussi la satisfaction de l'exigence humaine essentielle d'avoir un foyer. »[13] Je laisserai de côté les détails de la politique du logement en Irlande, d'abord pour des raisons constitutionnelles, dans le sens physique du terme, j'entends, mais surtout parce que Catríona Crowe a réuni un excellent panel pour en discuter ce soir. J'aimerais cependant ajouter deux remarques de principe d'ordre plus général.

D'abord, Dr Kenna souligne un aspect absolument fondamental. C'est effectivement une vérité morale qui reflète les luttes dans notre histoire. Même si l'on considère les lois agraires comme une réponse a minima, elles ont toutefois été accompagnées d'une série de lois sur les ouvriers agricoles, votées après une action concertée, dans le but de fournir des subventions d'état aux autorités locales qui ont permis la construction de nouvelles habitations à un juste prix pour les paysans dépourvus de terre en Irlande. Entre 1883, l'année de la première loi, et 1914, près de 50 000 cottages ont été construits par les autorités locales, donnant un toit à plus d'un quart de million de personnes.

Il ne faut pas sous-estimer ce changement de cap remarquable par rapport à la réalité du laissez-faire d'alors. Bien que tardive, il s'agissait bien d'une victoire partielle pour les tenants, au sein de la Ligue agraire, d'une ligne plus émancipatrice. La perte de cohésion sociale allait se révéler être la source d'une nouvelle énergie mobilisatrice, l'autre source étant le besoin de main d'œuvre. Dans les villes irlandaises, les autorités locales ont été plus lentes à appliquer la loi sur le logement des classes ouvrière, l'équivalent urbain de la loi sur les ouvriers agricoles.

Il n'existait bien évidemment aucun droit légal au logement en tant que tel, mais un droit moral avait été établi et en partie reconnu. C'était l'affirmation qu'une maison est une entité plus grande qu'un abri et pas seulement une solution temporaire. Il s'agit ici de l'acquisition d'un moyen pour faire partie de la communauté et participer à la vie de la société, la tête haute, pour reprendre une terminologie que ne renierait pas Amartya Sen. Au jour d'aujourd'hui, aucun droit au logement opposable ne figure dans l'organisation juridique irlandaise. Je me réjouis cependant des discussions de la Convention constitutionnelle sur la possible intégration des droits sociaux et économiques dans notre Constitution. Ce débat doit continuer et être approfondi en prenant notamment en compte les travaux du Professeur P.J. Trudy, de Des Collins, et d'autres comme Dr Kenna. Pouvons-nous et devons-nous réellement intégrer la dimension du droit au logement dans notre droit et dans les politiques que nous menons ?

Deuxièmement, si nous reconnaissons que, dans notre société, le logement est une nécessité première pour la création d'un foyer, il est de notre devoir de réfléchir sérieusement à tous les éléments constitutifs de notre système de logement. J'emploie à dessein le terme « système » car le terme de marché immobilier peut masquer le rôle nécessaire et crucial joué par l'état qui met en place des mesures fiscales et monétaires ou d'autres types de politiques. Cela concerne toutes les différentes parties du système, du permis de construire au financement de la construction, en passant par la conception et la régulation de la construction sans oublier les différents mécanismes pour ce qui est du financement de l'occupation de la maison, qu'il s'agisse d'une location ou d'une maison achetée.

Combien de maisons nouvelles devraient-être construites chaque année ? Quels devraient-être les moyens de financement ? Comment concevoir les espaces de vie ? Quels sont les différents types de logement adaptés à notre société ? De même pour le type de structure de propriété, qu'elle soit municipale, privée ou collective. Il nous faut élargir le débat et nous donner les moyens de répondre politiquement avec la volonté d'éviter tout obstacle idéologique dans un ensemble de politiques le plus vaste possible.

La relecture du *Livre blanc sur le logement*, publié en 1964, est en cela instructive. Son récapitulatif historique rappelle comment l'état a pris la décision de lancer un vaste plan de construction en 1933, au cœur de la Grande Dépression. En conséquence, le nombre de maisons construites par les autorités locales a dépassé celui des constructions privées durant quinze ans, entre 1933 et 1948. C'était un choix de politique publique et l'état a été très clair et transparent dans ses objectifs.

A cette même période, les démocrates sociaux suédois ont mis en avant un remarquable idéal politique, le *folkhemmet*, c'est-à-dire, la maison du peuple. Cette locution renferme l'idée de maison en tant que communauté politique, en tant qu'ensemble de relations basées sur la solidarité. Ce schéma est similaire aux modèles des villages irlandais, le *clochán* ou *baile*, dont l'organisation politique exigeait, à l'époque comme d'ailleurs encore de nos jours, la mise à disposition pour tous de logements accordés de droit.

Dans notre époque d'Anthropocène, nous avons la capacité et même le devoir de maintenir l'idéal de la maison comme communauté politique, attachée à une vision de la justice s'appuyant sur le droit. Pour que cela soit possible, nos horizons ne peuvent cependant se limiter à une communauté politique qui repose sur une territorialité unique. Nous tous sur cette planète partageons ce que le pape François a appelé « notre maison commune ».

Si nous voulons relever le défi posé par cette maison commune, il est impératif d'élargir notre perspective de la maison pour englober tous les habitants de cette terre.

Le XXIe siècle ne saurait tolérer une solidarité au rabais, que cette solidarité soit nationale ou européenne. Une solidarité internationale s'impose, dépouillée des antagonismes nationaux. Une solidarité internationale ouverte, où nous sommes disposés à coopérer là où nous le pouvons et à faire des sacrifices là où nous le devons. Pour l'Europe, il se peut bien que ce siècle soit un autre siècle d'immigration. Un renversement de la grande vague d'émigration vers le Nouveau monde et les colonies que nous avons connue au XIXe siècle.

Cet argument n'est pas seulement politique ou moral, c'est aussi un argument pratique. Il est vrai que les taux de natalité sont très en-deçà des seuils de renouvellement des générations partout dans l'Union européenne et le recours à l'immigration pratiqué actuellement pour soutenir les économies des pays du Nord continuera d'attirer des immigrés sur nos rivages.

De même, au regard de la présente situation en ce qui concerne les émissions de gaz à effet de serre et en dépit des promesses des Accords de Paris sur le climat, des millions de gens vont venir chercher refuge sous nos latitudes, tentant ainsi d'échapper à un environnement dégradé et à l'épuisement des ressources naturelles. Nous devrons faire face à ce défi de solidarité et nous serons jugés sur notre volonté d'accueillir ceux qui fuient les catastrophes climatiques, les guerres et les persécutions.

Nombreux sont les défis auxquels nous sommes confrontés qui mettront à l'épreuve notre capacité et notre volonté à engager une réflexion collective pour distinguer le bien commun et les actions à entreprendre pour y arriver. L'histoire des peuples indigènes constitue un héritage qui met en jeu notre capacité, en tant qu'êtres humains à forger des conceptions collectives de l'idée de « maison ». Des conceptions qui peuvent servir de fondations aux politiques gouvernementales. Nous ne devons pas oublier notre passé collectif et en tirer les meilleurs enseignements possibles. Nous devons inventer ensemble un avenir partagé pour tous les peuples de notre maison commune.

Traduit par Dominique Le Meur

Die Zukunft Europas: Ökologie, Wirtschaft und Ethik – Eine neue Balance finden

Rede an der Universität Leipzig, 4. Juli 2019.

Alle guten Universitäten teilen ein Bekenntnis zur Bildung, und ebenso dazu, zukunftsorientiert auf Errungenschaften der Vergangenheit aufzubauen. Viele sind stolz auf ihre prächtigen Vorlesungssäle und prestigeträchtigen historischen Gebäude. Nur wenige jedoch haben den Mut und die Vorstellungskraft, einen Ort wie dieses Paulinum zu schaffen; es ist dies wirklich eine großartige Leistung, zu der ich die Universität, die Stadt und das Land Sachsen beglückwünsche; es ist ein Raum, der harmonisch das Alte mit dem Neuen, das Religiöse mit dem Säkularen verbindet.

Man sagte mir, dass der große Komponist Johann Sebastian Bach – mit seinem Respekt für den langen Atem der Geschichte und seinem Bewusstsein für das Dauerhafte und Universelle – während seiner Leipziger Zeit sein Interesse am Komponieren neuer Musik gerade in der St. Pauli-Kirche verlor, die damals an dieser Stelle stand, eine der vier Kirchen, für die er verantwortlich war. Er war enttäuscht, so heißt es, dass die Stadt ihm nicht genügend Mittel zur Verfügung stellte. Diese Klage kann ich nur allzu gut verstehen!

Dennoch bin ich mir sicher, dass der begabte Komponist diesen Raum hier zu schätzen gewusst hätte.

Wie am Paulinum ersichtlich, ist es eine bestens bekannte und in Leipzig wohlverstandene Herausforderung, Neues im Schlagschatten der Vergangenheit zu erschaffen; für die Zukunft zu bauen mit den Materialien, die uns heute zur Verfügung stehen, und gleichzeitig Vergangenes zu würdigen. Ein ethischer Umgang mit der Vergangenheit in all ihrer Komplexität ist eine zwangsläufig moralische Aufgabe, die, so glaube ich, uns befähigt, die Gegenwart zu erhellen, die imaginierten Umrisse von etwas Besserem zu erkennen und uns zu einer harmonischeren Existenz einlädt auf der Suche nach einer erfüllten Zukunft.

Dies ist ein Thema, das ich als Präsident von Irland zu verschiedenen Anlässen in der Vergangenheit angesprochen habe. Es ist eine dauernde Herausforderung für uns alle als Staatsbürger und ein Thema, welches von der Europäischen Union und ihren Mitgliedstaaten in der sich entfaltenden Architektur ihrer Institutionen angemessen berücksichtigt und bedacht werden muss, und damit die Frage nach dem Verhältnis zu ihren eigentlichen Zielsetzungen und Aufgaben und inwiefern ihre Entscheidungen auf der europäische Straße ein Echo finden oder zu dortigen Befindlichkeiten in Dissonanz stehen.

Ich habe Leipzig schon zuvor besucht und bin mir des kulturellen Erbes der Stadt bewusst. Leipzig hat nicht nur in der deutschen, sondern auch in der europäischen Geschichte eine bedeutende Rolle gespielt. Mein heutiger Besuch ist der erste offizielle wie auch inoffizielle Staatsbesuch eines irischen Präsidenten in Sachsen, ja im östlichen Teil Deutschlands außerhalb Berlins überhaupt. Ich hoffe aufrichtig, dass mein Besuch eine neue und tiefere Beziehung zu Ihnen sowie zu Ihren Nachbarstaaten einleitet. Mein Besuch als Präsident von Irland spiegelt Irlands Absicht wider, die irische Präsenz deutschlandweit zu vertiefen und auszuweiten. Es ist unser Wunsch, neue Freundschaften aufzubauen.

Ich möchte auch die besondere Rolle würdigen, die diese Universität bei der Förderung und dem Schutz von Minderheitssprachen gespielt hat. Ich weiß, dass hier die Erforschung der sorbischen Sprache betrieben wird, und ich freue mich insbesondere, dass die Universität auch zu einem Zentrum

VI. A Multilingual Europe – Translations into Irish, French and German

für irische Sprachstudien in Deutschland geworden ist. Unsere jeweiligen Sprachen bereichern unser Leben in Europa, jede auf ihre besondere Art und Weise. Wir haben eine generationenübergreifende Verpflichtung, unsere Sprachen zu pflegen und sicherzustellen, dass sie für zukünftige Generationen lebendig und ausdrucksvoll bleiben. Dass wir heute die irische Sprache benutzen und sie auch heute noch auf dem irischen Lehrplan steht, verdanken wir der Unterstützung, die Dr. Douglas de hÍde[14] von einer Anzahl deutscher Gelehrter erhielt. Unter ihnen war Dr. Kuno Meyer, der 1919 in Leipzig starb. Ich möchte Professor Sabine Asmus und ihre Studenten und Studentinnen, die heute hier anwesend sind, für ihre Bemühungen in dieser Hinsicht danken. *Gabhaim buíochas libh agus treaslaím libh as bhur n-iarrachtaí.*[15]

Auch fühle ich mich geehrt, dass ich im Anschluss an diesen Empfang heute morgen die Möglichkeit haben werde, die Nikolaikirche zu besichtigen, um den Mut der Demonstranten vor dreißig Jahren zu würdigen, deren furchtlose Entschlossenheit den Weg ebnete für jene seismischen, geopolitisch-kontinentalen Verschiebungen, und deren friedliche Aktionen zur deutschen Wiedervereinigung und einer neuen Ära der Partnerschaft in Europa führen sollten. Heute sind wir in der Europäischen Union wieder an einem wichtigen Zeitpunkt angelangt. Angesichts neuer Herausforderungen innerhalb und jenseits der Union sind wir aufgefordert, unser Bekenntnis zum Zusammenstehen als Union zu erneuern und einen angemessenen Diskurs zu gestalten über dringend notwendige Veränderungen, die uns Mut abverlangen werden, wenn wir die Spielräume ernsthafter intellektueller Auseinandersetzung verteidigen wollen und die Freiheit des Diskurses sowie politische Veränderungen möglich machen wollen.

Da ich heute morgen zu Ihnen über die Zukunft Europas sprechen werde, möchte ich die Gelegenheit nutzen, einige radikale Veränderungen vorzuschlagen, die wir in unserem Denken und politischen Handeln vornehmen müssen. Ich bin davon überzeugt, dass wir dringend neue Beziehungen zwischen Ökologie, Ökonomie und Ethik finden müssen, nicht nur zum Wohle der Europäischen Union, sondern auch zum Schutz unseres gemeinsamen zerbrechlichen Planeten, dass wir neue Wege finden müssen, auf denen wir im Interesse aller unserer Bürger voranschreiten können. Meine Kritik und meine Vorschläge gehen über lediglich kleinere Justierungen, über eine reine (ökologische oder humanitäre) Neuperspektivierung bestehender Politik oder existierender Paradigmen wirtschaftlicher Entwicklung hinaus. Ein solches Vorgehen wird immer wieder versucht und rhetorisch behandelt, hat aber keinen Erfolg gezeitigt. Keine authentische Strukturierung einer solch begrenzten Herangehensweise in Hinsicht auf ihre Umsetzung hat bisher stattgefunden oder ist im offiziellen oder institutionellen Diskurs wahrnehmbar, noch, was am wichtigsten ist, hat sie den Weg auf die europäische Straße gefunden, wo das Vertrauen in Worte und Taten dringend zurückgewonnen werden muss, um eine überzeugende Authentizität der Politik zu bewirken. Wir, als globale Gemeinschaft, müssen auf die Auswirkungen des Klimawandels und die zwingende Notwendigkeit der Nachhaltigkeit eine Antwort finden, um eine radikale Veränderung in Richtung neuer ökonomischer Denkmuster in einer dekarbonisierten Welt zu erreichen. Eine ökosoziale politische Ökonomie ist notwendig zur Umsetzung dessen, worauf wir uns nur prinzipiell geeinigt haben.

Da ich in einer Universität spreche, möchte ich betonen, dass die notwendigen Paradigmenwechsel der Spielräume erkenntnistheoretischer Freiheit in unseren Forschungsinstituten bedürfen. Hiermit meine ich, dass Lehrenden und Studierenden das selbstständige Denken gestattet werden muss, den Hochschullehrern die Freiheit zumindest pluralistisch zu lehren und grundsätzlich frei, das derzeitige orthodoxe kapitalistische System zu hinterfragen, welches regel- und verantwortungslos sich nicht um seine gesellschaftlichen und sozialpolitischen Auswirkungen schert. Veränderung ist nicht möglich, wenn es nicht erlaubt ist, deren Umrisse diskursiv abwägend zu behandeln und ihre Grundsätze zu lehren. Jedoch stößt die notwendige Veränderung auf Widerstände seitens einer geballten Macht von Ängstlichen, Verstummten oder intellektuell Lethargischen sowie unternehmerischen Machthabern, Gegnern staatlicher Regulierung und einer Minderheit der Bevölkerung, die lediglich froh ist, Zugang zu einem immer unersättlicher werdenden Akkumulationsprozess gefunden zu haben.

Das Ausmaß der notwendigen Veränderung entspricht meiner Meinung nach der Veränderung, die in den späten 1980er Jahren und frühen 1990er Jahren in Mittel- und Osteuropa stattgefunden hat; der Ruf nach eine moralischen, friedlichen Zukunft ist in Umfang, Tragweite und Bedeutung vielleicht dem *Manifest von Ventotene* ähnlich. Diese von Altiero Spinello und Ernesto Rossi 1941 verfasste programmatische Schrift wurde zum Programm der (italienischen) Europäischen Föderalisten-Bewegung. Die außerordentliche Vision sprach die Bedürfnisse und Ziele der Menschen grenzübergreifend an und hatte zum Hauptziel die Schaffung eines stabilen übernationalen Staates. Nachdem die nationale Unabhängigkeit erreicht war, sollte sie als Instrument zur Erreichung internationaler Einheit dienen. Europäischer Föderalismus und Weltföderalismus erscheinen im *Manifest von Ventotene* als ein Weg zukünftige Kriege zu verhindern. Das Manifest gilt gemeinhin als Geburtsort des europäischen Föderalismusgedankens.

Die vielzitierte Schuman-Erklärung erinnerte uns ihrerseits daran, dass ‚Europa [...] sich nicht mit einem Schlage herstellen [lässt] und auch nicht durch eine einfache Zusammenfassung'.[16] Mir ist bewusst, dass viele unter den Entmutigten oft mit Wehmut an solche Deklarationen aus den Tagen der Pioniere der Europäischen Union zurückdenken, an Robert Schuman, Konrad Adenauer, Jean Monnet und andere, Momente der Inspiration, als solche neuen Ideen die Stimmung erfassten und Wirklichkeit wurden. Es ist wichtig uns zu vergegenwärtigen, dass diese Politiker zusammenkamen, um ein gemeinsames Ziel zu erreichen, das aus ihren unterschiedlichen Interessen entstanden war, sie aber zugleich transzendierte, den Samen zu sähen für friedliche Kooperation und politische Einheit. Jedoch müssen wir Nostalgie mit Vorsicht beggnen. Nostalgie ist oft unsere Antwort, wenn wir uns neuen Herausforderungen nicht gewachsen fühlen, Vorspiel eines Eingeständnisses von Versagen oder Verzweiflung im Glauben, dass wir angesichts fehlender erkennbarer oder aus gegenwärtiger intellektueller Arbeit uns zustehender Hoffnung die Zukunft nur meistern können im Rückgriff auf die Vergangenheit, als ob die Werkzeuge von gestern genügten die Bedürfnisse der Zukunft zu bewältigen. Jede Generation ist verpflichtet, die Instrumente für ihre Selbstanalyse und ihr Leben in der Komplexität ihrer jeweiligen Zeit zu finden, oder neu zu erfinden. Dies ist für mich die große Leistung von Jürgen Habermas, als er sich vom Pessimismus, der in den Werken Theodor W. Adornos fühlbar wird, lossagte.

Wir stehen weder am Ende der Geschichte noch am Ende der Ideen. Dies war ein anmaßendes Konstrukt Francis Fukuyamas, das in skandalöser Weise

Die Zukunft Europas: Ökologie, Wirtschaft und Ethik – Eine neue Balance finden

von zu vielen geteilt wurde und nie wirklich zurückgenommen wurde. Eine weitere Gefahr besteht darin, dass wir die Gegenwart rationalisieren durch eine entstellte oder begrenzte Vorstellung von der Vergangenheit, dass Ursprünge aus gemischten Motivationen heraus konstruiert werden. Wie immer man auch Texte wie den Schuman-Plan interpretieren mag, sie stehen als Beispiel, als Herausforderung für zukünftige Generationen, sich verändernde Umstände zu antizipieren, sich ihnen anzupassen und neuen Anforderungen gerecht zu werden. Diese Herausforderungen müssen eine gemeinsame Perspektive bedingen aufgrund unserer Interdependenz, einer gegenseitigen Abhängigkeit, die weit über reinen Import und Export hinausgeht. Es sind dies gemeinsame Herausforderungen, die einer gemeinsamen grenzüberschreitenden Antwort bedürfen. Ein Rückgriff auf die enge Sichtweise des Nationalismus, ist nicht mehr, wie vielleicht in der Vergangenheit, Ausdruck einer Forderung nach Freiheit einer Nation, sondern einer verzweifelten Verteidigung enger Eigeninteressen. Interessen, die Ungleichheit und hemmungslose Kapitalakkumulation von Wenigen auf Kosten von Vielen ermöglichen.

Noch können wir in internationalen Beziehungen eine Rhetorik oder gar praktische Vorbereitungen dulden für einen Krieg zwischen Schwerstbewaffneten als Ersatz für engagierte und verbindliche Diplomatie. Frieden zu schaffen und zu bewahren – zu diesen Zwecken wurden die Vereinten Nationen gegründet. Wie Deutschland ist auch Irland ein überzeugter Unterstützer der Vereinten Nationen und die UN-Mitgliedschaft hat stets eine wichtige Rolle in unserer jeweiligen politischen Evolution gespielt. Durch unsere Mitgliedschaft fördern unsere beiden Nationen nicht nur eine faire regelbasierte Ordnung internationaler Angelegenheiten, sondern wir leben, überleben und gedeihen auch gerade aufgrund dieser Ordnung. In den Bereichen Friedenssicherung, Abrüstung, nachhaltige Entwicklung, Klima, Ernährung, Menschenrechte und humanitäre Hilfe sind wir gemeinsam bestrebt, unseren Worten Taten und Geldmittel folgen zu lassen und multinationale Strukturen zu unterstützen. Auch wenn das UN-System Mängel hat, teilen Irland und Deutschland die Überzeugung, dass es keinen besseren Weg gibt, die uns gemeinsamen Möglichkeiten zu nutzen und Bedrohungen entgegenzutreten. Die Vereinten Nationen stellen den besten Raum für deren Aushandlung dar, den wir verteidigen und fördern müssen.

VI. A Multilingual Europe – Translations into Irish, French and German

Ich habe mich entschieden nach Leipzig zu kommen um diese Überzeugungen zu präsentieren, weil ich glaube, dass die Arbeit an der Neukonzeptionierung, Erneuerung, oder Zukunftsfähigkeit der EU nicht ausschließlich in Konferenzen in den Hauptstädten der Mitgliedstaaten stattfinden sollte. Ein Gespräch über Europa muss breit angelegt und inklusiv sein und von Institutionen und Bürgern getragen werden, denen privilegiert Raum für intellektuelle Arbeit dieser Art bereitgestellt werden muss. Europa ist nicht exklusiv eine Union von Hauptstädten, sondern eine von allen Menschen in unseren Großstädten, Städten, Dörfern und ländlichen Gebieten getragene. Wir haben zwischen unseren Völkern zwar die Fähigkeit zu kommunizieren entwickelt, aber unter den bestehenden Bedingungen machen wir oft nur die Erfahrung einer individualisierten, privatisierten Kommunikation, einer flüchtigen, trivialen Kommunikation, die nicht die ehemalige und nunmehr fragil gewordene gemeinsame Welt des öffentlich-rechtlichen Rundfunks, den Medien-Pluralismus, die öffentlichen Reden in der *Agora* ersetzen kann. Wir sind gezwungen, unsere derzeitige Lage und unsere mögliche gemeinsame Zukunft unter den neuen Bedingungen zu diskutieren, aber wir sollten nicht pessimistisch sein. Wir haben eine Ressource: den Respekt für intellektuelle Arbeit, und dazu – und zur Beförderung der Vernunft – die Musik des Herzens. Dass Deutschland und Irland ihren Respekt für Ideen miteinander teilen, ist ebenso wichtig wie gemeinsame Innovationen und gemeinsamer Handel; beides gehört zusammen. Es gibt keinen besseren Ort die Zukunft Europas zu diskutieren als Leipzig, wo der große deutsche Dichter Friedrich Schiller den Text seiner wundervolle Ode „An die Freude" verfasste. Einige seiner Worte wurden von Beethoven für den vierten Satz seiner meisterhaften Neunten Sinfonie vertont, diesen wunderschönen mitreißenden Ausdruck musikalischer Brillanz, den die uns gemeinsame Europäischen Union zu ihrer Hymne erkor.

Aus diesem Geiste heraus möchte ich eine grundsätzliche Überlegung über die Bedeutung der Worte ‚Europa' und ‚europäisch' in unseren Diskursen anstellen. Sprechen wir nur über die geografischen Koordinaten des Kontinents und der Inselstaaten an der Peripherie, aus denen Europa im physischen Sinn besteht? Sprechen wir von einem Block von Konsumenten oder von einem Handelsblock? Wie oft sprechen wir von einem sozialen

Die Zukunft Europas: Ökologie, Wirtschaft und Ethik – Eine neue Balance finden

Europa, wenn wir über die Europäische Union reden? Mit anderen Worten, was bedeutet es für uns Heutige und für die noch kommenden Generationen, die in der von uns so genannten Union leben werden, wenn wir im frühen 21. Jahrhundert vom ‚Europäer sein' reden? Welche gemeinsamen Werte und welche gemeinsame Ethik wollen wir als Europäer aufrechterhalten, verteidigen, als Basis nehmen und in unseren Mitgliedstaaten sowie der restlichen Welt befördern?

Wenn auch unser Kontinent, der über Jahrhunderte durch Krieg und Leiden befleckt wurde, in der Geschichte viele Leistungen erbracht hat, stellt doch die Europäische Union aufgrund ihres philosophischen Erbes, ihres Bestehens auf intellektuellen Diskurs, ihrer Bereitschaft, die Fesseln der Imperien abzuwerfen und Imperialismus zu bekämpfen, sowohl eine einmalige Chance als auch eine Verpflichtung dar, ihre Gründungswerte von Demokratie, Zusammenhalt, gemeinsamer Zukunft, Menschenrechten und Rechtsstaatlichkeit zu behaupten und, falls notwendig, wieder geltend zu machen in einer Welt, in der diese Werte in Frage gestellt werden. Diese Werte sind weder abstrakt, noch sind sie optionale Extras oder durch Grenzen eingeschränkt. Sie sind das Kernstück und müssen von allen Mitgliedstaaten respektiert und aufrechterhalten werden. Im Zentrum dieser Werte und deren Verteidigung stehen Idee und Praxis der Personenfreizügigkeit, die es Menschen ermöglicht ihre Hoffnungen zu erfüllen wie auch ihre Geschichten und ihr kulturelles Erbe in die neue Umgebung miteinzubringen. Migration, aus dem und ins Ausland, ist seit Jahrhunderten ein Schlüsselaspekt europäischer Geschichte. Migration gab es lange vor der Gründung des Gemeinsamen Marktes und der Europäischen Wirtschaftsgemeinschaft. Aus- und Einwanderung hat uns als Europäer geformt, unsere Werte, unsere Empfindungen beeinflusst, ja auch die Grundlagen unseres Wohlstands mitgeschaffen.

Jedoch kann dieser Wohlstand, der auf der Annahme von unbegrenztem und sich stets beschleunigendem Wachstum aufgrund unendlicher Ressourcen basiert, nicht die von ihm selbst bewirkten Konsequenzen vermeiden, wie Klimawandel und dessen Auswirkungen. Vielleicht ist es lehrreich, wenn wir ein wenig Abstand nehmen und die Merkmale einer Ära Revue passieren lassen, die eine so große Auswirkung auf unseren Planeten und uns selbst gehabt hat. Das Zeitalter des Anthropozän, in dem wir jetzt leben, hat neue existenzielle Herausforderungen mit sich gebracht, die das Überleben der Menschheit auf diesem Planeten gefährden. Wenn wir annehmen, dass die rezentesten Auswirkungen des Anthropozäns mit dem Beginn der Industriellen Revolution, also etwa den 1760er Jahren, einsetzten, können wir erkennen wie diese Zeit den Beginn eines Zyklus von Ereignissen markiert, der zu der ökologischen Krise geführt hat, die uns heute konfrontiert. Die Industrielle Revolution, die in Großbritannien ihren Anfang nahm, resultierte darin, dass dieses Land ein globales Handelsimperium beherrschte mit Kolonien in Nordafrika, der Karibik und politischem Einfluss auf dem indischen Subkontinent. Die Entwicklung von Handel und Wirtschaft gehörten zu den treibenden Kräften der Industriellen Revolution. Letztere stellt einen Wendepunkt in der Geschichte dar, nahezu jeder Aspekt des täglichen Lebens wurde auf die eine oder andere Art und Weise von ihr beeinflusst. Besonders die Durchschnittseinkommen und die Bevölkerung begannen beispiellos und nachhaltig zu wachsen. In diese Periode fällt auch der Aufstieg der Industriestädte wie etwa Manchester. Jeder Lebensbereich veränderte sich, nicht nur die Verbindung zwischen Heim und Arbeit. Zeit und Raum wurden neu definiert, oder ‚kolonisiert', wie Michel Foucault es vielleicht formuliert hätte.

Im kontinentalen Europa setzte die Industrielle Revolution ein wenig später als in Großbritannien ein. Aufgrund seiner Führungsrolle in der Chemieforschung in Universitäten und in Industrielaboratorien übernahm das 1871 vereinigte Deutschland im späten 19. Jahrhundert eine dominierende Rolle in der chemischen Industrie. Deutschland konzentrierte sich auf die Förderung der Industrialisierung und bald durchzog ein Netz von Eisenbahnlinien das Ruhrgebiet und andere industrielle Zentren; es entstanden gute Verbindungen zu den wichtigen Häfen Hamburg und Bremen.

Warum nahm die Industrielle Revolution ihren Ursprung in Europa? Der Wirtschaftshistoriker Joel Mokyr hat argumentiert, dass gerade die politische Fragmentierung (d.h. die Existenz vieler Einzelstaaten) die Entwicklung heterodoxer Ideen beflügelte; Unternehmer, Erfinder, Ideologen und Ketzer konnten ohne Schwierigkeiten in einen Nachbarstaat flüchten, falls der eigene ihre Ideen und Aktivitäten zu unterdrücken suchte. Dieser ständige Aus- und

Einfluss unterschied Europa von den technologisch entwickelten Reichen China und Indien, da Migration, Innovation und geistige Erneuerung, unerschöpfliche Neugier und *technos*, als ‚Versicherung gegen ökonomische und technologische Stagnation' dienten, wie Mokyr es ausdrückt. China besaß beides, eine Druckerpresse und bewegliche Einzellettern, und Indien war auf ähnlich hohem Niveau wie das Europa um 1700 was wissenschaftliche und technologische Errungenschaften betrifft, aber die Industrielle Revolution fand in Europa statt und nicht in China oder Indien. In Europa war die politische Fragmentierung mit einem ‚integrierten Markt der Ideen' gekoppelt, wobei die Intellektuellen die Verkehrssprache Latein benutzten und damit eine gemeinsame intellektuelle Basis in Europas klassischen Erbe in der pan-europäischen ‚Republik der Gelehrten' hatten.

Der Historiker Peter Stearns weist darauf hin, dass ‚Europas industrielle Revolution zum großen Teil von Europas Fähigkeit herrührte, in überproportionalem Maße globale Ressourcen zu nutzen'. Die neue Welt der Industrie war untrennbar verknüpft mit Kolonisation, imperialer Herrschaft und einer Ideologie, die etwaige kulturelle Unterschiede bestenfalls als Rückständigkeit betrachtete. Darüber hinaus sollten wir auch nicht die schier unüberblickbare Menge der im Druck erschienenen philosophischen Werke ignorieren.

Ich muss die Betrachtung des Zusammenspiels von Enteignung, Eroberung, Beherrschung, Ausbeutung und kultureller Auslöschung, das dies alles möglich machte, auf einen anderen Anlass verschieben. Die Auswirkungen dieser Aneignung und Ausbeutung von Ressourcen sind heute natürlich nur allzu offenbar, wo die ökologischen und sozialen Folgen der Ausbeutung der natürlichen Schätze der Erde deutlich werden. Neben Stimmen der Aufklärer gegen die Imperien wie Denis Diderot, Immanuel Kant und Johann Gottfried Herder gab es während dieser Periode auch Gegenstimmen, die im Allgemeinen dem ‚Bereich der Kunst' zugeordnet werden. Während der Industriellen Revolution entwickelte sich in Verbindung mit der romantischen Bewegung eine intellektuelle und künstlerische Feindschaft der Industrialisierung gegenüber. Diese kritisierte, dass das, was sie sahen, lediglich eine Version des Lebens wie es sein *würde* entwickelte, nicht aber wie es sein *könnte*, nämlich ein Leben, das die Suche nach Schönheit in der Form beinhaltete und das Schöne in der Natur und ländlicher Vertrautheit feierte. Die

VI. A Multilingual Europe – Translations into Irish, French and German

Romantik bevorzugte den Traditionalismus ländlichen Lebens und schreckte zurück vor den Umwälzungen, die Industrialisierung, Urbanisierung und das Elend der Arbeiterklasse mit sich brachten. Deren wichtigste Vertreter in englischer Sprache waren der Künstler und Poet William Blake, die Dichter William Wordsworth, John Keats, Lord Byron und Percy Bysshe Shelley und andere. Die Bewegung hob die Bedeutung der Natur in Kunst und Sprache hervor, im Gegensatz zu den ‚gespenstischen (*monstrous*)' Maschinen und Fabriken, den ‚Dark satanic mills' in Blakes Gedicht ‚And Did Those Feet in Ancient Time'. Mary Shelleys Roman *Frankenstein* spiegelt die Bedenken der Zweischneidigkeit wissenschaftlichen Fortschritts gegenüber wider. Auch die französische Romantik stand der Industrie kritisch gegenüber. In einer späteren Periode sollte sie sich vom Realismus der ländlichen Existenz zu dem anti-urbanen Mythos einer idealisierten ländlichen Existenz fortentwickeln und das schaffen, was Raymond Williams ‚false pastoral' nannte. In seiner reaktionärsten Form sollte es dann eine anti-städtische Ideologie schüren helfen. Josiah Strong drückte es so aus: ‚Gott erschuf den Menschen in einem Garten. Die Stadt ist das Ergebnis des Sündenfalls.'

Es ist interessant, dass in der derzeitigen Debatte über die Zukunft der Europäischen Union die Nutzbarmachung der in der literarischen Fantasie existierenden Ideen sowie der intellektuellen Kultur im Allgemeinen kaum je artikuliert, ja nicht einmal anerkannt wird, eine Nachlässigkeit, für die die Europäische Union einen hohen Preis hat zahlen müssen. *Ideas matter*. Zum Beispiel ist es unmöglich, soziale und politische Theorie in ihrer Beziehung zu Wirtschaft und politischer Praxis zu lehren, ohne auf die Frankfurter Schule zu verweisen, deren Gelehrte einige der besten ‚kritischen Theorien' zur Wirtschaft, dem Selbst und der Gesellschaft hervorgebracht haben.

Während zur Zeit der Industriellen Revolution *Empires* geformt und ausgebaut wurden, wurde Europa zugleich Zeuge des aufkommenden Nationalismus. Im 19. Jahrhundert schwappte eine Welle des romantischen Nationalismus über den europäischen Kontinent und transformierte Länder und Völker. Die Erfindung einer symbolischen nationalen Identität wurde europaweit zum Anliegen rassischer, ethnischer und sprachlicher Gruppen, die den Aufstieg der Politik der Massen und den Verfall der traditionellen, meist ausbeuterischen sozialen Eliten sowie breitgestreute Diskriminierung und Fremdenfeindlichkeit zu bewältigen suchten. In dieser Zeit wurden die Ideale des europäischen Nationalismus weltweit exportiert und begannen sich nun weiterzuentwickeln und mit den die Kolonial-Imperien beherrschenden europäischen Nationalstaaten zu konkurrieren und diese zu bedrohen. Die darauf folgende Phase brachte, aus den Trümmern und dem Wettbewerb zwischen irrationalen Imperien resultierend, das Aufkommen des extremen Nationalismus und des Faschismus, und Europas Niedergang durch zwei katastrophale Weltkriege; sie sollten uns vor den heimtückischen Gefahren warnen, die aus engstirnig nationalistischen, über Demokratie und utopische Ideale uninformierten Bewegungen resultieren können, besonders dann, wenn wirtschaftliche und soziale Verwerfungen mit ihnen einhergehen.

Dieser kurze Überblick über die europäische Geschichte der letzten zweieinhalb Jahrhunderte erinnert uns auch daran, dass es vor seiner industriellen Entwicklung einen europäischen Geist gab, ein Europa des geistigen Lebens, der Musik und der Philosophie, dass vor dem Europa von Stahl und Kohle ein Europa blühte ohne übertriebene und unersättliche Ausbeutung seiner natürlichen Grundlagen und Bodenschätze. Die Revolution des frühkapitalistischen Handels, die der industriellen Revolution vorausging, war von einem Anstieg der Handelstätigkeit und einem Wachstum finanzieller Dienstleistungen, wie Bankenwesen, Versicherungen und Investitionen gekennzeichnet. Es gab sogar eine moralisch fundierte Literatur über die Ethik von Wirtschafts- und Handelstransaktionen. Die Geschichte zeigt uns, dass es tatsächlich ein Europa jenseits von Stahl und Kohle geben kann während wir im Anthropozän fortschreiten, und lässt uns hoffen, dass es fundamentale Veränderungen geben kann und damit ein grünes Europa, das fähig ist, seine Völker weiterhin zu ernähren ohne die feine ökologische Balance des Planeten und seiner 7,5 Milliarden menschlichen Bewohner und 8,7 Millionen Gattungen unwiderruflich zu schädigen, und damit eine Version von Gesellschaft, in der Ökologie, Ökonomie und Kultur zusammenkommen und die in sozialer Gerechtigkeit, Humanität und Ethik wurzelt.

Um diese Vision von Europa zu erreichen braucht es meiner Ansicht nach nicht weniger als einen Paradigmenwechsel in Gesellschaftstheorie, Politik und Praxis. In der neuesten Literatur zu diesen Themen wird uns die Berücksichtigung neuer, auf ökonomischer Heterodoxie basierter ökologisch-

VI. A Multilingual Europe – Translations into Irish, French and German

sozialer Denkmuster zugänglich gemacht, etwa in den Arbeiten von Professor Ian Gough und anderen, die sich der Grenzen der natürlichen Ressourcen der Welt bewusst sind, sowie der Rolle, die hemmungslose Gier bei der Verursachung der Klimakrise gespielt hat. In seinem Buch *Heat, Greed and Human Need* – ich wünschte jeder Studierende der Sozialwissenschaften wäre im Besitz dieses Werkes – zeigt Gough auf, wie ein alternatives Paradigma im Konzept der Priorisierung menschlicher Bedürfnisse vor der Unersättlichkeit wurzeln kann. Das Paradigma, das er beschreibt, vertritt die Gedanken der Gleichberechtigung der Geschlechter, der Umverteilung von Einkommen, Reichtum und Ressourcen sowie eine neu konzipierte gesellschaftliche Konsum- und Investitionsstrategie, welche Mittel und Technologien von entwickelten Ländern in Entwicklungsländer transferiert, als Schlüssel zur Verwirklichung eines öko-sozialen Wohlfahrtsstaats. Die öko-sozialen Leitlinien, die solch ein ökonomisches Paradigma untermauern, müssen zugleich nach Fairness und sozialer Gerechtigkeit streben sowie auch nach Nachhaltigkeit und Suffizienz. Sie verlangen einen aktiven Innovationsstaat und erhebliche staatliche Investitionen und die Bereitschaft zu strengerer Regulierung und Planung. Des Weiteren sind auch sozio-ökonomische Maßnahmen notwendig, die nachteilige Auswirkungen der ökologischen Wende für die Ärmsten der Gesellschaft auszugleichen und eine Verbesserung statt einer Verschlimmerung der Ungleichheit zu erreichen suchen. Der Übergang mag schwierig sein, aber Gough bietet einen Ansatz, der als ernstzunehmender Versuch zur Erreichung generationenübergreifender Gerechtigkeit zunehmend Unterstützung gewinnt.

Goughs öko-soziale politische Ökonomie betont eine verantwortungsbewusste Wirtschaft, die erkannt hat, dass das Konzept des beschleunigten wirtschaftlichen Wachstums *ad infinitum* ein grundsätzlich mangelhaftes ist. Dabei haben Wissenschaftler wie Ian Gough einen Diskurs und eine Disziplin von politischer Ökonomie wiederentdeckt, die einer unkritischen Umarmung neoliberaler Mantras zum Opfer gefallen war. Er befürwortet ein Wirtschaftsmodell des Pluralismus, das die Endlichkeit der natürlichen Ressourcen der Erde betont wie auch die besondere Rolle reicher Nationen bei der Bewältigung der kritischen Lage, in der wir uns alle befinden. Wie es Gough selbst ausdrückt:

Konsum und konsum-basierten Emissionen, die von der Green Growth Agenda ignoriert werden, muss in der reichen Welt gleiche Aufmerksamkeit geschenkt werden. [...] Fragen der globalen Gerechtigkeit, die bisher in internationalen Klimaverhandlungen fast ausschließlich fehlen, müssen konfrontativ diskutiert werden. [...] Wohlstand hat sowohl eine Klassen- als auch eine nationale Dimension.

Kate Raworths Buch *Doughnut Economics* (dt. *Die Donut-Ökonomie*)[17] ist ein weiteres Beispiel von Werken, die einen erkenntnisträchtigen konzeptionellen Rahmen bereitstellen, in dem die sozialen und ökologischen Grenzen für die große Herausforderung der Menschheit im 21. Jahrhundert aufgezeigt werden, die Bedürfnisse aller Menschen mit den Möglichkeiten des Planeten in Einklang zu bringen. Mit anderen Worten, diese Arbeiten geben uns Hoffnung, indem sie uns zeigen, wie wir als globale Gemeinschaft sicherstellen können, dass niemand bei der Versorgung mit Lebensnotwendigem zurückbleibt (von Nahrung und Wohnraum bis zu Gesundheitsfürsorge und politischer Teilhabe), und gleichzeitig garantiert wird, dass wir die lebenserhaltenden Systeme der Erde, auf die wir grundsätzlich angewiesen sind, nicht überlasten – wie etwa ein stabiles Klima, fruchtbare Böden und eine schützende Ozonschicht.

Um zu unserer derzeitigen Lage und zur Europäischen Union und unserer gemeinsamen Zukunft zurückzukehren: Trotz der von der EU auferlegten, für alle Mitgliedstaaten verbindlichen Emissionsziele für 2020 und 2030, müssen wir in Europa darüber hinausgehen und eine vollständige Dekarbonisierung unserer Volkswirtschaften bis 2050 planen, und den Rest der Welt ermutigen, uns zu folgen. Wie müssen mit größtem Nachdruck die USA ermahnen, die Entscheidung für den Ausstieg aus dem Internationalen Pariser Abkommen über den Klimawandel zu überdenken, eine Entscheidung, die meiner Meinung nach unentschuldbar, schlecht informiert, zutiefst kurzsichtig ist und zukünftige Generationen mit katastrophalen Konsequenzen bedroht. Wenn wir uns mit sozio-ökonomischen Auswirkungen des Klimawandels befassen, müssen wir notwendigerweise einen ‚gerechten Übergang' (‚*just transition*') für Arbeitnehmer, Organisationen und Gemeinden ermöglichen und sicherstellen, dass wir alle an einer nachhaltigen kohlenstoffarmen Wirtschaft teilhaben und von vernünftigen und grünen Jobs profitieren können. In Irland

VI. A Multilingual Europe – Translations into Irish, French and German

und Deutschland bedeutet dies, dass zum Beispiel denjenigen, die von der Schließung karbon-intensiver Werke zur Elektrizitätsproduktion betroffen sind, Umschulungs-Möglichkeiten angeboten werden, die sie befähigen, angemessene Arbeitsplätze in anderen Bereichen wie der grünen Wirtschaft zu finden oder ihnen die Möglichkeit zu einem nachhaltigen Einkommen in anderen sozialen Bereichen geben. Darüber hinaus muss gute Sozialpolitik sicherstellen, dass staatsbürgerliche Mitwirkungsrechte nicht verloren gehen.

Ich möchte hervorheben, dass die Globalisierung, wie wir sie erlebt haben, d.h. ohne Berücksichtigung der sozialen Auswirkungen oder Konsequenzen, einen sich beschleunigenden negativen Einfluss auf den Klimawandel gehabt hat und noch hat: immer mehr Waren wurden produziert und verbraucht, immer mehr Waren wurden über lange Strecken transportiert, mit immer kürzeren Produktzyklen für eine immer mehr vom Konsum und Materialismus getriebene Gesellschaft. Für all diese Aspekte der Globalisierung wurde ein hoher Preis gezahlt, wenn man die Auswirkungen auf die begrenzten natürlichen Ressourcen und damit verbundenen CO_2-Emissionen bedenkt. Es war und ist gewiss nicht die Allgemeinheit, die von einem solch fehlerhaften Modell profitiert, weder jetzt noch in der Zukunft. Es profitiert eine Minderheit, die in der Verteidigung einer unersättlichen, unkontrollierten Akkumulation die Auswirkungen ihres eigenen Modells ignoriert, sowohl in klimatischer wie auch sozialer Hinsicht, eine Minderheit, die oft ungebunden ist und außerhalb der Reichweite staatlicher oder parlamentarischer Regulierung agiert. Das Wachstum von niemandem verantwortlichen, spekulativen Finanzkapital-Aktivitäten kann auch die Bemühungen von Regierungen zunichte machen. Das muss sich ändern. Die Demokratie verlangt danach. Wachstum von Verantwortungslosigkeit ist keine Ausübung von Freiheit. Es ist eine Bedrohung der Demokratie.

Es ist ermutigend, dass wir nach Jahrzehnten von Kommentaren der Mainstream-Wirtschaftsexperten, die darin ihren Glauben an unvermeidliche und oft extreme Versionen des Marktes, an Privatisierung sowie an eine lediglich kleine Rolle des Staates verfochten, nun dank einsichtsvoller Beiträge von Ökonomen, wie Mariana Mazzucato und Sylvia Walby im ökonomischen Diskurs so scheint mir an einem Wendepunkt angelangt sind. In ihren Büchern *The Entrepreneurial State* und *The Value of Everything* (dt. *Wie kommt der Wert in die Welt?*)[18] rügt Mazzucato die auf dem Prinzip der Austerität basierte Weltanschauung, nach welcher zur Wiederherstellung von Wachstum (nach der Finanzkrise von 2008) Haushaltsdefizite verringert und öffentliche Ausgaben reduziert werden müssen. Mazzucato argumentiert stattdessen, dass Staatsausgaben in Schlüsselbereichen wie Bildung, Forschung und Entwicklung Investitionsschwerpunkte sein müssen und das Wachstum befördern können. Zum Glück haben orthodoxe Institutionen wie der Internationale Währungsfond ihre Ansichten über Sparmaßnahmen als strategische Mittel langsam weiterentwickelt; auch sie gestehen ein, dass eine solche Politik schädigend und kontraproduktiv sein kann. Keynes argumentierte vor über achtzig Jahren, dass eine kurzlebige Rezession sich zu einer Depression auswachsen kann, wenn Regierungen während eines Konjunktureinbruchs Ausgaben kürzen. Genau das passierte 2008 in Irland, als eine Rezession 2009 in eine wirtschaftliche Depression mündete und es erst 2014 wieder zu einem verspäteten Wirtschaftsaufschwung kam.

In ihrem Buch *Germany and the European Union: Europe's Hegemon* argumentieren Bulmer und Paterson, dass Deutschland, aufgrund seiner neueren institutionellen Verträge, seiner Exportleistung und seines Einflusses sowie seiner langjährigen fiskalischen Solidität und der Attraktivität seines Modells der sozialen Marktwirtschaft die Fähigkeit hatte und immer noch hat, in wirtschaftlichen Angelegenheiten eine natürliche europäische Führungsrolle einzunehmen, welche auch die Durchsetzung eines neuen Paradigmas umfasst.

Viele Jahrzehnte vor den erwähnten zeitgenössischen politischen Ökonomen haben die geistigen Väter des kreativen Denkens im öffentlichen Sektor, Keynes und Polanyi, die politischen Entscheidungsträger aufgerufen, in der Wirtschaftspolitik nicht ausschließlich an antizyklische Ausgaben zu denken, wenn es darum geht die Auswirkungen von Rezessionen zu reduzieren oder Überhitzungen von Volkswirtschaften zu vermeiden, sondern auch strategisch zu denken und herauszuarbeiten, welche Investitionen helfen können, den Wohlstand der Bürger langfristig zu heben. In seinem Buch *The Great Transformation*[19] argumentiert Polanyi sogar, dass freie Märkte das Produkt staatlicher Interventionen sind, Resultate öffentlicher und privater Eingriffe, und keineswegs im Griff des Zwangsläufigen. Diese scharfsinnige Beobachtung ist von den auf Sparkurs basierenden neoliberalen

VI. A Multilingual Europe – Translations into Irish, French and German

Kommentaren zur noch nicht lange zurückliegende Wirtschaftskrise bequemerweise ignoriert worden. Das Instrument Staat muss von seinen Bürgern wieder in Besitz genommen werden, wenn wir die Gesellschaft zum Wohl der Bürger transformieren wollen, denn der Staat besitzt noch immer die Fähigkeit und den Großteil der Ressourcen, die demokratische Kontrolle von Wirtschaft und Finanzen einer Nation auszuüben. Dies ist nur eine Form der erkenntnistheoretischen Hinterfragung der neoklassischen ökonomischen Orthodoxie, welche starr rationales Denken und Individualismus als Kausalzusammenhang eines wirtschaftliches Gleichgewichts postuliert.

Die Rolle des Staates muss deshalb neu definiert werden, wie auch das Konzept der Souveränität, und zwar dergestalt, dass alle an beiden teilhaben und sie über Grenzen hinaus im Wohl der Bürger münden, und – denn wir befinden uns in einem Übergangsstadium in mehreren Ländern – sie auch eine vergleichende und regionale Eigenschaft haben, die beispielhaft für globale Wirtschaftssysteme sein kann. Das Konzept einer Souveränität, die auch grenzüberschreitende Verantwortung einschließt, könnte sogar noch stringenter definiert werden als ein Konzept, das grenzüberschreitendes *Bewusstsein* verlangt, um nicht in die Falle einer menschenleeren Technokratie oder Ignoranz gegenüber menschlichen Gefühlen zu geraten. Schließlich leben und teilen Nationen gleichermaßen Herzensanliegen wie das, was als ‚vernünftig' angesehen wird. Es ist diese Sensibilität, die den Ehrgeiz der Technokratie in Schranken verweist. Wir müssen den Mut aufbringen, die strukturelle Basis der Probleme, die uns konfrontieren, herauszuarbeiten.

Der Brexit-Entscheid im Vereinigten Königreich, die Wahl von Donald Trump in den Vereinigten Staaten, das Anwachsen nationalistischer und Anti-Immigrations-Parteien in Europa und aktueller die Gelbwestenbewegung in Frankreich werden oft dargestellt als Reaktionen auf steigende Ungleichheit, stagnierende Einkommen und wirtschaftliche Unsicherheit, die in vielen industrialisierten Ländern zu dominanten Trends geworden sind, wie John Evans in *Social Europe* scharfsinnig dargelegt hat:

> Sie spiegeln das Wachstum relativer Deprivation wider, wobei große Teile der Bevölkerung fühlen, dass sie und ihre Familien den Kürzeren gezogen haben, während andere von den wirtschaftlichen und sozialen Veränderungen profitierten – und sie befürchten eine noch unsicherere

Zukunft. Sich zuspitzende Spaltungen werden nach jahrzehntelanger Schwächung intermediärer Institutionen sichtbar, insbesondere der Gewerkschaften, deren Rolle es in wirtschaftlicher Hinsicht war, als Bremse gegen wachsende Ungleichheit zu fungieren und in politischer, denjenigen, die sich ungerecht behandelt fühlen, eine Stimme zu geben und für deren Beschwerden Lösungen auszuhandeln.[20]

Brexit, Trump und Straßengewalt, sie alle repräsentieren Reaktionen, die wir als schädlich empfinden, wenn es um die Frage geht: wie erarbeiten wir eine neuen Kontrakt über Verteilungsgerechtigkeit für diejenigen, die – entweder objektiv oder subjektiv – außen vor geblieben sind aufgrund von Globalisierung, technischen Innovationen (einschließlich Digitalisierung), sogenannter Innovation (einschließlich der Prekarisierung von Arbeit) oder Reaktionen auf den Klimawandel. Wie gewinnen wir Vertrauen zurück? Was sind die Konsequenzen eines Erbes weggefallener oder geschwächter vermittelnder Institutionen? Evans stellt fest:

> ein neuer Gesellschaftsvertrag an Arbeitsplätzen und in Gemeinden ist unerlässlich, um in zersplitterten Gesellschaften Vertrauen zurückzugewinnen. Er muss Einkommensungleichheiten reduzieren und Kaufkraft und mittlere Einkommen stützen, die Qualität der Arbeitsplätze thematisieren, der räumlichen Konzentration von Unzufriedenheit entgegenwirken. Vor allem aber beinhaltet dies eine Rekonstruktion und Stärkung mittelnder Institutionen wie zum Beispiel der Gewerkschaften, die den Benachteiligten Stimme und kollektive Lösungen anbieten können.

Jürgen Habermas hat einen zukunftsträchtigen Beitrag geleistet in seinen großen Sammlungen von Essays über die EU, einschließlich *Im Sog der Technokratie*. Habermas artikuliert eine schlüssige und weitreichende Verteidigung des europäischen Einigungsprojekts und mögliche gleichzeitige Entwicklungen auf eine politisch integrierte Welt und Gesellschaft hin. In seinen Schlüsselkonzepten Transnationalisierung der Demokratie und Konstitutionalisierung internationalen Rechts entwickelt Habermas mehrere wertvolle Anregungen, wie wir auf Umstände wie die aktuelle scheinbare Ausweglosigkeit reagieren können. Habermas kritisiert aufs Schärfste die von einigen Mitgliedstaaten befürwortete, inkrementelle technokratische Politik, die den wirtschaftlich schwächeren, krisengeschüttelten Mitgliedstaaten aufgezwungen wurde und weiterhin wird, und die Solidarität innerhalb der EU untergräbt. Er argumentiert für eine Alternative, in welcher der technokratische, auf Sparkurs fokussierte Ansatz durch eine Demokratisierung der europäischen Institutionen ersetzt wird, damit die EU die Chance bekommt, ihre Kern-Gründungsprinzipien zu erfüllen um sicherzustellen, dass ‚zügellose kapitalistische Marktwirtschaft auf supranationaler Ebene wieder unter Kontrolle gebracht werden kann'. Habermas definiert ein Kontinuum, in welchem Kapitalismus und Demokratie sich gegenüberstehen, wenn auch nicht unbedingt diametral, und er diskutiert mit erschreckender Präzision das bittere Elend einer national aufgestellten kapitalistischen Weltgesellschaft.

Bedeutet dies nun, dass sich eine fundamentale Unvereinbarkeit von Demokratie und Kapitalismus entwickelt oder vielleicht schon entwickelt hat, insbesondere ein Kapitalismus, der einer zügellosen Globalisierung eingeschrieben ist, welche für viele Bürger keinerlei Legitimation besitzt? Im Gegensatz zu Wolfgang Streeck, der, wie ich meine, eher pessimistische Schlussfolgerungen zieht, erklärt Habermas, dass zwei Interventionen das demokratische Fundament der Union verbessern können: gemeinsame Planung politischer Rahmenbedingungen und eine Überarbeitung des Lissabonner Vertrags, um die entsprechenden Kompetenzen demokratisch zu legitimieren ‚[...] insbesondere paritätische Beteiligung von Parlament und Rat bei Gesetzgebungsverfahren und gleiche Rechenschaftspflicht der Kommission gegenüber beiden Institutionen'.[21] In Habermas' Worten: ‚eine Generalisierung von Interessen, die nationale Grenzen überschreitet, ist nur möglich in einem Europäischen Parlament, das über parlamentarische Funktionen organisiert ist'. Er setzt sich ein für eine tiefgreifende politische Integration in Europa, die die Balance zwischen Politik und Markt neu justiert, welche sich bis zum heutigen Tag infolge der neoliberalen Selbstentmachtung der Politik verschoben hat.

Diese Selbstentmachtung der Politik wurde während der Finanzkrise 2008 sowie nachfolgenden wirtschaftlichen Rezessionen innerhalb der EU manifest, als auf die politisch fragmentierten nationalen Staatshaushalte seitens der Finanzmärkte Druck ausgeübt wurde, der zu einer kollektiven negativen Selbstwahrnehmung in der von der Krise besonders betroffenen Bevölkerungen führte. Habermas argumentiert, dass die Reaktion durch Märkte, Regierungen, wichtige internationale Organisationen und Kommentatoren aus dem neoliberalen Mainstream-Lager erheblich dazu beigetragen hat, dass den ‚Programm-Ländern Hilfe nur auf einer Bestrafungsbasis angeboten wurde, wobei „Geber" und „Empfänger"-Länder gegeneinander gesetzt wurden und dadurch Nationalismus geschürt wurde'. Eine Wiederholung einer solchen ausweglosen Situation könnte dadurch vermieden werden, dass pro-europäische Parteien gemeinsam transnationale Kampagnen durchführten gegen die Falschdarstellung, dass soziale Fragen nationale Fragen seien. Er verlangt auch, ‚die Währungsunion muss zu einer supranationalen Demokratie werden', die eine institutionelle Plattform bereitstellen kann den neoliberalen Trend der letzten Jahrzehnte umzukehren. Vor allem argumentiert Habermas (in *Europe: The Faltering Project* [dt. *Ach Europa*])[22] für eine graduelle Integration, in welcher Schlüsselentscheidungen über die Zukunft Europas in die Hände der Bürger gelegt werden und nicht in die der ‚neoliberalen Orthodoxie'.

Haben wir unsere Lehren gezogen aus der Wirtschaftskrise, dem ‚sich-selbst-regulierenden Markt', und der lange währenden, verheerenden Periode der Entbehrung, die Millionen von europäischen Bürgern aufgezwungen wurde? Ich glaube, es gibt viele – in der Politik, unter Entscheidungsträgern, Wissenschaftlern, Kommentatoren, Bürgern – die alte festsitzende Überzeugungen neu überdacht und eine neue Wertschätzung des Staates gefunden haben, eines Staates, der in allen Bereichen öffentlicher Ordnung eine wichtige Rolle zu spielen hat; dass gute Regeln wichtig ist, sei es im Finanzsektor, Bausektor oder im Gesundheitswesen – Sektoren, in denen wir in Irland die katastrophalen und manchmal tragischen Auswirkungen der Unter-Regulierung und/oder der mangelhaften Durchsetzung von Regeln gespürt haben.

Die Legitimationskrise ist nicht auf die Europäische Union oder ihre Mitglieder beschränkt. Die Rolle des Staates wird auch entscheidend sein, wenn es um Fragen wie Klimawandel und Nachhaltigkeit geht. Es besteht eine ernstzunehmende Lücke: wie behandeln wir Institutionen, die nicht dem Parlament, dem Volk oder den Gesetzen beider verantwortlich sind? Dieses Problem wurde vom Präsidenten Griechenlands Prokopios Pavlopoulos 2016 in seiner Aristoteles-Vorlesung angesprochen. Er sprach von nicht-staatlichen

VI. A Multilingual Europe – Translations into Irish, French and German

Einheiten mit internationaler Reichweite ohne demokratische Legitimität – die sogenannten Finanzmärkte, Kreditrating-Agenturen – und den Verfall von sozialer Fürsorge und Rechtsstaatlichkeit.

Wenn ich in die Zukunft blicke, stehen in der Vision meines Europas hervorragende öffentliche Dienste im Mittelpunkt. Gute Arbeitsplätze im öffentlichen Sektor bedeuten hochwertige Dienstleistungen für die Bürger. Wir müssen uns daran erinnern, dass die Dienstleistungen, die der öffentliche Dienst erbringt, keinen Kostenfaktor für die Gesellschaft darstellt, sondern eine Investition in unsere Gemeinschaft. Diese Botschaft muss im Herzen Europas ankommen. Ich möchte den Schluss nahelegen, dass spekulative, unersättliche Kapitalflüsse jenseits jeder Verantwortung stattfinden und eine globale, unkontrollierte und finanzialisierte Wirtschaftsform eine Bedrohung der Demokratie darstellt, die größte Quelle unvermeidlicher Konflikte und das größte Hindernis globale Armut auszumerzen oder Nachhaltigkeit zu erzielen.

Abschließend komme ich zum Anfang zurück, zu Schillers „An die Freude". Vor meiner Reise habe ich dieses Gedicht mit seiner wirkmächtigen Botschaft von Freiheit und Solidarität noch einmal gelesen. Schillers erste Strophe endet mit den eindringlichen Zeilen: ‚Alle Menschen werden Brüder, / Wo dein sanfter Flügel weilt.' Dieser Ausdruck von Solidarität und Toleranz erinnert uns nachdrücklich an Zweck und Leitprinzipien der Europäischen Union: Solidarität unter unseren Nationen und Solidarität mit anderen Menschen. Was verlangt Solidarität von uns heute? Sie muss generationenübergreifend sein, ein multidimensionales Konzept, das Ökosystem, Gesellschaft, Kultur und Wirtschaft (sowohl Handel wie Besteuerung) umfasst. Wir brauchen einen uns allen gemeinsamen Ansatz, das zu bekämpfen, was unverantwortlich ist, was öffentliches Vertrauen in die Demokratie untergräbt, was Bürger nur als unersättliche Konsumenten sieht.

Aber Solidarität ist nicht die einzige Botschaft, die wir Schillers Gedicht entnehmen, es ist ein längeres Werk und nur die ersten Strophen wurden von Beethoven vertont. Der Komponist selbst war sich wohl bewusst, dass nicht alle Strophen von seinen damaligen Herren geschätzt werden würden, da sie idealistische Aufrufe enthalten was für eine bessere Welt zu tun ist. In seiner Gesamtheit appelliert das Gedicht an Millionen eine bessere Welt zu erstreben:

Hilfe für die Unschuldigen, Freunden und Feinden die Wahrheit zu sagen, diejenigen zu würdigen, die es verdienen, und ein Ende denjenigen, die lügen.

Seinerzeit war es ein Ruf nach Rettung vor den Tyrannen, Gnade für Missetäter und Hoffnung bis in die Sterbestunden. Das Gedicht drückt die Essenz der europäischen Werte aus – zweifellos ideale Werte, aber Werte, nach deren Erfüllung wir weiterhin streben müssen. Die Ode „An die Freude" repräsentiert eine Moral, die zu einer konkreten, spürbaren Realität werden muss, die den Bürgern auf den Straßen Europas angeboten und von ihnen erfahren werden kann.

Zielgerichtetes Handeln zum Zwecke der notwendigen Transformation des Verhältnisses zwischen Wirtschaft und Gesellschaft, die ich in meiner Rede angesprochen habe, hat höchste Priorität in einer Zeit, in der es an angemessenem und integrativem Diskurs fehlt und die, wie ich glaube, als Konsequenz von einer wachsend erbitterten Rhetorik gekennzeichnet ist, eine Rhetorik, die zumeist auf Verzweiflung, Entfremdung, Anomie und Ausgrenzung gründet und Aussagen von Verantwortungslosigkeit produziert, die uns aufgrund ethnischer Zugehörigkeit, Religion oder Nationalität zu spalten versucht. Dieses Europa, das wir suchen, muss ein Europa sein, in welchem solch hasserfülltes Streiten ersetzt wird durch Offenheit, Inklusivität, Zusammenhalt, Solidarität und die Erkenntnis, dass wir nur gemeinsam, aber umgehend, den Wechsel hin zu einem neuen, gleichstellungspolitischen, ökologisch-sozialen Paradigma der Schaffung und Verteilung von Wohlstand anstreben können. Und dies nicht nur zu unserem Vorteil in der Europäischen Union, sondern auch zu dem zukünftiger Generationen, denen wir eine Heimat in einer friedlichen, harmonischen Welt wünschen, die auf einer nachhaltigen Vision für Wirtschaft und Gesellschaft gründet und von einer bunten Vielfalt der Kulturen bereichert wird.

Übersetzung: Rolf Höfig und Joachim Fischer.

Postscript on the COVID-19 Crisis

Towards a Europe Resolute in Its Vindication of the Most Vulnerable Among Us

From a letter to the President of the Hellenic Republic, 9 April 2020.

I have been watching with mounting concern and profound sadness as the people of Europe strive to tackle the cruel virus that is taking hold in so much of the world. It is just a few short months ago that members of the Arraiolos Group met in Athens [...]. How little did we imagine then that we would be faced with this crisis, which has cost the lives of so many of our citizens and stripped so many others of their livelihoods. As close friends, we mourn together as we come to terms with the losses that we have endured.

The example of citizens across the European Union has also served as an inspiration to us all through the courage and resilience that they have shown in the face of such adversity. The profound humanity demonstrated by people all across our great continent during these darkest of days gives such hope that as Europeans, as partners in the European Union, we can prevail.

These terrible events have exposed our shared vulnerability, but have also inspired such heart-warming acts of decency and solidarity among our people.

Though it may be difficult to look beyond the immediate emergency in which we find ourselves, as leaders within our Union, we must look ahead and take what instruction we can from this tragedy, in terms of a shared preparedness. We are called to be authentic to our citizens who can see how the very definition of a union with its promise of a shared vulnerability, social economy and responsible ecology, are all tested by our collective response or absence.

We must build on the solidarity being shown by our people and ensure that their example is reflected in how we act as Member States of the European Union. Like the financial crisis of a decade ago, this virus has exposed weaknesses in our Union. This is no time for us to withdraw behind our own borders, but rather we should learn from these events, and the frailties that they have uncovered, to drive forward, building on the vision of Altiero Spinelli, Robert Schuman, Jean Monnet and so many others to finally construct a Europe that speaks to all of its citizens and is resolute in its vindication of the most vulnerable among us.

Let us begin again bringing the wounded of all our peoples with us. The architecture of decision-making itself may have to change, as indeed the global architecture of the United Nations, and its institutions, must change and respond to what is a new moment in global history. The good news is that we can combine our preparedness for climate change and sustainability with our response to COVID-19 by, for example, setting about achieving universal basic services for all, which is so urgent in places such as Africa, Asia and Latin America, as well as on our own continent.

Yours sincerely

Michael D. Higgins
Uachtarán na hÉireann
President of Ireland

Bibliography

Adshead, Maura, 'European Union Politics and Ireland'. In: Brian Lalor (ed.), *The Encyclopedia of Ireland*. Dublin: Gill & Macmillan, 2003, pp. 364–5.

Aquinas, Thomas, *Summa Theologica*. https://oll.libertyfund.org/titles/aquinas-the-summa-theologica-of-st-thomas-aquinas-part-i-qq-i-xxvi-vol-1, 18 August 2020.

Arensberg, Conrad M. and Kimball, Solon T., *Family and Community in Ireland*. Cambridge, MA: Harvard University Press, 1940.

Arkins, Brian, *Hellenizing Ireland: Greek and Roman Themes in Modern Irish Literature*. Newbridge: Goldsmith Press, 2005.

Bachelard, Gaston (trans. Maria Jolas), *The Poetics of Space*. London, etc.: Penguin, 2014 (first publ. 1964).

Atkinson, Anthony, *Inequality: What Can Be Done?* Cambridge, MA and London: Harvard University Press, 2015.

Beckett, Samuel, *Happy Days*. London: Faber & Faber, 1962.

Beiner, Guy, 'Troubles with Remembering; or, The Seven Deadly Sins of Memory Studies'. *Dublin Review of Books*, 1 November 2017. https://www.drb.ie/essays/troubles-with-remembering-or-the-seven-sins-of-memory-studies, 10 July 2020.

Benedict. M.L. and Braithwaite, M., 'The Year of the Killer Flu'. *In the Face of Disaster: True Stories of Canadian Heroes from the Archives of Maclean's*. New York: Viking, 2000.

Bielefeld, Ulrich and Tietze, Nikola, 'In Search of Europe: An Interview with Jacques Delors'. 1 July 2011. https://www.eurozine.com/in-search-of-europe/, 13 July 2020.

Boccaccio, Giovanni (trans. G.H. McWilliam), *The Decameron*. London, etc.: Penguin, 1995.

Brennock, Mark, 'Harney opposed to closer integration of Europe'. *Irish Times*, 22 July 2000. https://www.irishtimes.com/news/harney-opposed-to-closer-integration-of-europe-1.295209, 21 January 2021.

Bibliography

Brown, Michael, *The Irish Enlightenment*. Cambridge, MA: Harvard University Press, 2016.

Bulmer, Simon and Paterson, William E., *Germany and the European Union: Europe's Reluctant Hegemon?* London: Red Globe Press, 2019.

Carbery, Genevieve, 'Ireland becoming anti-intellectual, academic editor says'. *Irish Times*, 28 June 2012. https://www.irishtimes.com/news/irelandbecoming-anti-intellectual-academic-editor-says-1.1069133, 7 July 2020.

Carmody, Pádraig and Fortuin, Alicia, '"Ride-sharing", virtual capital and impacts on labor in Cape Town, South Africa'. *African Geographical Review* 38/3 (2019), 196–208.

Casement, Roger, 'Speech from the Dock'. https://www.newstatesman.com/2010/03/ireland-law-england-irishmen, 17 August 2020.

Collini, Stefan, '"Every Fruit-Juice Drinker, Nudist, Sandal-Wearer …": Intellectuals as Other People'. In: Helen Small (ed.), *The Public Intellectual*. Oxford and Malden: Wiley-Blackwell, 2002, pp. 203–23.

Collins, Stephen, 'Labour on Europe: from No to Yes'. In: Paul Daly et al. (eds), *Making the Difference: The Irish Labour Party 1912–2012*. Cork: Collins Press, 2012, pp. 154–64.

Coote, Anna and Percy, Andrew, *The Case for Universal Basic Services*. London: Polity Press, 2020.

Corcoran, Mary P., 'Introduction: Challenging Intellectuals'. In: Mary P. Corcoran and Kevin Lalor (eds), *Reflections on Crisis: The Role of the Public Intellectual*. Dublin: RIA, 2012, pp. 3–11.

Cornewall-Lewis, George, *Remarks on the Third Report of the Irish Poor Inquiry Commissioners*. London: Charles Knight and Co., 1837.

Crouch, Colin, *Social Europe: A Manifesto*. Berlin: Social Europe Publishing, 2020.

Crowley, John, Smyth, William J. and Murphy, Mike (eds), *Atlas of the Great Irish Famine*. Cork: University Press, 2012.

Crosby, Alfred W., *Epidemic and Peace, 1918*. Westport, CT: Greenwood Press, 1976.

Crutzen, Paul, 'Geology of Mankind'. *Nature* 415/23 (2002). https://doi.org/10.1038/415023a, 14 July 2020.

Dabiri, Emma, 'Let's Talk about Race and Identity in Ireland'. *Dublin Inquirer*, 11 October 2017. https://www.dublininquirer.com/2017/10/11/emma-let-s-talk-about-race-and-identity-in-ireland, 22 July 2020.

Davis, Mike, *Late Victorian Holocausts: El Niño Famines and the Making of the Third World*. London: Verso, 2000.

Dawson, Asley, *Extinction: A Radical History*. New York: OR Books, 2016.

Delors, Jacques, 'Address to the Royal Institute of International Affairs, London, 7 September 1992'. https://ec.europa.eu/commission/presscorner/detail/en/SPEECH_92_81, 17 August 2020.

Drügh, Heinz, 'Pop-Intellektualität'. In: Jürgen Fohrmann and Carl Friedrich Gethmann (eds), *Topographien von Intellektualität*. Göttingen: Wallstein, 2018, pp. 58–81.

Duchêne, François, *Jean Monnet: The First Statesman of Interdependence*. New York: W.W. Norton and Company, 1980.

Duddy, Thomas, *A History of Irish Thought*. London and New York: Routledge, 2002.

Ellman, Richard, *James Joyce*. Oxford: University Press, 1959.

Eötvös, Baron József (trans. Paul Sohar and Lázló Bakas), *Poverty in Ireland 1837: A Hungarian's View*. Dublin: Phaeton, 1840.

Esping-Andersen, Gøsta, *The Three Worlds of Welfare Capitalism*. Princeton: University Press, 1990.

Evans, John, 'Inequality and unions: Brexit, Trump and "yellow vests"'. Social Europe, 23 January 2019. https://www.socialeurope.eu/inequality-and-unions, 20 July 2020.

Fanning, Bryan, *The Quest for Modern Ireland: The Battle of Ideas 1912–1986*. Dublin and Portland, OR: Irish Academic Press, 2008.

Ferriter, Diarmuid, 'Commemorations need political leadership'. *Irish Times*, 18 January 2020. https://www.irishtimes.com/opinion/diarmaid-ferriter-commemorations-need-political-leadership-1.4143053, 22 July 2020.

'Fight against desert locust swarms goes on in East Africa despite coronavirus measures'. 9 April 2020. https://news.un.org/en/story/2020/04/1061482, 20 July 2020.

Fischer, Joachim, 'Boston or Berlin? Reflections on a Topical Controversy, the Celtic Tiger and the World of Irish Studies'. *Irish Review* 48. Summer 2014, 81–95.

Foley, Caitriona, *The Last Irish Plague: The Great Flu Epidemic in Ireland 1918–19*. Dublin: Irish Academic Press, 2011.

Forster, E. M., *Pharos and Pharillon*. London: Hogarth, 1923, 75–9.

Fukuyama, Francis, *The End of History and the Last Man*. New York: Free Press, 1991.

Furlong, Sharon, '"Herstory" Recovered: Assessing the contribution of Cumann na mBan 1914–1923'. *The Past: The Organ of the Uí Cinsealaigh Historical Society* 30, 2010, 70–93.

Pope Francis, *Evangelii Gaudium*. http://www.vatican.va/content/francesco/en/apost_exhortations/documents/papa-francesco_esortazione-ap_20131124_evangelii-gaudium.html, 14 July 2020.

Pope Francis, *Encyclical Laudato Si' of the Holy Father Francis: On Care for our Common Home*. Vatican City: Vatican Press, 2015.

Pope Francis, 'Address to Participants in the 3rd World Meeting of Popular Movements, 5 November 2016'. https://w2.vatican.va/content/francesco/en/speeches/2016/november/documents/papa-francesco_20161105_movimenti-popolari.html, 18 August 2020.

Pope Francis, 'Address of His Holiness Pope Francis to the Heads of State and Government of the European Union, Rome, 24 March 2017'. http://www.vatican.va/content/francesco/en/speeches/2017/march/documents/papa-francesco_20170324_capi-unione-europea.html, 18 August 2020.

Friel, Brian, *Translations*. London: Faber & Faber, 1981.

Garvin, Tom, 'The Assault on Intellectualism in Irish Higher Education'. In: Mary P. Corcoran and Kevin Lalor (eds), *Reflections on Crisis: The Role of the Public Intellectual*. pp. 29–37, Dublin: RIA, 2012.

Guérot, Ulrike, *Why Europe Should Become a Republic! A Political Utopia*. Berlin: Dietz, 2019.

Bibliography

Guérot, Ulrike, 'Europe as a republic: the story of Europe in the twenty first century'. *Open Democracy*, 29 June 2015. https://www.opendemocracy.net/en/can-europe-make-it/europe-as-republic-story-of-europe-in-twenty-first-century, 23 July 2020.

Gough, Ian, *Heat, Greed and Human Need: Climate Change, Capitalism and Sustainable Well-being*. Cheltenham, UK and Northampton, MA: Edward Elgar, 2017.

Guterres, António, 'Opening remarks at virtual press encounter to launch the Report on the Socio-Economic Impacts of COVID-19', 31 March 2020. https://www.un.org/sg/en/content/sg/speeches/2020-03-31/remarks-launch-of-report-the-socio-economic-impacts-of-covid-19, 20 July 2020.

Habermas, Jürgen (trans. Ciaran Cronin), *The Lure of Technocracy*. Cambridge, UK and Malden, MA: Polity Press, 2015.

Habermas, Jürgen, *Im Sog der Technokratie*. Berlin: Suhrkamp, 2013.

Habermas, Jürgen (trans. Ciaran Cronin), *Europe: The Faltering Project*. Cambridge, UK and Malden, MA: Polity Press, 2009

Habermas, Jürgen, *Der gespaltene Westen*. Frankfurt am Main: Suhrkamp, 2004.

Hayward, Katy, 'Northern Ireland may find itself between a rock and a hard place after Brexit'. *Irish Times*, 13 January 2020. https://www.irishtimes.com/opinion/northern-ireland-may-find-itself-between-a-rock-and-a-hard-place-after-brexit-1.4137426, 22 July 2020.

Hayward, Katy, *Irish Nationalism and European Integration: The Official Redefinition of the Island of Ireland*. Manchester: University Press, 2009.

Hayward, Katy, 'From Visionary to Functionary: Representations of Irish intellectuals in the debate on "Europe"'. *Études irlandaises*. 34/2, 2009, 87–100. https://journals.openedition.org/etudesirlandaises/1650, 23 July 2020.

Heaney, Seamus, 'Varieties of Irishness: In the Element of his Genius'. *Irish Pages* 9/1 (2015), 9–20.

Heidegger, Martin, (trans. and introduction by Albert Hofstadter), *Poetry, Language, Thought*. New York: Harper & Row, 1971. Colophon ed. 1975.

Hennette, Stéphanie, Piketty, Thomas, Sacriste, Guillaume and Vauchez, Antoine, *How to Democratize Europe*. Cambridge, MA: Harvard University Press, 2019.

Higgins, Michael D., 'Out of the tragedy of coronavirus may come hope of a more just society'. *Social Europe*, 22 April 2020. https://www.socialeurope.eu/out-of-the-tragedy-of-coronavirus-may-come-hope-of-a-more-just-society, 24 August 2020.

Higgins, Michael D., 'We cannot ignore the impact of Covid-19 on Africa'. *Irish Times*, 23 April 2020. https://www.irishtimes.com/opinion/michael-d-higgins-we-cannot-ignore-the-impact-of-covid-19-on-africa-1.4235431, 24 August 2020.

Higgins, Michael D., 'Ireland in Europe 1992: Problems and Prospects for a Mutual Interdependence'. In: Richard Kearney (ed.), *Across the Frontiers: Ireland in the 1990s Cultural-Political-Economic*. Dublin: Wolfhound Press, 1988, pp. 58–77.

Higgins, Michael D., *When Ideas Matter: Speeches for an Ethical Republic*. London: Head of Zeus, 2016.

Hobson, Bulmer, 'Statement on IRB and Irish Freedom'. Bureau of Military History 1913–21. http://www.militaryarchives.ie/collections/online-collections/bureau-of-military-history-1913-1921/reels/bmh/BMH.WS0085.pdf, 17 August 2020.

Honigsbaum, Mark, *Living with Enza: The Forgotten Story of Britain and the Great Flu Pandemic of 1918*. London: Palgrave Macmillan, 2009.

Houman, Tim, '100 Years: Knowledge of the Spanish flu enhances our preparedness for future pandemics'. https://ruc.dk/en/news/100-years-knowledge-spanish-flu-enhances-our-preparedness-future-pandemics, 18 August 2020.

Hume, David, *The History of England: From the Invasion of Julius Caesar to the Revolution in 1688*. London: Jones & Company, 1829.

Humphries, Jane and Schneider, Benjamin, 'Spinning the Industrial Revolution'. *Economic History Review* 72/1, 2018, 126–55.

Isaacson, Walter, 'President and CEO Walter Isaacson delivers 2014 Jefferson Lecture'. https://www.aspeninstitute.org/blog-posts/president-ceo-walter-isaacson-delivers-2014-jefferson-lecture, 18 August 2020.

Joerges, Christian, 'The Market without the State? The "Economic Constitution" of the European Community and the Rebirth of Regulatory Politics'. *European Integration online Papers* 1/19 (1997). https://ssrn.com/abstract=302710 or http://dx.doi.org/10.2139/ssrn.302710, 20 August 2020.

Johnston, Alison and Regan, Aidan, 'Is the European Union Capable of Integrating Diverse Models of Capitalism?' *New Political Economy* 23/2 (2018), 145–59.

Kay, Joseph, *Free Trade in Land*. London: Ballantyne Press, 1877.

Kearney, Richard, *The Irish Mind*. Dublin: Wolfhound Press, 1985.

Kehrbaum, Tom, 'Ein soziales und ein demokratisches Europa neu denken!' In: Ulrike Guérot, Oskar Negt, Tom Kehrbaum and Emanuel Herold, *Europa jetzt! Eine Ermutigung*. Göttingen: Steidl, 2018, pp. 11–38.

Kenna, Padraic, *Housing and Human Rights: International Encyclopedia of Housing and Home*. Oxford: Elsevier, 2011.

Klein, Naomi, *No Logo*. New York: Picador, 2000.

Komlosy, Andrea, (trans. Jacob K. Watson), *Work: The Last 1,000 Years*. London and New York: Verso, 2018.

Krastev, Ivan, *After Europe*. Philadelphia: University of Pennsylvania, 2020.

Krastev, Ivan, *Ist heute schon morgen? Wie die Pandemie Europa verändert*. Berlin: Ullstein, 2020.

Laffan, Brigid, 'Ireland may have to sacrifice sacred cows to survive Brexit'. *Irish Times*, 16 May 2017. https://www.irishtimes.com/opinion/ireland-may-have-to-sacrifice-sacred-cows-to-survive-brexit-1.3083791, 22 July 2020.

Laffan, Brigid and O'Mahony, Jane, *Ireland and the European Union*. London: Palgrave Macmillan, 2008.

Laski, Harold, 'Revolution by Consent'. *The Nation*, 152, 22 March 1941.

Bibliography

Lee, J.J., *Ireland 1912–1985: Politics and Society*. Cambridge: University Press, 1989.

Leggewie, Claus, *Europa Zuerst! Eine Unabhängigkeitserklärung*. Berlin: Ullstein, 2017.

Lenehan, Fergal, *Intellectuals and Europe: Imagining a Europe of the Regions in Twentieth Century Germany, Britain and Ireland*. Trier: Wissenschaftlicher Verlag Trier, 2014.

Lindley, Robin, 'The Forgotten American Pandemic: Historian Dr. Nancy K. Bristow on the Influenza Epidemic of 1918'. *History News Network*, 6 November 2012. http://hnn.us/article/146655, 10 July 2020.

Llosa, Mario Vargas (trans. Edith Grossman), *The Dream of the Celt*. London: Faber & Faber, 2012.

Locke, John, *An Essay Concerning Toleration: And Other Writings on Law and Politics, 1667–1683*. Oxford: University Press, 2006.

Longo, Michael and Murray, Philomena, *Europe's Legitimacy Crisis: From Causes to Solutions*. London: Palgrave Macmillan, 2015.

Lopes, Carlos and Kararach, George, *Structural Change in Africa: Misperceptions, New Narratives and Development in the 21st Century*. London: Routledge, 2020.

Losurdo, Domenico, *Liberalism: A Counter-History*. London and New York: Verso, 2014.

Luxemburg, Rosa (trans. George Shriver), *The Letters of Rosa Luxemburg*, Georg Adler, Peter Hudis and Annelies Laschitza (eds). London and New York: Verso, 2011.

Mahaffy, J.P., *Rambles and Studies in Greece*. Gerrards Cross: Colin Smythe, 2012.

Margalit, Avishai, *The Ethics of Memory*. Cambridge, MA and London: Harvard University Press, 2004, pp. 51–4.

Mathew, James Charles, 'Mathew, Theobald'. In Sidney Lee (ed.), *Dictionary of National Biography*. 37. New York: Macmillan, 1894, pp. 32–4.

Mathew, Father Theobald, 'House of Lords Testimony'. http://www.capuchinfranciscans.ie/wp-content/uploads/2018/07/5.-Descriptive-List-Web-Fr.-Theobald-Mathew-Research-and-Commemorative-Papers.pdf, 17 August 2020.

Mazzucato, Mariana, *The Value of Everything: Making and Taking in the Global Economy*. New York: Public Affairs, 2018.

Meehan, Paula, 'Crossing the Threshold'. https://www.dcu.ie/news/news/2020/Jun/Crossing-Threshold-poet-Paula-Meehan-marks-DCU-Virtual-Graduation.shtml, 18 August 2020.

McGrath, Dominic, 'Millennials for Michael D: Why young people are backing a Higgins presidency'. https://www.thejournal.ie/millennials-and-michael-d-higgins-presidency-4257246-Sep2018/, 21 July 2020.

Menasse, Robert, *Der europäische Landbote: Die Wut der Bürger und der Friede Europas*. Vienna: Zsolnay, 2012.

Milne, Ida, *Stacking the Coffins: Influenza, War and Revolution in Ireland, 1918–19*. Manchester: University Press, 2018.

Miłosz, Czesław, 'Incantation'. In: Czesław Miłosz, *Collected Poems 1931–1987*. London: Harper Collins, 1988.

Mitchell, William and Fazi, Thomas, *Reclaiming the State: A Progressive Vision of Sovereignty for a Post-Neoliberal World*. London: Pluto Press, 2017.

Mokyr, Joel, 'Secular Stagnation? Not in Your Life'. In: Coen Teulings and Richard Baldwin (eds), *Secular Stagnation: Facts, Causes and Cures*. London: Centre for Economic and Policy Research, 2014, pp. 83–90.

Morrissey, Carla R., 'The Influenza Epidemic of 1918'. *Navy Medicine* 77, 3 (May–June 1986), 11–17.

Mouzelis, Nicos, 'Class and Clientelistic Politics: The Case of Greece'. *Sociological Review*, 26/3 (1978), 471–98.

Müller-Armack, Alfred, 'The Principles of the Social Market Economy'. 19 December 1962. https://ghdi.ghi-dc.org/sub_document.cfm?document_id=926, 17 July 2020.

Muthu, Sankar, *Enlightenment against Empire*. Princeton: University Press, 2003.

National Economic and Social Council Report, 'Addressing Employment Vulnerability as Part of a Just Transition in Ireland'. Dublin: NESC, 2020. https://www.nesc.ie/publications, 24 August 2020.

Negt, Oskar, *Gesellschaftsentwurf Europa: Plädoyer für ein gerechtes Gemeinwesen*. Göttingen: Steidl, 2012.

Newman, John Henry, *An Essay on the Development of Christian Doctrine*. http://www.newmanreader.org/works/development/index.html, 13 July 2020.

O'Connor, Pat, 'Reflections on the Public Intellectual's Role in a Gendered Society'. In: Mary P. Corcoran and Kevin Lalor (eds), *Reflections on Crisis: The Role of the Public Intellectual*, pp. 55–73, Dublin: RIA, 2012.

O'Dowd, Liam, 'Public Intellectuals and the "Crisis": Accountability, Democracy and Market Fundamentalism'. In: Mary P. Corcoran and Kevin Lalor (eds), *Reflections on Crisis*, pp. 77–102, Dublin: RIA, 2012.

O'Leary, John, *The Writings of James Fintan Lalor and a Memoir*. Dublin: T.G. O'Donoghue, 1895.

O'Rourke, Fran, *Aristotelian Interpretations*. Sallins: Irish Academic Press, 2016.

O'Sullivan, T.F., *The Young Irelanders*. Tralee: The Kerryman, 1944.

O'Toole, Fintan, 'Unpresidented'. *New York Review of Books*, 23 July 2020. https://www.nybooks.com/articles/2020/07/23/trump-unpresident-unredeemed-promise/ 23 July 2020.

O'Toole, Fintan, 'The Union Without Qualities'. *New York Review of Books*, 24 October 2019, 14-16.

O'Toole, Fintan, *Heroic Failure: Brexit and the Politics of Pain*. London: Head of Zeus, 2018.

O'Toole, Fintan, *Ship of Fools: How Stupidity and Corruption Sank the Celtic Tiger*. London: Faber & Faber, 2009.

Padoa-Schioppa, Tommaso, *The Road to Monetary Union in Europe*. Oxford: University Press, 1994.

Polanyi, Karl, *The Great Transformation: The Political and Economic Origins of Our Time*. Boston: Beacon Press, 2001.

Raworth, Kate, *Doughnut Economics: Seven Ways to Think Like a 21st-Century Economist*. White River Junction, VT: Chelsea Green Publishing, 2017.

Bibliography

'Report on Citizens' Consultations on the Future of Europe in Ireland', p. 4. https://www.dfa.ie/our-role-policies/ireland-in-the-eu/future-of-europe/news/newsarchive/report-on-citizens-consultations-on-the-future-of-europe-in-ireland.php, 20 September 2020.

Ricoeur, Paul (trans. Kathleen Blamey and David Pellauer), *Memory, History, Forgetting*. Chicago and London: University of Chicago Press, 2004.

Roll, Evelyn, *Wir sind Europa! Eine Streitschrift gegen den Nationalismus*. Berlin: Ullstein, 2016.

Rosa, Hartmut (trans. James Wagner), *Resonance: A Sociology of Our Relationship to the World*. Cambridge, UK and Medford, MA: Polity Press, 2019.

Runde, Daniel F., 'The Role of the AfDB and the Future of Africa'. https://csis-website-prod.s3.amazonaws.com/s3fs-public/publication/191011_RundeandBandura_AfDB.pdf, 20 July 2020.

Said, Edward W., 'The Public Role of Writers and Intellectuals'. In: Helen Small (ed.), *The Public Intellectual*, pp. 19–39, Oxford and Malden: Wiley-Blackwell, 2002.

Schuman, Robert, 'Declaration of 9 May: The Schuman Plan for European Integration'. https://www.robert-schuman.eu/en/declaration-of-9-may-1950, 17 August 2020.

Scott, James C., *Against the Grain: A Deep History of the Earliest States*. New Haven: Yale University Press, 2017.

Sen, Amartya, *Poverty and Famines: An Essay on Entitlement and Deprivation*, Oxford: University Press, 1981.

'Social Action Programme'. *Bulletin of the European Communities Supplement* 2/74. COM(73) 1600,24 October 1973. http://aei.pitt.edu/1253/1/social_action_program_COM_73_1600.pdf, 20 August 2020.

Soskice, David and Hall, Peter A., *Varieties of Capitalism*. Oxford: University Press, 2001.

Spinelli, Altiero and Rossi, Ernesto, The *Ventotene Manifesto*. https://www.federalists.eu/uef/library/books/the-ventotene-manifesto/, 10 July 2020.

Stearns, Peter, *The Industrial Revolution in World History*. Boulder, CO: Westview Press, 1998.

Strong, Josiah, *The Challenge of the City*. New York: Baker and Taylor, 1907.

Sullivan, Moynagh, 'Raising the Veil: Mystery, Myth, and Melancholia in Irish Studies'. In: Patricia Coughlan and Tina O'Toole (eds), *Irish Literature: Feminist Perspectives*. Dublin: Carysfort Press, 2008, pp. 245–78.

Sutherland, Peter D., 'Our Great Migration Challenge: The Littleton Memorial Lecture, presented by Peter Sutherland in Dublin on 17 December 2015'. https://www.thecairoreview.com/essays/our-great-migration-challenge, 18 August 2020.

Thomas, William L. and Znaniecki, Florian, *The Polish Peasant in Europe and America: Monograph on an Immigrant Group*. 5 vols. Boston: Richard G. Badger, 1918–20.

Trauth, Mary Philip, *Italo-American Diplomatic Relations, 1861–1882: The Mission of George Perkins Marsh, First American Minister to the Kingdom of Italy*. Washington, DC: Catholic University of America Press, 1958.

'UNHCR welcomes "unprecedented force and resonance" of New York Declaration'. https://www.unhcr.org/en-ie/news/press/2016/9/57dff34f4/unhcr-welcomes-unprecedented-force-resonance-new-york-declaration.html, 18 August 2020.

Valéry, Paul, 'The Crisis of the Mind'. In: Paul Valéry, *An Anthology*. Princeton, NJ: University Press, 1977, pp. 94–107 (translator not given).

Walby, Sylvia, *Crisis*. Cambridge, UK and Malden, MA: Polity Press, 2015.

Weldon, Duncan, 'The British Model and the Brexit Shock: Plus ça Change?' *The Political Quarterly* 90/2, 2019, pp. 12–20. https://onlinelibrary.wiley.com/doi/full/10.1111/1467-923X.12625, 10 July 2020.

Williams, Raymond, *The Country and the City*. Oxford: University Press, 1973.

Woodham-Smith, Cecil, *The Great Hunger: Ireland 1845–1949*. New York: Harper & Row, 1962.

World Bank, *Doing Business: Going Beyond Efficiency*. https://www.doingbusiness.org/content/dam/doingBusiness/media/Annual-Reports/English/DB15-Full-Report.pdf, 18 August 2020.

Wyschogrod, Edith, *An Ethics of Remembering: History, Heterology and the Nameless Others*. Chicago and London: University of Chicago Press, 1998.

Notes

FOREWORD

1. See, for example, Ian Gough, *Heat, Greed and Human Need: Climate Change, Capitalism and Sustainable Wellbeing*. Cheltenham, UK and Northampton, MA: Edward Elgar, 2017.
2. See, for example, Mariana Mazzucato, *The Value of Everything: Making and Taking in the Global Economy*. New York: Public Affairs, 2018.
3. See, for example, Sylvia Walby, *Crisis*. Cambridge, UK and Malden, MA: Polity Press, 2015.
4. See, for example, Kate Raworth, *Doughnut Economics: Seven Ways to Think Like a 21st-Century Economist*. White River Junction, VT: Chelsea Green Publishing, 2017.
5. Francis Fukuyama, *The End of History and the Last Man*. New York: Free Press, 1991.
6. Anna Coote and Andrew Percy, *The Case for Universal Basic Services*. London: Polity Press, 2020.
7. Ian Gough, *op. cit.*
8. Michael D. Higgins, 'Out of the tragedy of coronavirus may come hope of a more just society'. *Social Europe*, 22 April 2020. https://www.socialeurope.eu/out-of-the-tragedy-of-coronavirus-may-come-hope-of-a-more-just-society, 24 August 2020; and Michael D. Higgins, 'We cannot ignore the impact of Covid-19 on Africa', *Irish Times*, 23 April 2020. https://www.irishtimes.com/opinion/michael-d-higgins-we-cannot-ignore-the-impact-of-covid-19-on-africa-1.4235431, 24 August 2020.
9. National Economic and Social Council Report, 'Addressing Employment Vulnerability as Part of a Just Transition in Ireland'. Dublin: NESC, 2020. https://www.nesc.ie/publications, 24 August 2020.
10. Altiero Spinelli and Ernesto Rossi, *The Ventotene Manifesto*. https://www.federalists.eu/uef/library/books/the-ventotene-manifesto, 10 July 2020.

INTRODUCTION

1. The speeches in Florence and Kaunas in this volume, pp. 66–78, 150–9.
2. https://www.dfa.ie/our-role-policies/ireland-in-the-eu/future-of-europe/news/newsarchive/report-on-citizens-consultations-on-the-future-of-europe-in-ireland.php, 30 September 2020.
3. https://ec.europa.eu/commfrontoffice/publicopinion/index.cfm/Survey/getSurveyDetail/instruments/STANDARD/surveyKy/2255, 7 September 2020.
4. Brigid Laffan und Jane O'Mahony, *Ireland and the European Union*. London: Palgrave Macmillan, 2008, 30ff.
5. Mark Brennock, 'Harney Opposed to Closer Integration of Europe'. *Irish Times*, 22 July 2000 https://www.irishtimes.com/news/harney-opposed-to-closer-integration-of-europe-1.295209, 21 January 2021.
6. Maura Adshead, 'European Union Politics and Ireland'. In: Brian Lalor (ed.), *The Encyclopedia of Ireland*. Dublin: Gill & Macmillan, 2003, pp. 364–5.
7. 'Report on Citizens' Consultations on the Future of Europe in Ireland', p. 4. https://www.dfa.ie/our-role-policies/ireland-in-the-eu/future-of-europe/news/newsarchive/report-on-citizens-consultations-on-the-future-of-europe-in-ireland.php, 20 September 2020.
8. There is also some space available during the Junior Cycle within the Civil, Social & Political Education (CSPE) course.
9. Stephen Collins has meticulously documented the party's dissensions on the issue of Europe. See: Stephen Collins, 'Labour on Europe: from No to Yes'. In: Paul Daly et al. (eds), *Making the Difference: The Irish Labour Party 1912–2012*. Cork: Collins Press, 2012, pp. 154–64.
10. *Irish Times*, 14 May 1987; *Irish Times*, 20 May 1992.
11. See, for example, Michael D. Higgins, 'Ireland in Europe 1992: Problems and Prospects for a Mutual Interdependency'. In: Richard Kearney (ed.), *Across the Frontiers: Ireland in the 1990s Cultural-Political-Economic*. Dublin: Wolfhound Press, 1988, pp. 58–77.
12. *Irish Times*, 30 November 1991.
13. See, for example, Evelyn Roll, *Wir sind Europa! Eine Streitschrift gegen den Nationalismus*. Berlin: Ullstein, 2016.
14. Ivan Krastev, *After Europe*. Philadelphia: University of Pennsylvania, 2020, pp. 117–18.
15. Ivan Krastev, *Ist heute schon morgen? Wie die Pandemie Europa verändert*. Berlin: Ullstein, 2020, p. 28, pp. 74–7.
16. https://pulseofeurope.eu/en/; http://www.whoifnotus.eu/about/; https://diem25.org/about/; https://we-are-europe.org/en/events-and-campaigns/; and https://www.standupforeurope.org/about/our-mission, 28 July 2020.
17. Claus Leggewie, *Europa Zuerst! Eine Unabhängigkeitserklärung*. Berlin: Ullstein, 2017, p. 8.
18. Leggewie, pp. 212–66.

19. Ulrike Guérot, 'Europe as a republic: the story of Europe in the twenty first century'. *Open Democracy*, 29 June 2015. https://www.opendemocracy.net/en/can-europe-make-it/europe-as-republic-story-of-europe-in-twenty-first-century, 23 July 2020. See also: Robert Menasse, *Der europäsische Landbote: Die Wut der Bürger und der Friede Europas*. Vienna: Zsolnay, 2012.
20. Ulrike Guérot, *Why Europe Should Become a Republic! A Political Utopia*. Berlin: Dietz, 2019 (German orig. 2018).
21. See the review by Fintan O'Toole in the *New York Review of Books*, 24 October 2019.
22. Stéphanie Hennette, Thomas Piketty, Guillaume Sacriste, Antoine Vauchez, *How to Democratize Europe*. Cambridge, MA: Harvard University Press, 2019.
23. See: Mary P. Corcoran, 'Introduction: Challenging Intellectuals' pp. 3–11, p. 4; Tom Garvin, 'The Assault on Intellectualism in Irish Higher Education', pp. 29–37, p. 31; and Pat O'Connor, 'Reflections on the Public Intellectual's Role in a Gendered Society', pp. 55–73, p. 57. In: Mary P. Corcoran and Kevin Lalor (eds), *Reflections on Crisis: The Role of the Public Intellectual*. Dublin: RIA, 2012.
24. Edward W. Said, 'The Public Role of Writers and Intellectuals'. In: Helen Small (ed.), *The Public Intellectual*. Oxford and Malden: Wiley-Blackwell, 2002, pp. 19–29, p. 31.
25. Heinz Drügh, 'Pop-Intellektualität'. In: Jürgen Fohrmann and Carl Friedrich Gethmann (eds), *Topographien von Intellektualität*. Göttingen: Wallstein, 2018, pp. 58–81, p. 63, p. 64.
26. Stefan Collini, '"Every Fruit-Juice Drinker, Nudist, Sandal-Wearer…": Intellectuals as Other People'. In: Helen Small (ed.), *The Public Intellectual*, pp. 203–23, p. 214.
27. J. J. Lee, *Ireland 1912–1985: Politics and Society*. Cambridge: University Press, 1989, p. 577, and Genevieve Carbery, 'Ireland becoming anti-intellectual, academic editor says'. *Irish Times*, 28 June 2012. https://www.irishtimes.com/news/irelandbecoming-anti-intellectual-academic-editor-says-1.1069133, 7 July 2020.
28. For exceptions, see: Richard Kearney, *The Irish Mind*. Dublin: Wolfhound Press, 1985; Thomas Duddy, *A History of Irish Thought*. London and New York: Routledge, 2002; Michael Brown, *The Irish Enlightenment*. Cambridge, MA: Harvard University Press, 2016; Bryan Fanning, *The Quest for Modern Ireland: The Battle of Ideas 1912–1986*. Dublin and Portland, OR: Irish Academic Press, 2008; Mary P. Corcoran and Kevin Lalor (eds), *Reflections on Crisis: The Role of the Public Intellectual*; Fergal Lenehan, *Intellectuals and Europe: Imagining a Europe of the Regions in Twentieth-Century Germany, Britain and Ireland*. Trier: Wissenschaftlicher Verlag, 2014.
29. Dominic McGrath, 'Millennials for Michael D: Why young people are backing a Higgins presidency'. https://www.thejournal.ie/millennials-and-michael-d-higgins-presidency-4257246-Sep2018/, 21 July 2020.
30. https://www.drb.ie/contributors, 22 July 2020.
31. Moynagh Sullivan, 'Raising the Veil: Mystery, Myth and Melancholia in Irish Studies'. In: Patricia Coughlan and Tina O'Toole (eds), *Irish Literature: Feminist Perspectives*. Dublin: Carysfort Press, 2008, pp. 245–8, p. 246.

32. Liam O'Dowd, 'Public Intellectuals and the "Crisis": Accountability, Democracy and Market Fundamentalism'. In: Mary P. Corcoran and Kevin Lalor (eds), *Reflections on Crisis*, pp. 77–102, p. 88.
33. See, for example, Diarmuid Ferriter, 'Commemorations need political leadership'. *Irish Times*, 18 January 2020. https://www.irishtimes.com/opinion/diarmaid-ferriter-commemorations-need-political-leadership-1.4143053, 22 July 2020; and Emma Dabiri, 'Let's Talk about Race and Identity in Ireland'. *Dublin Inquirer*, 11 October 2017. https://www.dublininquirer.com/2017/10/11/emma-let-s-talk-about-race-and-identity-in-ireland, 22 July 2020.
34. See, for example, Brigid Laffan, 'Ireland may have to sacrifice sacred cows to survive Brexit'. *Irish Times*, 16 May 2017. https://www.irishtimes.com/opinion/ireland-may-have-to-sacrifice-sacred-cows-to-survive-brexit-1.3083791, 22 July 2020; and Katy Hayward, 'Northern Ireland may find itself between a rock and a hard place after Brexit'. *Irish Times*, 13 January 2020. https://www.irishtimes.com/opinion/northern-ireland-may-find-itself-between-a-rock-and-a-hard-place-after-brexit-1.4137426, 22 July 2020.
35. See, for example, Fintan O'Toole, *Ship of Fools: How Stupidity and Corruption Sank the Celtic Tiger*. London: Faber & Faber, 2009; Fintan O'Toole, *Heroic Failure: Brexit and the Politics of Pain*. London: Head of Zeus, 2018; and Fintan O'Toole, 'Unpresidented'. *New York Review of Books*, 23 July 2020. https://www.nybooks.com/articles/2020/07/23/trump-unpresident-unredeemed-promise, 23 July 2020.
36. Katy Hayward, 'From Visionary to Functionary: Representations of Irish Intellectuals in the debate on "Europe"'. *Études irlandaises*. 34/2, 2009, 87–100. https://journals.openedition.org/etudesirlandaises/1650, 23 July 2020.
37. Lenehan, *Intellectuals and Europe*, pp. 82–92, 117–18.
38. Katy Hayward, *Irish Nationalism and European Integration: The Official Redefinition of the Island of Ireland*. Manchester: University Press, 2009, p. 8.
39. Lenehan, *Intellectuals and Europe*, pp. 95–118. On the role of Europe and Europeanism in the field of Irish Studies, see Joachim Fischer, 'Boston or Berlin? Reflections on a Topical Controversy, the Celtic Tiger and the World of Irish Studies', *Irish Review* 48. Summer 2014, 81–95.
40. Jürgen Habermas, 'Der 15. Februar Oder: Was uns Europäer verbindet'. In: Habermas, *Der gespaltene Westen*. Frankfurt am Main: Suhrkamp, 2004, pp. 43–51, here pp. 48–51.
41. Jürgen Habermas, 'Drei Gründe für "Mehr Europa"'. In: Habermas, *Im Sog der Technokratie*. Berlin: Suhrkamp, 2013, pp. 132–7, here pp. 133–4.
42. https://www.socialeurope.eu/ 24 July 2020. Colin Crouch, *Social Europe: A Manifesto*. Berlin: Social Europe Publishing, 2020 provides a good summary of the present state of the debate.
43. The social philosopher Oskar Negt and the trade unionist Tom Kehrbaum have also published texts that present, essentially, social democratic visions of Europe. Oskar Negt,

Gesellschaftsentwurf Europa. Göttingen: Steidl, 2012; and Tom Kehrbaum, 'Ein soziales und ein demokratisches Europa neu denken!' In: Ulrike Guérot, Oskar Hegt, Tom Kehrbaum and Emanuel Herold, *Europa jetzt! Eine Ermutigung*. Göttingen: Steidl, 2018, pp. 11–38.

44. See, for example, the conclusion of the Leipzig speech.

I. EUROPEAN HISTORY AND MEMORY

1. Bulmer Hobson, 'Statement on IRB and Irish Freedom'. Bureau of Military History 1913–21. http://www.militaryarchives.ie/collections/online-collections/bureau-of-military-history-1913-1921/reels/bmh/BMH.WS0085.pdf, 17 August 2020.
2. Casement was unwilling to send those men to fight to Ireland: 'I shall not have said that I handed these men to the hangman,' he insisted.
3. Roger Casement, 'Speech from the Dock'. https://www.newstatesman.com/2010/03/ireland-law-england-irishmen, 17 August 2020.
4. *Ibid*.
5. *Ibid*.
6. Mario Vargas Llosa (trans. Edith Grossman), *The Dream of the Celt*. London: Faber & Faber, 2012.
7. It is estimated that roughly 60 million people left Europe during the period 1860–1914.
8. Engl. transl.: These centenary commemorations, then, are an invitation to pay full attention to the fundamental moral questions that Roger Casement was calling on his contemporaries to face, questions that still confront us in our own times. Today we take great pride in recalling Roger Casement's idealism, his passionate defence of the human dignity of those who were the victims of a brutal world order, and his commitment to the cause of freedom, in Ireland and abroad.
9. Roger Casement, 'Speech from the Dock'. https://www.newstatesman.com/2010/03/ireland-law-england-irishmen, 17 August 2020.
10. William L. Thomas and Florian Znaniecki, T*he Polish Peasant in Europe and America: Monograph on an Immigrant Group*. 5 vols. Boston: Richard G. Badger, 1918–20.
11. On 25 October 1849 George Boole (1815–64) wrote his first letter home from his new place of residence, the city of Cork. Boole's letter was addressed to his sister Mary Ann and is now housed in UCC Library as part of the George Boole Papers in Library Archives. The digital collection is available at http://georgeboole.ucc.ie. 17 August 2020.
12. Baron József Eötvös (trans. Paul Sohar and Lázló Bakas), *Poverty in Ireland 1837: A Hungarian's View*. Dublin: Phaeton, 1840.
13. George Cornewall Lewis, *Remarks on the Third Report of the Irish Poor Inquiry Commissioners*. London: Charles Knight and Co., 1837. Also printed in vol. ii of the Parliamentary Papers for 1837, pp. 253–90.
14. John Crowley, William J. Smyth and Mike Murphy (eds), *Atlas of the Great Irish Famine*. Cork: University Press, 2012.

15. Joseph Kay, *Free Trade in Land*. London: Ballantyne Press, 1877.
16. *Times*, as cited in: *The Nation*, May 1860.
17. Father Theobald Mathew, 'House of Lords Testimony'. http://www.capuchinfranciscans.ie/wp-content/uploads/2018/07/5.-Descriptive-List-Web-Fr.-Theobald-Mathew-Research-and-Commemorative-Papers.pdf, 17 August 2020.
18. See, for example, 'On the State of Democracy in Our Changing World: The Aristotle Address 2019', The Stoa of Attalos at the Ancient Agora of Athens, 10 October 2019; in this book in Section III (pp. 81–94).
19. On 15 December 1846 Mr Nicholas Cummins, the well-known magistrate of Cork, had paid a visit to Skibbereen and the surrounding district, and had been horrified by what he saw. He appears to have written to the authorities, but without result, because on 22 December 1846 he addressed a letter to the Duke of Wellington, who was an Irishman, and also sent a copy to the *Times*. It was published on 24 December 1846 and is reproduced in: Cecil Woodham-Smith, *The Great Hunger: Ireland 1845–1949*. New York: Harper and Row, 1962.
20. James Charles Mathew, 'Mathew, Theobald'. In Sidney Lee (ed.). *Dictionary of National Biography*. 37. New York: Macmillan, 1894, pp. 32–4.
21. Cited in: Cecil Woodham-Smith, *The Great Hunger*.
22. See: Mike Davis, *Late Victorian Holocausts: El Niño Famines and the Making of the Third World*. London: Verso, 2000; and Amartya Sen, *Poverty and Famines – An Essay on Entitlement and Deprivation*. Oxford: University Press: 1981.
23. Mark Honigsbaum, *Living with Enza: The Forgotten Story of Britain and the Great Flu Pandemic of 1918*. London: Palgrave Macmillan, 2009.
24. Manchester: University Press, 2018.
25. Engl. transl.: The book tells of how the pandemic created a stillness in cities and towns as it passed through, closing schools, courts and libraries, quelling trade, cramming hospitals, and stretching medical doctors to their limit as they treated hundreds of patients each day.
26. Alfred W. Crosby, *Epidemic and Peace*, 1918. Westport, CT: Greenwood Press, 1976. Republished as *America's Forgotten Pandemic*; and Caitriona Foley, *The Last Irish Plague: The Great Flu Epidemic in Ireland 1918–19*. Dublin: Irish Academic Press, 2011.
27. Guy Beiner, 'Troubles with Remembering; or, The Seven Deadly Sins of Memory Studies'. *Dublin Review of Books*, 1 November 2017. https://www.drb.ie/essays/troubles-with-remembering-or-the-seven-sins-of-memory-studies, 10 July 2020.
28. Paul Ricoeur (trans. Kathleen Blamey and David Pellauer), *Memory, History, Forgetting*. Chicago and London: University of Chicago Press, 2004.
29. Viet Thanh Nguyen, *Nothing Ever Dies: Vietnam and The Memory of War*. Cambridge, MA: Harvard University Press, 2016, p. 12.

30. Avishai Margalit, *The Ethics of Memory*. Cambridge, MA and London: Harvard University Press, 2004, pp. 51–4.
31. Edith Wyschogrod, *An Ethics of Remembering: History, Heterology and the Nameless Others*. Chicago and London: University of Chicago Press, 1998, p. xi.
32. Carla R. Morrissey, 'The Influenza Epidemic of 1918'. *Navy Medicine* 77, 3 (May–June 1986), 11–17.
33. M.L. Benedict and M. Braithwaite, 'The Year of the Killer Flu'. *In the Face of Disaster: True Stories of Canadian Heroes from the Archives of Maclean's*. New York: Viking, 2000.
34. *Epidemic and Peace, 1918*. Westport, CT: Greenwood Press, 1976.
35. See here: Tim Houman, '100 Years: Knowledge of the Spanish Flu enhances our preparedness for future pandemics' https://ruc.dk/en/news/100-years-knowledge-spanish-flu-enhances-our-preparedness-future-pandemics, 18 August 2020.
36. Robin Lindley, 'The Forgotten American Pandemic: Historian Dr. Nancy K. Bristow on the Influenza Epidemic of 1918'. *History News Network*, 6 November 2012. http://hnn.us/article/146655, 10 July 2020.
37. The Great (Irish) Famine.
38. Samuel Beckett, *Happy Days*. London: Faber & Faber, 1962.
39. http://www.claimscon.org/wp-content/uploads/2018/04/Holocaust-Knowledge-Awareness-Study_Executive-Summary-2018.pdf, 5 November 2020.
40. https://edition.cnn.com/interactive/2018/11/europe/antisemitism-poll-2018-intl, 5 November 2020.

II. TOWARDS A SOCIAL EUROPE

1. Duncan Weldon, 'The British Model and the Brexit Shock: Plus ça Change?' *The Political Quarterly* 90/2, 2019, 12–20. https://onlinelibrary.wiley.com/doi/full/10.1111/1467-923X.12625, 10 July 2020.
2. Alison Johnston and Aidan Regan, 'Is the European Union Capable of Integrating Diverse Models of Capitalism?' *New Political Economy* 23/2 (2018), 145–59.
3. https://www.federalists.eu/uef/library/books/the-ventotene-manifesto, 10 July 2020.
4. https://www.president.ie/en/media-library/speeches/speech-by-president-higginsat-the-inaugural-event-of-the-brexit-institute, 31 August 2020.
5. Robert Schuman, 'Declaration of 9 May: The Schuman Plan for European Integration'. https://www.robert-schuman.eu/en/declaration-of-9-may-1950, 17 August 2020.
6. Jacques Delors, 'Address to the Royal Institute of International Affairs, London, 7 September 1992'. https://ec.europa.eu/commission/presscorner/detail/en/SPEECH_92_81, 17 August 2020.
7. Hartmut, Rosa (trans. James Wagner), *Resonance: A Sociology of our Relationship to the World*. Cambridge, UK and Medford, MA: Polity Press, 2019, p. 317.
8. Michael Longo and Philomena Murray, *Europe's Legitimacy Crisis: From Causes to Solutions*. London: Palgrave Macmillan, 2015.

9. Karl Polanyi, *The Great Transformation: The Political and Economic Origins of Our Time*. Boston: Beacon Press, 2001 (1944).
10. Sylvia Walby, *Crisis*. Cambridge, UK and Malden, MA: Polity Press, 2015.
11. Mariana Mazzucato, *The Value of Everything: Making and Taking in the Global Economy*. New York: Public Affairs, 2018.
12. Ian Gough, *Heat, Greed and Human Need: Climate Change, Capitalism and Sustainable Wellbeing*. Cheltenham, UK and Northampton, MA: Edward Elgar 2017.
13. Gough, *Heat, Greed and Human Need*, p. 199.
14. Sylvia Walby, *Crisis*.
15. Naomi Klein, *No Logo*. New York: Picador, 2000.
16. Pádraig Carmody and Alicia Fortuin, '"Ride-sharing": Virtual Capital and Impacts on Labor in Cape Town, South Africa'. *African Geographical Review* 38/3 (2019), 196–208.
17. World Bank (2015). *Doing Business: Going Beyond Efficiency*. https://www.doingbusiness.org/content/dam/doingBusiness/media/Annual-Reports/English/DB15-Full-Report.pdf, 18 August 2020.
18. William Mitchell and Thomas Fazi, *Reclaiming the State: A Progressive Vision of Sovereignty for a Post-Neoliberal World*. London: Pluto Press, 2017.
19. Anthony Atkinson, *Inequality: What Can Be Done?* Cambridge, MA and London: Harvard University Press, 2015.
20. Andrea Komlosy (trans. Jacob K. Watson), *Work: The Last 1,000 Years*. London and New York: Verso, 2018.
21. Robert and Edward Skidelsky, *How Much is Enough? Money and the Good Life*. London: Penguin, 2013.
22. Gøsta Esping-Andersen, *The Three Worlds of Welfare Capitalism*. Princeton: University Press, 1990.
23. Mitchell, *Reclaiming the State*, 2017.
24. For more on the London Bridge attack of June 2017, see: https://www.bbc.com/news/uk-england-london-40147164, 6 November 2020.
25. Pope Francis, 'Address of His Holiness Pope Francis to the Heads of State and Government of the European Union, Rome 24 March 2017'. http://www.vatican.va/content/francesco/en/speeches/2017/march/documents/papa-francesco_20170324_capi-unione-europea.html, 18 August 2020.
26. Engl. transl.: Cooperation is the key, not fragmentation. A united Europe, and not a cacophony of competing voices, is our best chance to shape the global agenda, to infuse it with the values we cherish, to make it more hospitable to dignified human life, and to life in all its form.
27. Giovanni Boccaccio (trans. G.H. McWilliam), *The Decameron*. London, etc.: Penguin, 1995.
28. John Henry Newman, *An Essay on the Development of Christian Doctrine*. http://www.newmanreader.org/works/development/index.html, 13 July 2020.

29. Robert Schuman, 'Declaration of 9 May: The Schuman Plan for European Integration'. https://www.robert-schuman.eu/en/declaration-of-9-may-1950, 17 August 2020.
30. Ulrich Bielefeld and Nikola Tietze, 'In Search of Europe: An Interview with Jacques Delors'. 1 July 2011. https://www.eurozine.com/in-search-of-europe/, 13 July 2020.

III. THINKING ABOUT EUROPE

1. Brian Arkins, *Hellenizing Ireland: Greek and Roman Themes in Modern Irish Literature*. Newbridge: Goldsmith Press, 2005
2. Sallins: Irish Academic Press, 2016.
3. Paul Valéry, 'The Crisis of the Mind'. In: Paul Valéry, *An Anthology*. Princeton, NJ: University Press, 1977, pp. 94–107 (translator not given).
4. Kate Raworth, *Doughnut Economics: Seven Ways to Think Like a 21st-Century Economist*. White River Junction, VT: Chelsea Green Publishing, 2017.
5. Hartmut Rosa (trans. James Wagner), *Resonance: A Sociology of Our Relationship to the World*. Cambridge, UK and Medford, MA: Polity Press 2019.
6. Jürgen Habermas (trans. Ciaran Cronin), *The Lure of Technocracy*. Cambridge, UK and Malden, MA: Polity Press, 2015.
7. Keynote address at a meeting at the Royal Irish Academy on state funding for research, 17 November 2014.
8. 'Three quarks for Muster Mark!' (James Joyce, *Finnegans Wake*. London: Faber & Faber, 1939.)
9. Walter Isaacson, 'Walter Isaacson Delivers the 2014 Jefferson Lecture, 14 May 2014'. https://www.aspeninstitute.org/blog-posts/president-ceo-walter-isaacson-delivers-2014-jefferson-lecture/ 18 August 2020.
10. Pope Francis, 'Address to Participants in the 3rd World Meeting of Popular Movements, 5 November 2016'. https://w2.vatican.va/content/francesco/en/speeches/2016/november/documents/papa-francesco_20161105_movimenti-popolari.html, 18 August 2020.
11. Pope Francis, *Evangelii Gaudium*. http://www.vatican.va/content/francesco/en/apost_exhortations/documents/papa-francesco_esortazione-ap_20131124_evangelii-gaudium.html, 14 July 2020.
12. Martin Heidegger (trans. and introduction by Albert Hofstadter), *Poetry, Language, Thought*. New York: Harper & Row, 1971.
13. Gaston Bachelard (trans. Maria Jolas), *The Poetics of Space*. London, etc.: Penguin, 2014 (first publ. 1964).
14. Conrad M. Arensberg and Solon T. Kimball, *Family and Community in Ireland*. Cambridge, MA: Harvard University Press, 1940.
15. Paul Crutzen, 'Geology of Mankind'. *Nature* 415/23 (2002), https://doi.org/10.1038/415023a, 14 July 2020. The word 'Anthropocene' is derived from the Greek words

ἄνθρωπος (anthropos), for 'man' and καινός (kainos) for 'new', coined and made popular by biologist Eugene Stormer and chemist Paul Crutzen in 2000. See: Asley Dawson, *Extinction: A Radical History*. New York: OR Books, 2016, p. 19.

16. In 1873 Stoppani acknowledged the increasing power and impact of humanity on the earth's systems and referred to the 'anthropozoic era', an idea that was possibly based on George Perkins Marsh who lived in Italy and whose work, *Man and Nature*, was translated into Italian in 1872. See: Paul Crutzen, 'Geology of Mankind'; and Mary Philip Trauth, *Italo-American Diplomatic Relations, 1861–1882: The Mission of George Perkins Marsh, First American Minister to the Kingdom of Italy*. Washington, DC: Catholic University of America Press, 1958.

17. James C. Scott, *Against the Grain: A Deep History of the Earliest States*. New Haven: Yale University Press, 2017.

18. Jane Humphries and Benjamin Schneider, 'Spinning the Industrial Revolution'. *The Economic History Review* 72/1, 2018, 126–55.

19. John Locke, *An Essay Concerning Toleration: And Other Writings on Law and Politics, 1667–1683*. University Press: Oxford, 2006.

20. Domenico Losurdo, *Liberalism: A Counter-History*. London and New York: Verso, 2014.

21. David Hume, *The History of England: From the Invasion of Julius Caesar to the Revolution in 1688*. London: Jones & Company, 1829, p. 454.

22. Cited in: T.F. O'Sullivan, *The Young Irelanders*. Tralee: The Kerryman, 1944; and John O'Leary, *The Writings of James Fintan Lalor and a Memoir*, Dublin: T.G. O'Donoghue, 1895.

23. Parnell reportedly said these famous lines at his speech having become president of the newly-founded Land League in October 1879.

24. Cited in: Sharon Furlong, '"Herstory" Recovered: Assessing the contribution of Cumann na mBan 1914–1923'. *The Past: The Organ of the Uí Cinsealaigh Historical Society* 30, 2010, 70–93.

25. Padraic Kenna, *Housing and Human Rights: International Encyclopedia of Housing and Home*. Oxford: Elsevier, 2011.

IV. CONNECTING EUROPEAN CULTURES

1. Prokopis Pavlopoulos, President of Greece March 2015 – March 2020.
2. Paula Meehan, 'Crossing the Threshold'. https://www.dcu.ie/news/news/2020/Jun/Crossing-Threshold-poet-Paula-Meehan-marks-DCU-Virtual-Graduation.shtml, 18 August 2020.
3. Fran O' Rourke, *Aristotelian Interpretations*. Sallins: Irish Academic Press, 2016.
4. J. P. Mahaffy, *Rambles and Studies in Greece*. Gerrards Cross: Colin Smythe, 2012.
5. Brian Friel, *Translations*. London: Faber & Faber, 1981.
6. Seamus Heaney, 'Varieties of Irishness: In the Element of his Genius'. *Irish Pages* 9/1 (2015), 9–20.
7. E. M. Forster, *Pharos and Pharillon*. London: Hogarth, 1923.

8. Peter D. Sutherland, 'Our Great Migration Challenge: The Littleton Memorial Lecture', presented by Peter Sutherland in Dublin on 17 December 2015. https://www.thecairoreview.com/essays/our-great-migration-challenge, 18 August 2020.
9. 'UNHCR welcomes "unprecedented force and resonance" of New York Declaration'. https://www.unhcr.org/en-ie/news/press/2016/9/57dff34f4/unhcr-welcomes-unprecedented-force-resonance-new-york-declaration.html, 18 August 2020.
10. Nicos Mouzelis, 'Class and Clientelistic Politics: The Case of Greece'. *Sociological Review*, 26/3 (1978), 471–98.
11. Engl. transl.: A flash of inspiration can transcend all limits. Artists can be soulmates regardless of a time or culture barrier.
12. Saoi ('wise one') is the highest honour bestowed by Aosdána, the state-supported association of Irish creative artists. The title is awarded for life and held by at most seven people at a time.
13. In June 2020 Ireland was indeed elected as a non-permanent member of the UN Security Council.
14. The President of Ireland received the academic regalia of Honorary Doctor from Vytautas Magnus University.
15. Thomas Aquinas, *Summa Theologica*. https://oll.libertyfund.org/titles/aquinas-the-summa-theologica-of-st-thomas-aquinas-part-i-qq-i-xxvi-vol-1, 18 August 2020.
16. 'Beacons at Bealtaine', poem delivered at EU Enlargement Ceremony by Nobel Laureate Seamus Heaney, Phoenix Park, May Day 2004.
17. Seamus Heaney, 'Varieties of Irishness: In the Element of his Genius'. *Irish Pages* 9/1 (2015), 9–20.
18. Pope Francis, 'Address of His Holiness Pope Francis to the Heads of State and Government of the European Union, Rome, 24 March 2017'. http://www.vatican.va/content/francesco/en/speeches/2017/march/documents/papa-francesco_20170324_capi-unione-europea.html, 18 August 2020.
19. See also pp. 174–5.
20. Pope Francis, *Encyclical Laudato Si' of the Holy Father Francis: On Care for our Common Home*. Vatican City: Vatican Press, 2015.
21. Czesław Miłosz, 'Incantation'. In: Czesław Miłosz, *Collected Poems 1931–1987*. London: Harper Collins, 1988.
22. Richard Ellman, *James Joyce*. Oxford: University Press, 1959.
23. See, Paul Ricoeur, *Memory, History, Forgetting*. Chicago: University of Chicago Press, 2000.

V. THE FUTURE OF THE EUROPEAN UNION

1. Paul Valéry, 'The Crisis of the Mind'. In: Paul Valéry, *An Anthology*. Princeton, NJ: University Press, 1977, pp. 94–107 (translator not given).
2. Francis Fukuyama, *The End of History and the Last Man*. New York: Free Press, 1991.

3. Harold Laski, 'Revolution by Consent'. *The Nation*, 152, 22 March 1941.
4. Alfred Müller-Armack, 'The Principles of the Social Market Economy'. 19 December 1962. https://ghdi.ghi-dc.org/sub_document.cfm?document_id=926, 17 July 2020.
5. David Soskice and Peter A. Hall, *Varieties of Capitalism*. Oxford: University Press, 2001.
6. Gøsta Esping-Andersen, *The Three Worlds of Welfare Capitalism*. Princeton: University Press, 1990.
7. See: François Duchêne, *Jean Monnet: The First Statesman of Interdependence*. New York: W.W. Norton and Company, 1980. Duchêne writes this was stated in a conversation between Jean Monnet and one of his advisers at the end of November 1955 in the run-up to the Treaty of Rome.
8. 'Social Action Programme'. *Bulletin of the European Communities Supplement* 2/74. COM(73) 1600. 24 October 1973. http://aei.pitt.edu/1253/1/social_action_program_COM_73_1600.pdf, 20 August 2020.
9. Tommaso Padoa-Schioppa, *The Road to Monetary Union in Europe*. Oxford: University Press, 1994.
10. See, for example, Fritz W. Scharpf, 'The asymmetry of European integration, or why the EU cannot be a "social market economy"'. *Socio-Economic Review* 8/2, April 2010, 211–50.
11. Christian Joerges, 'The Market without the State? The "Economic Constitution" of the European Community and the Rebirth of Regulatory Politics'. *European Integration online Papers* 1/19 (1997). https://ssrn.com/abstract=302710 or http://dx.doi.org/10.2139/ssrn.302710, 20 August 2020.
12. Rosa Luxemburg (trans. George Shriver), *The Letters of Rosa Luxemburg*, eds. Georg Adler, Peter Hudis and Annelies Laschitza. London and New York: Verso, 2011.
13. The Paulinum is a reconstructed meeting space at the University of Leipzig, inspired by an earlier Pauline church, which stood at this spot until 1968, when it was blown up by the GDR authorities.
14. Engl. transl. Thank you, and I congratulate you for your efforts.
15. Francis Fukuyama, *The End of History and the Last Man*. New York: Free Press, 1991.
16. Friedrich. Schiller, 'An die Freude' ('To Joy'), first published in *Thalia* magazine in 1786.
17. Joel Mokyr, 'Secular Stagnation? Not in Your Life'. In: Coen Teulings and Richard Baldwin (eds), *Secular Stagnation: Facts, Causes and Cures*. London: Centre for Economic and Policy Research, 2014, pp. 83–90.
18. Peter Stearns, *The Industrial Revolution in World History*. Boulder, CO: Westview Press, 1998, p. 36.
19. Raymond Williams, *The Country and the City*. Oxford: University Press, 1973.
20. Josiah Strong, *The Challenge of the City*. New York: Baker and Taylor, 1907.
21. The Frankfurt School of thought was founded at the university in 1923 by Theodor Adorno, Herbert Marcuse and others. It draws on the work of Marxist, Freudian and Hegelian thought in the development of its critical theory. The theorists fled Germany during the

National Socialist period, with Adorno returning to a professorial chair in 1949. Jürgen Habermas was later also associated with the Frankfurt School.
22. Cheltenham, UK and Northampton, MA: Edward Elgar, 2017.
23. White River Junction, VT: Chelsea Green Publishing, 2017.
24. London: Penguin, 2018; New York: Public Affairs, 2018.
25. Simon Bulmer and William E. Paterson, *Germany and the European Union: Europe's Reluctant Hegemon?* London: Red Globe Press, 2019.
26. John Evans, 'Inequality and unions: Brexit, Trump and "yellow vests"'. *Social Europe*, 23 January 2019. https://www.socialeurope.eu/inequality-and-unions, 20 July 2020.
27. Jürgen Habermas (trans. Ciaran Cronin), *The Lure of Technocracy*. Cambridge, UK and Malden, MA: Polity Press, 2015.
28. Jürgen Habermas (trans. Ciaran Cronin), *Europe: The Faltering Project*. Cambridge, UK and Malden, MA: Polity Press, 2009.
29. London: Routledge, 2020.
30. Lopes and Kararach, p. 1.
31. *Ibid*.
32. Princeton: University Press, 2003.
33. 'The Irish, from the beginning of time, had been buried in the most profound barbarism and ignorance; as they were never conquered or even invaded by the Romans, from whom all the western world derived its civility, they continued still in the most rude state of society, and were distinguished only by those vices to which human nature, not tamed by education or restrained by laws, is for ever subject.' See: David Hume, *The History of England: From the Invasion of Julius Caesar to the Revolution in 1688*. London: Jones & Company, 1829, p. 454.
34. https://csis-website-prod.s3.amazonaws.com/s3fs-public/publication/191011 _RundeandBandura_AfDB.pdf, 20 July 2020.
35. António Guterres, 'Opening remarks at virtual press encounter to launch the Report on the Socio-Economic Impacts of COVID-19', 31 March 2020. https://www.un.org/sg/en /content/sg/speeches/2020-03-31/remarks-launch-of-report-the-socio-economic-impacts -of-covid-19, 20 July 2020.
36. 'Fight against desert locusts swarms goes on in East Africa despite coronavirus crisis measures'. 9 April 2020. https://news.un.org/en/story/2020/04/1061482, 20 July 2020.
37. Lopes and Kararach, p. 123.

VI. A MULTILINGUAL EUROPE – TRANSLATIONS INTO IRISH, FRENCH AND GERMAN

1. Tá an Saoi ar an onóir is airde a bhronann Aosdána Aosdána, cumann ealaíontóirí cruthaitheacha na hÉireann a bhfuil tacaíocht ón stát aige. Bronntar an teideal ar feadh an tsaoil agus ní bhíonn níos mó nach seachtar a mbíonn an teideal orthu ag am ar bith.

2. Oifig na nOibreacha Poiblí.
3. Aucune source en français identifiée. La version française est celle du traducteur (NdT).
4. Martin Heidegger, *Essais et conférences*, traduit de l'allemand par André Préau. Gallimard : 1980.
5. Gaston Bachelard, *La poétique de l'espace*. Paris: Les Presses universitaires de France, 1957.
6. Conrad M. Arensberg and Solon T. Kimball, *Family and Community in Ireland*. Cambridge, MA: Harvard University Press, 1940.
7. David Hume, *Histoire d'Angleterre*. Paris: Hyppolyte Boisgard Éditeur, 1853.
8. Aucune source en français identifiée. La version française est celle du traducteur (NdT).
9. Idem.
10. Idem.
11. Home Rule (1870–1914) : projet de loi proposant une certaine autonomie de l'Irlande au sein du Royaume-Uni (NdT).
12. Aucune source en français identifiée. La version française est celle du traducteur (NdT).
13. Idem.
14. Douglas Hyde, Keltologe und Volkskundler, erster Präsident des Freistaates Irland.
15. Ich danke Ihnen und schätze Ihre Bemühungen.
16. https://europa.eu/european-union/about-eu/symbols/europe-day/schuman-declaration_de; 29 September 2020.
17. *Die Donut-Ökonomie: Endlich ein Wirtschaftsmodell, das den Planeten nicht zerstört*. München: Hanser, 2018.
18. *Wie kommt der Wert in die Welt? Von Schöpfern und Abschöpfern*. Frankfurt am Main: Campus Verlag, 2019.
19. *The Great Transformation. Politische und ökonomische Ursprünge von Gesellschaften und Wirtschaftssystemen*. (Dt. Übersetzung von Heinrich Jelinek). 8. Auflage. Frankfurt am Main: Suhrkamp, 1973.
20. Übersetzung RH/JF.
21. Jürgen Habermas, *Im Sog der Technokratie*. Frankfurt am Main: Suhrkamp, 2013.
22. Frankfurt am Main: Suhrkamp, 2008.

Index

Aboriginal Australians 112–13, 115–16
Adenauer, Konrad 170, 191
Adorno, Theodor W. 191
Adshead, Maura xviii
Africa xii, xxix, 8, 76–7, 152
    colonization of 207–8, 216–17
    and the European Union 75–7, 206–21
    and imperialism 209, 216–17
    and Ireland 208–11
    national boundaries 217
    structural problems 213–16
African Development Bank 210–11
African Development Fund 210
'African Enlightenment' 217–20
African Union 219
Agenda for Sustainable Development 159
agriculture 12, 108, 115, 142, 148, 182, 210, 215, 217, 220
Albertus Magnus 151
Almqvist, Bo Gunnar 145
Amazon region 7–8
Anderson, Perry 35, 178
Angola 214
Anthropocene era 50, 107–8, 119, 194, 197

anthropology 207, 221
anti-fascist movements 157, 175–6
anti-immigration parties 201
anti-Semitism 24–8
Arendt, Hannah 19, 21, 28, 152, 208
Arensberg, Conrad M. 107
Aristotle 83–4, 109, 125
Arkins, Brian 82, 125
arms trade 27, 76
Asmus, Sabine 189
Athens 109, 124
Athens Democracy Forum 81
Atkinson, Tony 57
Aud 4–5
Auden, W.H. 133
Augustin, Wilhelm 5
Auschwitz-Birkenau 24–5, 28–9
austerity ix, xviii, 55–6, 91–2, 163, 174, 185, 200–2, 204
    consequences of 27, 44, 48, 52, 86, 91, 94
Australia *see also* Aboriginal Australians
    immigrants to 13, 15, 115
    and imperialism 112, 115–16

Index

Bach, Johann Sebastian 188
Bachelard, Gaston 106–7, 110, 117
Bailey, Daniel 4
Beckett, Samuel 23
Beethoven, Ludwig van 193, 205
Beiner, Guy 19–20
Benedict, M.L. 22
Bentham, Jeremy 113–14
Bergman, Ingmar 145–6
Bernhard of Lippe-Biesterfeld, Prince 141
bird flu 19
Black Death 16
Blake, William 196
Bluebell, HMS 5
Boccaccio, Giovanni 67
bogs 141
Böll, Heinrich 135
Bonaventure 151
Boole, George 11
Bord na Móna 141
borders, national 62, 64, 161, 201, 203, 213
Borges, Jorge Luis 21, 25
Bosnia-Herzegovina 161
Bourguignon, Jean-Pierre 97
Boyle, Robert 98
Braithwaite, M. 22
Bretton Woods system 179, 181–2, 185
Brexit ix, xv–xvii, 37, 56, 61, 68, 70–1, 102, 135, 140, 160, 172, 201–2
    and Ireland 155
    and neo-nationalism xxi
Bristow, Nancy K. 22–3
British Relief Association 11
Bulmer, Simon 200
Burke, Christy 15
Burren, Co. Clare 148
Butler, Hubert xxvi
Byron, Lord 196

Callan, Nicholas 98
capitalism xx, xxvi–xxvii, xxx, 52, 58, 92, 178, 190, 202–3, 216
    and democracy 45, 203
    models of 35, 176, 186
carbon taxes 147
Carmody, Pádraig 54
Carr, Marina 82
Casement, Roger 3–9, 208
Catholicism xxvi, xxx, 112
Cavafy, Constantine 127
Celtic Tiger xviii, 59
Chadwick, Edwin 14
Charles, Prince of Wales 148
Charter of Fundamental Rights *see* European Union
Childers, Erskine 7
China 195, 215, 220
Church, Richard 129
Cicero 109
Citizens' Consultations xvii, xix
city-states 109–10
civil society xv, 41, 218–19
class inequality 13, 44–5, 51–2, 54, 89, 196, 198, 217
class system 107, 109, 111, 116
clientelism 128
Climate Act 2018 (Sweden) 147
Climate Action Plan 136
climate change 34, 49–51, 54–5, 62, 64, 95, 119–20, 142, 154, 158, 174, 187, 190, 194, 204, 213
    consequences of 38, 136, 199, 219–20
    denial 97
    and globalization 199
    response to 72, 77, 92, 135–6, 147, 197–8, 202, 207, 272
collective memory 19–22, 25–6, 28 *see also* ethical remembering

Index

Collini, Stefan xxiv
Collins, Des 118
colonialism xxii, 7, 9, 115–16, 152, 197, 214, 216–19 *see also* imperialism
colonization 195, 208 *see also* Africa; Ireland; South Australia, colonization of
Commercial Revolution 197
Commissariat général du Plan 175, 178
Common Agricultural Policy 182
Common Market 170, 178–9, 194
Congo 4, 7–8
Congo, Democratic Republic of 207
Congo Reform Association 3
Connolly, James 114
Constitution of Ireland xxx, 118
Coote, Anna xii
Corcoran, Mary xxiii, xxiv
Corless, Catherine 116–17
Cornwall Lewis, George 12
COVID-19 pandemic ix–xiv, xvii, xxi, 210–13, 271–2
Cox, Pat xviii
Crane Bag xxiv
Croatia
    joins EU 160, 162
    relations with Ireland 160–5
Crosby, A.W. 19, 22
Crutzen, Paul 108
culture xiii, 67–8, 82–4, 196–7 *see also* German culture; Greek culture; Irish culture; Swedish culture
    shared 58, 126, 143, 153, 205–6, 213
    threats to 24, 207, 209

Davis, Mike 15
Davitt, Michael 114
Day, Catherine xviii
de Buitléir, Eamon 141
de Híde, Douglas (Douglas Hyde) 189

de Rossa, Proinsias xx
Decade of Centenaries 152
decarbonization 51, 136, 147, 190, 199
debt 39, 76, 213–14, 207, 212–14
debt cancellation 210, 218
debt crisis 85
Delors, Jacques 37, 71, 185
democracy 81–94, 156, 163–4, 186, 199, 202–3, 211
    industrial 180
    parliamentary 61–5, 91
Democracy in Europe Movement 25 (DiEM25) xxi
Demosthenes 109
depression, economic 55, 119, 200 *see also* financial crisis (2008); Great Depression; recession
deregulation 55, 73, 181, 215
Desmond, Barry xx
development 53, 64, 77, 103, 124, 190, 194, 207, 210–11, 218–20 *see also* sustainable development
development planning 215–16
Diamond, Suzi 24
diaspora 12–14, 127
dictatorship 70, 176
Diderot, Denis 93, 196
Dionysius the Areopagite 124
Dionysus, Festival of 83
disarmament 147, 192
dispossession 12, 111, 113, 116, 124, 127, 195 *see also* colonization
Dixie, USS 18
Dougan, Edmond 105
Drudy, P.J. 118
Drügh, Heinz xxiv
Dublin Lockout (1913) 47
Dublin Review of Books xxv
Dunker, Hans 5

299

Index

Durkheim, Émile 112
Dutch Foundation for the Conservation of Irish Bogs 141

Easter Rising 4–6
  commemorations xxix
ecological issues x–xii, xiv, xxii, xxvii, xxix, 37, 42, 64, 77, 88–9, 93, 101, 103, 111, 146, 163, 190, 194, 206–7, 209, 213–14, 218, 272 *see also* climate change; eco-social model
economic growth 38, 55, 89, 171–2, 180, 183, 188–205, 210, 215 *see also* green growth; inclusive growth
economic and monetary union 74, 172, 174, 181–3, 185, 203
economics 44, 68, 188–205 *see also* market economy
  behavioural 87
  and ecology 197–8
  new 70, 89, 136, 190, 200
  pluralist 51, 89, 198
  teaching 43, 45–6
eco-social model 49–51, 56, 58, 89–90, 94, 136, 190, 197–8, 205, 220
Eden, Anthony 170
education xix, 42, 74, 82, 96, 113, 139, 151, 175, 208–9 *see also* universities
  investment in 55, 200
Egypt 17, 170
Einstein, Albert 46
Ellman, Richard 161
emigration 13–15, 115, 146, 161 *see also* diaspora; immigration; migration
employment 73, 183 *see also* work, concept of; workers' rights
  precarious 38, 53–4, 73–4
Enlightenment 93
environmental degradation 108–9, 119–20
Eötvös, Baron József 11

equal pay 36, 178–80
Erasmus xxviii
ERASMUS Programme xxxii, 139–40, 171
Eriugena, John Scotus 124–5
Esping-Andersen, Gøsta 59, 176
Estonia 153
ethical remembering 19–23, 164, 170
ethics xxix, 34, 64, 76–7, 100–3, 111, 142, 152, 188–205
Ethics Initiative 19
Ethiopia 216
Eurobarometer xvii
Europe, concept of 192–3
Europe of the Regions xxvi
European Association of Former Members of Parliament 61
European Central Bank xvii, 158
European Coal and Steel Community 177–8
European Commission 71, 162, 172, 180, 203
European Court of Auditors xx
European Cyclists' Federation xxii
European Economic Community 178–9, 181–2
  Common Agricultural Policy 182
European Federalist Movement 191
European Federation of Public Service Unions (EPSU) 48
European Green Deal xxi, xxvii
European Monetary System 182
European Movement Ireland xxii
European Parliament 64–5, 91, 175, 203
European People's Party xx
European Pillar of Social Rights 74, 146
European Project 68–9
European Republic xxii–xxiii
European Research Council (ERC) 95, 97–8
European Semester 183
European Union *see also* Brexit
  acquis 164, 174, 179, 184–5

300

Index

and Africa 75–7, 206–21
anthem 193
Banking Union 74
Charter of Fundamental Rights 69, 171, 184
Council 203
Court of Justice 184
decision-making in 69
diversity: xxviii, 34, 42, 83, 123, 176–7, 186, 191; cultural 67, 76, 187, 205
early period 177
economic policy 172–84
expansion (2004) xviii, 153, 160, 162
foundation 169–70
founding principles 35–7, 40–2, 62, 67–70, 72, 78, 86, 93, 153, 156–8, 164, 171, 186, 193–4, 202, 204–5
founding states 170
future of xv–xvi, 34, 41, 68, 70, 86–7, 94, 99, 102–3, 157–9, 164–5, 172–4, 196, 204
integration xv, xxi, xxvi, 33–7, 92, 176–8, 184–6, 203–4
internal market 42, 182, 185–6
international relations 75–7
Member States: peripheral 85; weaker 92
policymaking 154–5
social aims *see* social Europe
threats to 37, 162–3
European Union, Treaty on 69, 171
European Union, Treaty on the Functioning of the 36, 179
European University Institute 68
euro-scepticism xviii, xx, 86
Evans, John 201–2
evictions 12–13, 114–15
extremism 26–8

factories 53, 111–12, 196
Fagel Collection 141
Fair Trade 142
famine *see* Great Famine
far right movements 27, 172
farming *see* agriculture
fascism 28, 129, 197
Fazi, Thomas 56, 60
federalism xxi, xxvi, 178, 191
Fianna Fáil xxxi
film 145
financial crisis (2008) ix, 40, 43–5, 55, 59, 85–6, 92, 156, 163, 200, 203–4 *see also* austerity; recession
bailout xviii–xix
Fine Gael xix–xx, xxxi
Fintan Lalor, James 114
Fiscal Compact 183
Fiscal Stability Treaty 183
fishing industry 148–9
Flower, Robin 130–1, 133
Foley, Caitriona 19
folklore 144–5
food security 210–13
Forster, E.M. 127
Fortuin, Alicia 54
Foucault, Michel 105
Fourth Republic (France) 178–9
France xxiii, 179, 180, 201
post-war development 175
Francis, Pope 65, 77, 100–1, 103–4, 119, 156, 158
Frankfurt School 196
free movement 36, 178, 184, 194
Friedman, Milton 88
Friel, Brian 82, 126
frontier research 97–8
Fukuyama, Francis xi, 174, 192
Future of Europe, White Paper on (2017) xv–xvi, 172

301

Index

G7 210
Gaelic Athletic Association (GAA) 143
Galileo 72
Gallagher, Archbishop Paul 102
Garvin, Tom xxiii
gender equality xxvii, 44, 49, 89, 94, 146, 198, 205, 208, 210
gender inequality xxv, 44–5, 48, 52, 128
    pay gap 52
gender relations 111–12, 117
Geneva Conventions 26
German culture 134–5
Germany
    constitution 136–7
    post-war development 175–6
    relations with Ireland 134–7
    reunification xviii, 137, 190
Giustizia e Libertà 157, 175
Glaucon 59
global south 76, 170
globalization xxi, 37, 52–5, 63, 70, 174, 181, 199, 203
Goldsmith, Oliver 141
Good Friday Agreement xvii, 71, 155
Gorta Mór, An *see* Great Famine
Gough, Ian xi–xii, 49, 51, 72, 89, 197–8
Grabar-Kitarović, Kolinda 164
Great Depression 119
Great Famine 11–15, 23, 113, 128
Great Flu Epidemic (1918–19) x, 16–23
    mortality rates 16–17
Great Green Wall 219
Greece xxii
    independence 84, 128–9
    recession 91
    relations with Ireland 123–9
Greece, ancient 81–3, 109–10, 123–4
Greek citizenship 127
Greek Civil War 129
Greek culture 126
Greek diaspora 127
green economy xxii, 51, 136, 199
green growth 51, 89, 198, 210
greenhouse gases 38, 51, 119
    emissions targets 136, 147, 199
Grotius, Hugo 140
growth *see* economic growth; green growth; inclusive growth
Growth and Stability Pact 183
Guérot, Ulrike xxii–xxiii
gun-running 4–5, 7
Guterres, António 77, 212

Habermas, Jürgen xxvi–xxvii, 42, 58, 63, 91–2, 157, 163, 191, 202–4
Hague Conventions 140
Halbwachs, Maurice 19, 21
Hall, Peter 176
Halligan, Brendan xx
Hamilton, William Rowan 98
Händel, Georg Friedrich 134
Harney, Mary xviii, xxxi
Hayward, Katy xxv–xxvi
Heaney, Seamus 82, 126, 133, 144, 153–4
Hearn, John 4
hedge schools 82, 126
Heidegger, Martin 106
Hennette, Stéphanie xxiii
Herder, Johann Gottfried von 93, 196
Higgins, Sabina 146
Hillery, Patrick 179
HIV/AIDS 16
Hobson, Bulmer 3, 7
Holocaust 24–9
home 105–20
Home Rule 7, 115
Homer 82, 125
homophobia xxii, 50

Index

Hone, Evie 141
Hone, Nathaniel, the Elder 141
Hong Kong flu 18
Honigsbaum, Mark 17–18
housing 89–90, 101, 116–19, 198
    insecure x, 43
Housing, White Paper on (1964) 119
Housing Law, Rights and Policy Research, Centre for (NUI Galway) 117
housing policy 117–19
Housing of Working Classes Acts 118
human rights xxviii, 8–9, 41, 46, 53, 60, 67, 72, 76, 85, 128, 135–8, 140, 147, 153, 158, 162, 192, 194
Hume, David 113, 207
Hume, John xxvi
Humphries, Jane 111
Hungary xxi–xxii
Hyde, Douglas (Douglas de Híde) 189

identity 24, 49, 60, 107, 128, 196–7
immigrant communities 10, 14, 26
immigration 119, 146 *see also* emigration; migration
imperialism 3, 6, 8–9, 10, 90, 111, 125, 153, 161, 194, 196, 216, 220 *see also* Africa; Australia; colonialism
    struggle against 85, 93, 170, 193–4, 196
inclusive growth 41, 55, 208, 210
inclusivity 36, 43, 45–6, 49–50, 72, 76, 84, 86, 97, 103, 123, 138, 152, 162, 173, 192–3, 205, 211, 218
income 43, 54, 57–8, 194, 198, 199, 201, 215
    minimum xxii, 146
    sustainable 51, 136, 199
income inequality 38, 49, 158, 171, 180, 202, 214
India 15–17, 195
indigenous peoples 8–9, 116, 120, 217 *see also* Aboriginal Australians; Native Americans

individualism xii, 56, 59, 88, 90, 201
Industrial Revolution 108, 111, 194–6
industrialization 111–12, 194–6, 214–16, 218, 220
inequality 38, 158, 201 *see also* class inequality; gender inequality
Institute of European Affairs xx
Institute of International and European Affairs xx
intellectualism xxiii–xxvii
International Holocaust Remembrance Alliance 29
International Labour Organization (ILO) 35, 50, 94, 178
International Monetary Fund 200
Internet 211
Inuit 17
Ireland
    colonization of 113–14
    independence 128, 151–2
    international relations: 75; Africa 208–11; Croatia 160–5; Germany 134–7; Greece 123–9; Lithuania 150–9; the Netherlands 138–43; Sweden 144–9
    joins EEC xviii, 179
    neutrality xx
    recession 91
    relations with EU xvi–xx
Irish Aid 208
Irish border xvii, 155, 161
Irish Brigade 5
Irish Citizen Army 6
Irish citizenship 127
Irish Civil War 23, 129
Irish College, Rome 100
Irish culture xxiv–xxv, xxxi, 126, 134–5, 144–5
Irish diaspora 12–14, 127
Irish Folklore Commission 145
Irish language xxx, 139, 189

303

Index

Irish mythology 144–5
Irish Research Council 98
Irish Review xxiv
Isaacson, Walter 99

Jaśkowiak, Jacek 15
Joerges, Christian 185
Johnston, Alison 35
Joyce, James 84, 98–9, 125, 146, 161
Joynt, Rachel 132
Juncker, Jean-Claude xv, 172

Kant, Immanuel 93, 196
Kararach, George 207, 214–16, 218–20
Kay, Joseph 12–13
Kearney, John A. 4
Kearney, Richard xxvi, 19, 152
Keats, John 196
Kenna, Padraic 117–18
Kennedy, Kish 133
Kennelly, Brendan 82
key workers x
Keynes, John Maynard 48, 55–6, 200
Kimball, Solon T. 107
Klein, Naomi 52–3
kleptocracy 217
Kohl, Helmut xviii, xx
Kolb, Annette 134–5
Komlosy, Andrea 57
Krastev, Ivan xxi

labour rights *see* workers' rights
Labour Party xx, xxvi–xxvii, xxxi
Labourers Acts 117–18
Ladies' Land League 115
Laffan, Brigid xviii, xxv
Lally, Mick 133
Land Acts 115–17
Land League 114, 118

Land War 114–15
language xxviii, 189 *see also* Irish language
Laski, Harold 175
Latvia 153
Laval cases 184
Lee, Joseph xxiv
Leggewie, Claus xxii
Leipzig 189, 188, 192
Leopold II, King of Belgium 8
Liberia 216
life expectancy 17
Lindley, Robin 23
Linkevičius, Linas Antanas 155
Lisbon, Treaty of xviii, xxvii, 40, 184–5, 203
Lithuania
    independence 150–1
    occupation 152–3
    relations with Ireland 150–9
Lithuanian community in Ireland 154
Locke, John 112–13
locusts 213
London Bridge attack 62
Longley, Michael 82
Longo, Michael 41
Lopes, Carlos 207, 214–16, 218–21
Losurdo, Domenico 113
Luxembourg Compromise (1966) 184

Maastricht Treaty xx, 183, 185
Mabo judgment 112
McGuinness, Máiréad xviii
MacNeill, Eoin 5, 7
MacNeill, Josephine 143
Macron, Emmanuel xxiii, 68, 173
Mahaffy, J.P. 125
Manning, Mary 47
Margalit, Avishai 19, 21
market economy 39–40, 59, 73, 86, 90, 92, 95, 116, 181, 184, 204

marriage equality xxii, 49
Marsh, George Perkins 108
Marsh, Patricia 18
Marx, Karl 112
Mathew, Fr Theobald 14
Mazzucato, Mariana xi, 45, 55, 89, 200
Meehan, Paula 124
memory/forgetting, social 20 *see also* collective memory; ethical remembering
Menasse, Robert xxiii
Mercator projection 207
Merkel, Angela xx
Meyer, Kuno 189
Michelangelo 66, 78
migrants 27, 52, 77–8, 154, 164 *see also* emigrants; immigrant communities
migration 10, 12–13, 64, 72, 106–7, 126–7, 194 *see also* diaspora; emigration; immigration
Milne, Ida 18
Miłosz, Czesław 159
minorities xxviii, 25–6, 29, 76, 189
Mitchell, William 56, 60
Mitteleuropa 161
Mokyr, Joel 195
Mollet, Guy 170
monetary union *see* economic and monetary union
Monnet, Jean 35–6, 40, 43, 178, 180, 191
Monteith, Robert 4
Montez, Lola 134
Montreal Protocol 136
Moore, Thomas 129
Morgan, Lady 129
Morin, Edgar xxiii
Morrissey, Carla 22
mother and baby homes 117
Mouzelis, Nicos 128
Müller-Armack, Alfred 176

multilateralism xiii, xv, 26, 53, 63, 75–6, 128, 135, 137, 140, 147, 159, 192, 211–13, 219
multinationals 48, 53, 174
Murphy, Tom 82
Murray, Philomena 41
Muthu, Sankar 208
Myrdal, Gunnar 44, 147
mythology 82, 144–5

National Economic and Social Council (NESC) xiii
National Folklore Collection (UCD) 145
nationalism xx–xxii, xxvi–xxvii, 26–7, 35, 60, 92, 127–8, 157–9, 172, 175, 192, 196–7, 201–3, 208
nationalization 175
Native Americans 112–13
nativism 60, 86
neo-liberalism x, xx, xxvii, xxx, 51, 56, 59, 87–9, 92, 94, 181, 183–5, 198, 201, 203–4
Neolithic period 108–11
neo-nationalism xxi, 26–7, 86
Neoplatonists 110
Netherlands, relations with Ireland 138–43
'New Jerusalem' 175
New York Declaration for Refugees and Migrants 77–8, 127
Newman, John Henry 67
Nguyen, Viet Thanh 20
Nice, Treaty of xviii
nomadic peoples 106–7
Norse mythology 144–5
Northern Ireland 7, 102–3, 155, 161
nostalgia 191
Nugent, Laval 161

O'Connor, Frank 133
O'Connor, Pat xxiii–xxiv
O'Dowd, Liam xxv

Ó Duilearga, Séamus 145
Ó Faoláin, Seán xxvi
Ohlin, Bert 35, 178–9
Ohlin Report (1956) 35–6, 178–9, 181
Old Dutch 139
O'Mahony, Jane xviii
Orbán, Viktor xxii
ordoliberalism 175–6
O'Reilly, Bernard 4
O'Reilly, Emily xviii
O'Rourke, Fran 82, 84, 125
O'Sullivan, David xviii
O'Toole, Fintan xxv
Oxfam 213

Padoa-Schioppa, Tommaso 182
Palme, Olof 147
pandemics 16, 25, 64, 213 *see also* COVID-19 pandemic; Great Flu Epidemic
Pangur Bán (poem and sculpture) 130–3
Paris, Treaty of 177
Paris Climate Agreement 45, 51, 77, 119, 136, 159, 199
parliamentary democracy *see* democracy
Parnell, Anna 114
Parnell, Charles Stewart 114
Parolin, Cardinal Pietro 102
Parsons, William 98
Paszko, Kinga 24
Paterson, William E. 200, 263
Paulin, Tom 82
Paulinum, University of Leipzig 188
Pavlopoulos, Prokopis 204
peace, sustaining 27, 36, 50, 71, 76, 88, 102, 137, 140, 148, 152–3, 155, 158–9, 164–5, 186, 191–2
Pearse, Patrick 114
peatlands 141
Percy, Andrew xii
Phelan, Edward 48

philosophy 40, 43, 82, 87, 103, 124–6
 principles of xxix, 46
Piketty, Thomas xxiii
plantations, in Ireland 12
pluralism 19, 38–9, 41, 43, 63, 67, 84, 99, 157, 193 *see also* economics, pluralist
Poland xxi–xxii, 10
Polanyi, Karl 44, 55–6, 200–1
Polish community
 in Ireland 10
 in the USA 14
political economy 33–46, 68, 87–90, 111, 113, 115, 171 *see also* eco-social model
Poor Law Unions 11
Popular Front (France) 179
populism xxvii, 27, 73, 86, 140, 162, 172, 201
poverty x, 15, 78, 111, 208, 211, 215–16
 global xiv, 204, 209–10
President of Ireland Initiatives 19
privatization 39, 55, 200, 215
Proclamation of the Irish Republic 6
pro-cycling associations xxii
pro-European movements xxi
property rights 113–16
Ptolemy, Claudius 124
public sector xiv, 55, 59, 200, 204
public services xi, xiv, 48, 50, 57, 59, 204
Pulse of Europe xxi
Putin, Vladimir xxii
Putumayo 7–8
Pytheas of Massalia 123–4

racism 24, 28–9, 50, 60, 172, 207, 209, 216–17
Raworth, Kate xi, 89, 198
recession 48–9, 52, 55–6, 85, 91–2, 200 *see also* depression, economic; financial crisis (2008)
referenda xv, xviii, xxii, 49, 71, 172
refugees 26–7, 71, 77–8, 127–8, 158, 164, 174

Regan, Aidan 35
regulation 49, 53–4, 59, 88–9, 92, 118, 185, 198–9, 204
    opposition to 38, 191
Reichenthal, Tomi 24
remembering *see* collective memory; ethical remembering
renewable energy 210–11
research 55, 95–9, 200
resources, natural 49–51, 55, 89, 148–9, 194–5, 197–9, 217–18
    depletion 38, 119–20
Ricardo, David 115
Ricoeur, Paul 19–21, 23, 25, 152, 164
Rieff, David 152
Roma xxii, 25
Romania, anti-corruption movement in xxii
Romanticism 196
Rome, ancient 109–10
Rome, Treaty of xxvii, 156, 169–70, 181
Rosa, Hartmut 39, 41, 91
Rossi, Ernesto xiii, 35, 157, 175, 191
Royal Irish Academy 98
rubber industry 8
Ruggiero, Paul 125
Runde, Daniel F. 211
Russian flu 18

Said, Edward xxiv
St Brendan 124
St Kilian 134
St Thomas Aquinas 150–1, 157
St Willibrord 138
Scharpf, Fritz 184
Schiller, Friedrich 193, 204–5
Schmitz, Friedrich 5
Schneider, Benjamin 111
Schouten, Matthijs 141–2
Schumacher, Kurt 178

Schuman, Robert 36, 69, 191
Schuman Declaration 69, 177, 191–2
Scott, James C. 109
Scottish Highland Potato Famine 11
'scramble for Africa' 216–17
sea levels, rising 142
Sen, Amartya 15, 118
Shaw, Elizabeth 135
Shaw, George Bernard 82
Shelley, Mary 196
Shelley, Percy Bysshe 196
Simonsen, Lone 22
Single European Act (1987) xx, 179, 182, 185
single market 74
Sinn Féin xx
Skidelsky, Edward 58
Skidelsky, Robert 58
slave trade 216
slavery 109
Social Action Programme 180
social cohesion 49–50, 69, 74–5, 103, 154, 171–2, 174, 177
    loss of xii, 34, 36–8, 40, 86, 93, 118, 163
social contract 41, 54, 59–60, 220
Social Democratic Party (Germany) 177–8
social Europe xx, xxvi–xxvii, 86, 99, 156–7, 179–81, 193
Social Europe xi, 201
social justice 41–2, 49–50, 69, 87, 89–90, 171, 177, 187, 197–8, 221
social protection x, 50, 60, 183, 185
social rights 74, 94, 114, 118, 146, 176, 184
Social Summit for Fair Jobs and Growth (2017) xvi, 73–4
Socrates 124
solidarity
    European 40–2, 64–5, 66–78, 93, 135, 155–6, 162–3, 272
    international xii–xiv, 119, 153–4, 158, 170–1, 186, 204–5, 212, 218, 221

Index

Soskice, David 176
South Australia, colonization of 115–16
sovereignty xi, 56, 128, 201
    shared xx, 171
Spanish flu *see* Great Flu Epidemic
Spindler, Captain Karl 5
Spinelli, Altiero xiii, 35, 69, 86, 157, 175, 191
Stalin, Joseph xxii
Stand Up for Europe xxi
Stearns, Peter 195
Steinmeier, Frank-Walter 137
Stoa of Attalos 81
Stockholm Declaration 29
Stokes, George Gabriel 98
Stoney, George Johnstone 98
Stopford Green, Alice 7
Stoppani, Antonio 108
Strategic and International Studies, Centre for 211
Streeck, Wolfgang 42, 203
Strindberg, August 146
Strong, Josiah 196
Strzelecki, Paul (Paweł) 10–11, 13–15
Stuart, Imogen 130–3, 135
student protests (1968) 180
subsidiarity 42
substantivism 44
sustainable development 71–2, 95, 101, 140, 147–8, 158–9, 163–4, 174, 192, 207, 213, 215, 218 *see also* United Nations, Sustainable Development Goals
Sutherland, Peter xviii
Sweden, relations with Ireland 144–9
Swedish culture 144-5
swine flu 18
Switzerland xxii
Synge, John Lighton 98
Synge, John Millington 82

Taisce, An 141
tariffs 36, 178, 217
technocracy 91–2, 177, 201–2
Teilifís na Gaeilge xxx
terrorism 62
TG4 xxx
Themistocles 109
Therborn, Göran 147
Thomas, William 10
Thomson, George 82
Times 13
Torrens, Robert 115
Torrens, Robert Richard 115–16
totalitarianism 21, 26
trade, terms of 209
trade unions 47–60, 185, 201–2
Troubles, the 155
Trump, Donald ix, xxii, 56, 201–2
Tyndall, John 98

U2 135
U19 4
Ulster Unionists 7
Ulster Volunteers 7
unemployment 48, 73, 216
United Nations (UN) xiii, 26, 76, 135, 140, 147, 148, 158, 192, 209, 212, 213, 219
    High Commissioner for Refugees 127–8
    Human Rights Council 127, 140
    peacekeeping role 148
    Security Council 76, 128, 140, 209, 219
    Sustainable Development Goals 45, 76, 207
universities 34, 66-7, 87, 90, 188–91
University College Dublin (UCD) 34–5, 134, 145

Valéry, Paul 85, 169–70
van Gelderen, Gerrit 141
Venclova, Tomas 157
Ventotene Manifesto xiii, 35, 38, 69, 86, 157–8, 174–5, 186, 191
Victoria, Queen 14
Vienna, Congress of 129
Viking period 144
von Hayek, Friedrich 88

Wadding, Luke 100
Walby, Sylvia xi, 44–5, 52, 55, 89, 91, 200
Walter, Otto 5
Walton, Ernest 98
War of Independence (Ireland) 19, 23
We Are Europe xxi
Weisbach, Raimund 5
Weldon, Duncan 34
welfare state 42, 49, 89, 93, 175–6, 179, 186, 198, 204
Werner Plan 182–3
Western Samoa 17
Wiesel, Eli 28
Wilde, Oscar 125
Willem the Silent 139

Williams, Raymond 196
women xxvii, 22–3
    economists 44
women's rights *see* gender equality
Wood, Robert 125
work, concept of 57, 103 *see also* employment
worker participation 180
workers' rights 50, 53–4, 59, 103, 180, 184, 201
workshops 111
World Bank 55, 87, 207
World Happiness Report 59
World War I 6, 16, 22, 50, 85, 186, 197
World War II 26, 40, 169, 175, 197
Wyschogrod, Edith 21–2
Wyse Power, Jennie 115

xenophobia 24, 27–8, 197

Yeats, William Butler 82
yellow vest movement 201
Young European Collective xxi
Young Ireland 114
Yugoslav federation 165

Znaniecki, Florian 10